The Reasoning Criminolo

This book is a tribute to the work of criminologist Professor Ronald V. Clarke, in view of his enormous and enduring contribution to criminology and crime science. Clarke is best known for his development of the theory and application of situational crime prevention, although he also played a major part in the establishment of the British Crime Survey, in discussions of evaluation methodology and in improving the knowledge base and tools for problem-oriented policing. He has consistently emphasised the need for crime studies to be practical as well as academically rigorous.

In this major collection of original essays, Tilley and Farrell bring together leading criminologists from around the globe – they profess to have 'inadvertently invited only world-class scholars. Oops.' – all of whom are colleagues or ex-students of Clarke.

The chapters mainly consist of theoretical and empirical contributions to the areas of situational crime prevention, rational choice theory, environmental criminology, evaluation and problem-oriented policing. The largely biographical introduction 'Ronald V. Clarke – the quiet revolutionary' is based on interviews with Clarke.

Nick Tilley is Professor in the Department of Security and Crime Science at UCL. He is also Emeritus Professor of Sociology at Nottingham Trent University.

Graham Farrell is Professor of Criminology and Director of the Midlands Centre for Criminology and Criminal Justice at Loughborough University, and Senior Research Fellow at the Institute for Canadian Urban Research Studies, Simon Fraser University.

Crime Science Series
Edited by Richard Wortley, UCL

Crime science is a new way of thinking about and responding to the problem of crime in society. The distinctive nature of crime science is captured in the name.

First, crime science is about crime. Instead of the usual focus in criminology on the characteristics of the criminal offender, crime science is concerned with the characteristics of the criminal event. The analysis shifts from the distant causes of criminality – biological makeup, upbringing, social disadvantage and the like – to the near causes of crime. Crime scientists are interested in why, where, when and how particular crimes occur. They examine trends and patterns in crime in order to devise immediate and practical strategies to disrupt these patterns.

Second, crime science is about science. Many traditional responses to crime control are unsystematic, reactive, and populist, too often based on untested assumptions about what works. In contrast crime science advocates an evidence-based, problem-solving approach to crime control. Adopting the scientific method, crime scientists collect data on crime, generate hypotheses about observed crime trends, devise interventions to respond to crime problems, and test the adequacy of those interventions.

Crime science is utilitarian in its orientation and multidisciplinary in its foundations. Crime scientists actively engage with front-line criminal justice practitioners to reduce crime by making it more difficult for individuals to offend, and making it more likely that they will be detected if they do offend. To achieve these objectives, crime science draws on disciplines from both the social and physical sciences, including criminology, sociology, psychology, geography, economics, architecture, industrial design, epidemiology, computer science, mathematics, engineering, and biology.

1. **Superhighway Robbery**
   Graeme R. Newman and Ronald V. Clarke

2. **Crime Reduction and Problem-oriented Policing**
   Edited by Karen Bullock and Nick Tilley

3. **Crime Science**
   New approaches to preventing and detecting crime
   Edited by Melissa J. Smith and Nick Tilley

4. **Problem-oriented Policing and Partnerships**
   Implementing an evidence-based approach to crime reduction
   Karen Bullock, Rosie Erol and Nick Tilley

5. **Preventing Child Sexual Abuse**
   Stephen Smallbone, William L. Marshall and Richard Wortley

6. **Environmental Criminology and Crime Analysis**
   Edited by Richard Wortley and Lorraine Mazerolle

7. **Raising the Bar**
   Preventing aggression in and around bars, pubs and clubs
   Kathryn Graham and Ross Homel

8. **Situational Prevention of Organised Crimes**
   Edited by Karen Bullock, Ronald V. Clarke and Nick Tilley

9. **Psychological Criminology**
   An integrative approach
   Richard Wortley

10. **The Reasoning Criminologist**
    Essays in honour of Ronald V. Clarke
    Edited by Nick Tilley and Graham Farrell

The Reasoning Criminologist

Essays in honour of Ronald V. Clarke

Edited by
Nick Tilley and Graham Farrell

Routledge
Taylor & Francis Group
LONDON AND NEW YORK

First published 2012
by Routledge
2 Park Square, Milton Park, Abingdon, Oxon OX14 4RN

Simultaneously published in the USA and Canada
by Routledge
711 Third Avenue, New York, NY 10017

Routledge is an imprint of the Taylor & Francis Group, an informa business

© 2012 Nick Tilley and Graham Farrell for selection and editorial matter; the contributors for their chapters

The right of Nick Tilley and Graham Farrell to be identified as editors of this work has been asserted by them in accordance with the Copyright, Designs and Patent Act 1988.

All rights reserved. No part of this book may be reprinted or reproduced or utilised in any form or by any electronic, mechanical, or other means, now known or hereafter invented, including photocopying and recording, or in any information storage or retrieval system, without permission in writing from the publishers.

Trademark notice: Product or corporate names may be trademarks or registered trademarks, and are used only for identification and explanation without intent to infringe.

British Library Cataloguing in Publication Data
A catalogue record for this book is available from the British Library

Library of Congress Cataloging in Publication Data
The reasoning criminologist : essays in honour of Ronald V. Clarke/ edited by Nick Tilley and Graham Farrell. – 1st ed.
  p. cm.
  1. Clarke, R. V. G. 2. Criminologists – Great Britain – Biography.
  3. Crime prevention – Great Britain. 4. Criminology – Great Britain – History.
  I. Clarke, R. V. G. II. Tilley, Nick. III. Farrell, Graham.
  HV6023.C53R43 2011
  363.25092–dc23
  2011022741

ISBN: 978-0-415-68851-2 (hbk)
ISBN: 978-0-415-68852-9 (pbk)
ISBN: 978-0-203-15440-3 (ebk)

Typeset in Times New Roman by
Swales & Willis Ltd, Exeter, Devon

Printed and bound in Great Britain by
TJ International Ltd, Padstow, Cornwall

Contents

List of illustrations ix
Notes on contributors xi
Series editor's foreword xx

Introduction: Ronald V. Clarke – the quiet revolutionary 1
GRAHAM FARRELL AND NICK TILLEY

1 **Situational crime prevention: the Home Office origins** 15
PAT MAYHEW AND MIKE HOUGH

2 **On being crime specific: observations on the career of R.V.G. Clarke** 30
DEREK B. CORNISH AND MARTHA J. SMITH

3 **Ferruginous ducks, low hanging fruit and Ronald V. Clarke's world of crime science** 46
NICK ROSS

4 **Happy returns: ideas brought back from situational crime prevention's exploration of design against crime** 52
PAUL EKBLOM

5 **Linking situational crime prevention and focused deterrence strategies** 65
ANTHONY A. BRAGA AND DAVID M. KENNEDY

6 **Situational crime prevention makes problem-oriented policing work: the importance of interdependent theories for effective policing** 80
JOHN E. ECK AND TAMARA D. MADENSEN

7 **Ron Clarke's contribution to improving policing: a diffusion of benefits** 93
MICHAEL S. SCOTT AND HERMAN GOLDSTEIN

8	**Vulnerability of evaluators of problem-oriented policing projects** JOHANNES KNUTSSON	108
9	**Evaluation for everyday life** MIKE MAXFIELD	119
10	**Using rational choice and situational crime prevention to inform, interpret, and enhance public surveillance efforts: a three-city study** NANCY LA VIGNE	131
11	**Spatial displacement and diffusion of crime control benefits revisited: new evidence on why crime doesn't just move around the corner** DAVID WEISBURD AND CODY W. TELEP	142
12	**Suicide and opportunity: implications for the rationality of suicide** DAVID LESTER	160
13	**Ron and the Schiphol fly** KEN PEASE AND GLORIA LAYCOCK	172
14	**Exploring the person–situation interaction in situational crime prevention** RICHARD WORTLEY	184
15	**A rational choice analysis of organized crime and trafficked goods** MANGAI NATARAJAN	194
16	**The structure of angry violence** MARCUS FELSON	205
17	**Extending the reach of situational crime prevention** GRAEME R. NEWMAN AND JOSHUA D. FREILICH	212
18	**Contrasting hotspots: did the opportunist make the heat?** KATE BOWERS AND SHANE JOHNSON	226
19	**Situating situational crime prevention: anchoring a politically palatable crime reduction strategy** PAUL J. BRANTINGHAM AND PATRICIA L. BRANTINGHAM	240
	Index	252

Illustrations

Figures

8.1	Contextual configurations for conducting problem-oriented policing	111
11.1	Eighteen trajectories of crime incidents in Seattle	146
11.2	Location of medium to high juvenile arrest incident trajectory blocks	147
14.1	Reciprocal relationship between person and situation	185
14.2	Relationship between the person, situation and behaviour in the non-interactive model	187
14.3	Relationship between the person, situation and behaviour in the interactive model	187
14.4	Probability of crime for a hypothetical person + situation model	188
14.5	Probability of crime for a hypothetical person × situation model	188
14.6	Hypothetical interaction between provoked, mundane and predatory offenders and the situation	191
17.1	The two-stage situational prevention model	215
18.1	Journey to crime distribution for prolific and occasional offender groups	232
18.2	Occasional offender and prolific offender hotspots in the county of Dorset, UK	233
18.3	Journey to crime for prolific hotspot P6	235
18.4	Occasional offender and prolific offender hotspots, and burglary density in the county of Dorset, UK	236

Tables

5.1	Focused deterrence, situational crime prevention, and street group homicides	71
6.1	Problem types and situational methods	84
6.2	Percentage of situational interventions	86
6.3	Percentage of offender-, victim- and place-based interventions	87
8.1	Assessments in problem-oriented policing projects by practitioner and academic respectively	113

x *Illustrations*

8.2	Evaluations of treatment programmes and problem-oriented policing projects respectively	114
9.1	Two cultures	120
10.1	Significant average monthly changes in crime, downtown Baltimore	136
10.2	Significant average monthly changes in crime, Humboldt Park, Chicago	136
15.1	Hypothetical CRAVED scores for selected goods that are internationally trafficked	198
15.2	Choice structuring properties of trafficking offenses	200
17.1	Twenty-five techniques of SCP	214
17.2	Classification of precipitation-control strategies	215
18.1	Summary statistics for the occasional and prolific groups	231
18.2	Offence data summaries for prolific-generated and occasional-generated hotspots	233
18.3	Census data for the prolific and occasional hotspots	234

Notes on contributors

Kate Bowers is Reader at the Department of Security and Crime Science, UCL. She has worked in the field of environmental criminology for eighteen years. Her research has generally focused on applying quantitative methods to crime analysis and to studies of crime prevention. Some of her previous work has involved examining spatial and temporal patterns in crime, evaluating the effectiveness of crime prevention schemes and investigating business crime. She is also very interested in the development of products and procedures that help to design out crime. Her work has been funded by a variety of organisations including the Home Office, the police, the NPIA, the DfES, the ESRC and the AHRC. She has published almost sixty papers and book chapters in criminology, the vast majority being peer-reviewed. She has also guest edited a special edition of a journal and a *Crime Prevention Studies* volume and co-edited a book on crime mapping. She has acted on journal editorial boards and has presented her work many times to national and international audiences.

Anthony A. Braga is Professor in the School of Criminal Justice at Rutgers University and Senior Research Fellow in the Program in Criminal Justice Policy and Management at Harvard University. His research involves collaborating with criminal justice, social service and community-based organisations to address illegal access to firearms, reduce gang and group-involved violence, and control crime hot spots.

Patricia L. Brantingham is RCMP University Professor of Computational Criminology, Director of the Institute for Canadian Urban Research Studies (ICURS) and Associate Member of the School of Computing Science at Simon Fraser University. She is a member Simon Fraser University's Interdisciplinary Research in Mathematics and Computing Science Centre (IRMACS) and a director of its Modelling of Complex Social Systems program (MoCSSy). She has worked as a systems analyst for such major corporations as Johnson & Johnson and Norton Simon, Inc. and served as Director of Programme Evaluation for the Department of Justice Canada. Dr Brantingham holds degrees in theoretical mathematics from Columbia University and Fordham University and in Urban and Regional Planning from Florida State University. She is the author or editor of two dozen books and scientific monographs and more than

100 articles and scientific papers. She is one of the founders of environmental criminology and is currently the leader of an international collaboration in *computational criminology* linking fourteen university research laboratories around the world. She is known widely for development of crime pattern theory. She has twice been keynote speaker at NIJ Maps Conferences. She is a recipient of the R.V.G. Clarke Award from the Environmental Criminology and Crime Analysis Symposium and of the President's Award from the Western Society of Criminology. Her current research includes the analysis of prolific offender travel directionality and the use of computational topology in understanding the structure of crime patterns.

Paul J. Brantingham is RCMP University Professor of Crime Analysis at Simon Fraser University and Associate Director of ICURS. He received degrees in government and law at Columbia University and in Criminology at Cambridge University. He is a member of the California Bar. Prof. Brantingham has background and interest in linking the policy research needs within government with the criminological and legal skills within universities. He served as Director of Programme Evaluation and Special Reviews at the Public Service Commission of Canada and has served as a faculty dean and as a department head at Simon Fraser University. He currently is an academic advisor for Canadian Centre for Justice Statistics, is on the editorial board of numerous criminology journals and is the author of over 100 scientific papers, policy documents, articles, monographs and books. His most recent book is *Classics in Environmental Criminology* (co-edited with Martin Andresen and Bryan Kinney). Prof. Brantingham is a past president of the Western Society of Criminology and a past program chair for the American Society of Criminology. He is co-developer of crime pattern theory, originator of crime gravity indexing as an alternative measure of crime problems faced by police in different communities and a primary developer of several crime analysis tools prototyped at ICURS including the Crime Analysis System-Pacific Region (CAS-PR) for tracking crime trends in detail and a criminal case analysis system, Cour-BC. His current research is focused on development of measures of the complexity of police work.

Derek B. Cornish and Ron first met in 1959 as students at Bristol University, and later worked together at the Home Office. Derek joined the London School of Economics in 1978 to teach psychology, criminology and research methods, taking early retirement in 2002. Ron and Derek have collaborated on many projects connected with offender rehabilitation, the rational choice perspective and situational crime prevention over the years.

John E. Eck is Professor of Criminal Justice at the University of Cincinnati. He received his Masters of Public Policy from the University of Michigan in 1977 and his doctorate in Criminology from the University of Maryland in 1994. Dr Eck specializes in police effectiveness and crime prevention. He is particularly interested in the study of high-crime locations and the development of methods for preventing crimes at places. He has written numerous articles and books on policing, crime patterns, drug control, crime mapping, research methods and computer simulation of crime patterns. Many of his publications are designed to assist police in their efforts to reduce crime.

Paul Ekblom is Professor of Design Against Crime at the Design Against Crime Research Centre, Central Saint Martin's College of Art & Design, University of the Arts London. Besides involvement in design and crime, he holds Ron Clarke entirely responsible for a career in the theory, practice and evaluation of situational crime prevention, crime prevention arms races and the capture and dissemination of knowledge of good practice.

Graham Farrell is Professor of Criminology and Director of the Midlands Centre for Criminology and Criminal Justice at Loughborough University, Senior Research Fellow at the ICURS at Simon Fraser University, and an associate of the Jill Dando Institute of Crime Science at University College London. He has conducted research on various areas of crime prevention and criminal justice, particularly repeat victimisation and situational crime prevention.

Marcus Felson has been a leader not only in crime theory ('the routine activity approach') but also in applying that theory to reducing crime. His central argument is that everyday legal activities set the stage for the illegal activities that feed on them. He is Professor of Criminal Justice at Texas State University, and has also been a professor at the University of Illinois at Urbana-Champaign, Rutgers University and University of Southern California. Prof. Felson has been Visiting Scholar at the University of Stockholm and the Free University of Amsterdam, where he is a member of the Royal Academy. He received his BA from the University of Chicago and his PhD from the University of Michigan. Prof. Felson has been a guest lecturer in over twenty nations, including Australia, Belgium, Canada, Denmark, England, Finland, Hungary, Italy, the Netherlands, Norway, Poland, Scotland, Spain, Sweden and Switzerland. Author of more than eighty professional papers, including 'Redesigning hell: preventing crime and disorder at the Port Authority Bus Terminal', he is co-editor (with Ronald V. Clarke) of *Business Crime and Routine Activity* and *Rational Choice* and co-author of *Opportunity Makes the Thief*. A recent book of his, *Crime and Nature*, extends crime theory as part of the life sciences.

Joshua D. Freilich is the Acting Director of the Criminal Justice PhD programme and a member of the Criminal Justice Department at John Jay College, the City University of New York. He is a lead investigator for the National Consortium for the Study of Terrorism and Responses to Terrorism (START), a Center for Excellence of the US Department of Homeland Security (DHS); a member of the Terrorism Research and Analysis Project (TRAP), sponsored by the Federal Bureau of Investigation's (FBI) Behavioral Science Unit (BSU); and a member of the Global Terrorism Database's (GTD) Advisory Board. Freilich's research focuses on causes of and responses to terrorism and criminological theory, particularly environmental criminology. His research has been funded by DHS directly as well as through START. Freilich is currently the principal investigator (with Steven Chermak) on the United States Extremist Crime Database (ECDB) study, a large-scale data-collection effort that is building the first-of-its-kind relational database of crimes committed by far-right, Al-Qaeda directed and influenced, and animal rights and environmental rights extremists in the United States reported in an open source.

Herman Goldstein is Professor Emeritus at the University of Wisconsin-Madison Law School and the original architect of the problem-oriented approach to policing. His first experiences in working with the police were in Philadelphia as a graduate student in governmental administration at the University of Pennsylvania and subsequently as an assistant to the city manager of Portland, Maine. He spent two years observing the on-the-street operations of the police in Wisconsin and Michigan as a researcher with the American Bar Foundation's Survey of the Administration of Criminal Justice, and then participated in the analysis phase of that landmark project. From 1960 to 1964, he was Executive Assistant to the superintendent of the Chicago Police Department, O.W. Wilson, the widely recognized architect of the professional model of policing. Prof. Goldstein has published widely on problem-oriented policing, the police function, police discretion, the political accountability of the police and the control of police misconduct. He was co-author of the American Bar Association Standards Relating to the Urban Police Function. His 1977 book, *Policing a Free Society*, is among the most frequently cited works on the police. He first described the problem-oriented approach to policing in a 1979 article, which he expanded upon in his 1990 book, *Problem-oriented Policing*. Prof. Goldstein's research and writings have inspired many efforts to implement and advance problem-oriented policing in police agencies around the world.

Mike Hough is Co-Director of the Institute for Criminal Policy Research at Birkbeck, University of London. Prof. Hough has published on a range of criminological topics including probation work, youth justice, policing, crime prevention and community safety, anti-social behaviour, probation and drugs. Current studies include research on sentencing, on youth justice and on public trust in justice.

Shane Johnson is Professor and Deputy Head of Department at the UCL Department of Security and Crime Science. He has published over sixty papers on topics including predictors of victimisation risk, crime and design, the impact of prevention strategies on crime, space-time patterns of insurgent attacks, and offender foraging activity. He has received funding from a range of sponsors including the British Academy, the Arts and Humanities Research Council (AHRC), the Engineering and Physical Research Council (EPSRC), the UK Home Office and the UK National Police Improvement Agency (NPIA).

David M. Kennedy is Director of the Center for Crime Prevention and Control at John Jay College of Criminal Justice in New York City. He directed the Boston Gun Project, whose 'Operation Ceasefire' intervention was responsible for a more than 60 per cent reduction in youth homicide victimisation and won the Ford Foundation Innovations in Government Award, the Herman Goldstein International Award for Problem Oriented Policing and the International Association of Chiefs of Police Webber Seavey Award. He developed the 'High Point' drug market elimination strategy, which also won an Innovations in Government Award. He helped design and field the Justice Department's Strategic Approaches to Community Safety Initiative, the Treasury Department's Youth Crime Gun Interdiction Initiative and the Bureau of Justice Assistance's Drug Market Intervention Program. He is Co-Chair of the National Network for Safe Communities, which includes more than 50 jurisdictions – among them Los Angeles, Chicago, Milwaukee, Cincinnati, Boston, Providence, High Point, North Carolina, Newark and the states of California and North Carolina – and is dedicated to reducing crime, reducing incarceration and addressing the racial conflict associated with traditional crime policy. He is the author of *Deterrence and Crime Prevention: Reconsidering the Prospect of Sanction*, co-author of *Beyond 911: A New Era for Policing* and author of a wide range of articles on gang violence, drug markets, domestic violence, firearms trafficking, deterrence theory and other public safety issues. His next book, *Don't Shoot*, will be published by Bloomsbury in the autumn of 2011.

Johannes Knutsson is a professor of Police Research at the Norwegian Police University College. Dr Knutsson is also a visiting professor at Jill Dando Institute of Crime Science, University College London. His research interests have been policing, problem-oriented policing, crime prevention and the evaluation of crime preventive measures.

Nancy La Vigne is Director of the Justice Policy Center at the Urban Institute, where she leads a staff of over thirty-five researchers and oversees a research portfolio of more than three dozen active projects spanning a wide array of crime, justice and public safety topics. Before being appointed as Director, Dr La Vigne served for eight years as a senior research associate at the Urban Institute, directing projects on prisoner re-entry, crime prevention and the evaluation of criminal justice technologies. Prior to joining the Urban Institute, Dr La Vigne was the founding director of the Crime Mapping Research Center (since renamed the Mapping and Analysis for Public Safety Program) at the National Institute of Justice, the research, technology and evaluation arm of the US Department of Justice (DOJ). She later served as Special Assistant to the Assistant Attorney General for the Office of Justice Programs within DOJ. She has held positions as Research Director for the Texas sentencing commission, Research Fellow at the Police Executive Research Forum, and Consultant to the National Council on Crime and Delinquency. Her research interests focus on criminal justice evaluation, prisoner re-entry, crime prevention and the spatial analysis of crime and criminal behaviour. She has published widely on these topics, appearing in a variety of scholarly journals and practitioner publications. Dr La Vigne holds a BA in Government from Smith College, a Master's degree in Public Affairs from the LBJ School of Public Affairs at the

University of Texas-Austin, and a PhD from the School of Criminal Justice at Rutgers, the State University of New Jersey.

Gloria Laycock OBE graduated in psychology from University College London in 1968 and completed her PhD there in 1975. She worked in the Home Office for over thirty years of which almost twenty years were spent on research and development in the policing and crime prevention fields. She has extensive research experience in the UK and has acted as a consultant on policing and crime prevention in North America, Australia, New Zealand, Israel, South Africa and Europe. In 1999 she was awarded an International Visiting Fellowship by the United States DOJ based in Washington DC. She returned to the UK in April 2001 from a four-month consultancy at the Australian Institute of Criminology in Canberra to become Director of the University College London's Jill Dando Institute of Crime Science. She was awarded an OBE in the Queen's Birthday Honours 2008 for services to crime policy. Prof. Laycock is now Director of the Community Policing and Police Science Institute in Abu Dhabi, United Arab Emirates.

David Lester has doctoral degrees from Cambridge University in Social and Political Science and Brandeis University in Psychology. He is currently Distinguished Professor of Psychology at the Richard Stockton College of New Jersey in Pomona. He is also President-Elect of the American Association of Suicidology, and he is a former president of the International Association for Suicide Prevention. He has published extensively on suicide, murder and other issues in thanatology. His recent books include *Mass Murder* (2004), *Katie's Diary: Unlocking the Mystery of a Suicide* (2004), *Is There Life after Death?* (2005), *A Multiple-self Theory of Personality* (2009), and *Preventing Suicide: Why We Don't and How We Might* (2010).

Tamara D. Madensen is an environmental criminologist and assistant professor in the Department of Criminal Justice at the University of Nevada, Las Vegas. Her research examines the impact of place management and police strategies on crime. She has co-authored two problem-oriented policing guides and recently co-edited and authored a *Crime Prevention Studies* volume focused on preventing crowd violence.

Mike Maxfield is Professor of Criminal Justice at John Jay College. He is the author of articles and books on a variety of topics – victimisation, policing, homicide, community corrections, auto theft and long-term consequences of child abuse and neglect. He is the co-author (with Earl Babbie) of the textbook, *Research Methods for Criminal Justice and Criminology*, now in its sixth edition, and currently serves as the editor of the *Journal of Research in Crime and Delinquency*. Formerly a professor at Rutgers University, Maxfield received his PhD in Political Science from Northwestern University.

Pat Mayhew worked for much of her career as a researcher in the Home Office. She joined the Home Office Research Unit at about the time that Ron Clarke

Contributors xvii

did, and she worked with him until his departure in 1984. She was a visiting fellow at the National Institute of Justice in Washington, DC in the late 1980s, and was the consultant criminologist at the Australian Institute of Criminology between 2002 and 2003. Between 2004 and 2008 she was Director of the Crime and Justice Research Centre at Victoria University of Wellington, New Zealand. Since then, she has worked as a freelance criminologist consultant.

Mangai Natarajan is Professor in the Department of Criminal Justice at John Jay College of Criminal Justice. She is an active policy-oriented researcher who has published widely in four areas: drug trafficking; women police; domestic violence; and international criminal justice. Her recent publications include *International Crime and Justice* (2011) and *Crime Opportunity Theories: Routine Activity, Rational Choice and their Variants* (2011). She is currently studying burn and acid attacks on young women in India.

Graeme R. Newman is Distinguished Teaching Professor at the School of Criminal Justice, University at Albany and Associate Director of the Center for Problem-Oriented Policing. He has known Ron Clarke for an awfully long time and is honoured to count him among his best friends. The friendship has even survived the co-authoring of several articles and books, which include *Super Highway Robbery* (2003), *Outsmarting the Terrorists* (2006), *Designing out Crime from Products and Systems* (2006) and *Policing Terrorism: An Executive's Guide* (2008). Newman's recent major works include *Crime and Immigration* with Joshua Freilich (2006), *Perspectives on Identity Theft* with Megan McNally (2008), a new translation of Cesare Beccaria's *On Crimes and Punishments* with Pietro Marongiu (2009), *Reducing Terrorism through Situational Crime Prevention* with Joshua Freilich (2010) and *Crime and Punishment around the World* in four volumes (2010).

Ken Pease OBE, a forensic psychologist by training, is currently Visiting Professor at University College London and the Universities of Chester, Loughborough and Manchester. Before retirement, he held chairs at the Universities of Manchester and Saskatchewan where he worked in the maximum security Regional Psychiatric Centre (Prairies). He has acted as Head of the Police Research Group at the Home Office and has been a member of the Parole Board for England and Wales. He was a member of the Home Office Design and Technology Alliance and sat on the Steering Group of the DBERR review of Home Office science.

Nick Ross is a British broadcaster and journalist best known for the top-rated BBC police appeal show *Crimewatch* which he presented for twenty-three years. Dismayed by traditional criminology's failure to create solutions to crime, and inspired by Ron Clarke and Ken Pease especially, he coined the term 'crime science' and founded the University College London's Jill Dando Institute, which is named after his *Crimewatch* co-presenter who was murdered in 1999. He has served on several UK government advisory boards, was for many years an adviser to Victim Support and Crime Concern along with other crime-related xviii *Contributors*

charities and is a board member of Crimestoppers. He has several honorary titles (he is an honorary fellow and visiting professor at University College London, has an honorary doctorate from Queen's University Belfast and is an honorary fellow of the Academy of Experimental Criminologists) but no academic qualifications beyond a forty-year-old psychology degree. Apart from crime and victimisation, his other abiding interests include the promotion of evidence-based public policy (he is a trustee of Sense About Science) and in particular evidence-based medicine (he is President of HealthWatch and is Chairman or a board member of several other healthcare organisations).

Michael S. Scott is Director of the Center for Problem-Oriented Policing and Clinical Professor at the University of Wisconsin Law School. He currently chairs the judging committee for the Herman Goldstein Award for Excellence in Problem-Oriented Policing. Scott was formerly chief of police in Lauderhill, Florida; served in various civilian administrative positions in the St Louis, Missouri, Metropolitan, Ft Pierce, Florida, and New York City police departments; and was a police officer in the Madison, Wisconsin, police department. He was a senior researcher at the Police Executive Research Forum (PERF) in Washington, DC. In 1996, he received PERF's Gary P. Hayes Award for innovation and leadership in policing. Scott holds a law degree from Harvard Law School and a bachelor's degree from the University of Wisconsin-Madison.

Martha J. Smith received a JD from New York University and then attended Rutgers University, School of Criminal Justice, where Ron Clarke served as her dissertation chair on a study that looked at vandalism decision making. She and Dr Clarke have worked together on a number of different situational crime prevention projects since then, including papers on crime on public transport, anticipatory benefits and the development of the situational crime prevention typology. Currently, she is an associate professor at Wichita State University.

Cody W. Telep is a doctoral student in the Department of Criminology, Law and Society at George Mason University and a research assistant in the Center for Evidence-Based Crime Policy. His research interests include innovations in policing, police education and evidence-based policy. His recent work includes a Campbell Collaboration systematic review on the effectiveness of problem-oriented policing, the Evidence-Based Policing Matrix, and a study of the impact of police officer education on abuse of authority attitudes.

Nick Tilley OBE is Director of the Security Science Doctoral Research Training Centre at University College London. He is also Emeritus Professor of Sociology at Nottingham Trent University. His research interests lie in policing, crime prevention and programme evaluation methodology. He was awarded an OBE for services to policing and crime reduction in the 2005 Queen's Birthday Honours. He was elected to the Academy of the Social Sciences in 2009.

David Weisburd is the Walter E. Meyer Professor of Law and Criminal Justice and Director of the Institute of Criminology of the Hebrew University Faculty of Law in Jerusalem, and a Distinguished Professor of Criminology, Law and Society at George Mason University and Director of its Center for Evidence-Based Crime Policy. Prof. Weisburd is a member of a number of prestigious international committees including the Scientific Advisory Committee of the Office of Justice Programs; the Campbell Crime and Justice Group (as Co-Chair); and the Committee on Crime, Law and Justice of the US National Academies of Science. Prof. Weisburd received the 2010 Stockholm Prize in Criminology for his research on policing and crime 'hot spots'. In 2011 he received the Klachky Family Award for the Advancement of the Frontiers of Science. He is author or editor of eighteen books and more than 100 scientific articles.

Richard Wortley joined University College London in August 2010 as Director of the Jill Dando Institute for Security and Crime Science, and Head of the Department of Security and Crime Science. He was previously Head of the School of Criminology and Criminal Justice at Griffith University (Australia). He began his career as a prison psychologist and is a former chair of the Australian College of Forensic Psychologists. His research interests centre on the role that immediate environments play in behaviour, especially in criminal, corrupt and antisocial acts. Funded research areas include official misconduct in prison, whistleblowing in the public sector, child sexual abuse, the investigation of internet child exploitation, and intimate partner homicide.

Series editor's foreword

I am especially delighted to write the foreword for this celebration of the work of Ron Clarke. Crime science can trace no single lineage but rather it has evolved from a number of environmental theories of crime that began appearing from the 1970s. Nevertheless, few would disagree that the most influential of these seminal approaches as far as crime science is concerned was Ron Clarke's model of situational crime prevention.

I am assuming that if you have picked up this book then you will have at least some familiarity with the contributions that Ron Clarke has made to the theory and practice of crime prevention. You will certainly have a better appreciation of just what an important and much-admired figure he has been in crime prevention after you have read the book. So I won't go into details about his work here. But I would like to highlight two lessons from Ron Clarke that have been guiding principles in the development of crime science.

The first lesson is to be specific. There are many models of crime prevention; what distinguishes Clarke's approach is the focus on the minutia of specific crime events. Clarke realised that preventing 'crime' was an impossible task. Preventing 'a' crime however, was a different matter. He was among the first to realise that the secret to crime prevention was the careful and detailed analysis of the micro-environments associated with particular crimes. Where others might have talked vaguely about crime being caused by bad neighbourhoods, Clarke demanded to know precisely what crimes, and what particular aspects of the neighbourhood were allowing these crimes to occur – the what, where, when, why, who and how. Situational crime prevention is characterised by a methodical, problem-solving approach. It is this approach derived from the scientific method that forms the basis of crime science.

The second lesson is to make an impact. Clarke's writings from the very beginning have been designed to inform practice. Those who know him will know that he is scathing of criminological papers that are inaccessible and self-indulgent, and that ultimately serve no practical purpose. He has a tenacious, single-minded commitment to reducing crime. Moreover, he has always sought to make his ideas clear and memorable – to choose just the right word, to crystallise concepts into summary tables, to invent a catchy acronym. Some of his most important writings have been guidebooks intended for use by front-line practitioners. But mark well, in his writing he may strive for simplicity but the content of his writing is far from simplistic. Clarke is an outstanding academic and I have little doubt that he has made a major and enduring contribution to crime prevention and to the field of criminology more generally.

As crime science has evolved over the last ten years its scope has broadened. To the traditional focus on crime prevention has been added a focus on crime detection – in the event that a crime does occur let us also bring the scientific method to bear of the task of apprehending the offender as swiftly as possible. Crime science has also sought more explicitly to draw in contributions from the physical sciences as well as the social sciences. Situational crime prevention, however, remains a core focus of crime science. I can think of no fitter book to join the Crime Science series than this one.

Introduction
Ronald V. Clarke – the quiet revolutionary

Graham Farrell and Nick Tilley

This book was conceived in late summer 2009 as we walked the coastline cliffs of Whitby in the northeast of England. Neither sun nor wind distracted us from agreement on two issues. The first was that Ron Clarke was probably the only living criminologist whose work would still be read in 100 years, and the second was that acknowledgement of his contribution by colleagues was seldom seen in print. Before we reached the café at Sandsend it was clear we needed a *Festschrift*. It is, we hope, a small gesture in the right direction. For Clarke's contribution is, we would argue, ample to be considered that of a disciplinary founding parent.

The other pieces fell quickly into place. At our first editorial brainstorming session we laughed at the notion of a volume title that parodied *The Reasoning Criminal*, his landmark book with Derek Cornish (Cornish and Clarke 1986). Then we paused as it dawned on us that the task of identifying a title was complete. We thank many of the contributors for their unsolicited confirmations that it is apt.

The contributor list almost wrote itself but we apologise to the many others we were unable to ask. Those who have written chapters are all Clarke collaborators or students. Thereafter, we congratulated ourselves that, as editorial tasks go, ours would be simple because we had inadvertently invited only world-class scholars. Oops. And we owe some of them an apology because they were so speedy and efficient that they outpaced us.

Rich Allinson and Brian Willan, former owners of Criminal Justice Press and Willan Publishing respectively, immediately saw the book's potential and sent a contract. This almost certainly reflected their admiration for Clarke accrued during years of collaboration on the *Crime Prevention Studies* peer-reviewed series, which Clarke founded and built as series editor. The series has become a principal reference point in the twenty or so years since its foundation. When Rich and Brian both sold their successful businesses shortly after this project began, Taylor & Francis had purchased Willan Publishing and happily continued the project. Julia Willan shepherded the book through its copy-editing stages and was a pleasure to work with. We thank them all.

After soliciting contributions and a contract we determined to consult Ron Clarke. A key benefit was being able to tell him we would interview him later in the process. By the time the interview took place it was clear many of the chapters would portray his professional contributions and context better than we could hope to here. Ron had also sent us the brief autobiographical account which is shown in the box 'My intellectual development', which squares well with the accounts in many of the chapters that follow.

During the years that we have known Ron, we have witnessed him nurture talent and provide assistance (advice, a contact, an idea) on many occasions, and have ourselves benefited from those activities. Ron is a private person, but we have come to know that the brilliant academic is a modest and compassionate man, considerate in thought and deed. So our contribution here is to offer readers a brief biographical account.[1] And while we caution against reading across from personal life to professional work, we hope some readers will enjoy this indulgence on our part. After undertaking this work we learned that Josh Freilich and Mangai Natarajan (2010) had written an enjoyable biographical note that, thankfully, largely corresponds with ours.

My intellectual development

Ronald V. Clarke[2]

I obtained a degree in the United Kingdom as a behavioural psychologist before being trained at London University's Maudsley Hospital as a clinical psychologist. On completing the training, I decided that research was more interesting than clinical practice and took a job as the first, and for a few years, the only full-time research officer in the UK system of training schools for delinquent boys. I was based in a large regional assessment centre where I was viewed with considerable suspicion by most of the staff, who constantly questioned the practical use of my work to the schools that employed me. This was a highly salutary experience, especially as the results of my early work (subsequently turned into a PhD dissertation) on predicting absconders from the schools produced so few usable results – those who ran away from the schools turned out to be little different from other residents in terms of their scores on a wide range of psychological tests and background variables. During this work, I made a discovery that led me to turn my back on my clinical training: despite the few differences between those who absconded and those who did not, there were enormous differences in rates of absconding among the eighty-eight schools in the system. This suggested that school environments were much stronger determinants of absconding than the dispositions of the residents and also suggested that changes made to the regimes and environments could substantially reduce absconding rates. Unfortunately, this discovery came too late in the research for its implications for the training schools to be fully explored.

My decision to abandon clinical psychology was reinforced by the results of another early study, a randomised controlled trial of a therapeutic regime in one training school, that I undertook with Derek Cornish (Clarke and Cornish 1972; Cornish and Clarke 1975). No significant differences were found between the reconviction rates of the boys in the therapeutic community and those in the control house and, like many other similar studies of the time (Martinson 1974), these findings showed that modifying criminal dispositions was very difficult.

On obtaining a PhD, pursued part-time, I obtained a post in the Home Office Research Unit (subsequently renamed the Research and Planning Unit) – the British government's criminological research department, which was by far the largest employer of criminologists in the country. Here, again, I was constantly challenged to make my research relevant to policy and practice – pressure that intensified as I moved up the ranks during my tenure in the Home Office from 1968–84, and as I became increasingly responsible for justifying the government's investment in criminological research in the bleak financial conditions of the times. This meant that every proposed research project had to be justified in advance by its contribution to Home Office business. This was often irksome to the researchers in the department because it imposed considerable discipline on them, and as much as I also squirmed under this yoke at the time, in retrospect I consider this to have been a very valuable and formative experience. Though I have been working now in universities for more than twenty years, I have never abandoned this research goal of policy relevance.

Some five or six years after joining the Home Office, I was put in charge of a section responsible for developing a programme of research intended to help to reduce crime. By then, an avalanche of negative evaluations published in the United States and the UK had all but destroyed the rehabilitative ideal that had guided Home Office policy and research for so many years. Other research, mostly from the United States, had also cast doubt on the ability of the courts or the police to do much to reduce crime (see Clarke and Cornish 1983). At around the same time, however, two books appeared – Oscar Newman's (1972) *Defensible Space* and C. Ray Jeffrey's (1971) *Crime Prevention through Environmental Design* – that reinforced in my mind the lessons of my absconding research: situational factors were powerful determinants of crime and they could likely be changed to reduce the opportunity for crime and hence its commission.

These ideas were tentatively explored in *Crime as Opportunity*, a Home Office research study authored together with several of my section members (Mayhew, Clarke, Sturman and Hough 1976) and subsequently developed in *Designing Out Crime* (Clarke and Mayhew 1980) and a *British Journal of Criminology* article on 'situational crime prevention' (Clarke 1980).

Personal development

We write this introduction in early 2011, which coincides with the seventieth anniversary of Ronald Clarke's birth. That event took place in the small town of Tanga in Tanganyika (now Tanzania), East Africa, on 24 April 1941, to a German mother and a British father. Tanganyika had been a German colony, becoming a British protectorate after the First World War. Ron's maternal grandfather had brought his family to Africa as a missionary bishop of the Moravian Church. Their daughter, Ron's mother, trained as a dentist at Tübingen University in Germany. She never liked dentistry and quit soon after meeting Ron's father on her return to Tanganyika, whereafter she developed a keen interest in wildlife. Ron's father had moved to Tanganyika around 1930 as a civil engineer after being in the British army since the age of sixteen.

Young Ronald was more fluent in Swahili than English, and the middle child to an older sister Veronica and younger brother Robin. When their parents separated in 1950 the three of them moved with their mother to the British coastal town of Teignmouth. The sea wall at Teignmouth had been extensively bombed during the war (the main railway line from London to Plymouth ran by the sea wall), and life for a newly arrived single mother with a pronounced German accent was not without difficulty at that time. Shortly after arrival, Ronald passed the exams that facilitated entry to the local grammar school. He recalls that his background made him somewhat of an outsider and how on one occasion some older girls, convinced that he was lying, grilled him on why he was not black if he was born in Africa! From school, Ronald went to university first in Bristol and then London and moved back to Bristol where, in 1966, he married Sheelagh. They have now lived in Milburn, New Jersey, in the United States, for many years, and have a cottage in Wimbledon, London. They have three children – Henry, George and Marianne – and seven grandchildren who, at the time of writing, are all aged under seven. Seven under sevens, Ron noted, with evident enjoyment of the symmetry.

Ron's younger brother Robin trained as an entomologist and, under the auspices of the UK's Overseas Development Agency, visited Bolivia in the mid-1970s to study crop beetles. He stayed on, was influential in setting up the Amboro National Park, and owns an eco-hotel about 100 miles from Santa Cruz. Robin courted controversy during his career for his outspoken stance on the need for better protection of parrots. We note a familiar theme yet, while Ron has visited Robin several times, as of the time of writing he had not yet sent him a copy of his recent works on the prevention of parrot poaching (Pires and Clarke 2011a, b). We would encourage him to do so and follow it with a copy of this volume because Ron took the photograph of the Rainbow Lorikeet that is on the cover, on 4 January 2003 in Lakes Entrance, Victoria, Australia. We suspect Robin would be proud that his elder brother has followed in at least some of his footsteps.

Older sister Veronica graduated in psychology from University College London. She lectured in psychology for many years at London Metropolitan University and is now retired. As a child she had contracted polio, which, as often happens with that disease, affects her more as she grows older. When we interviewed

Ron at University College London for this editorial on 18 March 2011, he was on his way to visit her home in the north of the city that afternoon.

For many years Ron has pursued a keen interest in bird photography. He may take six or seven hundred photographs in a morning. He has travelled widely in pursuit of this hobby, often with Johannes Knutsson (the author of Chapter 8 in this volume). They have visited places including Zimbabwe, Tanzania and Botswana along the way. Johannes also has some good photography gear, Ron quipped, but a little heavier and not quite as quick as his, and so not quite as good for capturing fast-moving targets. When pressed on whether his work had been exhibited, Ronnie – as Sheelagh calls him – was more modest but clearly proud that his work had been shown in their long-term home town of Milburn.

In Tanzania on one of their ornithological travels, Clarke and Knutsson visited Arusha, the small town where Ron last lived in Tanganyika. While the countryside was similarly beautiful, the town had changed beyond recognition into a sprawling city. Ron observed, however, that he almost certainly travelled along roads that his father, a civil engineer, had built.

Around 100 miles north of Arusha is the famous archaeological site of Olduvai Gorge where Mary and Louis Leakey discovered fossilised hominid remains, leading to the site sometimes being referred to as 'the Cradle of Humankind'. Their second son Richard Leakey, born in Nairobi, Kenya, in 1944, subsequently became Wildlife Minister for Kenya, an active conservationist and, at the time of writing, director of WildlifeDirect, the charity that helped saved gorillas in the Congo in 2007. He met Ron Clarke in the mid-1990s and Leakey talked of the need to evaluate the effect of the international ban on the ivory trade. Clarke identifies this as the origins of his recently published evaluation of that ban and its effects on elephant poaching in Africa (Lemieux and Clarke 2009).

Among the more influential components of Clarke's body of work is the set of twenty-five techniques of situational prevention. The set has evolved in his published work, from a crude eight techniques in the late 1970s, into the benchmark set of twelve in 1992, sixteen in 1997, then twenty-five in 2003 (for details, see Mayhew and Hough, Chapter 1 in this volume). When we challenged Ron on the fact that they are grouped lists of techniques but that they are not a matrix, even though each iteration appears as such visually, Ron grinned. Why did the length of each list always match? He suggested it probably reflected his somewhat compulsive desire for order and symmetry, but perhaps also, he added, the symmetry of the name of his father's car when Ron was about twelve – a Wolseley 4/44 (four cylinders, 44 horse power). We noted later that this would have directly mapped onto the breakthrough set of twelve techniques of the 1990s that consisted of four techniques for increasing the effort, four for increasing the risk, and four for reducing the rewards of crime, or 444.

The chapters and their story

Befitting a *Festschrift*, significant parts of Clarke's professional story are told directly and indirectly in the chapters that follow. This is not entirely coincidence, and in many instances we offered topic suggestions to authors in areas we hoped were appropriate and stimulating. Between them, the authors of this volume account for the bulk of editorships of the *Crime Prevention Studies* series that Ron Clarke founded. Several have known and worked with Clarke for decades. All acknowledge the influence of his thinking upon theirs.

Pat Mayhew and Mike Hough provide what to us is the intellectually thrilling story of their 'early days' working with Clarke at the Home Office, which saw them co-author landmark studies on situational crime prevention. Clarke was their line manager and influential in starting up the British Crime Survey that Mayhew and Hough made into what is almost certainly the best crime victimisation survey of its type.

Derek Cornish and Martha Smith focus on crime specificity, one of the cornerstones of the situational approach. Cornish's and Clarke's names will always be linked to the pioneering set of models and concepts that apply rational choice theory to crime prevention. Smith has co-authored various studies with Clarke on car theft and other crimes. Cornish and Smith, now married for many years, met when Cornish was a visiting professor at Rutgers University during Clarke's tenure as Dean at which time Smith was a mature research student.

British broadcaster and journalist Nick Ross provides a personal angle on his work with Clarke. For more than a decade they have been key driving forces in the development of the Jill Dando Institute of Crime Science at University College London. Much of the work of that institute relates to designing-out crime, which is closely associated with situational crime prevention and the subject of Paul Ekblom's chapter. Ekblom is professor of designing-out crime and traces his intellectual roots to his early work with Clarke in London at the Home Office.

Several of our chapters note the range of Clarke's influence upon various aspects of policing and crime prevention. Clarke chaired Anthony Braga's doctoral committee at Rutgers University, to which the latter has recently returned. Braga's chapter with David Kennedy links their influential Harvard-based work on deterring gun crime and gang violence to Clarke's framework of situational crime prevention techniques. John Eck is most known for his pioneering work on problem-solving policing and a series of theoretical and conceptual developments relating to routine activity theory and crime prevention. Among other things he collaborated with Clarke on their path-breaking manual, *Become a Problem-solving Crime Analyst in 55 Steps*, now reprinted around the world in many different languages. Tamara Madensen completed her doctoral work with Eck's guidance and recently completed an edited book on preventing crowd violence with Knutsson (Madensen and Knutsson 2011). Michael Scott and Herman Goldstein write, perhaps not surprisingly, on problem-oriented policing (POP). POP was Goldstein's brain-child and Scott has built the Centre for Problem-Oriented Policing into an invaluable resource with a major online presence (www.popcenter.org). Along with Eck and Madensen they chart and explore Clarke's significant influence upon POP. Scott and Goldstein offer the compelling and topically appropriate argument that Clarke's influence upon POP is an example of a diffusion of the benefits of situational crime prevention.

POP is also one of the areas in which Johannes Knutsson has made significant contributions. Ever professional, Knutsson's chapter on evaluation fails to mention his long friendship with Clarke and their global travels in pursuit of the ornithological, often in the wake of one of the annual symposiums on Environmental Criminology and Crime Analysis (ECCA). Mike Maxfield, author of the best-known criminal justice research methods text, worked at Rutgers for many years after bring recruited by Clarke. We were thrilled to be able to encourage Maxfield to expound on the issue of evaluation research methodology.

Nancy La Vigne, now Director of the Justice Policy Centre at the Urban Institute, was a Clarke doctoral student at Rutgers. Her chapter on CCTV reflects an enduring situational influence. David Weisburd was a young assistant professor in the Rutgers School of Criminal Justice when Clarke was appointed as Dean. Weisburd's chapter with Cody Telep portrays Clarke's major influence upon the area of crime displacement and in developing the concept of the diffusion of crime control benefits.

We thank David Lester for his most eloquent contribution on suicide prevention. The links with situational crime prevention and the inspiration for the series of co-authored publications with Clarke on the subject are in evidence. Ken Pease and Gloria Laycock both worked with and were influenced by Clarke at the Home Office in the 1970s and 1980s. Here they suggest that both psychology and behavioural economics may provide a broad theoretical foundation for situational crime prevention. Richard Wortley's chapter on person–situation interactions brings the attention to detail that has made him a leader in this area. Among his many contributions, Wortley's critiques of Clarke's work drove the growth of the situational crime prevention techniques from sixteen to twenty-five.

Mangai Natarajan's chapter explores how Clarke's CRAVED hypothesis, which denotes the characteristics of frequently stolen goods (they are Concealable, Removable, Available, Valuable, Enjoyable and Disposable) can be applied to goods that are trafficked such as illicit drugs. Natarajan was also a former doctoral student of Clarke's at Rutgers. Marcus Felson, long-term collaborator of Clarke and colleague at Rutgers for many years, will need little introduction to most readers. Felson is the intellectual driving force behind routine activity theory that is now closely linked with situational crime prevention. His chapter on the instrumental aspects of angry violence has his hallmark originality. Graeme Newman has co-authored many studies with Clarke in recent years including their books on preventing e-crime (Newman and Clarke 2003) and preventing terrorism (Clarke and Newman 2006). Newman's chapter with Josh Freilich describes how the scope of situational crime prevention has expanded in ways that were at one time unforeseen.

In our penultimate chapter, Kate Bowers and Shane Johnson, who together continue to drive much of the development of crime science at University College London, make a further contribution to their body of work on crime hotspots. The final chapter of the book is by Paul and Patricia Brantingham. They coined the term 'environmental criminology' over breakfast at the 1977 meeting of the American Society of Criminology. Along with Clarke they have worked to build the symposia and network of ECCA that continues to nurture much of the work in the area of environmental criminology and situational crime prevention. Their chapter suggests that Clarke's situational crime prevention may need to be situated in a portfolio of other strategies to be politically palatable.

Concluding note and a thesis

Ronald V. Clarke's work has already had a massive impact in many areas of criminological theory and practice. We judge the most important of his intellectual contributions to include:

- the twenty-five techniques of situational crime prevention;
- models and concepts for a rational choice perspective on offending;
- opportunity theory and its implications for crime prevention;
- recognition of the importance of situational relative to dispositional factors in offending;
- theoretical contributions to the study of displacement;
- the concept of diffusion of crime control benefits;
- the CRAVED hypothesis of the characteristics of frequently stolen products;
- delineation of the roles of routine and special precautions against crime;
- numerous case studies that analyse and inform the prevention of many specific types of crime;
- exemplary studies of POP;
- a series of guides for policy-makers and practitioners;
- provision of much of the thinking behind the development of crime science as a discipline.

Clarke has also facilitated progress in criminology and crime science in very practical ways by:

- setting up the *Crime Prevention Studies* series;
- helping to found the ECCA symposium and network;
- playing a key role in kick-starting the British Crime Survey;
- playing a central part in establishing the Home Office Crime Prevention Unit;
- influencing much policy and practice as Head of the Home Office Research and Planning Unit;
- influencing academia as Dean of the School of Criminal Justice at Rutgers University;
- advising and working on the development of crime science and the Jill Dando Institute at University College London;
- co-directing the Centre for Problem-Oriented Policing.

It may appear crude to attempt to summarise Clarke's contributions in two short lists. They are not exhaustive and we would argue that it is not their length but the quality of the contributions by which their merit should be gauged. Many are broad categories or titles that often belie a series of contributions or the development of a new field of study.

However, we would argue that Ronald V. Clarke's overarching contribution has been to develop a body of practical theory and evidence that informs policy and practice to prevent crime. This has involved some institution building along the way. The result is that he has, to our minds, re-shaped much of the field of criminology and guided the growth of the emerging discipline of crime science. Crime science, unlike most criminology, has crime prevention as its objective and aims to achieve it by incorporating the hard as well as the soft sciences. This is the natural culmination of Clarke's long-term disenchantment with the aims of much of criminological theory, which he argued should be 'not "understanding" crime in the abstract, but rather understanding to help control a variety of mostly selfish acts injuring society and often, in time, the perpetrators themselves' (Clarke and Felson 1993: 13). This was re-stated more recently as:

> [U]nless a criminological theory leads to clear and practical preventive policy it should be regarded as suspect. This would be heretical thinking to many criminologists who believe that theory should be free from 'correctional' ambitions because these limit and distort the understanding of crime. However, our view would be that, if a theory cannot be tested in the real world of crime control, this allows its proponents to make unsupported claims about its power and significance.
>
> (Clarke and Felson 2010)

We conclude by proposing a thesis that is summarised in the title of this chapter. It is that Clarke has been a quiet revolutionary. In around forty-five years of work to date he has, patiently and persistently, changed the direction of criminology. His work has been far more radical and critically insightful than any who typically claim the 'radical' or 'critical' monikers. We propose that Clarke's work will also prove far more durable. We therefore believe that we are a long way from yet experiencing the full impact he will have on crime-related theory, research, policy and practice.

Notes

1 We have both published more academic studies elsewhere that examine aspects of Clarke's work – see Tilley (2004) and Farrell (2010).
2 This is adapted from Clarke and Felson (2010).

References

Clarke, R.V. (1980) 'Situational crime prevention: theory and practice'. *British Journal of Criminology*, 20: 136–47.
Clarke, R.V. and D.B. Cornish. (1972) *The Controlled Trial in Institutional Research*. Home Office Research Studies No. 15. London: HMSO.

Clarke, R.V. and D.B. Cornish. (1983) *Crime Control in Britain – A Review of Policy Research*. Albany, NY: State University of New York Press.

Clarke, R.V. and P.M. Mayhew. (1980) *Designing Out Crime*. London: HMSO.

Clarke, R.V. and M. Felson. (1993) *Routine Activity and Rational Choice* (Advances in Criminological Theory, vol. 5). New Brunswick, NJ: Transaction.

Clarke, R.V. and M. Felson. (2010) 'The origins on the routine activity approach and situational crime prevention' in F. Cullen, C. Jonson, A. Myer and F. Adler (eds) *The Origins of American Criminology*. New Brunswick: Transaction Press.

Clarke, R.V. and G. Newman. (2006) *Outsmarting the Terrorists*. New York: Praeger.

Cornish, D.B. and R.V. Clarke. (1975) *Residential Treatment and its Effects on Delinquency*. Home Office Research Studies No. 32. London: HMSO.

Cornish, D.B. and R.V. Clarke. (1986) *The Reasoning Criminal: Rational Choice Perspectives on Offending*. New York: Springer-Verlag.

Farrell, G. (2010) 'Situational crime prevention and its discontents: rational choice and harm reduction versus "cultural criminology"'. *Social Policy and Administration*, 44(1): 40–66.

Freilich, J. and M. Natarajan. (2010) 'Ronald Clarke 1941–' in K. Hayward, S. Maruna and J. Mooney (eds) *Fifty Key Thinkers in Criminology*. London: Routledge.

Jeffrey, C.R. (1971) *Crime Prevention through Environmental Design*. Beverly Hills, CA: Sage Publications.

Lemieux, A.M. and R.V. Clarke. (2009) 'The international ban on ivory sales and its effects on elephant poaching in Africa'. *British Journal of Criminology*, 49(4): 451–71.

Madensen, T. and J. Knutsson. (eds) (2011) *Preventing Crowd Violence*. London: Lynne Rienner.

Martinson, R. (1974) 'What works? – questions and answers about prison reform'. *The Public Interest*, Spring: 22–54.

Mayhew, P., R.V. Clarke, A. Sturman and J.M. Hough. (1976) *Crime as Opportunity*. Home Office Research Studies No. 34. London: HMSO.

Newman, Graeme R. and R.V. Clarke. (2003) *Superhighway Robbery. Preventing Ecommerce Crime*. Cullompton: Willan Publishing.

Newman, O. (1972) *Defensible Space: Crime Prevention through Urban Design*. New York: Macmillan.

Pires, S.F. and R.V. Clarke. (2011a) 'Are parrots CRAVED? An analysis of parrot poaching in Mexico'. *Journal of Research in Crime and Delinquency*, Advanced Access, published online 15 March 2011.

Pires, S.F. and R.V. Clarke. (2011b) 'Sequential foraging, itinerant fences and parrot poaching in Bolivia'. *British Journal of Criminology*, 51(2): 314–35.

Tilley, N. (2004) 'Karl Popper: a philosopher for Ronald Clarke's situational crime prevention'. *Israel Studies in Criminology*, 8: 39–56.

Left: Ron's maternal grandparents, Bishop Oskar Gemuseus (Moravian Church) and Mathilde, in Tanganyika, in the 1930s. *Right*: Ron's father, Henry Leonard Clarke, in the Indian Army in the early 1920s.

Ron's sister Veronica, Ron aged 13, his brother Robin and his father with their dog and the Wolesley 4/44 car in Bukoba, in Tanganyika, August 1954.

Ron aged 11.

Robin, Veronica and Ron (aged 15) in Teignmouth, Devon, 1956.

Ron aged 17, mother Barbara, sister Veronica, brother Robin and father, Teignmouth.

Ron and Sheelagh's marriage, 19th August 1966.

Tom Lodge, Ron, and John Croft at the Home Office, February 1983.

Ron in Wellington, New Zealand for the 2004 ECCA Symposium.

Brasil, 16 July 2009, after ECCA in Santiago, Chile. Photos on this page by Johannes Knutsson.

Ron holds up traffic in South Africa, 13 January 2009.

1 Situational crime prevention
The Home Office origins

Pat Mayhew and Mike Hough

Introduction

This chapter tells the story of how Ron Clarke developed his thinking on situational crime prevention (SCP) at the Home Office, and how SCP became integrated into Home Office thinking about ways of reducing crime. To summarise a complex story, Ron saw criminal policy at the time as overly focused on attempts to reduce offending through rehabilitation or social welfare. In contrast to the assumptions underpinning this approach, Ron saw crime as a diverse set of behaviours best explained by the interaction of criminal propensity (or disposition) and situational opportunities, with the latter – in his view – considerably more amenable to policy intervention than the former. He thus promoted SCP as a way of focusing on the immediate circumstances under which crime occurs, by using mechanisms to block obvious criminogenic opportunities and to alter the balance of risks and rewards for offenders. In the decade following his departure from the Home Office in 1984, this approach became quite well institutionalised in the Home Office and beyond. This chapter focuses on the early development of SCP, which took form on the basis of a number of studies that Ron started in the Home Office in the 1970s. We begin with a résumé of Ron's career in the Home Office, moving onto the development of his research agenda, the criminological context in which Ron's 'manifesto' for SCP was launched, and how the research he initiated fundamentally changed the discourse about crime prevention in the Home Office and related agencies. We also deal with the advent of the British Crime Survey and how this fitted into Ron's agenda. Our assessment – not, incidentally, shared by Ron himself – is that he was enormously successful in promoting the SCP perspective and in making it part of the everyday currency of crime control policy.

We should preface the story by saying something about our own role in it, as we can hardly claim to be dispassionate observers. We worked closely with Ron from the mid-1970s to the mid-1980s, first on SCP research and then on the British Crime Survey. Both together and separately we co-authored a number of publications with him. In relation to SCP, at least, we were foot-soldiers working to his agenda rather than our own. We both had – and retain – considerable sympathy for this agenda. We have also benefitted greatly in professional terms from our association with Ron and from the opportunity to work on a significant programme of work. On the other hand, neither of us has sustained a professional interest in SCP to the same extent as some of the other contributors to this volume. One of us (PM) has accumulated extensive experience in the UK and internationally in surveys of victimisation – to which SCP has some, but not central, relevance. The other (MH) has been increasingly promiscuous in his research interests, including work on rehabilitation, on drug treatment and compliance theories, all of which might considered to be tarnished with the 'dispositional' tendency in criminology that Ron found objectionable. We leave it to the reader to decide whether this renders us well or badly qualified to offer a history of the early days of SCP.

Ron Clarke's Home Office career

Ron worked for the Home Office between 1964 and 1984, when he 'brain drained' to the United States to take up a post at Temple University in Philadelphia. Between 1964 and 1968, he was employed as a researcher by the Home Office at Kingswood Approved School.[1] Here, he worked on the *Kingswood Controlled Trial of Residential Treatment for Delinquents*, which is returned to. Ron moved to London in 1968 to join the Home Office Research Unit (HORU) as a senior research officer. He stayed in the Home Office until 1984 except for a period as Visiting Professor at the State University of New York at Albany between 1981/2. He became the head of the Home Office Research and Planning Unit (RPU) in 1983. RPU had come into being in 1981 as a revamp of HORU designed to give a greater focus on policy analysis. It thus took over some of the remit of the Crime Policy Planning Unit, which was established in the early 1970s but closed in 1981 when HORU changed into RPU.

Ron has described his Home Office career as extremely rewarding, albeit with frustrations. It is fair to say that he preferred his academic workload to managerial and personnel tasks. It is also fair to say, though, that he performed these diligently enough. His decision to move to the US was prompted by personal considerations (his wife had strong American ties), and the lure of greener and less constrained academic pastures. Ron was also bruised by a prolonged battle within the Home Office over the publication of *Crime and Police Effectiveness* (Clarke and Hough, 1984) – to which his administrative colleagues eventually and very reluctantly agreed.[2] But the experience probably confirmed him in his decision to leave.

Throughout Ron's time in the Home Office, under the leadership first of John Croft and then Ron himself, HORU/RPU was a dominant force in British criminology, employing more criminologists than any other institution in the country. Their business was to (1) undertake in-house research of policy relevance on topics negotiated with Home Office administrative units; (2) manage Home Office-funded research in universities; and (3) provide 'on tap' advice to administrators and ministers. The reputation of the Unit was strong, helped by a sustained output of reports dealing with in-house research on a variety of topics in the Home Office's area of business. These reports appeared in both the Home Office's own research series and as academic publications. There was a stronger tradition of publication in academic outlets then than now. Ron always supported this – and he added considerably to the list of academic publications by government criminologists. He saw no contradiction with his belief that the main purpose of social research was for it to be relevant to policy, especially as 'applied' research in his judgement needed to be grounded in theory.

This is not to say that HORU/RPU had a comfortable relationship with academic criminology. In the 1970s, the discipline had become quite sharply polarised between the traditional 'positivist' approach and the emergent radicalism associated with the National Deviancy Conference (NDC). Governmental criminology was seen to be closely aligned with the 'positivists' – which was a term of abuse at the time.

Ron's belief in the importance of social research conducted for policy purposes was a major strength of his work in the Home Office but it was not without costs for him. For one, he had to cope with the fact that many researchers he worked with and managed had considerable sympathy for the emerging academic radicalism of the 1970s – with its inherent detachment from policy concerns. More importantly, though, as key academics in the NDC movement later regrouped into 'New Realists' in the early 1980s and themselves began to engage effectively in policy research, researchers in the RPU were given the disparaging label of 'administrative criminologists'. Ron became to be seen as one of the main faces of administrative criminology, which was criticised for being a-theoretical and politically compromised, in the sense that it was institutionally debarred from engaging with explanations of crime that paid heed to the 'basic social and economic problems of a divided society' (Young, 1997: xii).[3] For many government criminologists at the time, the 'administrative' label – with its connotations of being mere functionaries – was probably less comfortable to wear than those placed on us when criminology was in its heyday of radicalism. It was certainly a brilliant marketing tactic on the part of the New Realists as they embraced the idea of policy relevance (Lea and Young, 1984).

The early research agenda

Ron's early academic work was initially aligned with the criminological agenda that characterised the work of HORU and the Cambridge Institute since their establishment in the 1950s: principally, the 'causes' of offending, and the effectiveness of treatment for those who offended. However, he moved away from the then widely shared presupposition that crime could be best controlled by rectifying the criminal predispositions of individuals before they became involved in crime, or afterwards through effective use of the criminal justice system.

Ron worked with Derek Cornish on *the Kingswood Controlled Trial of Residential Treatment for Delinquents*. It compared the relative effectiveness in reducing offending of a 'therapeutic community' approach with a traditional training regime (Cornish and Clarke, 1975). The finding that there was no difference in outcomes was seen by Ron as testament to the overriding influence of the post-release social and physical environment. This presented 'opportunities' and 'situational inducements' to offend that Ron saw as undermining any effects of treatment. Ron also lauded Ian Sinclair's (1971) work that showed that whether or not boys absconded or re-offended while in probation hostels depended more on the way hostels were managed than on the boys' histories. Likewise, his own work on boys absconding from approved schools showed that the only factor explaining different absconding rates was the opportunity to abscond presented by either the physical security of the premises or elements of the regime (Clarke and Martin, 1971). This early work prompted Ron to believe that immediate situational influences were important in both understanding and reducing crime.

If Ron was moving rapidly away from the positivist tradition of rehabilitative criminology, he was by no means the only person to be doing so in the 1970s. Both in Britain and North America there was a growing pessimism about the capacity of 'people-changing' professionals to have any benign effect whatsoever – whether in education, social work, psychiatry or criminal justice.[4] Within the Home Office, Stephen Brody's (1976) report, *The Effectiveness of Sentencing*, pulled together the evidence on the effectiveness of the various penal disposals: for instance, fines, community service orders, borstals, approved schools, prisons, parole and probation, reaching conclusions that echoed the 'nothing works' message from America (Lipton et al., 1975; Martinson, 1974).

What differentiated Ron's position from the 'impossibilism' of those arguing that 'nothing works' was that he had a very clear belief that some crime control strategies *did* work, in the shape of SCP. In other words he had something to offer policy that promised to fill the vacuum left by the research – broadly accepted at the time – that had undermined the rehabilitative aspirations of the 1950s and 1960s.[5] The Brody Report had been particularly influential within the Home Office. It led to a marked shift in Home Office research, in large part orchestrated by Ron, away from evaluating penal treatments towards, principally, research on crime prevention – i.e. interventions before rather than after crime had occurred. We now look at Ron's work in developing SCP, then move onto associated policing research, although in fact they ran in tandem and overlapped.

The development of SCP

As our focus is on Ron's development of SCP in the Home Office, we restrict ourselves to a brief overview of SCP itself, although there are now numerous accounts of its underlying theoretical base and practical application.

The terms in which Ron currently describes SCP have not changed from the early days:

> SCP is the science of reducing opportunities for crime. It focuses on specific forms of crime or disorder and analyses the opportunity structure giving rise to these problems – in particular, the immediate settings in which they occur. It then seeks to identify the changes in the design and management of these settings that will reduce crime with fewest economic and social costs. These changes are intended to discourage potential offenders by increasing the risks

or difficulties of crime, making it less rewarding or excusable and reducing temptations or provocations.

(Clarke, 2010: 879–83)

Ron in fact lays no claim to inventing the term 'situational crime prevention', although he was happy to adopt it. It originated, as far as we can tell, in discussions in the late 1970s in a working group set up by the Home Office Crime Policy Planning Unit, led by Chris Train. Before that, 'physical' crime prevention was the favoured term – used for instance in the first publication promoting SCP, *Crime as Opportunity* (Mayhew et al., 1976). 'Situational crime prevention', though, was in use by the time *Designing Out Crime* appeared in 1980 (Clarke and Mayhew, 1980). 'Environmental crime prevention' and 'crime prevention through environmental design' (CPTED) also got a look-in as terms seen as largely synonymous with SCP, although Ron sees these more about dealing with *anticipated* problems in design on the basis of previous experience, as against SCP's focus on *existing* problems (Clarke, 2009).

Now that SCP has clocked up innumerable successes and is increasingly accepted as being on a firm theoretical base, it is easy to forget the cool reception it got in many quarters early on. Recently, Wortley (2010) has listed the criticisms in full. The main ones are as follows. First, SCP ignored the macro-level, sociocultural and individual dispositional factors that cause offending, treating it simply as a person–situation interaction. Second, it lacked theoretical sophistication, amounting to little more than a simplistic response to complex social problems. Third, SCP would not stop offending, but merely displace it in time, place or form – perhaps even making matters worse by encouraging offenders to escalate their efforts. Fourth, while SCP might be appropriate in reducing acquisitive crime, it would not cope well with 'irrational' crimes, crimes of passion or ones involving strong drives. Finally, SCP was seen as invasive and oppressive, leading to a 'fortress society'.

Ron (and indeed others, including Wortley) has responded to these criticisms in robust fashion (see, more recently, Clarke, 2005, 2009). The purpose here is not to address the criticisms on Ron's behalf, but note them as challenges that he faced at the time. Arguably, these challenges were a consequence of Ron's strategy for promoting SCP. Many people would readily accept that situational measures have their place in a broad church of preventive strategies. But Ron tended to frame the policy options in terms of 'either situational *or* social prevention' rather than 'both/and' – stemming from his deep-seated conviction that SCP outperforms social prevention. Setting up this sort of competition between the two forms of prevention probably helped embed SCP successfully in policy thinking – but at the same time it may have engendered some resistance to the otherwise acceptable idea that reducing opportunities for crime will, in very many situations, actually reduce crime.

The early publications on SCP

The 1976 publication, *Crime as Opportunity* (Mayhew et al., 1976), was the first to set out the case for SCP. It had discursive introductory and concluding chapters, with two empirical studies sandwiched in between. One was on the introduction of steering columns locks (SCLs) on new cars in the UK. The other was a study of the location of vandalism on different types of buses, which showed that there was more damage on buses without conductors and in parts of the bus with low supervision. (The first study is more memorable than the second.) The introductory chapter of *Crime as Opportunity* discussed one piece of evidence that struck Ron particularly forcefully. This was the dramatic fall in coal-gas suicides, following a substantial reduction in the toxic content of domestic coal gas. The fall in coal-gas suicides (a common method of suicide at the time) was reflected in an overall drop in suicide rates in the UK. This suggested to Ron that despite suicide being seen as behaviour determined by strong internal motivations, a simple change in the opportunity for killing oneself could have a marked effect on suicide rates. Ron saw this as crucial to the 'displacement' argument, since it suggested that blocking one opportunity to commit suicide did not necessarily lead those with suicidal intent to choose another more unpleasant alternative.

The second piece of evidence that carried weight with Ron at the time was the substantial fall in thefts and unauthorised taking of cars in the Federal Republic of Germany after legislation requiring *all* cars to be fitted with an SCL. This was the spur for the first of the two studies reported in *Crime as Opportunity*, looking at the effectiveness of UK legislation in 1971 that required all *new* cars in the UK to be fitted with an SCL. The results showed a different picture to the German experience. There were lower theft rates for new cars, but little change in the overall number of thefts. This, it was argued, was because there were plenty of older vehicles to keep car thieves in business. Displacement (in this case) was easy. With hindsight, the prescience of the SCL study can be seen as remarkable given that rates of car thefts have fallen substantially as a result of increasingly effective in-built security, SCLs being the beginning.

A number of other SCP Home Office Research Studies (HORS) followed *Crime as Opportunity*. They contained studies of various forms of SCP as well as evaluations of other crime prevention strategies popular at the time, such as publicity campaigns. The first publication after *Crime as Opportunity* was *Tackling Vandalism* (HORS 47, Clarke, 1978). One study, set in two London housing estates, tested the 'defensible space' hypothesis of the New York architect, Oscar Newman. Newman's ideas struck a chord with Ron. Essentially, Newman (1972) proposed that residential environments should be designed in ways to reduce crime by adhering to two principles in particular: 'territoriality' (sub-dividing buildings and grounds in ways to discourage outsiders from entering and encourage residents to defend their areas); and 'surveillance' (designing buildings to allow easy observation of territorial areas). In this, Newman was on Ron's wavelength: changing the environment rather than offenders. Moreover, it helped Ron's case immensely that Newman's ideas got unusually wide coverage in the popular press and were adopted by local planners in the UK.

Crime in Public View appeared in 1979 (HORS 49, Mayhew et al., 1979). It assessed the effects of 'natural surveillance' on telephone kiosk vandalism in a London borough,[6] and evaluated the experimental introduction of CCTV at four stations of the London Underground – perhaps the first evaluation of CCTV in the UK. *Crime Prevention and the Police* followed next, also in 1979 (HORS 55, Burrows et al., 1979), consisting of two studies. One study evaluated a 'truancy sweep' by Bristol police – considered a form of 'environmental management'. The second study examined the (non-existent) effect of a publicity campaign by Plymouth police to persuade car owners to lock their cars. Two further evaluations of crime prevention publicity campaigns appeared in the next publication, *Crime in Public View* (HORS 63, Riley and Mayhew, 1980). Finally, *Co-ordinating Crime Prevention Efforts* (HORS 62, Gladstone, 1980) reported on a 'demonstration project' mounted by the Home Office Crime Prevention Unit (CPU) to test interagency co-operation in dealing with vandalism in Manchester schools. (One lesson of this was that SCP measures were often favoured at local level, but there was also residual support for 'social' remedies, even though these proved more difficult to get off the ground.)

The studies in HORS 34 were drawn together in *Designing Out Crime* (Clarke and Mayhew, 1980). An introductory chapter started the first of several subsequently developed typologies of different types of SCP measures. In *Designing Out Crime*, there were eight; there are now twenty-five (Clarke, 2009: 267).

The later Home Office publications

Work in which Ron was involved produced further publications after he left the Home Office. Some but not all of these focused on policing in relation to crime prevention. The year 1986 saw a volume edited by Kevin Heal and Gloria Laycock that developed the theoretical ideas behind SCP, with rational choice theory getting an early airing by Ron (Heal and Laycock, 1986). It then presented a number of applications of crime analyses and situational preventive measures. It noted the still evident tension between social and situational prevention, as well as problems of interagency implementation, a theme that Hope (1985) had also developed on the basis of some early interagency projects.

Policing research

Ron's programme of policing research in the 1970s and early 1980s resulted in both another 'bad news' message, but also in a new focus for policing, which Ron aligned to SCP. The 'bad news' message was about the limited preventive impact of traditional patrolling, and putting 'more police on the ground' (Clarke and Hough, 1980, 1984). It was seen as a controversial conclusion (with Margaret Thatcher promising to increase police numbers) and one that posed difficulties for the Home Office (*plus ça change*). At the same time, though, it revealed both the paucity of thinking of a 'more patrols/more police' approach to reducing crime, and (letting the police off the hook somewhat) helped cement the idea that responsibility for crime prevention lay with other agencies beyond the police.[7] This led to a significant change in Home Office crime prevention policy, as will be seen.

Although crime prevention has always been a stated function of the police in the UK, it was rarely seen as 'real' policing (Reiner, 1992). To be sure, there was a different strand of crime prevention work in the police at the time, done by (rather low status) crime prevention officers and slightly later by crime prevention panels, which were led by the police. Ron would not have derided all that they did, but in his terms much of it achieved little (publicity campaigns for instance).

Ron pushed forward policing research, notably in relation to what he called 'situational policing'. He promoted this as a more targeted form of policing to (1) analyse crime problems better; (2) identify the places and institutions that attract a disproportionate amount of crime; and (3) put in place (along with other agencies) mechanisms to reduce opportunities for crime, and increase risks. One early example was a study of street attacks in city centres (Poyner, 1980). Situational policing was in the same stable as problem-oriented policing (POP). This was being promoted at the same time in the US by Herman Goldstein as a method of policing in which officers were encouraged to use problem-solving techniques to deal innovatively with crime problems using the technique of SARA (scanning, analysing, responding and assessing). As these things go, the British police were somewhat over-awed by these American developments with the result that situational policing enjoyed some synergy with POP.

In the RPU, policing research continued to some extent after Ron left, with a study of police effectiveness in investigating burglary published in 1986 for instance (Burrows, 1986). With time, however, the term situational policing lost currency, although its basic principles were carried forward in the work of the Home Office CPU, set up in the Police Department in 1983, later becoming the Police Research Group (PRG). Both CPU and PRG were staffed largely by researchers originally recruited to RPU, but with policy personnel and seconded police officers on board too. They were headed initially by Kevin Heal and then by Gloria Laycock, who went on in 2001 to become the Director of the Jill Dando Institute of Crime Science. The PRG was closed down in 2002, as research resources were 'streamlined'. Later, police research in the Home Office emerged actively again but largely with an emphasis on improving confidence in the police, through 'reassurance policing' and neighbourhood policing for instance.

The integration of SCP into the mainstream

As said, one outcome of policing research in the 1970s and early 1980s was that it cemented the idea that responsibility for crime prevention should be shared between the police, other local agencies and indeed ordinary citizens – a process dubbed by David Garland (2001) as that of 'responsibilisation'. There had been much lip-service to this before of course, but it began to get much stronger and more forceful articulation. An inter-departmental working group on crime reduction was set up by the Home Secretary William Whitelaw in 1982, which endorsed a new approach in which SCP got prominent billing (Home Office, 1983). More importantly, this was followed by Circular 8/84 (issued to Chief Constables and others by the Home Office and other government departments (Home Office et al.,

1984), which Bottoms described as 'the cornerstone of most subsequent official policies on crime prevention' in England and Wales (Bottoms, 1990: 3)).

Circular 8/84 again endorsed the delivery of crime prevention through multi-agency partnerships, essentially within an SCP framework. SCP was also high on the agenda of a crime prevention seminar in 1985, chaired by the Prime Minister. (One item was the design of prepayment gas and electricity coin meters, a common target of burglaries on poor housing estates.) This led to a ministerial group on crime prevention in 1986. In 1988, core funding support was given for a large-scale Safer Cities programme, in which local partnerships had to deliver initiatives to address local concerns – see Tilley (1993) for background and results. Government funding was also given in 1988 to a new voluntary agency, Crime Concern, to support crime prevention at the local level, largely involving the private sector. In 1990, there was a further Home Office Circular again encouraging partnership working and providing examples of good practice (Home Office, 1990). The Morgan Report followed with the suggestion that crime prevention should be a statutory responsibility (Home Office, 1991) – albeit rejected at the time. In 1995, a challenge fund was set up for CCTV in town centres, marking the beginning of what has been a momentous expansion of CCTV in the UK.

After the election of the Labour government in 1997, the stakes were raised with the Crime and Disorder Act (1998). This placed a statutory duty on local police, in partnership with local government, to create crime and disorder reduction partnerships (CDRPs) and to develop (and publish) strategic plans to reduce crime and disorder, based on crime audits and local consultation. There was wide variability in the quality of the work conducted by CDRPs, but most of them drew eclectically on a mix of situational and social prevention strategies. It is questionable whether or not Ron would have approved of this eclecticism. What is beyond question is that by 2000 SCP and 'designing out crime' were ideas that had thoroughly permeated the emerging 'community safety' profession. This is not the place to review the outcomes of the CDRPs (for which see, e.g., Hough, 2006, 2007). But suffice it to say that the intention behind them reflected at least one of the principles of SCP: to gather and analyse data about the precise nature of local crime problems.

The year 1998 also saw the announcement of the three-year Crime Reduction Programme, with an original budget of £250m. Partly behind this was a Home Office report, *Reducing Offending*, which reviewed the 'what works' literature (Goldblatt and Lewis, 1998). Rehabilitative treatment (especially cognitive behaviour therapy) made an appearance, along with other approaches, including SCP. In any event, the aims of the Crime Reduction Programme were ambitious: to produce a sustained reduction in crime, and improve and mainstream knowledge of the most cost-effective practices (Homel et al., 2004). Two of the five thrusts of the programme reflected Ron's contribution. One was tackling high-volume crime such as domestic burglary, where a key theme was to develop local infrastructure and skills to identify the nature of different problems. The other was the development of products and systems that are resistant to crime, which went under the 'Foresight' programme. Again, the outcome of this massive injection of funds into reducing crime is not our business here, although the Crime Reduction Programme clearly and extensively underachieved on its ambitions, largely because of implementation failure (see, e.g., Hough, 2004; Maguire, 2004).

The British Crime Survey

The development of the British Crime Survey (BCS) took place when SCP was beginning to bed down in the Home Office. Discussion about the survey started in 1977, but gained impetus after a workshop in Cambridge early in 1981 at which 'big guns' from abroad helped make the case. There was yet further impetus after the Brixton riots in mid-1981, which propelled issues of 'law and order' even more into the spotlight. The first sweep of the BCS went into the field in early 1982 and results were published a year later (Hough and Mayhew, 1983).

Ron was heavily instrumental in promoting the BCS as a new way of measuring crime that would overcome the increasingly recognised deficiencies of police records. The obvious political risk was that a national victimisation survey would reveal a substantial and hitherto hidden amount of unrecorded crime (see Hough and Maxfield, 2007). For Ron, however, the political risks of documenting a large 'dark figure' of crime were worth taking, given the prize in prospect of BCS findings that would strengthen the case for more work on preventing crime as it ordinarily impacted on the public, rather than as the police knew it. In Ron's view, the 'truer' picture of crime from the BCS would show how (1) the majority of crime involved property loss or damage, which was (2) committed by offenders because of the everyday opportunities presented by often ill-secured targets.

Our recollection is that Ron saw the case for a national victimisation survey as persuasive in its own terms, and not simply a means for advancing SCP. Nonetheless, the BCS served him well in this respect:

- The BCS raised RPU's profile in the Home Office and thus possibly gave Ron's more specific SCP interests a more sympathetic hearing.
- The survey shifted attention away from the needs of offenders to the consequences of crime for victims.
- The BCS showed the extent to which crimes went unknown to the police and therefore lay beyond the reach of the criminal justice system. This result in particular fitted with the message of Circular 8/84, which appeared shortly after the first BCS results.
- Through questions on self-reported offending in some of the earlier sweeps, the BCS showed the overlap between offending and victimisation at the individual level (Mayhew and Elliott, 1990). This dented the notion of offenders being a distinctly special population, and lent weight to the 'lifestyle' perspective that underlying common denominators such as being young, male, residence in an urban area, and having an active night-time social life increase both exposure to victimisation and the likelihood of getting into trouble.

- The survey exposed the phenomenon of repeat victimisation. This generated a number of studies in the SCP mould, the *Kirkholt Burglary Prevention Demonstration Project* being the best known (Forrester et al., 1988). In due course, the reduction of repeat victimisation became a performance measure for the police.
- The BCS also tracked how the common targets of theft changed over time, showing how the simple availability (and desirability) of targets could determine crime patterns. Mobile phones were one case in point (Harrington and Mayhew, 2001).

After he had left the Home Office, Ron remained a strong supporter of the BCS. He used the 1984 BCS himself to demonstrate how the risks of vehicle crime varied by location. His purpose was to show how better management of private car parking spaces could reduce vehicle crime. The route to this involved a complicated module of questions in the BCS to measure the duration for which household cars were parked in different locations, with actual thefts at these locations then computed to give 'exposure-adjusted' risks. (Dealing with the inevitable complexity of the questions and analysis was typical of Ron's persistence.) Results showed that, allowing for the parking time at each location, cars parked in public car parks were four times more vulnerable than cars parked outside the driver's home or workplace, and 40 per cent more vulnerable than cars parked on any other street (Clarke and Mayhew, 1998).

A stocktaking

By the time Ron left the Home Office in 1984, SCP had gained acceptance within policy units and was well-embedded in the research agenda of CPU, and then PRG. Ron himself continued to contribute to Home Office research, doing various pieces of work for PRG, including one on 'hot products' (Clarke, 1999) – analogous to the notion of 'hot spots', which he had promoted before.

After Ron's departure from the Home Office, others apart from us continued to develop SCP. It is fair to say that Mary Tuck, Ron's successor as the director of RPU, was sceptical about several aspects of SCP, and work on this within RPU largely stopped – though Paul Ekblom continued with a programme of relevant work until he moved to PRG. It was within PRG that most SCP work was focused from the mid-1980s until the early 2000s. Thereafter, the development of SCP in the UK occurred mainly in academic settings – notably in the Jill Dando Institute at University College London, although important work was also done in Huddersfield, Keele, Loughborough, Nottingham Trent, Manchester and elsewhere. And it was, of course, taken forward by Ron himself on US soil – with the same energy and dogged persistence. In RPU, the inventive in-house research that Ron was so good at withered rather, as the research agenda became increasingly framed by policy officials.

Ron's own interest in policing remained after he left the Home Office. He became a co-director of the Center for Problem-Oriented Policing whose publications are distributed by the US Department of Justice Office of Community Oriented Policing Services (COPS Office). He has also regularly worked and written for the Jill Dando Institute, which is concerned with police training among other things, and whose notion of 'crime science' is much akin to SCP although expanded to include the work of catching offenders.

More than twenty-five years after Ron left it, the old Home Office responsibilities have been divided between the Ministry of Justice and a slimmed-down Home Office, which retains policing responsibilities and much (though not all) of the work of reducing crime. There seems little research on SCP now emanating from the Home Office, although a 2006 report from the Economics and Resource Analysis Strategic Policy Team, *Changing Behaviour to Prevent Crime*, discusses how to design security features into new products, reduce crime on industrial estates, and reduce theft of old cars (Home Office, 2006). All this is very much along SCP lines – albeit it does not mention the term or once cite Ron. Broadly put, Home Office research has moved towards monitoring performance (rather than evaluating it), and expanding victimisation survey work. There is also considerably more research on drugs and immigration issues. The re-location of researchers to policy units after 2004 also arguably dissipated the intellectual thrust of Home Office research. The academic critique of 'administrative criminology' is perhaps more apposite now than it was in Ron's time.

The principles of SCP, however, are evident in recent policy messages from the Home Office. For instance, SCP featured in the 2007 Home Office *Cutting Crime* Strategy, although well-padded by correctional and law enforcement strategies, as well as social reformist ones (early intervention much to the fore). Moreover, 'crime analysts' are now firmly embedded in the police. One recent development has been the setting up of a Design and Technology Alliance panel headed by Sebastian Conran to identify emerging crime problems and develop solutions. More generally, the practice of SCP is now institutionalised in the burgeoning community safety 'industry' associated with the work of local CDRPs. It is often so routine as to be unnoticed – for instance in the design and management of transportation systems – an area which Ron has actively researched (see Smith and Clarke, 2000). It is hard to see how this could have come about without the work Ron started in the Home Office.

We see Ron's promotion of SCP as a remarkable achievement. The situational approach to crime control has become institutionalised within police forces and CDRPs, and is woven tightly into government policy about crime – even if its antecedents go unrecognised. In discussions that we have had with Ron on this subject, he takes a more pessimistic view: that take-up of his ideas has been partial and limited. This stubborn pessimism is perhaps a pointer to the reasons for his success. The pessimism reflects ambitions for SCP that were, and remain, very high indeed – and are arguably unachievable. If he had simply promoted SCP as one of several strategies for tackling crime – best deployed in combination with social prevention and rehabilitative work with offenders – few people would have taken issue with his ideas. But probably few would have taken much notice of them, either.

Notes

1 Approved schools were open institutions, in contrast to borstals, which were secure. The former have been relabelled as community homes, and the latter as young offender institutions.
2 The publication was a review of the literature on police effectiveness that challenged the orthodoxy of the day that there was a close relationship between police activity and crime levels – a message that some judged to be politically unpalatable. This is discussed further later in the chapter.
3 It must be remembered that these developments were happening against the backdrop of Thatcherite economic policies – even if the then Home Secretary was quietly pursuing a socially liberal policy agenda.
4 The idea of 'radical non-intervention' (Schur, 1973) was by no means restricted to criminology. The anti-psychiatry movement in particular exercised a strong cultural pull on related fields.
5 This position was reversed from the mid-1990s onwards, as policy recognised the overstatements of the 'nothing works' position.
6 Providing one of us (MH) with the – probably unique but unrewarding – experience of visiting every public telephone kiosk in Greenwich.
7 It contained the much-quoted statistic that a police officer patrolling randomly on foot in an average beat could expect to come within a hundred yards of a burglary in progress once every eight years (Clarke and Hough, 1984: 7).

References

Bottoms, A.E. (1990). 'Crime prevention facing the 1990s'. *Policing and Society*, 1, 3–22.
Brody, S. (1976). *The Effectiveness of Sentencing*. Home Office Research Study No. 35. London: HMSO.
Burrows, J. (1986). *Investigating Burglary: The Measurement of Police Performance*. Home Office Research Study No. 88. London: HMSO.
Burrows, J., Ekblom, P. and Heal, K. (1979). *Crime Prevention and the Police*. Home Office Research Study No. 55. London: HMSO.
Clarke, R.V. (ed.) (1978). *Tackling Vandalism*. Home Office Research Study No. 47. London: HMSO.
Clarke, R.V. (1999). 'Hot products: understanding, anticipating and reducing the demand for stolen goods'. Police Research Group Paper No. 112. London: Home Office.
Clarke, R.V. (2005). 'Seven misconceptions of situational crime prevention'. In N. Tilley (ed.), *Handbook of Crime Prevention and Community Safety*. Cullompton: Willan Publishing.
Clarke, R.V. (2009). 'Situational crime prevention: theoretical background and current practice'. In M.D. Krohn, A.J. Lizotte and G.P. Hall (eds), *Handbook on Crime and Deviance*. New York: Springer Science+Business Media.
Clarke, R.V. (2010). 'Situational crime prevention'. In, B.S. Fisher and S.P. Lab (eds), *Encyclopaedia of Victimology and Crime Prevention*. London: Sage.
Clarke, R.V. and Hough, M. (eds) (1980). *The Effectiveness of Policing*. Farnborough: Gower.
Clarke, R.V. and Hough, M. (1984). *Crime and Police Effectiveness*. Home Office Research Study No. 79. London: HMSO.
Clarke R. G. and Martin, D. (1971). *Absconding from Approved Schools*. London: HMSO.
Clarke, R.V. and Mayhew, P. (eds) (1980). *Designing Out Crime*. London: HMSO.
Clarke, R.V. and Mayhew, P. (1998). 'Preventing crime in parking lots: what we know and

need to know'. In *Crime Prevention through Real Estate Management and Development.* Washington, DC: Urban Land Institute.
Cornish, D. and Clarke, R. V. (1975). *Residential Treatments and its Effects on Delinquency.* London: HMSO.
Forrester, D., Chatterton, M. and Pease, K. (1988). *The Kirkholt Burglary Prevention Demonstration Project.* London: Home Office CPU.
Garland, D. (2001). *The Culture of Control: Crime and Social Order in Contemporary Society.* Chicago: University of Chicago Press.
Gladstone, F. (1980). *Co-ordinating Crime Prevention Efforts.* Home Office Research Study No. 62. London: HMSO.
Goldblatt, P. and Lewis, C. (1998). *Reducing Offending: An Assessment of Research Evidence on Ways of Dealing with Offending Behaviour.* Home Office Research Study No. 187. London: Home Office
Harrington, V. and Mayhew, P. (2001). *Mobile Phone Theft.* Home Office Research Study No. 235. London: Home Office.
Heal, K. and Laycock, C. (1986). *Situational Crime Prevention: From Theory into Practice.* London: HMSO.
Home Office. (1983). *Crime Reduction: Report of an Interdepartmental Working Group.* London: HMSO.
Home Office. (1990). *Crime Prevention: The Success of the Partnership Approach.* London: HMSO.
Home Office. (1991). *Safer Communities: The Local Delivery of Crime Prevention Through the Partnership Approach* (the Morgan Report). London: HMSO.
Home Office. (2006). *Changing Behaviour to Prevent Crime: An Incentives-based Approach.* Economics and Resource Analysis Strategic Policy Team. Home Office Online Report 05/2006. Available at: www.homeoffice.gov.uk/rds/pdfs06/rdsolr0506.pdf (accessed 4 March 2011).
Home Office, Department of Education and Science, Department of the Environment, Department of Health and Social Security and Welsh Office. (1984). *Crime Prevention.* Home Office Circular 8/84. London: Home Office.
Homel, P., Nutley, S., Webb, B. and Tilley, N. (2004). *Making it Happen from the Centre: Managing for the Regional Delivery of Local Crime Reduction Outcomes.* Home Office Online Report 54/04. Available at: http://rds.homeoffice.gov.uk/rds/pdfs05/rdsolr5404.pdf (accessed 4 March 2011).
Hope, T. (1985). *Implementing Crime Prevention Measures.* Home Office Research Study No. 86. London: HMSO.
Hough, M. (2004). 'Special edition: evaluating the Crime Reduction Programme in England and Wales' (guest editor). *Criminal Justice*, 4(3).
Hough, M. (2006). 'Not seeing the wood for the trees: mistaking tactics for strategy in crime reduction initiatives'. In J. Knuttson and C. Clarke (eds), *Putting Theory to Work.* Monsey, NY: Criminal Justice Press.
Hough, M. (2007). 'Hands on or hands off? Central government's role in managing CDRPs'. In E. Hogard, R. Ellis and J. Warren (eds), *Community Safety: Innovation and Evaluation.* Chester: Chester Academic Press.
Hough, M. and Maxfield, M. (2007). 'Introduction'. In M. Hough and M. Maxfield (eds), *Surveying Crime in the 21st Century. Crime Prevention Studies.* Vol. 22. Cullompton: Willan Publishing.
Hough, M. and Mayhew, P. (1983). *The British Crime Survey: First Report.* Home Office Research Study No. 76. London: HMSO.

Lea, J. and Young, J. (1984). *What Is to Be Done about Law and Order?* Harmondsworth: Penguin.
Lipton, D., Martinson, R. and Wilks, J. (1975). *The Effectiveness of Correctional Treatment: A Survey of Treatment Valuation Studies*. New York: Praeger Press.
Maguire, M. (2004). 'The Crime Reduction Programme: reflections on the vision and the reality'. *Criminal Justice*, 4(3): 213–38.
Martinson, R. (1974). 'What works? – Questions and answers about prison reform'. *The Public Interest*, Spring: 22–54.
Mayhew, P. and Elliott, D.P. (1990). 'Self-reported offending, victimization, and the British Crime Survey'. *Victims and Violence*, 5: 83–96.
Mayhew, P., Clarke, R.V., Sturman, A. and Hough, J. (1976). *Crime as Opportunity*. Home Office Research Study No. 34. London: HMSO.
Mayhew, P., Clarke, R.V., Burrows, J., Hough, J. and Winchester, S. (1979). *Crime in Public View*. Home Office Research Study No. 49. London: HMSO.
Newman, O. (1972). *Defensible Space: Crime Prevention through Urban Design*. New York: Macmillan.
Poyner, B. (1980). *A Study of Street Attacks and their Environmental Settings*. London: Tavistock Institute of Human Relations.
Reiner, R. (1992). *The Politics of the Police*. Hemel Hempstead: Harvester Wheatsheaf.
Riley, D. and Mayhew, P. (1980). *Crime Prevention Publicity: An Assessment*. Home Office Research Study No. 63. London: Home Office.
Schur, E.M. (1973). *Radical Non-intervention – Rethinking the Delinquency Problem*. Englewood Cliffs, NJ: Prentice Hall.
Sinclair, I. (1971). *Hostels for Probationers*. London: HMSO.
Smith, M.J. and Clarke, R.V. (2000). 'Crime and public transport'. In M. Tonry (ed.), *Crime and Justice. A Review of Research*. Vol. 27. Chicago: University of Chicago Press.
Tilly, N. (1993). 'Crime prevention and the Safer Cities story'. *Howard Journal*, 32: 40–57.
Wortley, R. (2010). 'Situational crime prevention, critiques of'. In B.S. Fisher and S.P. Lab (eds), *Encyclopaedia of Victimology and Crime Prevention*. London: Sage.
Young, J. (1997). 'Foreword'. In R. van Swaaningen, *Critical Criminology: Visions from Europe*. London: Sage Publications.

2 On being crime specific
Observations on the career of R.V.G. Clarke

Derek B. Cornish and Martha J. Smith

Introduction

Over the last thirty years or so situational crime prevention (SCP) has become a major field of theory, research and practice within the broader areas of environmental criminology and crime science. In very large measure, its emergence, growth and present status is due to the efforts of one particular individual, Ron Clarke, whose talents have shaped and fostered its development from its earliest beginnings. Looking back on what is now such a substantial body of theory, research and practical work, it is impressive to see just how many of the arguments and ideas that currently drive its development were already present, though not fully formed, from the start. Of these seminal themes, that of the need to be crime-specific when thinking about SCP is perhaps the most important.

This chapter traces the influence of this analytic strategy on the development of SCP, from its emergence as an early component of research and practice to its incorporation as one of the core concepts of the rational choice perspective, and beyond. Novel approaches to crime-control need strong advocates if they are going to prosper in the criminological market-place, so this chapter provides a small window on the ways in which Ron Clarke's talents have enabled him, working collaboratively with a wide variety of other researchers in the field, to establish the situational perspective as one of the most important practical criminological enterprises of recent years. The story of Ron Clarke as academic entrepreneur remains to be written.

Why were we not always crime-specific?

For a great many years both criminologists and deviancy sociologists have published studies of the lives, lifestyles and criminal activities of offenders. These have often included descriptions of particular kinds of crimes and accounts, sometimes detailed, of how they are committed. But it is only in the last few decades that environmental criminology and crime science have explicitly highlighted the importance of such crime-specific information for crime control purposes, gathered it more systematically, and used it to design effective SCP (Clarke 2010). So why did it take so long to translate this knowledge into usable crime prevention policy and practice?

Human agency

There seem to be a number of interconnected reasons for the delay. These involve issues of human agency, human interest, and politics. Since crimes are committed through human agency, it seems only natural to pay especial attention to issues of motivation and criminal responsibility and more broadly to those personal characteristics of the offender that might have caused him or her to offend. This 'dispositionist bias' is a well-known one in social psychology (Ross and Nisbett 1991) and tends to draw attention away from other possible causal factors, such as those supplied by the environment. Likewise, academic criminology has tended to equate crime prevention with the reduction of criminality, and reducing the problem of crime to the problem of criminality has often led to a preoccupation with identifying types of offender, while ignoring types of crime. Locating all the interesting and important causes of crime in the offender inevitably takes attention away from the offending act itself, and from considering crimes as events with a wider range of causes than simply those contributed by the offender.

Human interest

Second, most crimes are relatively simple to commit, and boring to relate. To put it bluntly, they lack human interest. It is to the reasons and motives for the offender's actions, therefore, that the observer turns for enlightenment or entertainment. Human interest requires that offences either be extraordinary in some way – whether because of their seriousness, rarity or horrific nature – or that their essential banality be located within the context of an exciting criminal lifestyle, or used to showcase the work of forensic science. Since crime prevention, on the other hand, is about how these various entertaining narratives can be stopped from unfolding rather than described, detected and punished, it inevitably appears colourless, boring and banal in contrast to these more muscular endeavours. Perhaps also the regulation of behaviour from the outside, by reducing opportunities and inducements to offend, is seen as undermining personal autonomy, moral responsibility and freedom of choice to live or reject the virtuous life.

Politics

Lastly, the specific nature of criminal events gets neglected whenever they are bundled together for political or academic purposes. Given the enormous variety of human actions and their impact on the common weal, there is a natural tendency to want to impose some measure of order by identifying common elements of the behaviours in question and sorting them into relatively general and abstract categories (crime, disease, poverty) for debate or social action. Such categories may be used as general indicators of social malaise; and politicians, aided and abetted by the media, may employ them to convey messages of political toughness, determination and commitment to their solution. The rhetoric of waging wars on 'crime', 'drugs' and 'terror' or being 'tough on crime; tough on the causes of crime' conveys purposeful bustle and the imminence of action without risking too much in the way of specifics about how this will be achieved. Furthermore, the bundling of discrete concrete problems into more abstract packages – essentially the task of making complex problems look simple – enables the actual job of dealing with the problems to be passed on to others.

The practitioner's art

When social problems are handed on to those whose task it is to get something done about them, the move from politics to policy-implementation and practice characteristically involves some measure of disaggregation, and the crime (or drugs, terror, health, etc.) problem becomes a collection, or rag-bag, of discrete problems again. Here, if anywhere, is the point at which attention to the specifics of criminal activity might be expected to take place. But how and how far this process of analysis and separation proceeds, and at what point the quest for greater specificity begins or ends, depends very much on the ways of thinking and working of whichever groups of applied social scientists or practitioners are responsible for solving the problem in question. Since criminology is a multidisciplinary field, each academic or professional speciality with an interest in crime – for example, sociology, law, economics, psychology, psychiatry, geography, architecture, planning, policing, corrections – brings its own perspectives and agendas to the job of deciding where and how best to make its contributions.

For practitioners from disciplines such as psychology, the challenge of focusing on crime problems has involved having to abandon traditional disciplinary preoccupations in order to develop more appropriate theory and practice. Clarke's academic background was in psychology and his professional training was as a clinical psychologist. As a science and as one of the helping professions, psychology was already well-established in post-war Britain, but it was a relative latecomer to criminology. Before, during and after the Second World War, the most influential contributions to theory and practice in the UK were being made by those following a medico-psychological approach to the study and treatment of offenders and, in particular, by those working from within a broadly psychoanalytic perspective (see, e.g., Glover 1960; and, for a more detailed historical discussion, Clarke and Cornish 1983).

By the 1950s, when psychologists were beginning to enter the fields of criminology and criminal justice in greater numbers, the influence of psychoanalysis was waning. Its relationship to psychology, as opposed to its impact upon psychiatry or social work, had in any case always been an uneasy and contested one. Yet although psychologists were to bring to criminology and criminal justice new ways of thinking and working, those who became practitioners – and especially those undertaking postgraduate training in educational, vocational or clinical psychology – were inevitably influenced by the pressures of being members of a helping profession. As such their role as problem-solvers tended to be a person-centred one – that is, one of working primarily with individuals to bring about changes in their behaviour. Since criminal behaviour was regarded as the outcome of stable personality traits and dispositions, the focus of change efforts – whether in relation to prevention or rehabilitation – took the form of assessing and then attempting to change these criminal dispositions. In this respect, psychology continued to work broadly within the existing medico-psychological framework. As Clarke put it:

> In that personality can provide a convenient focus and rationale for treatment it is understandable that psychologists have been preoccupied by the concept; after all, their help has generally been sought (within the context of child guidance clinics, community homes, borstals and prisons) in the treatment of offenders rather than the prevention of crime.
>
> (Clarke 1977: 282)

The ethos of being a helping profession has also influenced psychological approaches to crime and criminal behaviour in more subtle ways. With the professional obligation to intervene in people's lives comes a recognition of the limited relevance of existing theory and practice to this task, the knowledge that intervention can as easily harm as help, and that windows of opportunity for action open and close rapidly, often without much likelihood that mistakes can be rectified or that a second chance will become available. The pressure to act responsibly leads to two cautionary principles: a present-centred preference for changes that have an immediate positive impact on individuals' lives, and a preference for tinkering (or, less disparagingly, piecemeal social engineering) at the individual or micro-level of intervention, rather than engaging in or awaiting the outcomes of larger-scale, longer-term society-changing efforts that may leave individuals without the benefit of help in a timely fashion. These are fundamental obligations that, incidentally, explain some of the mutual impatience of psychologists and sociologists with each other (see Clarke 2005).

Changing focus: from disposition to environment

By the 1960s, psychologists were to be found within the two most powerful UK research centres of the time – the Home Office's own Research Unit (HORU) and the Cambridge Institute of Criminology. At HORU, a significant proportion of its research until the mid-1970s was treatment-oriented, and involved studying the social and psychological characteristics of offenders, and evaluating institutional and community treatment programmes. While it would be a caricature to suggest that psychology was uninterested in the effects of the environment on behaviour, in criminology it was true that much time was taken up in making psychological assessments of offenders, and with designing typologies and classifications. And where treatments were applied, they were assumed to bring about changes in behaviour by way of their effects on the attitudes and personalities of offenders.

But already forces from outside and from within psychology had begun to challenge the dominance of the medico-psychological model. Moving into a new multidisciplinary field such as criminology exposed psychologists to competing explanations of criminal behaviour. Sociological accounts, in particular, normalised rather than pathologised offending, and provided compelling explanations at micro- and macro-levels. These took as given that, whatever role psychological factors might or might not play in offending, the interaction of the individual with his or her environment – whether family, community, society or culture – was of equal importance. As Brunswick (see Bonnes and Secchiaroli 1995: 35) lamented in 1957, however, 'psychology has forgotten that it is a science of organism–environment relationship, and has become a science of the organism . . .'. It is true that pioneer ecological psychologists, such as Barker and Wright, were conducting field research on the interactions between people and the environments and were struck by the active influence of everyday environments – what they called the 'coerciveness' (1951: 206) of such behaviour settings – on their inhabitants. This interactional stance was strikingly different from that taken by the medico-psychological one, which viewed behaviour as primarily a function of longstanding personal predispositions, stable across settings and over time.

Within mainstream psychology, too, an interest in the influence of the environment on behaviour had existed since the early years of the twentieth century in the form of theories to explain how organisms adapted to their environments through processes of learning. One simple but powerful model of learning to which students were being exposed was Skinner's radical behaviourism. This viewed behaviour as shaped by environmental contingencies, particularly those of rewards and punishments, and dispensed entirely with any consideration of intrapersonal variables such as personality traits as causes of behaviour – and it tested its hypotheses using simple behavioural responses of a very specific nature (bar-pressing by rats, token-pecking by pigeons, etc.). Perhaps most disconcerting of all, however, were the criticisms being made by personality theorists such as Vernon (1964) and Mischel (1968) who pointed to the growing evidence for the variability of behaviour across situations and over time – a view that questioned traditional notions concerning the stability of personality traits and dispositions as the pre-eminent causes of behaviour in favour of considering the influence of the settings within which behaviour occurred. For psychologists about to embark upon clinical research or practice this was an unwelcome message, especially when it came from eminent figures in their field. Clarke, reflecting back on the completion of his clinical training in the mid-1960s, recalled the visit of one such bearer of bad news, Professor Jack Tizard:

> His message was that he doubted the value of much of the training we had received. . . . In his experience . . . attempting to change environments could be of much greater benefit to patients than attempting to change their personalities or habitual modes of behaviour.
>
> (Clarke 1985: 505)

Changing focus: from criminality to crime events

Armed with this unpromising news, Clarke began working in November 1964 as a researcher for Kingswood Classifying and Training Schools, part of the 'approved schools' system, a national network of residential institutions for delinquents funded and regulated by the Home Office. Of the two major research programmes that he established, one (the subject of his PhD) was to become particularly important to the development of SCP. This involved the study of absconding – a source of much concern, frustration and inconvenience to those managing approved schools – in a series of studies conducted by Clarke and Martin (1971). What is interesting about the project is that it required an answer to a practical question: how to reduce incidents of absconding during treatment. Clarke's and Martin's behavioural orientation shaped their approach to this problem in two major respects: first, it was a perspective that was designed to explore specific behaviours. The fact that absconding was easily differentiated from other types of institutional misbehaviours in terms of its motives, purposes, behavioural form and situational contingencies, made it a particularly apt choice from a theoretical viewpoint, behavioural specificity being a requirement of behavioural analysis. By focusing on a specific act as their primary unit of analysis, these studies enabled the researchers to move away from the traditional preoccupation with criminality – i.e. with criminal dispositions as causes of criminal behaviour. Second, their behavioural perspective was one that emphasised the influence of the current environment on the expression of specific behaviours, and this opened the way to the sort of problem-oriented psychology advocated by Tizard: one that emphasised the need to examine the role of environmental variables in the occurrence of specific behaviours.

By the mid-1960s Clarke had begun reporting the effects of punishment, weather conditions and other factors on absconding behaviour. The results of absconding studies by Clarke and colleagues (reported in detail in Clarke and Martin 1971, 1975; and Clarke and Cornish 1983) were to have far-reaching effects on the direction of his later thinking and research. They indicated that while there were few individual differences between absconders and non-absconders that could account for whether they absconded or not, there was strong evidence that environmental factors such as stress, opportunities to abscond, and the extent to which the action was rewarded or punished had a major role in its production. In addition, studies of persistent absconders indicated that this was learned behaviour. These findings suggested a two-component explanation of absconding to which they gave the name 'environmental/learning theory' (ELT), and absconding became the first example of a specific delinquent act for which situational factors had been identified, and situational solutions proposed. The rule-breaking nature of absconding also suggested later that such an approach might be applicable to specific criminal behaviours as well.

ELT also offered a way of explaining the failure of another major project established by Clarke at Kingswood – a controlled trial of two contrasting residential treatment regimes (Cornish and Clarke 1975) to produce differences in post-treatment reconviction rates – or, indeed, much evidence of effectiveness at all. By the mid-1970s the theoretical and practical bankruptcy of existing rehabilitation programmes as forms of crime control had led HORU to explore a number of alternative policy options (see Clarke and Cornish 1983: 7, Fig. 1), one of which was that of exploring the situational determinants of offending as a means of preventing crimes. For a psychologist at that time, such a direction meant abandoning the profession's preoccupation with individual differences, and entailed a move to the periphery of the discipline if not out of it. In many respects, however, the focus of the new project on preventing criminal acts or events rather than changing persons still reflected many of the traditional values of a helping profession. The need for a gradualist approach with defined and limited environmental interventions, a present-centred orientation that worked to change current environmental factors at the micro-level (within the local interactional field, as it has been described), the focus on immediate impact, a pragmatic approach and willingness to tinker – all these reflected a concern for the timescales of individual lives that characterises a helping profession rather than a professional reformer. In many ways it also reflected the policy-oriented credo of the HORU at that time: 'pragmatic, interdisciplinary, correctional, reformist and positivist' (Clarke and Cornish 1983: 12).

Theory from practice

In his Foreword to *Crime as Opportunity* in October 1975, John Croft, head of HORU, introduced the first collection of what were then known as studies of 'physical' crime prevention by commenting

> that a closer study of opportunity (in the physical sense) might help to redress an imbalance in criminology brought about by concentration on the social and psychological characteristics of known offenders. It might also help to provide a sounder basis for those crime prevention measures, also in the physical sense, which seek to reduce opportunities for crime.
>
> (Mayhew et al. 1976: iii)

Thus began one of the most theoretically coherent and practically fruitful long-running research programmes in the Unit's history, and it is interesting to see in retrospect just how many of the later theoretical developments of the mid-1980s and beyond were strongly prefigured in the Unit's earliest publications, and those of colleagues outside. For the years until the first discussions of the rational choice perspective were published (Clarke and Cornish 1985; Cornish and Clarke 1986), were as much about the development of theory as of practice. After the important initial impetus given by ELT (see, e.g., discussions in Cornish and Clarke 1975; and Mayhew et al. 1976), practical considerations indicated that the theory would need to be simplified and clarified for crime prevention purposes. Early advocates of SCP faced a number of difficulties when trying to apply the insights of ELT to understanding and preventing crimes. The most important of these centred on the place of offender motivation and learning in the new theory.

Understanding the place of offender motivation and learning in SCP

The traditional importance of distal factors such as differences in backgrounds and personality in directly motivating a current behaviour such as absconding had already been somewhat undermined by ELT. Instead, the theory highlighted the importance of proximal factors in the individual's current circumstances, such as stressful stimuli like anxiety, frustration and boredom. It was these often temporary states of affairs that created the needs and motives that 'motivated' the individual to seek ways, means and the opportunities to satisfy them. But while the proximal motivating factors for specific behaviours might be identified and perhaps regulated in capsule environments such as institutions with relatively small populations about whom much was known,[1] the task is a much more challenging one in the environment of everyday life with its multiplicity of stresses, wide range of possible behavioural responses (including criminal ones), and variety of potential offenders. In the absence of hard information about sources of proximal motivation, discussion of possible factors was inevitably speculative. All SCP researchers had to work with was perhaps some basic data about the characteristics of likely offenders, gleaned from police, court records and previous criminological research and what might be gleaned from the criminal behaviour itself, considered as an instrumental act or series of acts intended to bring about a particular objective. This might provide some relevant information about its purpose as one way of satisfying a particular motive; and, as Clarke (1977: 280) pointed out, the type of crime would also provide information about its seriousness in terms of its consequences. Both of these pieces of information were crucial to an understanding of the particular crime in question, and some estimate of the likely strength of the offender's motivation, and hence the nature of the challenge to SCP. As for the rest, however, *Crime as Opportunity* tended to assume that the motives behind purposive criminal activities were unexceptional, and much like those governing all human behaviour (see, for example, the list of common motives for crime later listed by Clarke 1995: 62). In *Crime as Opportunity* comparatively little further attention is given to issues of motivation, therefore, except to assume the availability of motivated potential offenders for particular crimes, while recognising that the strength of their motivation might vary from one potential offender to the next and according to the nature of the crime. In the cases used by the authors, for example, causing damage on buses was viewed as governed largely by ephemeral motives and easy opportunities to satisfy them. In the case of car theft, variations in the purpose of the theft were considered to have implications for the likely strength of motivation involved: stealing vehicles for parts or resale was regarded as the work of more painstaking, professional thieves as opposed to taking temporarily for joyriding or personal transport, which was regarded as more casual and opportunistic.

Developing 'good-enough theory'

As far as the influence of learning was concerned, ELT had suggested that persistent absconding was more likely to occur where it was rewarded, a finding that suggested that whatever the original distal or proximal motivation for a particular behaviour, its continuation and refinement would be motivated largely by its success at achieving its purpose. Variations in motivation might, therefore, also reflect not only differences specific to the purposes and requirements of particular crimes, but also differences in the degrees of skill and experience brought by offenders to the particular crime in question. Recognising the existence of these differences had both positive and negative implications for SCP. On the one hand, since the mission of SCP was to design ways to prevent or disrupt particular crimes, it made sense to plan its countermeasures in the light of how the more successful offenders carried out their crimes, since measures aimed at preventing or slowing down these offenders would be even more likely to foil less well-thought-out or novice attempts.[2] On the other hand, the existence of determined and relatively effective criminals raised the question of how effective situational prevention would be for this group, given the likelihood that growing skills at identifying and manipulating opportunities would increase the offenders' abilities to circumvent situational strategies, and when necessary to change their methods, or even their type of crime.

For supporters of SCP as a form of crime-control the existence of committed and determined offenders and the threat of displacement were to present continual challenges to the utility and reach of the enterprise. Well before outside criticisms such as those from Maguire (1980) were raised, however, *Crime as Opportunity* was laying the groundwork for some pre-emptive rebuttals, (1) taking a motivated offender as given, (2) assuming variations in its strength within the pool of potential offenders for any crime, (3) recognising but downplaying the importance of learning and commitment by concentrating much of its early attention on forms of crime such as vandalism that could be construed as casual and opportunistic rather than determined and planned, and (4) calling attention to casual as well as professional forms of car crime. Initially, these steps were taken in order to provide some initial plausibility to the goals of SCP. Later, as it became clear that, in cases of determined offenders, SCP might provide one of the few realistic options for slowing down and disrupting their activities, the need to stress the casual and opportunistic nature of offending became less pressing. While the factors highlighted by ELT remained of theoretical importance, therefore, SCP as practised simply assumed the existence of motivated offenders and focused its attention on the offence itself: how and for what purpose it was being carried out, and the role played by situational opportunities. Concentrating on those aspects of the theory most immediately useful to practice later became known as the process of developing 'good-enough theory'.

Using the everyday language of 'choice'

One more subtle departure from ELT took place. This involved a gradual move away from the concepts and vocabulary of behavioural psychology towards the everyday language of desires, beliefs and actions. This treated the offender as a decision-maker with purposes to achieve, choices to make about means of achieving them, opportunities to be assessed, and decisions to make about whether to take them, based on the likely efforts, risks and rewards involved. Many of these concepts were already implicit in *Crime as Opportunity* – for example, assumptions about the determination and skills of professional offenders in the case of more serious crimes – and they were give a progressively more systematic treatment by Clarke (1977, 1980, 1983; Clarke and Cornish 1983: 49–50, 1985) who introduced the notion of a 'choice' perspective or 'choice model of crime' that emphasised the importance of criminal decision-making while stressing its 'limited rationality'. This made it easier to argue for the instrumental nature of crime-commission and – while recognising the existence of many variations in skills, experience and commitment among potential offenders – to suggest that the default assumption of a 'reasoning criminal' was most likely to clarify the best in crime-commission practices along with the best in SCP techniques.

The development of models

In parallel with the change of language, Clarke developed ways of diagramming this move. As well as being intended to map out the range of variables contributing to the occurrence of particular crimes, they were also designed to indicate the difficulties of reducing criminal motivation, distal or proximal, and the benefits of concentrating instead on reducing the opportunities for motivation to be translated into successful action. Although early diagrams were based on ELT (see Clarke and Martin 1975: 270), they already incorporated aspects of the choice perspective. Those about vandalism (Clarke 1978; Clarke and Mayhew 1980) are interesting on two counts: first, because of their somewhat crime-specific nature – although Clarke (1978: 77) suggests that the term 'vandalism' conceals many different forms of behaviour that require separate treatment; and, second, because they anticipate the forms to be taken by later decision-making models, although in the present case the instrumental decisions and actions of the crime event itself are yet to be spelled out, and take place off-stage. And, while at this point, the diagrams deal only with initial involvement, and therefore do not directly address the influence of successful crime-commission on further offending, these early models do achieve some separation of motivation from opportunity. Clarke's (1977) original but more general diagram, 'Elements Contributing to the Occurrence of a Criminal Event', is particularly interesting for its title and accompanying text, which suggests that viewing crimes as events like road accidents, rather than simply as behaviours, directs attention to current person–situation interactions. This enables those involved in preventing crimes to exploit the potential for opportunity-reduction through modifying settings in place of continuing psychology's preoccupation with attempts to modify the criminal personality.

The core mission of SCP

The initial working assumptions about motivation and learning described above enabled early researchers to simplify the application of ELT to SCP. As Mayhew et al. (1976: 6) put it: 'We believe that criminal behaviour consists of a number of discrete activities which are heavily influenced by particular situational inducements and by the balance of risks and rewards involved.' And 'crime as opportunity' became a shorthand for its concentration upon opportunity reduction. By taking the existence of the motivated offender as given, researchers could concentrate their attention on the crimes themselves, considered as specific instrumental behaviours in the service of particular criminal purposes. Identifying these specific instrumental behaviours, the opportunities that enabled them to take place, and devising the means of preventing them became the goals of SCP. In these respects it remained true to ELT's behavioural roots.

Defending against assertions of the inevitability of displacement

As well as having to establish its credentials as a new approach to crime prevention, SCP had at the same time to anticipate the likely objections of critics. *Crime as Opportunity* identified two linked lines of argument. The first involved the familiar assertion that, since offending was driven by deep-seated criminal dispositions, merely reducing opportunities could only postpone rather than prevent the inevitable offence. The second allowed for the variations in the strength of motivation to offend but suggested that the existence of plentiful supplies of opportunities would render attempts at opportunity-reduction largely futile: offenders would simply switch their attentions to those that still existed – the issue of 'displacement'. In order to counter these objections, Mayhew et al. (1976) developed two main counter-arguments, one asserting the sensitivity of allegedly overwhelmingly strong, or even pathologically motivated, behaviours to changes in the nature of opportunities available for their performance, and the other suggesting some likely limits to the phenomenon of displacement. Both depended for their arguments on asserting the crime-specific nature of offending behaviour.

Taking suicide as an example of behaviour commonly thought resistant to change, they noted that reducing the toxicity of domestic coal-gas in Birmingham, UK, had contributed substantially to a fall in the rates of suicides (see a much later article by Clarke and Mayhew 1988, for a thorough discussion of the issues). This indicated that even strongly motivated behaviours might sometimes be prevented by reducing access to certain means of commission. It also raised intriguing questions about the nature of the behaviour itself: were behaviours like suicide that responded to changes in situational contingencies, such as the non-availability of a preferred method, exhibiting elements of choice, decision-making and rationality? And did this sensitivity to availability of methods also suggest that suicide might sometimes be less deeply motivated and more influenced by ephemeral proximal stimuli together with the availability of easy opportunities than had hitherto been thought? Both these notions raised the possibility that suicide itself might be better considered as a collection of ostensibly similar behaviours with different purposes and preferences rather than as a unitary phenomenon.

The issue of displacement raised some similar themes. Since Reppetto (1976) had only just published his comprehensive classification of types of displacement, it seems unlikely that the authors of *Crime as Opportunity* were yet aware of his work (the Home Office monograph was sent for printing sometime in late 1975). But their discussion of the contrasting implications for opportunity-reduction strategies of specific displacement (the greater likelihood of displacement occurring within groups of crimes similar in modus operandi and purpose) – and general displacement (the lesser likelihood of displacement occurring to crimes of different types and/or purposes) – made distinctions that were consistent with those of Reppetto's more comprehensive analysis.

Examining crime specifically, rather than broadly

These initial forays into how crimes differ, and the implications of such differences for the development and defence of SCP, were an early indication of the central role that the need to be crime-specific would play in its future. Efforts in three directions occurred over the following years. First, in keeping with much earlier attempts to produce more detailed 'situational' classifications of offences broadly categorised as robberies (McClintock and Gibson 1961), Barry Poyner (1983) indicated that broad categories of crime, such as street attacks, could usefully be broken down into smaller, more specific groupings, such as thefts in markets and covered shopping malls, violence after drinking, pickpocketing at bus stops and crime in pedestrian subways. Identifying those aspects of the locations that facilitated the offences in question might provide useful information to those designing ways of reducing opportunities for crime. Clarke and Hope's (1984) edited book on *Coping with Burglary*, which indicated the growing body of research on different aspects of the crime, noted the many different types of burglary – described as 'a collection of different problems' – and argued for the need to be very crime-specific in designing SCP responses, citing many differences between housing types, areas, goods sought and methods used.

Offender accounts and choice-structuring properties of crime

Second, the burgeoning research on more closely defined crimes such as residential burglary by researchers at the Cambridge Institute of Criminology (see, for example, Maguire and Bennett 1982; Bennett and Wright 1984) was producing some of the first detailed descriptions of how offenders perceived opportunities for burglary and went about committing their crimes. These studies provided designers of SCP with helpful examples of criminal decision-making in relation to crime-specific offending. Third, as mentioned earlier, the discussion of displacement in *Crime as Opportunity* had suggested that this was more likely to occur where crimes involved similar purposes and methods. This alerted those interested in determining the likely limits of displacement to the need for a means of specifying the similarities and differences between ostensibly similar crimes. The concept of the choice-structuring properties of crimes (Cornish and Clarke 1987), based on previous work by Weinstein and Deitch (1974) on the structural characteristics of different forms of gambling, was developed to assist in this task. It enabled individual forms of criminal activity (e.g. pickpocketing, bank robbery or mugging) within a broader group of crimes with a similar purpose (e.g. theft involving cash) to be compared and contrasted on a wide range of factors. These factors related to the requirements necessary for committing the crime (need for co-offenders, transport, weapons, planning, expertise, use of instrumental violence and so on) and the nature of the risks and rewards involved. Since many of these factors also related to the skills, experience and personal preferences of the potential offender, two different scenarios were possible. Where the profiles of crimes being compared differed widely, then it was assumed that the chances of displacement occurring between the crimes would tend to be low; and where the profiles were similar – for example where they merely involved small changes in modus operandi – then displacement would be a much easier proposition. Choice-structuring properties can also provide useful ways of identifying the specific qualities of products that make them especially attractive to offenders (Clarke 1999), and they can, indeed, be used to analyse any feature of a crime that is relevant to its commission.

Consolidations in theory and practice

By 1980 a small group of researchers in the Home Office had assembled a useful body of research on the theory and practice of SCP (see, for example, the extracts from some of the earlier studies in Clarke and Mayhew 1980), and were beginning to search out and make contact with a range of outside researchers with compatible interests. This provided additional empirical data and ideas from a growing group of colleagues. Before leaving the Home Office, Clarke had already positioned SCP both as a new direction in criminological theory (see Clarke and Cornish 1983: 7, Fig. 1), and as a promising new departure for crime prevention policy. By this time the Office's Crime Prevention Unit was publishing SCP research from a variety of sources, internal and external, with a view to informing the police and other practitioners.

Ten years on from *Crime as Opportunity* it was time to take stock again. The development of the rational choice perspective (RCP) in 1985 was intended to integrate some of the scattered advances in the theory and practice of SCP by providing an overarching explanatory framework – however sketchy – within which the ideas driving SCP could be located and explored further. In that respect it represented another stage in the ongoing process of explaining, diagramming and defending the utility of SCP.

In particular, it was intended that RCP should carve out a separate space for the crime-commission process itself – this being the primary focus of SCP's activities. The following is a selective list of 'positions' taken by RCP that were relevant to this purpose:

- its adoption – for the purpose of designing effective prevention measures – of a view of the offender as a rational decision-maker, and its rejection of explanations of crime-commission that deny its instrumental nature;
- its use of appropriately crime-specific models to sketch out the processes of involvement in particular crimes;

- its use of an appropriately crime-specific model to sketch out the decision-making processes of crime-commission that constitute a crime event;
- its maintenance of clear distinctions between the decision-making processes of becoming *ready* to commit a specific crime and those of actually *committing* the crime itself;
- its outlining of successive crime-specific stages of involvement (initial, continuing and desistance), so that the contribution of initially and/or repeatedly successful offending to continued involvement, and initially and/or repeatedly unsuccessful offending to desistance could be demonstrated. This acknowledged the role of learning – and, hence, the essential role that successful SCP efforts could play in reducing involvement.

SCP itself was also engaged in similar processes of consolidating its theory and practice. It was recognised from the start that SCP achieved the reduction of opportunities to commit specific crimes by way of three broad mechanisms: increasing the effort required, raising the risks and reducing or eliminating the rewards. A series of Home Office monographs from Mayhew et al. (1976) to Clarke and Mayhew (1980) had gradually identified a growing number of opportunity-reduction techniques suitable for use by situational prevention. In his first book of case studies in situational prevention, Clarke (1992) began to classify the twelve techniques in terms of the three mechanisms by way of which the techniques achieved their effects in reducing opportunities. For each technique crime-specific examples of its use were also given. By 2008, twenty-five techniques were being classified in terms of five mechanisms, following the addition of two more ('reduce provocations' and 'remove excuses') (Clarke 2008).

From the late 1970s the practice of SCP had benefited from a five-stage action research methodology developed for identifying and dealing with specific crime problems. As Clarke (1992) commented at the time, similar methodologies, such as the SARA (scanning, analysis, response and assessment) model (Eck and Spelman 1987), had been developed for use in problem-oriented policing and these soon found their way into SCP practice. Some sense of the distance that SCP has travelled since the early days recalled in this chapter can be found in the pages of a recent handbook for training crime analysts (Clarke and Eck 2005). Thanks in large measure to the personal talents, extraordinary productivity, entrepreneurial skills and networking abilities of its founder, SCP has now moved from the outer limits of academic criminology to play a central role in the new mainstream of crime science.

Notes

1 The absconding research, for example, suggested likely proximal motivating factors and possible ways of reducing their impact. Later research would show how other capsule environments – relatively permanent ones such as prisons, and temporary ones such as railway stations, bars and football crowds – might create frustrations, pressures and provocations.
2 Studying attempts, of course, can yield useful information about the success of SCP techniques.

References

Barker, R.C. and Wright, H.F. (1951) 'The psychological habitat of Raymond Birch', in J.H. Rohrer and M. Sherif (eds) *Social Psychology at the Crossroads*. New York, NY: Harper and Brothers.

Bennett, T. and Wright, R. (1984) *Burglars on Burglary*. Aldershot: Gower.

Bonnes, M. and Secchiaroli, G. (1995) *Environmental Psychology: A Psycho-social Introduction*. London: Sage.

Clarke, R.V.G. (1977) 'Psychology and crime'. *Bulletin of the British Psychological Society*, 30: 280–3.

—— (ed.) (1978) *Tackling Vandalism*. Home Office Study No. 47. London: HMSO.

—— (1980) ' "Situational" crime prevention: theory and practice'. *British Journal of Criminology*, 20: 136–47.

—— (1983) 'Situational crime prevention: its theoretical basis and practical scope', in M. Tonry and N. Morris (eds) *Crime and Justice*, Vol. 4. Chicago: University of Chicago Press.

—— (1985) 'Jack Tizard memorial lecture: delinquency, environment and intervention'. *Journal of Child Psychology and Psychiatry*, 26(4): 505–23.

—— (1992) *Situational Crime Prevention: Successful Case Studies*. Albany, NY: Harrow and Heston.

—— (1995) 'Opportunity-reducing crime prevention strategies and the role of motivation', in P.O. Wikstrom, R.V. Clarke and J. McCord (eds) *Integrating Crime Prevention Strategies: Propensity and Opportunity*. Stockholm: Swedish National Council for Crime Prevention/Fritzes.

—— (1999) *Hot Products: Understanding Anticipating and Reducing Demand for Stolen Goods*. Police Research Series Paper 112. London: Home Office Policing and Reducing Crime Unit.

—— (2005) 'Seven misconceptions of situational crime prevention', in N. Tilley (ed.) *Handbook of Crime Prevention and Community Safety*. Cullompton: Willan Publishing.

—— (2008) 'Situational crime prevention', in R. Wortley and L. Mazerolle (eds) *Environmental Criminology and Crime Analysis*. Cullompton: Willan Publishing.

—— (2010) 'Crime science', in E. McLaughlin and T. Newburn (eds) *The Sage Handbook of Criminal Theory*. London: Sage.

—— and Cornish, D.B. (eds) (1983) *Crime Control in Britain: A Review of Policy Research*. Albany, NY: State University of New York Press.

—— and —— (1985) 'Modelling offenders' decisions: a framework for policy and research', in M. Tonry and N. Morris (eds) *Crime and Justice*, Vol. 6. Chicago, IL: University of Chicago Press.

—— and Eck, J.E. (2005) *Crime Analysis for Problem Solvers in 60 Small Steps*. Washington, DC: US Department of Justice, Office of Community Oriented Policing Services.

—— and Hope, T. (eds) (1984) *Coping with Burglary*. Boston: Kluwer-Nijhoff.

—— and Martin, D.N. (1971) *Absconding from Approved Schools*. Home Office Research Study 12. A Home Office Research Unit Report. London: HMSO.

—— and —— (1975) 'A study of absconding and its implications for the residential treatment of delinquents', in J. Tizard, I.A.C. Sinclair and R.V.G. Clarke (eds) *Varieties of Residential Experience*. London: Routledge and Kegan Paul.

—— and Mayhew, P. (eds) (1980) *Designing Out Crime*. London: HMSO.

—— and —— (1988) 'The British gas suicide story and its criminological implications', in M. Tonry and N. Morris (eds) *Crime and Justice: An Annual Review of Research*, Vol. 10. Chicago, IL: University of Chicago Press.

Cornish, D.B. and Clarke, R.V.G. (1975) *Residential Treatment and its Effects on Delinquency* Home Office Research Study No. 32. London: HMSO.

—— and —— (eds) (1986) *The Reasoning Criminal*. New York: Springer-Verlag.

—— and —— (1987) 'Understanding crime-displacement: an application of rational choice theory'. *Criminology*, 25: 933–47.

Eck, J.E. and Spelman, W. (1987) *Problem Solving: Problem Oriented Policing in Newport News*. Washington, DC: Police Executive Research Forum.

Glover, E. (1960) *The Roots of Crime: Selected Papers on Psycho-analysis*, Vol. II. London: Imago Publishing Company.

McClintock, F.H. and Gibson, E. (1961) *Robbery in London*. London: Macmillan.

Maguire, M. (1980) 'Burglary as opportunity.' *Research Bulletin*, 10: 6–9. London: Home Office Research Unit.

—— and Bennett, T. (1982) *Burglary in a Dwelling*. London: Heinemann.

Mayhew, P., Clarke, R.V.G., Sturman, A. and Hough, J.M. (1976) *Crime as Opportunity*. Home Office Research Study 34. A Home Office Research Unit Report. London: HMSO.

Mischel, W. (1968) *Personality and Assessment*. New York: Wiley.

Poyner, B. (1983) *Design against Crime: Beyond Defensible Space*. London: Butterworth.

Reppetto, T.A. (1976) 'Crime prevention and the displacement phenomenon'. *Crime and Delinquency*, 22: 166–77.

Ross, L. and Nisbett, R.E. (1991) *The Person and the Situation: Perspectives of Social Psychology*. Philadelphia: Temple University Press.

Vernon, P. (1964) *Personality Assessment*. London: Methuen.

Weinstein, D. and Deitch, L. (1974) *The Impact of Legalized Gambling: The Socio-economic Consequences of Lotteries and Off-track Betting*. New York: Praeger.

3 Ferruginous ducks, low hanging fruit and Ronald V. Clarke's world of crime science

Nick Ross

I would never have taken Ron Clarke to be a bird fancier. But perhaps I should have seen the clue. He has a lot of patience. And he needs to. Ron has been pioneering and pointing out some obvious truths for decades, while almost nobody takes notice.

But then he's always hard to pigeonhole. A Brit who has lived in New Jersey for decades but still sticks resolutely to a Wimbledon accent. Such a serious fellow who is so often wreathed in smiles. A career civil servant with his own sense of direction and conviction. A long-term faculty dean who prefers just doing his own thing. An iconoclast who can be doggedly faithful to a single idea.

It's not that Ron wrestles with contradictions. He's at ease with them. One day in Newark he can wax expertly on problems of the urban jungle, so why not another day sit on a remote lakeside shoreline looking for a ferruginous duck?

It's his engaging intellect that makes him so attractive. He knows so much but always listens out for new ideas. He always seems unruffled by dissent, is always patient with his explanations – and Ron is always, always interesting. So he should be. Clarke is truly one of the pioneers of a new way of thinking. Like his namesake, Arthur C. who grasped the prospect of geostationary satellites (and, incidentally, was also passionate for wildlife), Ron realised new possibilities, in his case for tackling a problem as old as humanity: crime.

His reasoning boils down to this: rather than simply blaming Adam and Eve, and then casting them out of the Garden, if we want to stop this sort of thing happening in future might we do well to address the unctuous and corrupting snake, and perhaps put all that low-hanging fruit further out of reach.

This didn't come to him in a flash of inspiration. The mundane truth is that Ron was the most conventional of people, a government official working in the most unglamorous of backroom offices, and quite a few passageways removed from the real corridors of power. There he did his best to ignore the daftest of ministerial knee-jerks and wrestle with some underlying problems, such as why does crime happen, and what should we do with people caught doing it?

It wasn't as though he was the first to consider these enigmas. Urukagina of Lagash of Mesopotamia, Ur-Nammu, the Neo-Sumerian king of Ur and Hammurabi, king of Babylon, had each had a crack at it four or five millennia previously, and even the Romans and Normans had got in on the issue one or two thousand years before Ron. These included some wise beards. They liked a sense of law and order, and of fairness (mostly only so long as you were rich), and they came up with ever more sophisticated codes, rules and protocols about how to deal with people who'd been naughty.

But none of these shrewd and judicious thinkers had pondered overmuch about the role of other factors. They might pray to their gods not to be led into temptation or, if tempted, at least to be delivered from evil; but in practical terms they really believed in deterrence. A bit of eye gouging, torture on the rack, disembowelment or hanging should keep most folk on the straight and narrow.

I suspect that, temperamentally, Ron was not averse to this. Well, maybe not the eye gouging, but if a slap on the wrist or a year in the slammer could stop someone from nastily victimising someone else, all well and good. The problem was that it didn't seem to work. In theory the bad guys ought to pull out slide rules and calculate the risk–reward ratios before committing an offence, but the dismal truth was that most crime is far from glamorous and there are few, if any, supervillainous Professor Moriarty masterminds.

So for Ron there was no Eureka moment. There was no conversion to a faith. It was a process of attrition. Each of the hallowed ideas for cutting crime that he picked up and inspected had failed to sort the problem. During his time at the Home Office (though I think this was coincidence) recorded crime was climbing at unprecedented and exponential rates. Burglary, vehicle crime, commercial theft, assault, woundings . . . you name your favourite bad behaviour and it was rocketing. You might challenge the police statistics, and Ron was so sceptical he played a key role in the development of an infinitely better measurement, the British Crime Survey. But the trend was too sharp and too consistent to be rejected as a whimsy. Homicide was climbing ominously too. This drift had been going on since more or less the end of the Second World War and, despite denials by social conservatives, the graphs didn't match changes in penal policy. If sentencing remained more or less the same how come there was such as epidemic, and why with some crimes so much more than others? Nor did the figures fit with economic expectations. If crime is the symptom of social deprivation, a theory beloved of liberals and the left, how come that wealth and crime were soaring hand in hand? Maybe something else was going on.

I really hate to say it, because for a while I thought I had come up with the idea myself that crime was largely driven by temptation and opportunity, but Ron was one of those who cottoned on to their importance long before I had even realised there was a problem that needed a solution. He, and a small but dogged band of researchers at the Home Office in London, began pursuing a research agenda that was way outside the political mainstream. He, together with like-minded colleagues such as Ken Pease, began to draw their eyes back from the big picture, the grand ideas such as deterrence and deprivation, and focus closer to the crime itself. They were like detectives. What had triggered the offence? Why here, why now, why this target rather than that one?

Ron was helping, in a big way, to lay the foundations for what would be called environmental or situational criminology, leading to his biggest single contribution along with his colleague Derek Cornish, the theory of rational choice. Ron and Derek had spotted what economists always suspected, that in general people will do what they perceive to be in their own interests, even if, being merely human, they are not always good at calculating the odds. Thus, if we take a bunch of individuals who all share the same disposition to act well or badly, those faced with great temptation are more likely to behave badly than those who are either not tempted or who are not given the chance to act in an antisocial way. It follows that it might be easier to change circumstances rather than citizens.

OK, I know you know all this, or you wouldn't be reading Ron's *Festschrift* compilation, but I need to rehearse it to explain my own sense of attachment to Professor Clarke. Back in the early 1980s, when Ron was coming to the end of his fifteen-year stint at the Home Office, I was a jobbing journalist presenting programmes for the BBC. My real interests lay in politics, health and the troubles in Northern Ireland where I had been at university; I had not the slightest curiosity about crime except what I read in the papers, and not really even then unless a headline story was unusually juicy. But largely by chance (another much more famous presenter was unavailable for the pilot programme) I was asked to anchor a police appeals series loosely based on a German show and aimed at recruiting viewers to help detect serious unsolved cases.

Crimewatch was an unexpected hit, attracting twelve million viewers and, to our immense relief, quite a lot of phone calls too, some of which led directly to detections. But after a few years it dawned on me that there had to be something better than chasing people after a crime had taken place. The police were so committed to detection and prosecution that chasing baddies was almost the only tool in their toolkit. So I began to look elsewhere for expertise – and was appalled. Politicians and their think-tanks started with ideologies and worked backwards to find convenient facts. But the criminologists were worse. Given the 'ology' in the title of their field I had expected to meet crime specialists who would be scientifically trained, dispassionate and evidence-led. Instead, what I saw was mostly self-indulgent waffle mixed with an achingly self-conscious 1960s Marxism – and without a practical solution in sight.

If only I had been introduced to Ron. But he and Sheelagh were then only just starting out on their adventure in America and, whatever Ron and his friends might be publishing in obscure academic journals, he had not got round to writing anything I might have read.

It was unexpected wisdom from the Far East that turned the lightbulbs on for me. As I describe it in a book I've been writing (more of which later, since Ron has played a big part in encouraging me to do it):

> Years ago, in central China as a reporter for the BBC, I stood on a top-floor balcony in sunshine with the local mayor and an interpreter. They proudly pointed out a hospital over to our left that we could just see through the trees, then the big secondary school across the road and, beyond the dusty high street, a prosperous cluster of new houses. 'Why,' I asked to make conversation, 'why are some of the new homes surrounded by barbed wire?' The

mayor was sorrowful: 'Burglaries,' he said. 'Televisions mostly.' I hadn't realised burglary was a problem in China. 'It wasn't,' said the mayor. 'My father never knew it, nor my grandfather.' 'So what changed?' I ventured: 'Why do you have burglaries now when you didn't have them then?'

As the interpreter translated the mayor recoiled slightly as though I had asked him a trick question. After a moment he responded gravely: 'We didn't have televisions.'

This simple exchange struck me as revelatory: television does indeed cause crime, though not in the way I had ever considered before. This new insight was scarcely a conversion on the road to Damascus (or in this case Wuhan) but it caused me to ponder about issues that had never much troubled me before.

Soon afterwards, and entirely by coincidence, I was invited to take part in a government review of crime reduction, chaired by an enthusiastic minister who, as is the way of politics, was swiftly shifted sideways to take charge of farming or some such distant portfolio. But before he went he challenged members of the group to come up with our predictions: where would the next crime wave emerge? It was a question which surprised me and excited me. It surprised me because the minister was tacitly, if not sentiently, acknowledging that crimes are not just caused by people but by circumstances that people find to hand. It excited me because it is so much easier to rearrange situations than it is to reprogramme people. We were off on an adventure that, unlike all that flimflam criminology, would take us close to the decisions people made before they listened to the whispering snake and reached up for the tempting apple.

I had still not been introduced to Ron, or even heard of him. That came from two people whom I met while serving on the ministerial committee, and who have become good friends and perpetual sages. One was Ken Pease, the diffident and brilliant psychologist-cum-crime-problem-solver who was a fellow member of the board, and who seemed to have an answer for every question. He still does. The other was a boffin, a backroom Home Office official, just as Ron had been, who came out to give us all a lecture. It was Gloria Laycock. I still remember where she stood and what she said, for I was mesmerised. She showed graphically how crime had risen in step with the economy, and how a river of crime gets filtered down to a trickle that result in prison or any other sanction that would be recognised by most people as a deterrent. Here was someone putting flesh on what, for me until then, had just been vague impressions.

It was still some time before I started reading about Ron Clarke, along with Marcus Felson, and what they were up to twenty miles or so southwest of Manhattan, and it was longer still before I met Ron. I not only liked and admired him, I was so impressed that I took a trip from the UK out to Rutgers to see what he was up to, to walk round his beloved campus library, to be taken out to lunch by him, and head home with another armful of books I ought to read.

By now I had resolved that there was no point in reforming criminology. Ron had been Dean of the School of Criminal Justice for a dozen years and even he had failed to shift its centre of gravity from theory to practical crime reduction, or from intrigue about offenders to concern about victims. I had resolved to start a fresh approach, one that would borrow from the experience of medicine where, after millennia of following clever but utterly flawed theories, scientific reasoning and experiment had transformed human health and life expectancy. Whereas physicians had been weaned off belief that disease was caused by imbalance of four humours, crime fighters had to be persuaded to give up belief in sin as the driving force in crime, and to give up trying to exorcise it. Just as doctors had learned to close the poisoned well, those tackling crime needed to shut off streams of needless temptations and opportunities.

Ron, along with Ken and Gloria, was all for it. Not just the principles, since mostly I was simply borrowing concepts they had been working on for years; but the notion of a new agenda, with a new label, a new brand identity. I called it crime science (though perhaps I should have called it The Reasoning Criminologist!). When at Environmental Criminology and Crime Analysis we tried proposing a change of name from criminology to crime science there was not a great deal of enthusiasm, but these three were in the forefront.

Perhaps that's because all of them are, or were, psychologists, as I was. All had had a training in quantitative science, and had then drifted from social psychology generally into crime issues per se. They had not been schooled in criminology and had no emotional attachments to the label. I still believe the name change is important. There are too many quacks, and even charlatans, in mainstream criminology, and so much sloppy methodology that public policymakers, and especially politicians, have almost zero confidence in what it says. If we want to have influence we need to differentiate ourselves.

The danger of a *Festschrift* is that the celebration of someone's achievements can easily begin to sound like the eulogy after they are dead. Ron has too much energy and too many ideas in him to give up for a long time yet. But obituaries are often hagiographies, and it's important to set on record that, at least in my view, Ron Clarke isn't quite a saint.

For one thing, he has a down on randomised trials. In Britain back in the 1970s Ron and Derek Cornish were involved in an expensive trial for the Home Office that, for all intents and purposes, seemed to fail. Delinquents had been randomly sent either to a traditional disciplinarian borstal or to a more liberal 'therapeutic' regime, but after two years there was no difference in reconviction. The researchers, naturally frustrated after all their work, cautioned others against from following their randomised approach, warning it was, 'unlikely that its widespread use at present would significantly advance our knowledge'. They were probably correct. Proving that offenders can be reformed has remained elusive ever since. But that does not mean the way we test it is wrong; indeed Ron and Derek had shown something important: they had confirmed the null hypothesis. Yet their pessimism about randomised control trials was influential and the Home Office stopped funding what I call 'fair tests' for many years.

It is true that randomised trials are not easily applied to many situational interventions; but the important point is that in the absence of cliff-edge effects they do have power to discriminate effects better than quasi-experiments, and much better than no formal comparisons at all. They are far from the gold standard in science – astronomy, physics, chemistry and many other disciplines barely use them at all – but they have transformed medicine, and they have powerful political currency, and I am reluctant to see crime science turn its back on them.

If lack of enthusiasm for randomised control trials can be considered a flaw, the only other fault I have ever detected in Ron is also a strength, just the flip side of it. He is such a champion for situational approaches that I fear sometimes he goes too far. In the admirable book he wrote with Graeme Newman, *Outsmarting the Terrorists*, he obliged us to see political crime just like any other and to search for situational remedies; but I sort of wished he had acknowledged the huge roles played by other interventions, notably intelligence and political sensitivity. His passion for designing out low-hanging fruit – a passion that will make his name ring out when obituary time eventually arrives – can be all-consuming.

But hey, I'm not complaining. Ron is one of the most prominent of that small band of intellectual entrepreneurs who has picked up crime fighting by its ears and shown it a new and better path. Now we simply have to get the policymakers to take heed.

And this is where the idea of a book comes in. Ron had always seen the need to engage the public in the revolution he was helping to foment. Hence he, together with Ken Pease, was always full of encouragement to get me, as a journalist, to write a pot-boiler that would bring crime science to a larger and more influential audience. He has spent hours helping to draft an outline and construct a shape and has been nothing but supportive. Alas, I am poacher who has almost turned into a gamekeeper. The draft became longer and longer until it would dwarf most earnest text books. The footnotes alone would be sufficient to fill a decent paperback. I am having to go back to the drawing board and do what Ron always persuaded me to do, to write for those who aren't converted, not those who are. I promise I'll do it, Ron, and soon.

Whenever I meet Ron he brings a sense of cheer to me. He is good company, a truly decent individual, which makes him a companionable mensch; but more than that, he is an inspiring one, and a bloody clever one. And, though he hasn't yet seen the world take up his ideas as forcefully and coherently as it should, one day it will.

Meanwhile, if he's as meticulous in his pastime as he is in his career, he'll know all about the ferruginous duck – or if he doesn't he soon will.

4 Happy returns

Ideas brought back from situational crime prevention's exploration of design against crime

Paul Ekblom

When lecturing on Design Against Crime (DAC) in design schools, I often introduce myself as a 'crime scientist fallen among designers'. But I didn't fall, I was pushed – by Ron Clarke himself. In 1978, when a novice researcher in the then Home Office Research Unit, Ron, my boss, suggested I write a kite-flying paper on the 'Crime-free car' to anticipate the possibilities design and technology might offer for preventing theft of/from vehicles, then a pressing policy problem. The article was duly written (Ekblom 1979)... and promptly sank without trace among policy colleagues,[1] like certain advanced vehicles, ahead of its time.

But designing products against crime inched up the research agenda, driven by vehicle theft. (The architectural design of environments against crime progressed more steadily but isn't covered here.) Roughly when Ron left the Home Office the original Crime Prevention Unit, another of his legacies, ran a study (Southall and Ekblom 1985) on the feasibility of improving car security during manufacture, as opposed to after-sale. Again, little consistent action followed until Gloria Laycock and Home Office colleagues commissioned the first Car Theft Index (Houghton 1992), awakening purchasers' interest in car security as a choice dimension. Combined with pressure from insurers and consumer organizations, the security of this one class of products has never looked back, with a European Directive of 1995 mandating the designing-in of electronic immobilizers on all new vehicles.

Research on the wider field of secure products came and went, but was significantly boosted by publication of *Hot Products* (Clarke 1999), whereby Ron introduced the world not only to *situational risk factors* as an adjunct to the opportunity approach to prevention, but also to the practice of eye-catching but tortuous acronyms. CRAVED (Concealable, Removable, Available, Valuable, Enjoyable, Disposable) was emulated for example by IN SAFE HANDS (mobile phone design security features – Whitehead et al. 2008) and EVIL DONE (Clarke and Newman 2006). Hot Products in turn influenced the design-oriented aspects of the UK Foresight Programme (DTI 2000), to which Ron contributed ever-practical views on, for example, a coding scheme for fostering product security (Clarke and Newman 2005a). That in turn inspired and informed a European-funded, international study (Project MARC – Armitage and Pease 2007) exploring practicalities of 'crime proofing' domestic electronic products at the design stage (testing whether their level of security was commensurate with the risks they were likely to encounter).

Other Home Office-funded research on DAC involved a widespread review of the field (Design Council 2000; Learmont 2005), guidance for designers issued by the UK Design Council (2003) and various student competitions. Ron gave useful encouragement and feedback on these behind the scenes; and stepped in when fickle Home Office interest diminished again (I was threatened with the sack if I continued to write in this area) to publish material from that programme as *Crime Prevention Studies 18* (Clarke and Newman 2005b).

When I eventually escaped the Home Office to the design world (2005), it became apparent that as a lone criminologist I, and my designer colleagues, needed a body of crime science collaborators to undertake joint research, development and evaluation. Twenty minutes' walk away from Central Saint Martin's College was the Jill Dando Institute (JDI) of Crime Science, brimming with just the right people. Of course, Ron Clarke had been a leading light in establishing JDI, and we now have a strong track record of collaborations both formal (e.g. www.bikeoff.org, www.grippaclip.com) and informal.

But Ron's contribution to DAC continues to play out in the policy domain too. 'Modifying criminogenic products: what role for government' (Clarke and Newman 2005c), directly influenced the instigation (2007) of the Design and Technology Alliance against Crime,[2] chaired by a Home Office minister, led by designers and with work commissioned by the UK Design Council. Products so far have included safer beer glasses and kitchen knives.

Historical twists and turns apart, though, the principal legacy from Ron Clarke has been, and will ever remain, that of situational crime prevention (SCP) in its entirety as *the* main theoretical underpinning of DAC.

Penetrating new ground has always affected the explorers themselves. As a member of a small scouting-party sent out, originally by Ron himself, to explore the enormous and diverse territory of design, what have we brought back to SCP, and how will it challenge and change things in the home discipline? I address this henceforward. I draw largely on my own experience in working in DAC with colleagues in a real art and design college, with real practitioners designing, making and testing things that work, are workable, have aesthetic appeal and are manufactured and deployed in the real world; but who are equally keen on theory, research and evaluation. Issues covered centre on the design process itself; visualization; discourses, co-evolution and innovation; and dynamics, scripts and script clashes.

From think thief to draw on design

Early forays into DAC centred on conveying the theory of SCP to designers, and the message 'think thief' (e.g. Ekblom 1995, 1997). Since designers are accustomed to 'user-centred' approaches (Norman 1998) this requirement to add the abuser perspective was challenging and, to some, distasteful. Arguably, the message is slowly sinking in, though pockets of resistance remain, centred as much on 'police state' fears[3] as on erroneous assumptions that criminocclusive design will inevitably be ugly and awkward.

To the extent that designers have now taken the point, crime prevention practitioners can increasingly deploy, or recommend to their customer/user communities, an array of products occupying many *niches* in the preventive ecosystem:

- *secure* products (such as the Vexed/Puma bike[4] with diagonal down-tube replaced by a lockable tensioned steel cable that both doubles as bike lock and acts as a value-reducer – cut the cable to steal the bike, and the bike becomes unusable);
- dedicated *security* products (e.g. locks, or ink-tags for spoiling the loot from shoplifting);
- *securing* products (with some other primary purpose, such as the Stop Thief chair,[5] primarily for sitting on, obviously, but with notches to hang one's bag behind the knees); and
- *security communications* conveying preventive messages in an attempt, say, to mobilize users to self-protect, to mobilize designers themselves (as with posters encouraging architects to design against terrorism[6]) or to deter offenders.

Hopefully, we're seeing the emergence of a market of preventive ideas and products, beyond the narrow domain of security products, where designers and practitioners negotiate supply and demand and each anticipates and exploits what the other needs or can offer. (This has its *market failures*, which governments have still not fully addressed – see Clarke and Newman 2005c.) Arguably, though, the *gold* brought home for crime prevention practice is not the *products*, but the *process*. Getting practitioners to *draw on design* is about transferring a design approach to the core problem-solving process that underlies SCP and problem-oriented policing. Practice-oriented researchers in this domain are accustomed to addressing the design of surveys, say, or of evaluations, but far less so the design of the intervention itself whether a product, procedure, service or system (although the architectural side is an exception in name at least). Here, the amorphous 'Response' stage of the problem-oriented policing process SARA (Scanning, Analysis, Response, Assessment) (Clarke and Eck 2003) both epitomizes and exacerbates the shortcoming. Even the attempt to adapt the problem-oriented approach to CPTED (Crime Prevention Through Environmental Design) (Zahm 2007) gives most emphasis to treatment of the 'Analysis' stage – necessary, but not sufficient.

One exception is the 5Is framework (Ekblom 2011),[7] in many ways a more detailed and inclusive equivalent of SARA. This was itself developed through a deliberate process of design.[8] Here, the Response stage is divided into three task streams – Intervention (planning the principles and methods with which to interrupt the causes of criminal events or frustrate offenders' plans), Implementation (converting plans into practical detail and making them happen) and Involvement (getting appropriate people and organizations to take responsibility, individually or in partnership, for implementing the intervention). Design enters in several additional ways:

- capturing user *demand* under Intelligence – and (like all good designers) *questioning* it before taking action;
- putting together Intervention principles in *workable and plausible combinations* fit for *problem and context*;
- realizing, testing and adjusting practical preventive methods in Implementation and Involvement – *further customization to context, innovation and iteration.*

Iteration – trial, improvement, new trial – is central to design, and ranges from generation and assessment of initial sketchy ideas to mock-ups, lab tests, field trials and formal impact evaluations. Such a process isn't a luxury extra for crime prevention; it's a fundamental necessity. The extreme context-dependency of prevention (Tilley 1993; Pawson and Tilley 1997; Ekblom 2011) means that converting even the most reliable and evidence-based 'what works . . .' knowledge into '. . . and what is workable' practice is far more like innovation than replication. Often, too, a trip to the knowledge cupboard will find it bare of well-evaluated precedent methods for *this* problem in *that* context. A related point is made by Eck (2002) in highlighting the importance of knowledge of principles of situational prevention, rather than of specific tactics, in generating solutions. Whether a preventive project involves customized replication or full-blown innovation creating a plausible effort based on first principles, the feedback and adjustment processes of design, including user trials, are vital. Yet these processes are rarely reported in project descriptions: not done or merely not described?

The process of converting principles to context-customized tactics is inescapably one of design, even if the practitioners don't realize it. And doing the design in a developed and professional way yields significant dividends. As experience shows, even elementary security products such as the table-mounted Grippa clip for protecting customers' bags against theft in bars, must be 'high performance' – robust, visible, cheap enough, aesthetically appropriate, safe, gaping wide for big bags, easy-clean, easily-mountable and so on. Likewise, the tricky process of trying to *mobilize* potential buyers and users of designs to actually buy and use them, may learn much from new approaches to social innovation and socially-responsive design.[9] The mobilization process itself has been captured (within 5Is, under Involvement) as CLAIMED (Clarify the preventive tasks/roles that need undertaking, Locate appropriate individuals/organizations to undertake them, then Alert, Inform, Motivate, Empower and Direct). Actually this framework, of general applicability in crime prevention, was distilled from earlier research on enablers and constraints in design against crime (Design Council 2000).

But knowledge transfer is two-way traffic. Conveying to designers awareness and understanding of *causal mechanisms* (Tilley 1993; Pawson and Tilley 1997; Ekblom 2002, 2011) of Intervention, Implementation or Involvement – *how* these processes work – renders the design process a far more scientific, and less hit-and-miss, affair. And designers have until recently had little experience of designing and conducting hard, prospective *impact evaluations* of their designs on crime. Attempts to bring these approaches together have included the Bikeoff project,[10]

56   *Paul Ekblom*

which demonstrated intermediate outcomes of improved secure locking behaviour by cyclists, in response to a new design of bike stand;[11] and the Grippa project, developing and trialling the above-mentioned clips. Although outside events frustrated (for now) the final evaluation of the clips, the process of designing both clips and their evaluation led to the development of a quantitative approach (Bowers et al. 2009) – CRITIC[12] – which combined the planning process for statistical power requirements of the scale of trial, with the costs of producing the prototype clips and coverage of particular bars.

Visualization

Embarrassingly, this chapter is no exception to the tendency for crime scientists and criminologists to neglect the visual dimension, a shortcoming first identified by Gamman and Pascoe (2004). (However, many links are included to appropriate graphics.) This is particularly significant as visualization seems the best way for crime prevention researchers and practitioners to communicate with designers. Designers are known to be highly visual in their thinking and more likely than the general population to be dyslexic (Gamman and Raein 2010),[13] so the textually heavy messages from conventional SCP experts face obstacles getting through.

There are, of course, some well-known graphical representations of abstract causal and/or practical relationships in SCP, such as the enhanced crime triangle at www.popcenter.org, my own Conjunction of Criminal Opportunity (e.g. Ekblom 2011 and www.designagainstcrime.com/files/crimeframeworks/06_cco_classic.pdf), and Ron Clarke's (1977) original diagram of the causes of a vandalism event. Books and manuals on CPTED such as *Safer Places* (ODPM 2004) bristle with pictures of buildings illustrating this or that point about, say, surveillance. But the latter tend to be over-detailed and often poor at conveying the key points – line drawings would be better; and the former remain isolated images, not always professionally done using the expertise of graphic/communications designers; they have yet to develop a consistent, rich and informative notation that helps convey the message and link together the field.

One promising area consistently used at the DAC Research Centre has been graphic illustration of modus operandi or perpetrator techniques. Examples include bag theft and bike theft, also in animated cartoon form.[14] The purposes of these illustrations have ranged from stimulating and informing designers to communicating 'these are the criminal methods to defend against' for the empowerment of, say, cyclists as potential preventers. Such approaches nicely fit the concept of scripts discussed later in the chapter.

Other visualization tools used by designers have included '3D prototyping' equipment, which takes computerized representations of designs (e.g. Grippa clips, fixed to the rim of tables in bars for preventing bag theft) and 'prints', in layers of plastic, realistic and life-size trial versions of the product. These can then be exposed to iterative tests and critiques from users, police and other stakeholders, trying out improvements before committing to the expensive manufacture process. Examples are on www.grippaclip.com/the-process-2/design-evolution (see

Iteration 3). Computer-aided design of buildings has similarly enabled 'virtual walk-throughs' of places to reveal vulnerabilities such as footholds for climbing or recesses for lurking. In both cases there is scope, still largely unexploited, for using such techniques with offenders and potential victims to explore the fine detail of what makes particular places feel safe and what makes them vulnerable to criminal misdeeds.

Ultimately this has potential to contribute to the development of 'configuration' knowledge (Ekblom 2004) – how criminogenic or fear-inducing properties are generated by (or emerge from) particular combinations of features. Underlying this are the dynamic interactions between theoretical components, which we know as causal mechanisms. Anything that helps SCP think about and test such interactions surely promises a major advance, whether using real humans, simulated agents (Liu and Eck 2008) or preferably both.

The one important exception in the visualization armoury of situational prevention is, of course, the advanced state of crime mapping. But even here design has further contributions to make. Approaches to 'co-design' (Sanders and Stappers 2008) emphasize bottom-up, participant-oriented techniques rather than exclusive reliance on top-down processes (and as such are a step beyond user-centred design). One such example is 'tag mapping', where, for example, cyclists can upload images and comments about the suitability and safety of particular locations for parking their bikes. An example is 'Bikeoff-TV'.[15]

Discourses

But there are verbal besides visual issues. Working in an art, design and cultural studies context one rapidly encounters concepts such as 'discourse analysis', and cannot avoid falling over references to French philosophical writers such as Foucault (1972) or Derrida (1970). By now many readers from the SCP field will have arched their backs, unsheathed claws and started hissing and spitting. But, in a closely defined way, the linguistical (as opposed to socio-cultural) side of discourse analysis may help SCP address language problems of its own, and help us articulate what we mean more self-consciously and deliberately, attuning our accounts to different purposes and allowing us to jump out of locked-in ways of viewing particular crime problems/solutions.

There are many alternative ways to describe a given preventive intervention. Take a simple burglary prevention project involving installation of alleygates protecting the insecure rear of terrace (row) houses:

- *purposive*: serving user (protecting householders), crime reduction (reducing burglary);
- *performance*: purpose plus ultimate quantitative crime reduction target criteria (e.g. reduce burglary in area by 10 percent) or intermediate outcome criteria (e.g. alleygate to resist attack by burglars for five minutes);
- *'reverse-purposive'*: frustrating offender's purpose (e.g. disrupting burglary plans);

- *problem-oriented*: tackling specific problem (burglary) in specific place, perhaps by specific method (e.g. gaining access via rear alleyways);
- *'ideal final result'*: *solution*-oriented descriptions in terms of all the purposes and/or performance criteria (e.g. reduce burglary cost-effectively while maintaining user convenience, safety, sustainability and aesthetic quality);
- *mechanistic*: how the intervention is supposed to work causally/theoretically (e.g. increasing effort and risk by creating target enclosures);
- *'reverse-causal'*: focusing on the causes of crime the intervention aims to remove, weaken or divert (e.g. tackling poorly defensible space, compensating for absent guardians);
- *technical/structural realization*: how the intervention is achieved through a practical procedure or product (e.g. creating enclosure with lockable wrought iron alleygates);
- *constructional/instructional*: how to manufacture, implement, install or operate method (e.g. alleygate customization, installation and locking procedure);
- *delivery*: targeting of interventions (e.g. 'primary, secondary, tertiary prevention' or as I prefer, 'universal, selected, indicated' (Ekblom 2011));
- *mobilization*: how to get people to implement the intervention (e.g. anti-burglary publicity campaign centring on acceptance and use of alleygates).

In everyday parlance of preventive folk these discourses are confused – it's common to see a publicity campaign, say, listed in a series of preventive methods alongside target-hardening, when the campaign could in fact be seeking to *mobilize* target-hardening. It's also obvious from the above list that there is no universally best discourse – some will be best for the strategic planning or impact evaluation stages, others for design, others for standard-setting, manufacture or gaining public acceptance. The important thing is for practitioners and researchers to be *self-aware* of which discourse they are using, which their collaborators are assuming and when is the appropriate occasion for a particular discourse.

Co-evolution and innovation

We cannot remain satisfied with victory in individual battles against offenders' moves and countermoves, but should aim to win sustained campaigns. My early explorations within DAC led to an awareness that what works now, may cease to work in future when adaptive offenders, perhaps exploiting new technology or social change, learn to circumvent current preventive methods or designs. 'What works' knowledge is a wasting asset (Ekblom 2002), albeit over a timescale rather longer than that of short-term displacement (Ekblom 2005). This awareness in turn engendered an interest in *arms races* between offenders and preventers (Ekblom 1997, 1999, 2005) and the tactics and strategy of how to run them. Strategies such as the pursuit of variety, incorporating upgradeability within product designs and so forth are vital for keeping up.

We have already seen how, *tactically*, replication in crime prevention must become more like innovation from first principles given the context-dependence

Happy returns 59

of intervention methods and the finite pool of successful case studies to emulate. Designers have an obvious *strategic* role too in helping preventers generate variety and keep up with those adaptive offenders.[16] But in turn, it's even *more* strategically important to build the capacity and motivation of designers, to *out-innovate offenders*. Developing such capacity to transfer to designers is a key aim of the DAC Research Centre (AHRC 2009). Capacity-building aside, *motivational* appeal to designers, design decision-makers and policy-makers comes partly from the powerful effects of visualization and physical handling, particularly of simple, blindingly obvious while thoroughly developed and sophisticated realizations as with the Stop Thief chair or the caMden bike stand.

One interesting approach to systematically boosting innovation is the Soviet 'Theory of Inventive Principles', TRIZ (Altshuller 1999). TRIZ was devised during the Second World War by a scientist examining thousands of patents for potential exploitation by the Soviet navy, and continued by him and colleagues during a spell in a labour camp. It identifies forty generic inventive principles observed to recur time and again in an enormous range of inventions. Principle 2, for example,[17] is:

> Taking out – Separate an interfering part or property from an object, or single out the only necessary part (or property) of an object.
>
> - Locate a noisy compressor outside building where compressed air is used.
> - Use fibre optics to separate hot light source from location where light is needed.
> - Use sound of barking dog, without the dog, as burglar alarm.

TRIZ also identifies thirty-nine generic 'contradiction principles' such as 'strength versus weight', and look-up tables identifying what inventive principles have previously helped to resolve particular contradictions.[18] 'Reverse-TRIZ'[19] changes the basic question from 'what went wrong?' with a product or system (e.g. vulnerable to crime), a checklist type of approach, to 'how do I *make* it go wrong?', conducive to a more active, 'saboteurial' analysis. TRIZ also identifies a series of 'evolutionary trends' in particular technological domains (e.g. a *fixed* linkage between components, to *hinged*, to *fully-flexible*, to *electric field-based*). These help anticipate where to expect the next innovation in a given product. Perhaps this could be applied to forecasting new perpetrator techniques?

The 'ideal final result' discourse above comes from TRIZ. The alleygate example referred to a range of conflicting or competing requirements or 'troublesome tradeoffs' between security, privacy and convenience. (Armitage and Monchuk (2009) describe an in-depth exploration of conflicts and synergies between security and sustainability of housing.) TRIZ maintains that, far from being obstacles, explicit statements of contradictions actually help the designer to focus on key issues to address. This facilitates the true creative leap, as with those fire escapes whose final run of steps is suspended above reach of intruders, and only slides

60　*Paul Ekblom*

down under the weight of fleeing occupants – thereby supplying both security *and* safety rather than forcing choice or compromise.

Besides these tradeoffs with other values, contradiction lies at the heart of the definition of a given crime. Hot products tend to be attractive to criminals for precisely the same reason as they appeal to legitimate owners/users, both for their inherent value and their stealability. Pocketability of music players, say, is good for both using and stealing; attempts to design against theft by making players bulky would be laughed out of court. Effective design thus relies on fine discrimination between user and abuser, much as anti-cancer drugs must finely discriminate between zapping tumours while leaving unharmed the nearly identical healthy tissue. Such discriminations must often use electronics although one could imagine, say, a mobile phone moulded to fit an individual user's ear.

Finally we should not neglect *criminal* creativity. Space precludes coverage but an excellent overview of the 'dark side' of creativity is in Cropley et al. (2010).

Dynamics, scripts and script clashes

Designers above all seek to understand their products *in use*. This means in practice that while static dissections of causes of crime such as the Crime Triangle or the Conjunction of Criminal Opportunity (CCO) are informative, they are insufficient to help designers address the *dynamics* of criminal events. Even the simplest snatch theft has such dynamics; the world of SCP has begun to capture them in terms of *scripts* (Cornish 1994).

Analysis of dynamics tends to be disruptive. It forced the modification of CCO (Ekblom 2011),[20] and questioned the universality of CRAVED (Ekblom and Sidebottom 2007). Concealability of the product, for example, is *helpful* to the thief at the 'flee' stage of his/her script; but *un*helpful at the 'seek' stage when it's hidden in the owner's pocket. This leads into the understanding that honest users have scripts too, and some script elements will centre on security, including perhaps 'hide music player in backpack before going out'. (Designers sometimes facilitate this hiding by, for example, incorporating 'earphone wire ports' in the backpack so the player stays protected from thieves or rain while the wires convey the music to the user's ears. At other times, they mess up – we all know what those fancy white wires advertise in terms of product value.) Offender and user scripts may co-evolve – imagine the first *bike-parking script* ('lean bike against shop wall, enter . . . return, find bike, ride off'), the first *bike theft script* ('see bike, get on, ride off'), and subsequent *elaborations* of move and countermove (including 'lock bike', 'obtain lever to break lock', etc.).

Considering the interplay between offender and user scripts leads naturally to the concept of *script clashes*, which neatly link with contradictions, introduced above:

- surveill vs. conceal;
- exclude vs. permit entry;
- wield force vs. resist;

- conceal criminal intent vs. detect;
- challenge suspect vs. give plausible response;
- surprise/ambush vs. warning;
- trap vs. elude;
- pursue vs. escape; and so on.

Understanding such script clashes is pivotal to SCP, which becomes an exercise in designing environments, products, procedures etc. to tip the balance to favour the good guys, while respecting all other requirements.

Conclusion

SCP theory and practice can learn plenty more lessons from design, which space precludes from covering (the limited space indicating Ron Clarke's *Festschriftwürdigkeit*). For example, there is the requirement to avoid producing 'paranoid products' (Gamman and Thorpe 2007) such as subway ticket machines with inbuilt explosives-sniffers or more generally to steer clear of 'vulnerability-led' design (Durodié 2002) in which the abuser-unfriendly tail wags the user-friendly dog. There is also the need to avoid rushing into superficial, awkward and inadequate 'technofixes', usually in response to a crime harvest (Pease 2001) that follows the original designer's neglect of security. And there is the possibility of connecting concepts of 'emotional design' (Norman 2003) to Wortley's (2008) situational precipitators that prompt, provoke, pressure or permit crime rather than simply providing instrumental opportunity.

The exploration of the design world by SCP has not been a simple case of 'grab the goodies and leave'. We're in an academic era where multidisciplinarity is favoured and the true merger of interdisciplinarity is considered a boon. Drawing on design means a real stirring of the multidisciplinary melting-pot, because some of the issues and examples covered above have involved ideas from SCP being taken across to the design world and then brought back again in a developed, and design-articulate form, to crime prevention practitioners.

Whether DAC and SCP should or could ever get as far as to produce a new interdiscipline is respectively for colleagues to opine and the future to reveal, but certainly the pursuit of that vision is an exciting one. Ron Clarke has drawn much of the map and continues to blaze the trail.

Notes

All websites in this chapter accessed 18/19 February 2011.

1 In one Home Office listing it was mislabelled 'A crime-free cat'.
2 www.designcouncil.org.uk/crime.
3 E.g. www.britishdesigninnovation.org/?page=newsservice/view&news_id=5454.
4 www.designagainstcrime.com/projects/puma-bike/.
5 www.designagainstcrime.com/projects/stop-thief-chair/.
6 http://designagainstterrorism.wordpress.com/work/.

62 Paul Ekblom

7 Intelligence, Intervention, Implementation, Involvement and Impact, and many sub-headings under these. See http://5isframework.wordpress.com.
8 5Is was not created in a direct leap from problem (implementation failure) to solution (5Is), but via an intermediate, design-like stage of problem to specification for knowledge framework to solution realizing specification.
9 E.g. www.designagainstcrime.com/methodology-resources/socially-responsive-design/.
10 www.bikeoff.org/.
11 www.designagainstcrime.com/projects/camden-stands/.
12 www.grippaclip.com/publications/academic-papers/critics-link-to-spreadsheet-calculator/.
13 Perhaps indicatively, a conference mug commissioned for Project MARC (Armitage and Pease 2007) presented CRAVED incorrectly, using 'Disposal' instead of 'Disposable'.
14 www.designagainstcrime.com/methodology-resources/perpetrator-techniques and www.bikeoff.org/design_resource/ABT_problem_who_steals.shtml.
15 http://bikeoff.beta.tagmap.co.uk/.
16 One assumes crooked designers exist too – as suggested by the use of 3D printers to produce realistic and accurately machined card-skimming add-ons to cash machines. http://i.materialize.com/blog/entry/attention-atm-skimming-device.
17 From www.triz-journal.com/archives/1997/07/b/index.html.
18 E.g. at www.triz40.com.
19 E.g. at www.innovationtools.com/Articles/ArticleDetails.asp?a=224.
20 And see www.bikeoff.org/wordpress/wp-content/uploads/2009/02/2007_thinking_thief_crime_frks_for_dac.pdf.

References

AHRC (2009) *Fighting Crime through More Effective Design*. Swindon: Arts and Humanities Research Council. Online. Available http://www.ahrc.ac.uk/About/Publications/Documents/DAC%20Brochure.pdf.

Altshuller, G. (1999) *The Innovation Algorithm, TRIZ, Systematic Innovation and Technical Creativity*. Worcester, MA: Technical Innovation Center, Inc.

Armitage, R. and Monchuk, L. (2009) 'Reconciling security with sustainability: the challenge for eco-homes', Special Edition of *Built Environment*, 35: 308–27.

Armitage, R. and Pease, K. (2007) 'Predicting and preventing the theft of electronic products', *European Journal on Criminal Policy and Research*, 14: 1–9.

Bowers, K., Sidebottom, A. and Ekblom, P. (2009) 'CRITIC: a prospective planning tool for crime prevention evaluation designs', Crime Prevention and Community Safety, 11: 48–70.

Clarke, R. (1977) 'Psychology and crime', *Bulletin of the British Psychological Society*, 27: 19–22.

—— (1999) *Hot Products: Understanding, Anticipating and Reducing Demand for Stolen Goods. Police Research Series Papers 112*. London: Home Office.

—— and Eck, J. (2003) *Become a Problem Solving Crime Analyst in 55 Small Steps*. Cullompton: Willan.

—— and Newman, G. (2005a) 'Secured by design. A plan for security coding of electronic products', in R. Clarke and G. Newman (eds) *Designing out Crime from Products and Systems. Crime Prevention Studies* 18. Cullompton: Willan.

—— and —— (eds) (2005b) *Designing out Crime from Products and Systems. Crime Prevention Studies* 18. Cullompton: Willan.

—— and —— (2005c) 'Modifying criminogenic products – What role for government?' in

R. Clarke and G. Newman (eds) *Designing out Crime from Products and Systems. Crime Prevention Studies* 18. Cullompton: Willan.

—— and —— (2006) *Outsmarting the Terrorists*. London: Praeger Security International.

Cornish, D. (1994) 'The procedural analysis of offending and its relevance for situational prevention', in R. Clarke (ed.) *Crime Prevention Studies* 3. Monsey, NY: Criminal Justice Press.

Cropley, D., Cropley, A., Kaufman, J. and Runco, M. (eds) (2010) *The Dark Side of Creativity*. Cambridge: Cambridge University Press.

Derrida, J. (1970) 'Structure, sign, and play in the human sciences', in R. Macksey and E. Donato (eds) *The Structuralist Controversy: The Languages of Criticism and the Sciences of Man*. Baltimore: The John Hopkins Press.

Design Council (2000) *Design Against Crime. A Report to the Design Council, The Home Office and the Department of Trade and Industry*. London: Design Council. Online. Available http://www.shu.ac.uk/schools/cs/cri/adrc/dac/designagainstcrimereport.pdf.

Design Council (2003) *Think Thief. A Designer's Guide to Designing out Crime*. London: Design Council.

DTI (2000) *Turning the Corner*. Report of Foresight Programme's Crime Prevention Panel. London: Department of Trade and Industry.

Durodié, B. (2002) 'Perception and threat: why vulnerability-led responses will fail', *Homeland Security and Resilience Monitor*, 1: 16–18.

Eck, J. (2002) 'Preventing crime at places', in L. Sherman, D. Farrington, B. Welsh and D. MacKenzie (eds) *Evidence-based Crime Prevention*. New York: Routledge.

Ekblom, P. (1979) 'A Crime Free Car?', *Home Office Research Bulletin* 7. London: Home Office.

—— (1995) 'Less crime, by design', *Annals of the American Academy of Political and Social Science*, 539: 114–29.

—— (1997) 'Gearing up against crime: a dynamic framework to help designers keep up with the adaptive criminal in a changing world', *International Journal of Risk, Security and Crime Prevention*, 2: 249–65.

—— (1999) 'Can we make crime prevention adaptive by learning from other evolutionary struggles?', Studies on Crime and Crime Prevention, 8: 27–51.

—— (2002) 'From the source to the mainstream is uphill: the challenge of transferring knowledge of crime prevention through replication, innovation and anticipation', in N. Tilley (ed.) *Analysis for Crime Prevention. Crime Prevention Studies* 13. Cullompton: Willan.

—— (2004) 'Reconciling evidence of what works, knowledge of crime reduction and community safety principles, and values', Annex 2 of *Safer Places: The Planning System and Crime Prevention*. London: Department for Communities and Local Government.

—— (2005) 'Designing products against crime', in N. Tilley (ed.) *Handbook of Crime Prevention and Community Safety*. Cullompton: Willan.

—— (2011) *Crime Prevention, Security and Community Safety Using the 5Is Framework*. Basingstoke: Palgrave Macmillan.

—— and Sidebottom, A. (2007) 'What do you mean, "Is it secure?" Redesigning language to be fit for the task of assessing the security of domestic and personal electronic goods', *European Journal on Criminal Policy and Research*, 14: 61–87.

Foucault, M. (1972) *Archaeology of Knowledge*. New York: Pantheon.

Gamman, L. and Pascoe, T. (eds) (2004) *Seeing is Believing, Crime Prevention and Community Safety Journal*, 6.

—— and Raein, M. (2010) 'Reviewing the art of crime: what, if anything, do criminals and artists/designers have in common?', in D. Cropley, A. Cropley, J. Kaufman and M. Runco (eds) *The Dark Side of Creativity*. Cambridge: Cambridge University Press.

—— and Thorpe, A. (2007) 'Profit from paranoia – design against "paranoid" products'. Paper presented at European Academy of Design conference on Dancing with Disorder: Design, Discourse, Disaster. Izmir, Turkey. Online. Available http://www.bikeoff.org/2007/04/30/profit-from-paranoia-design-against-paranoid-products/.

Houghton, G. (1992) *Car Theft in England & Wales. The Home Office Car Theft Index*. CPU Paper 33. London: Home Office.

Learmont, S. (2005) 'Design against crime', in R. Clarke and G. Newman (eds) *Designing out Crime from Products and Systems. Crime Prevention Studies* 18. Cullompton: Willan.

Liu, L. and Eck, J. (eds) (2008) *Artificial Crime Analysis Systems. Using Computer Simulations and Geographical Information Systems*. Hershey, PA: Information Science Reference.

Norman, D. (1998) *The Design of Everyday Things* (3rd edn). London: MIT Press.

—— (2003) *Emotional Design: Why We Love (or Hate) Everyday Things*. New York: Basic Books.

ODPM (2004) *Safer Places: The Planning System and Crime Prevention*. London: Department for Communities and Local Government.

Pawson, R. and Tilley, N. (1997) *Realistic Evaluation*. London: Sage.

Pease, K. (2001) *Cracking Crime through Design*. London: Design Council.

Sanders, E. and Stappers, P. (2008) 'Co-creation and the new landscapes of design', *CoDesign*, 4: 5–18.

Southall, D. and Ekblom, P. (1985) *Designing for Vehicle Security: towards a Crime Free Car. Crime Prevention Unit Paper 4*. London: Home Office.

Tilley, N. (1993) *After Kirkholt: Theory, Methods and Results of Replication Evaluations. Crime Prevention Unit Paper 47*. London: Home Office.

Whitehead, S., Mailley, J., Storer, I., McCardle, J., Torrens, G. and Farrell, G. (2008) 'IN SAFE HANDS: a review of mobile phone anti-theft designs', *European Journal on Criminal Policy and Research*, 14: 39–60.

Wortley, R. (2008) 'Situational precipitators of crime', in R. Wortley and L. Mazerolle (eds) *Environmental Criminology and Crime Analysis*. Cullompton: Willan.

Zahm, D. (2007) *Using Crime Prevention through Environmental Design in Problem Solving*. Tool Guide No. 8. Washington, DC: Center for Problem-Oriented Policing.

5 Linking situational crime prevention and focused deterrence strategies

Anthony A. Braga and David M. Kennedy

Introduction

The developing field of situational crime prevention has supported the problem-oriented policing movement since its genesis in the British government's Home Office Research Unit in the early 1980s (Clarke 1992). Instead of preventing crime by altering broad social conditions such as poverty and inequality, situational crime prevention advocates sought to make changes in local environments to decrease opportunities for crimes to be committed. Situational crime prevention techniques comprise

> opportunity-reducing measures that are, (1) directed at highly specific forms of crime (2) that involve the management, design, or manipulation of the immediate environment in as systematic and permanent way as possible (3) so as to increase the effort and risks of crime and reduce the rewards as perceived by a wide range of offenders.
>
> (Clarke 1992: 4)

The situational analysis of crime problems follows an action-research model that systematically identifies and examines problems, develops solutions, and evaluates results (Clarke 1992; Lewin 1947). Indeed, Goldstein's (1990) formulation of problem-oriented policing shares many similarities to the action-research underpinnings of situational prevention. The applications of situational crime prevention have shown convincing crime prevention results to a variety problems ranging from obscene phone callers (Clarke 1990) to burglary (Pease 1991) to car radio theft (Braga and Clarke 1994). This simple but powerful perspective is applicable to crime problems facing the police, security personnel, business owners, local government officials, and private citizens.

Situational crime prevention and problem-oriented policing are analytic approaches that have often, either explicitly or implicitly, taken the position that traditional law enforcement is not a desirable option in dealing with recurring crime problems. A number of US jurisdictions have been experimenting with new problem-oriented policing frameworks, generally known as focused deterrence strategies, to understand and respond to serious crime problems generated by chronically offending groups, such as gun violence among gang-involved offenders. Focused deterrence strategies honor core situational crime prevention ideas, such as increasing risks faced by offenders, while finding new and creative ways of deploying traditional and non-traditional law enforcement tools to do so. Focused deterrence strategies may be seen as a generally applicable framework for acting on the core set of situational crime prevention ideas. In this chapter, we explicitly map focused deterrence actions onto the base situational prevention ideas of increasing the effort, increasing the risks, reducing rewards, reducing provocations, and removing excuses.

The emergence of focused deterrence strategies

Pioneered in Boston to halt youth violence, the focused deterrence framework has been applied in many American cities, in part through federally sponsored violence prevention programs such as the Strategic Alternatives to Community Safety Initiative, Project Safe Neighborhoods (Coleman et al. 1999; Dalton 2002), and the Drug Market Initiative (e.g., see Kennedy 2009). In its simplest form, the approach consists of selecting a particular crime problem, such as youth homicide; convening an interagency working group of law enforcement practitioners; conducting research to identify key offenders, groups, and behavior patterns; framing a response to offenders and groups of offenders that uses a varied menu of sanctions (known as "pulling levers") to stop them from continuing their violent behavior; focusing social services and community resources on targeted offenders and groups to match law enforcement prevention efforts; focusing community normative expressions on targeted offenders and groups; and directly and repeatedly communicating with offenders to make them understand why they are receiving this special attention and what the special attention comprises (Kennedy 1997, 2006).

The Boston Gun Project was a problem-oriented policing enterprise expressly aimed at taking on a serious, large-scale crime problem – homicide victimization among young people in Boston in the 1990s. The trajectory of the Boston Gun Project, and the resulting Operation Ceasefire intervention, is by now well known and extensively documented (Braga et al. 2001; Braga and Winship 2006; Kennedy 1997, 2006; Kennedy et al. 1996, 1997). Briefly, a working group of law enforcement personnel, youth workers, and Harvard researchers diagnosed the youth violence problem in Boston as one of patterned, largely vendetta-like hostility among a small population of chronic offenders, and particularly among those involved in sixty-one loose, informal, mostly neighborhood-based "gangs." These sixty-one gangs consisted of some 1,300 members, representing less than 1 percent of the city's youth between the ages of fourteen and twenty-four. Although small in number, these gangs were responsible for more than 60 percent of youth homicide in Boston.

It is important to note here that Ronald Clarke's work on situational crime prevention influenced the problem analysis research pursued by the Harvard research team in direct and indirect ways. David Kennedy had long been a problem-oriented policing advocate who appreciated the need for deeper analysis of crime problems to frame appropriate prevention strategies. While pursuing his doctoral studies at Rutgers University in the early to mid-1990s, Anthony Braga was a student of Ronald Clarke. As such, Kennedy and Braga were very familiar with the joint efforts of Herman Goldstein and Ronald Clarke to improve the quality of problem analysis by importing lessons from situational crime prevention theory and practice (see, e.g., Goldstein 1990; Clarke and Goldstein 2002, 2003). Beyond providing important theoretical and conceptual insights on the dynamics of crime problems, situational crime prevention and its supporting theoretical perspectives have developed a number of data collection methodologies, such as offender interviews and detailed crime incident reviews, which can greatly enrich the understanding of crime problems and, in turn, result in more effective responses. Many of these techniques were applied to the analysis of youth homicide in Boston (Kennedy et al. 1997).

The Operation Ceasefire focused deterrence strategy was designed to prevent violence by reaching out directly to gangs, saying explicitly that violence would no longer be tolerated, and backing up that message by "pulling every lever" legally available when violence occurred (Kennedy 1997). The chronic involvement of gang members in a wide variety of offenses made them, and the gangs they formed, vulnerable to a coordinated criminal justice response. The authorities could disrupt street drug activity, focus police attention on low-level street crimes such as trespassing and public drinking, serve outstanding warrants, cultivate confidential informants for medium- and long-term investigations of gang activities, deliver strict probation and parole enforcement, seize drug proceeds and other assets, ensure stiffer plea bargains and sterner prosecutorial attention, request stronger bail terms (and enforce them), and bring potentially severe federal investigative and prosecutorial attention to gang-related drug and gun activity. Simultaneously, youth workers, probation and parole officers, and later churches and other community groups offered gang members services and other kinds of help. These partners also delivered an explicit message that violence was unacceptable to the community and that "street" justifications for violence were mistaken. The Ceasefire working group delivered this message in formal meetings with gang members (known as "forums" or "call-ins"), through individual police and probation contacts with gang members, through meetings with inmates at secure juvenile facilities in the city, and through gang outreach workers. The deterrence message was not a deal with gang members to stop violence. Rather, it was a promise to gang members that violent behavior would evoke an immediate and intense response. If gangs committed other crimes but refrained from violence, the normal workings of police, prosecutors, and the rest of the criminal justice system dealt with these matters. But if gang members hurt people, the working group concentrated its enforcement actions on their gangs.

The Ceasefire "crackdowns" were not designed to eliminate gangs or stop every aspect of gang activity, but to control and deter serious violence. To do this, the working group explained its actions against targeted gangs to other gangs, as in "this gang did violence, we responded with the following actions, and here is how to prevent anything similar from happening to you." The ongoing working group process regularly watched the city for outbreaks of gang violence and framed any necessary responses in accord with the Ceasefire strategy. As the strategy unfolded, the working group continued communication with gangs and gang members to convey its determination to stop violence, to explain its actions to the target population, and to maximize both voluntary compliance and the strategy's deterrent power.

A large reduction in the yearly number of Boston youth homicides followed immediately after Operation Ceasefire was implemented in mid-1996. A US Department of Justice-sponsored evaluation of Operation Ceasefire revealed that the intervention was associated with a 63 percent decrease in the monthly number of Boston youth homicides, a 32 percent decrease in the monthly number of shots-fired calls, a 25 percent decrease in the monthly number of gun assaults, and, in one high-risk police district given special attention in the evaluation, a 44 percent decrease in the monthly number of youth gun assault incidents (Braga et al. 2001). The evaluation also suggested that Boston's significant youth homicide reduction associated with Operation Ceasefire was distinct when compared to youth homicide trends in most major US and New England cities (Braga et al. 2001).

In subsequent reviews of the evaluation, some researchers have been less certain about the magnitude of the violence reduction effect associated with Ceasefire. Given the complexities of analyzing city-level homicide trend data, Ludwig (2005) and Rosenfeld et al. (2005) urged caution in making strong conclusions about Ceasefire's program effectiveness. Others reviewers, however, have been more supportive of the evaluation evidence on violence reductions associated with the Ceasefire intervention. The National Research Council's Panel on Improving Information and Data on Firearms (Wellford et al. 2005) acknowledged the uncertainty in specifying the size of violence reduction effect associated with Ceasefire by virtue of its quasi-experimental evaluation design. Nonetheless, the Panel concluded that the Ceasefire evaluation was "compelling" in associating the intervention with the subsequent decline in youth homicide. In their close review of the Ceasefire evaluation, Morgan and Winship (2007) found the analyses to be of very high methodological quality that provided a strong case for causal assertions.

The assertion that pulling levers focused deterrence strategies generate noteworthy violence prevention gains has been strengthened by subsequent replications of the Boston experience. A number of cities have experimented with the pulling levers framework and experienced some very encouraging results. Consistent with the problem-oriented policing approach, these cities have tailored the approach to fit their violence problems and operating environments. Quasi-experimental research designs have revealed noteworthy violence prevention gains in East Los Angeles, California (Tita et al. 2004); Indianapolis, Indiana (McGarrell et al. 2006); Lowell, Massachusetts (Braga et al. 2008b); and Stockton, California (Braga 2008).

Applying focused deterrence to individual offenders

A variation of the Boston model was applied by Papachristos and colleagues in Chicago, Illinois (Papachristos et al. 2007). Gun- and gang-involved parolees returning to selected highly dangerous Chicago neighborhoods went through "call-ins" where they were informed of their vulnerability as felons to federal firearms laws, with stiff mandatory minimum sentences; offered social services; and addressed by community members and ex-offenders. A quasi-experimental evaluation showed a neighborhood-level homicide reduction impact of 37 percent (Papachristos et al. 2007). Individual-level effects were remarkable. For offenders with gun priors but no evidence of gang involvement, for example, attendance at a call-in reduced return to prison at around five years from release from about half to about 10 percent (Fagan et al. 2008).

Applying focused deterrence to overt drug markets

There is less experience in applying the focused deterrence approach to other crime and disorder problems. In High Point, North Carolina, a focused deterrence strategy was aimed at eliminating public forms of drug dealing such as street markets and crack houses by warning dealers, buyers, and their families that enforcement was imminent (Kennedy 2006, 2009). With individual "overt" drug markets as the unit of work, the project employed a joint police-community partnership to identify individual offenders; notify them of the consequences of continued dealing; provide supportive services through a community-based resource coordinator; and convey an uncompromising community norm against drug dealing. This application of focused deterrence is generally referred to as the "Drug Market Intervention" (DMI) strategy.

The DMI strategy seeks to shut down overt drug markets entirely (Kennedy 2009). Enforcement powers are used strategically and sparingly, employing arrest and prosecution only against violent offenders and when nonviolent offenders have resisted all efforts to get them to desist and to provide them with help. Through the use of "banked" cases,[1] the strategy makes the promise of law enforcement sanctions against dealers extremely direct and credible, so that dealers are in no doubt concerning the consequences of offending and have good reason to change their behavior. The strategy also brings powerful informal social control to bear on dealers from immediate family and community figures. The strategy organizes and focuses services, help, and support on dealers so that those who are willing have what they need to change their lives. Each operation also includes a maintenance strategy.

A preliminary assessment of the High Point DMI found noteworthy reductions in drug and violent crime in the city's West End neighborhood (Frabutt et al. 2004). A more rigorous evaluation of the High Point DMI is currently being conducted. A quasi-experimental evaluation of a similar DMI strategy in Rockford, Illinois found noteworthy crime prevention gains associated with the approach (Corsaro et al. 2010). Study findings suggest that the Rockford strategy was associated with a statistically significant and substantive reduction in crime, drug, and nuisance offenses in the target neighborhood.

The links between situational crime prevention and focused deterrence strategies

Although situational crime prevention and pulling levers focused deterrence strategies developed separately, these approaches are complements in crime prevention and control. Focused deterrence strategies involve many elements that, at face value, appear very traditional and are thus hard to see and understand in the new light in which these strategies seek to use them. By identifying the links between the situational crime prevention and focused deterrence strategies, many of these new prevention ideas are made clearer to those seeking to these approaches to deal with crime problems. In this section, we build upon the prior work of Skubak Tillyer and Kennedy (2008) that located focused deterrence approaches within a situational prevention framework. Situational crime prevention and focused deterrence strategies both seek to change criminal decision making. We limit our discussion here to decisions to commit a criminal act, such as committing a gun homicide, rather than decisions to become involved in crime or decisions to persist or desist from criminal offending (Cornish and Clarke 2003). Drawing on the lessons learned in the prevention of group homicide, Table 5.1 provides a quick review of the links between the approaches in the core areas of increasing the effort, increasing risks, reducing rewards, reducing provocations, and removing excuses. We consider each of these core areas below.

Increasing risk

Increasing the risks faced by offenders to change their decisions to commit particular crimes is a central idea in both frameworks. Focused deterrence strategies aimed at "gangs," for example, are designed to alter the objective sanction environment by increasing enforcement risks faced by groups of offenders and accurately and directly communicating that change to a specific population of offenders in a manner that enhances the legitimacy of the strategy. Ongoing intelligence analysis reduces the anonymity of offending groups in the commission of their crimes. Triggering events, such as committing a homicide, results in a swift and certain enforcement response by law enforcement coupled with informal sanctions by community members intended to weaken pro-offending norms. Partnering criminal justice agencies mobilize a varied set of sanctions that are tailored to the specific crime dynamics associated with the offending group and to the varied offending behaviors of the individuals that comprise the targeted group. Beyond halting crime outbreaks by groups, the focused deterrence strategy seeks to prevent further offending by making it risky for criminal group members to encourage pro-offending norms and narratives within their social networks.

In addition, more traditional situational crime prevention techniques are often implemented as part of the core pulling levers work in focused deterrence strategies. Extending guardianship, assisting natural surveillance, strengthening formal surveillance, reducing the anonymity of offenders, and utilizing place managers can greatly enhance the range and the quality of the varying enforcement and

Linking situational crime prevention and focused deterrence strategies 71

Table 5.1 Focused deterrence, situational crime prevention, and street group homicides

Techniques of situational crime prevention (SCP)	Use of SCP technique in focused deterrence initiatives
Increase effort	Group-focused enforcement makes it more difficult for individuals to enlist necessary co-offenders (e.g., to provide weapons, act as lookouts, dispose of weapons, fence goods, etc.)
Increase risk	Committing a homicide virtually guarantees the combined resources of law enforcement to respond with certain and swift consequences Proactive intelligence gathering by law enforcement reduces the anonymity of criminal networks Mobilizing community in partnership with law enforcement weakens "no snitching" norms Informal sanctions from community leaders, peers, and other offenders are increased It is risky to encourage pro-offending norms and narratives within criminal relationships and networks
Reduce rewards	Violence that once won the respect of other group members now brings anger from or disassociation by one's peers, as individual violence increases police scrutiny of entire group Similarly, the rewards associated with encouraging pro-offending norms and narratives within criminal relationships and networks are drastically reduced
Reduce provocation	By leveraging the group members' rationality, members no longer encourage each other to be violent Because the message is communicated citywide, the "kill or be killed" norm is weakened or eliminated, as individuals recognize that their enemies will be operating under the new rules as well
Remove excuses	Community members effectively invalidate the excuses for violence by challenging the norms and narratives that point to racism, poverty, injustice, etc. as excuses for the targeted behavior Availability of social services invalidates excuses that there are no legitimate opportunities for employment

Source: Skubak Tillyer and Kennedy (2008: 79).

regulatory levers that can be pulled on offending groups and key actors in criminal networks. In High Point, North Carolina, the interagency working group conducted call-ins with landlords of drug houses to ensure that these place managers dealt with drug problems on their properties immediately or faced certain and swift law enforcement and civil code violations penalties. Similarly, the Cincinnati Initiative to Reduce Violence, a multi-agency community collaborative effort to apply focused deterrence principles to reduce group-based violence, used civil forfeiture techniques to close down a highly problematic bar that generated recurring serious violence.

A particularly interesting development within focused deterrence is the realization that the "guardians" so central to traditional situational crime prevention can themselves be offenders: who nonetheless can be brought to exercise powerful influences over other offenders. For instance, in Lowell, Massachusetts, the interagency working group recognized that they could systematically prevent street violence among Asian street gangs by targeting the gambling interests of older, influential members. When a street gang was violent, the Lowell Police targeted the gambling businesses run by the older members of the gang. The enforcement activities ranged from serving a search warrant on the business that houses the illegal enterprise and making arrests to simply placing a patrol car in front of the suspected gambling location to deter gamblers from entering. The working group coupled these tactics with the delivery of a clear message, "when the gang kids associated with you act violently, we will shut down your gambling business. When violence erupts, no one makes money" (Braga et al. 2006: 40). These possibilities have led to the idea of deliberately mobilizing even serious offenders as "intimate handlers" of other offenders along particular dimensions of their offending portfolio.

Reducing rewards

In many cities facing serious gun violence problems, chronic disputes among gangs and other criminally active groups generate the bulk of homicides and non-fatal shootings (Braga et al. 2002). These disputes are often personal and vendetta-like. In these settings, violence and a willingness to be violent often confers a very desirable status on particular members within group memberships and hierarchies. The rewards of violent behavior further encourage pro-offending norms and narratives within these criminal relationships and networks. Focused deterrence strategies attempt to reverse this problem by associating swift and certain negative consequences with behaviors, such as committing homicides and shootings, that once enhanced the reputation of individuals within a group and the group itself. The communications strategies explicitly make a "cause and effect" link between the actions of interagency working groups and the targeted criminal behavior by the group.

Focused deterrence strategies have extended the concept of denying the benefits of crime beyond those accrued by individual offenders to include these powerful group processes associated with repeat violent offending (Skubak Tillyer and Kennedy 2008). Nonetheless, there is considerable overlap and cross-fertilization between focused deterrence strategies and the various intervention ideas associated with particular situational prevention actions designed to reduce the rewards associated with offending. Ideas involving concealing and removing targets can be seen in the efforts of interagency working groups to use enforcement strategies, such as enhancing and monitoring probation conditions to limit their presence in high-risk places at high-risk times, and community-based actions, such as peace walks through gang turfs, to alter the presence of gang members in public places who are often the "targets" of retaliatory violence. Disrupting illegal drug markets can also produce desirable reward-reducing effects that can counter outbreaks of violence. Limiting the ability of group members to earn money when violence erupts can certainly reduce any benefits accrued to the group by violent behavior. Ideally, the violence that once won the respect of other group members would now bring anger and disassociation by one's peers.

Reducing provocation

In focused deterrence strategies, deterrent messages are framed to address the group context from which many crime problems emerge. The groups themselves can act as another internal communication vehicle for transmitting the actual sanction risk to other offenders. As Skubak Tillyer and Kennedy (2008) describe, meaningful enforcement actions and scrutiny by law enforcement agencies can leverage the rationality of group members to no longer encourage norms that provoke the outbreaks of violence. The citywide communication of the anti-violence message, coupled with meaningful examples of the consequences that will be brought to bear on groups that break the rules, can weaken or eliminate the "kill or be killed" norm as individuals recognize that their enemies will be operating under the new rules as well.

This perspective on reducing group-based provocations to commit violence developed as the Boston Gun Project unfolded. A central hypothesis within the working group was the idea that a meaningful period of substantially reduced youth violence might serve as a "firebreak" and result in a relatively long-lasting reduction in future youth violence (Kennedy et al. 1996). The idea was that youth violence in Boston had become a self-sustaining cycle among a relatively small number of youth, with objectively high levels of risk leading to nominally self-protective behavior such as gun acquisition and use, gang formation, tough "street" behavior, and the like: behavior that then became an additional input into the cycle of violence. If this cycle could be interrupted, a new equilibrium at a lower level of risk and violence might be established, perhaps without the need for continued high levels of either deterrent or facilitative intervention. The larger hope was that a successful intervention to reduce gang violence in the short term would have a disproportionate, sustainable impact in the long term.

Removing excuses

Community-based action in focused deterrence strategies helps to remove the excuses used by offenders to explain away their responsibility for the targeted behavior. In call-ins and on the street, community members effectively invalidate the excuses for criminal behavior by challenging the norms and narratives that point to racism, poverty, injustice, and the like. In Boston, for example, black clergy challenged gang members who attempted to use these excuses by countering that poverty, racism, and injustice were not linked to their decisions to fire shots in their neighborhoods and kill other young people who have experienced the same societal ills and life difficulties. Community members also work with law enforcement and social service agencies to set basic rules for group-involved offenders such as "don't shoot guns" and, hopefully, to alert the conscience of these offenders by appealing to moral values inherent in taking the life of another, causing harm to their neighborhood, or the pain that would be experienced by their mothers if they were killed or sent to prison for a long time in a very far away location.

The social service component of focused deterrence strategies serves as an independent good and also helps to remove excuses used by offenders to explain their offending. Social service providers present an alternative to illegal behavior by offering relevant jobs and social services. The availability of these services invalidates excuses that there criminal behavior is the result of a lack of legitimate opportunities for employment, or other problems, in their neighborhood.

A recent elaboration of these ideas has been to use persons of standing to explicitly challenge the "street code" (Anderson 1999) that in many places drives much or most "street" violence. This code has identifiable, if unwritten, elements with powerful criminogenic implications: that early death is inevitable; jail and prison are nothing to fear; disrespect must be met with violence; the enemy of my friend is my enemy; the failings of mainstream others justify violent offending; and the like. A long sociology of "techniques of neutralization" (Matza 1964) puts such exculpatory norms at the center of the etiology of street violence. When, for example, "original gangsters" respected by current offenders undercut such norms, it may in turn undercut felt justification for violence and other offending.

Situational crime prevention also seeks to reduce offending by making it easier for potential offenders to comply with laws and rules. Focused deterrence strategies also do so, in some very particular ways. To the extent that street norms stand against compliance, altering them for the better facilitates compliance: the law stands against violence, but the street honor code promotes it, so vitiating the honor code makes it easier to obey the law. Many potentially violent offenders do not wish to be violent, but are under very real peer pressure to be so; undercutting and even reversing group and network dynamics makes it easier for them to back off. Strengthening community norms against offending makes it easier to resist both internal and external pressure to offend. The original Boston project framed this "honorable exit" from violent offending as a possible consequence of changes in objective sanction risks and group dynamics.

A recent and potentially very important strain in focused deterrence thinking has focused explicitly on the gulf, often explicitly racialized, in the "norms and narratives" of law enforcement, affected communities, and offenders. These gulfs, rooted in historical and present experiences, understandings, and misunderstandings, can have powerful impacts on the ways in which these parties understand each other and on the perceived legitimacy of law enforcement, law, and informal rules and standards. If law enforcement is seen by the community and offender groups as a deliberate racial oppressor, for example, it will be difficult for community norms to support stands against drug dealing, and easier for offenders to break the drug laws. If those norms and narratives are effectively addressed – which usually includes changes in actual behavior on both sides – it becomes easier for community standards to support compliance, easier for offenders to comply, and harder for them not to (Kennedy 2009; Meares 2009; Tyler 1990).

These developments draw heavily on a rich literature addressing the "legitimacy" of law enforcement in the eyes of those subject to the law (Meares 2009; Tyler 1990). Very interestingly, one of the core findings in that literature is that even offenders obey the law most of the time. This empirical fact, of considerable theoretical and practical significance, stands in contrast to situational crime prevention's establishing assumption of the "motivated offender": the idea that we can take the presence of the impulse to offend as a given and for granted. That establishing assumption is just that – an assumption, explicitly deployed as a way to break with traditional criminology's pervasive, and for applied purposes not very helpful, search for the deep causal roots of individual offending. The emerging salience of legitimacy as an idea of profound practical significance could well lead to a reexamination, and refinement, of the idea of offending in situational crime prevention.

Increasing effort

Situational crime prevention seeks to increase the effort a criminal must expend to complete a crime through a variety of specific actions such as target hardening, controlling access to facilities, screening exits, deflecting offenders, and controlling tools and weapons (Clarke 1997; Cornish and Clarke 2003). In preventing and responding to outbreaks of serious violence by groups of offenders, many of these situational actions can be used to good effect in developing a "thicker" response to the offending groups in question. Focused deterrence responses benefit from changing the environments in which gangs and drug crews congregate, commit lesser offenses together, and launch plans for retaliation. Gang members are well known to commit a wide array of crimes (known as "cafeteria-style offending"; see Klein 1995). Making it more difficult to sell drugs at specific places, commit burglaries and car breaks, and rob passersby can be a powerful deterrent response to particular groups of offenders who rely on these illicit opportunities to generate income. Disrupting the ability of groups to associate with each other in space and time, through, for instance, controlling access to and screening exit from public housing, can slow down group processes that facilitate violence and make it more difficult for rivals to locate other group members targeted for retaliatory shootings.

Focused deterrence strategies seek to create similar dynamics. Changes in group norms and in objective risks associated with particular forms of misbehavior may, for example, make it more difficult to recruit peers for particular instances of co-offending. Ethnographic research on illicit gun markets in Chicago has shown that gangs' assessment of the law enforcement responses to gun violence leads them to withhold access to firearms for younger and more impulsive members (Cook et al. 2007). DMI strategy's goal of fundamentally disrupting overt drug markets can greatly enhance the difficulty of drug dealing: when buyers no longer routinely "cruise" once active markets, even a motivated street dealer may find it impossible to do business.

Concluding thoughts

Situational crime prevention is, in our opinion, one of the most powerful and robust of existing crime prevention heuristics. While demonstrably productive in the hands of those who understand it, those hands have been limited to a relatively small core of activist scholars and thoughtful practitioners. Our own focus, because of our concern about results on the ground, is on the latter: police officers and others who do not know about, understand, apply, and institutionalize the ideas of situational crime prevention will not realize its potential contributions to public safety. We believe that Ronald Clarke's creativity and imagination in his long-term development of this approach and his commitment to generating near-term crime reduction effects deserves to be highlighted and praised here.

In honoring Clarke, we attempted to clarify the links between base situational prevention ideas and focused deterrence strategies. However, there are some notable differences. Relative to the implementation of many situational measures, such as installing surveillance cameras, adding merchandise tags, and adopting Caller-ID systems, focused deterrence strategies can be more difficult to implement and sustain in the longer-term (Braga and Winship 2006; Braga et al. 2008a). Moreover, not all of the tactics used to induce focused deterrence are clearly situational in nature. For instance, certain tactics, such as customized communications with chronic offenders, do not contain the element of permanent (or near-permanent) change to the immediate environment posited by Clarke (1992) in his definition of situational crime prevention techniques. This raises the interesting issue of whether all of the twenty-five techniques are themselves inherently situational if non-situational tactics can be used to produce similar effects.[2] There is also the important distinction in conceptions of offender motivations to commit a crime described above. While beyond the scope of this brief chapter, crime prevention theory and practice could be enhanced by more careful consideration of the differences between these two complementary approaches.

One way of looking at focused deterrence is that it provides the practitioner with a (perhaps) simpler and more streamlined way of mobilizing some of the most central themes in situational crime prevention. For many crime problems, practitioners should look for core offenders, offending groups, and artifacts such as geographic markets; ways to substantially raise risks and to communicate those risks to offenders; ways to mobilize guardians; ways to reduce rewards; ways to reduce provocations; ways to remove excuses; and ways to increase effort. These steps, while far from simple, are perhaps easier than a wholesale and *de novo* problem analysis and intervention design. If so, focused deterrence may be a vehicle for easing some of the most important ideas of situational crime prevention into more widespread practice.

Notes

1 A "banked" case refers to a potential prosecution for narcotics sales, supported by audio and video evidence usually obtained through a controlled buy that is held in inactive

status unless the subject of the prosecution continues dealing, at which point an arrest warrant is issued and prosecution proceeds.
2 We would like to thank one of the anonymous reviewers for highlighting this distinction in his/her comments on an earlier version of this chapter.

References

Anderson, E. (1999) *Code of the Street: Decency, Violence, and the Moral Life of the Inner City*, New York: Norton.

Braga, A.A. (2008) "Pulling levers focused deterrence strategies and the prevention of gun homicide," *Journal of Criminal Justice*, 36: 332–43.

—— and Clarke, R.V. (1994) "Improved radios and more stripped cars in Germany: a routine activities analysis," *Security Journal*, 5: 154–9.

——, Hureau, D.M., and Winship, C. (2008a) "Losing faith? Police, black churches, and the resurgence of youth violence in Boston," *Ohio State Journal of Criminal Law*, 6: 141–72.

——, Kennedy, D.M., and Tita, G. (2002) "New approaches to the strategic prevention of gang and group-involved violence," in C.R. Huff (ed.) *Gangs in America* (3rd edn), Thousand Oaks, CA: Sage Publications.

——, ——, Waring, E.J., and Piehl, A.M. (2001) "Problem-oriented policing, deterrence, and youth violence: an evaluation of Boston's Operation Ceasefire," *Journal of Research in Crime and Delinquency*, 38: 195–225.

——, McDevitt, J., and Pierce, G.L. (2006) "Understanding and preventing gang violence: problem analysis and response development in Lowell, Massachusetts," *Police Quarterly*, 9: 20–46.

——, Pierce, G.L., McDevitt, J., Bond, B.J., and Cronin, S. (2008b) "The strategic prevention of gun violence among gang-involved offenders," *Justice Quarterly*, 25: 132–62.

—— and Winship, C. (2006) "Partnership, accountability, and innovation: clarifying Boston's experience with pulling levers," in D.L. Weisburd and A.A. Braga (eds) *Police Innovation: Contrasting Perspectives*, New York: Cambridge University Press.

Clarke, R.V. (1990) "Deterring obscene phone callers: preliminary results of the New Jersey experience." *Security Journal*, 1: 143–8.

—— (ed.) (1992) *Situational Crime Prevention: Successful Case Studies*, Albany, NY: Harrow and Heston.

—— (ed.) (1997) *Situational Crime Prevention: Successful Case Studies* (2nd edn), Albany, NY: Harrow and Heston.

—— and Goldstein, H. (2002) "Reducing theft at construction sites: lessons from a problem-oriented project," in N. Tilley (ed.) *Analysis for Crime Prevention* (*Crime Prevention Studies*, vol. 13), Monsey, NY: Criminal Justice Press.

—— and —— (2003) "Thefts from cars in center-city parking facilities: a case study in implementing problem-oriented policing," in J. Knutsson (ed.) *Problem-oriented Policing: From Innovation to Mainstream* (*Crime Prevention Studies*, vol. 15), Monsey, NY: Criminal Justice Press.

Coleman, V., Holton, W.C., Olson, K., Robinson, S., and Stewart, J. (1999) "Using knowledge and teamwork to reduce crime," *National Institute of Justice Journal*, 241: 16–23.

Cook, P.J., Ludwig, J., Venkatesh, S., and Braga, A.A. (2007) "Underground gun markets," *The Economic Journal*, 117: 558–88.

Cornish, D. and Clarke, R.V. (2003) "Opportunities, precipitators and criminal decisions: a reply to Wortley's critique of situational crime prevention," in M.J. Smith and D. Cornish (eds) *Theory for Practice in Situational Crime Prevention* (*Crime Prevention Studies*, vol. 16), Monsey, NY: Criminal Justice Press.

Corsaro, N., Brunson, R., and McGarrell, E. (2010) "Problem-oriented policing and open-air drug markets: examining the Rockford pulling levers strategy," *Crime & Delinquency* (forthcoming).

Dalton, E. (2002) "Targeted crime reduction efforts in ten communities: lessons for the Project Safe Neighborhoods initiative," *U.S. Attorney's Bulletin*, 50: 16–25.

Fagan, J., Meares, T., Papachristos, A.V., and Wallace, D. (2008) "Desistance and legitimacy: effect heterogeneity in a field experiment with high-risk offenders," paper presented at the annual meeting of the American Society of Criminology, St. Louis, MO, November.

Frabutt, J., Gathings, M.J., Hunt, E.D., and Loggins, T. (2004) *High Point West End Initiative: Project Description, Log, and Preliminary Impact Analysis*, Greensboro, NC: Center for Youth, Family, and Community Partnerships.

Goldstein, H. (1990) *Problem-Oriented Policing*, Philadelphia: Temple University Press.

Kennedy, D.M. (1997) "Pulling levers: chronic offenders, high-crime settings, and a theory of prevention," *Valparaiso University Law Review*, 31: 449–84.

—— (2006) "Old wine in new bottles: policing and the lessons of pulling levers," in D.L. Weisburd and A.A. Braga (eds) *Police Innovation: Contrasting Perspectives*, New York: Cambridge University Press.

—— (2009) "Drugs, race, and common ground: reflections on the High Point intervention," *National Institute of Justice Journal*, 262: 12–17.

——, Braga, A.A., and Piehl, A.M. (1997) "The (un)known universe: mapping gangs and gang violence in Boston," in D.L. Weisburd and J.T. McEwen (eds) *Crime Mapping and Crime Prevention* (*Crime Prevention Studies*, vol. 8), Monsey, NY: Criminal Justice Press.

——, Piehl, A.M., and Braga, A.A. (1996) "Youth violence in Boston: gun markets, serious youth offenders, and a use-reduction strategy," *Law and Contemporary Problems*, 59: 147–96.

Klein, M. (1995) *The American Street Gang: Its Nature, Prevalence, and Control*, New York and London: Oxford University Press.

Lewin, K. (1947) "Group decisions and social change," in T. Newcomb and E. Hartley (eds) *Readings in Social Psychology*, New York: Atherton Press.

Ludwig, J. (2005) "Better gun enforcement, less crime," *Criminology & Public Policy*, 4: 677–716.

McGarrell, E., Chermak, S., Wilson, J., and Corsaro, N. (2006) "Reducing homicide through a lever-pulling strategy," *Justice Quarterly*, 23: 214–29.

Matza, D. (1964) *Delinquency and Drift*, New York: John Wiley and Sons.

Meares, T. (2009) "The legitimacy of police among young African-American men," *Marquette Law Review*, 92: 651–66.

Morgan, S. and Winship, C. (2007) *Counterfactuals and Causal Models*, New York: Cambridge University Press.

Papachristos, A.V., Meares, T., and Fagan, J. (2007) "Attention felons: evaluating Project Safe Neighborhoods in Chicago," *Journal of Empirical Legal Studies*, 4: 223–72.

Pease, K. (1991) "The Kirkholt project: preventing burglary on a British public housing estate," *Security Journal*, 2: 73–7.

Rosenfeld, R., Fornango, R., and Baumer, E. (2005) "Did Ceasefire, Compstat, and Exile reduce homicide?" *Criminology & Public Policy*, 4: 419–50.

Skubak Tillyer, M. and Kennedy, D.M. (2008) "Locating focused deterrence approaches

within a situational crime prevention framework," *Crime Prevention and Community Safety*, 10: 75–84.
Tita, G., Riley, K.J., Ridgeway, G., Grammich, C., Abrahamse, A., and Greenwood, P. (2004) *Reducing Gun Violence: Results from an Intervention in East Los Angeles*, Santa Monica, CA: RAND Corporation.
Tyler, T. (1990) *Why People Obey the Law*, New Haven: Yale University Press.
Wellford, C., Pepper, J., and Petrie, C. (eds) (2005) *Firearms and Violence: A Critical Review*, Committee to Improve Research Information and Data on Firearms, Committee on Law and Justice, Division of Behavioral and Social Sciences and Education, Washington, DC: The National Academies Press.

6 Situational crime prevention makes problem-oriented policing work
The importance of interdependent theories for effective policing

John E. Eck and Tamara D. Madensen

> Lichens are unique in the world of vegetation in that they cannot be neatly be classified into any of the ordinary categories which we think of as "plants." The reason is simple: the lichen is not a single entity, but a composite of a fungus and an organism capable of producing food by photosynthesis. . . . The special biological relationship found in lichens is called symbiosis. The resulting composite of a fungus and its photosynthetic symbiont (photobiont, for short) has been such an evolutionary success that there are close to 14,000 species of lichens in the world, tremendously diverse in size, form, and color. They are found from the poles to the tropics, and from the intertidal zones to the peaks of mountains, and on every kind of surface from soil, rocks, and tree bark, to the backs of insects!
>
> (Brodo et al., 2001: 3)

Introduction

Today, the link between Ronald V. Clarke's situational crime prevention (Clarke, 1980) and Herman Goldstein's problem-oriented policing (Goldstein, 1979) is taken for granted by those involved in crime prevention. The Center for Problem-Oriented Policing contains educational materials on situational crime prevention (as well as other environmental criminology/crime sciences theories), and Ronald V. Clarke is one of the co-directors of the center. Most of the finalists' entries for either the Goldstein Awards for Problem-Solving Excellence or the UK's Tilley Awards for Problem-Solving Excellence contain elements of situational crime prevention. Not surprisingly, problem-solving training often has a hefty dose of situational crime prevention. The two crime analysis manuals for police devote a large proportion of the content to rational choice and situational crime prevention (Clarke and Eck, 2003, 2005). The annual Environmental Criminology and Crime Analysis conference routine has papers on problem-oriented policing. And the series *Crime Prevention Studies* (created and edited by Ronald V. Clarke) contains many papers on problem-oriented policing, including two of the twenty-six volumes explicitly devoted to problem-oriented policing.

Police researchers, on the other hand, typically overlook the contribution of situational crime prevention (and other crime science theories and research) and focus on Goldstein's theory of policing. And environmental criminologists approach problem-oriented policing from a crime sciences perspective, and generally ignore Goldstein's theory. In this chapter, we seek to make explicit the links between problem-oriented policing, rational choice perspectives and situational crime prevention. Our thesis is that without Clarke's theories of crime, problem-oriented policing would not have survived and continued to thrive after more than thirty years. Secondarily, we also propose that without a theory like problem-oriented policing, there would have been no institutional infrastructure for applying situational crime prevention, so this theory would not have thrived.

We make our argument in four parts. The next section describes two theories – developed independently – that require each other. They are, of course, problem-oriented policing and situational crime prevention. We then show, in the following section, how situational crime prevention has been incorporated into police problem-solving. We do this by examining the Goldstein Award database. In the third section, we show how situational crime prevention can be extended to deal with non-offenders in place-based problem-solving. In the final section we summarize our argument and suggest the "lichen conjecture": any enduring and successful theory of policing must attach itself to a valid theory of the issues that the police are required to address.

Two theories

Problem-oriented policing is a theory of policing agencies. It has descriptive and normative elements. The descriptive features make it scientifically testable. The normative features are not subject to empirical test (Eck, 2006). Like Bittner (1980), Goldstein (1979) claimed that the policing function could not be defined by crime control because the public demands that the police handle a diverse range of concerns. Bittner claimed that it is impossible to define the police function on the basis of ends (e.g., less crime), so the only alternative is to focus on the means of policing that distinguish policing from other institutions: use of force.

In contrast, Goldstein redefined the ends of policing, stating that the function of policing is to address "problems" that the public brings to police attention. It is, according to Goldstein (1979), the over attention to means and the neglect of ends that is at the heart of the policing dysfunctions. Goldstein's prescription is that police become scientific: that police identify problems, subject them to careful analysis, engage in a broad search for potential solutions and then determine if the implemented solutions reduced the problem. Sparrow (2000) extended Goldstein's ideas to apply to all government regulatory agencies, thus making the problem-oriented approach a general theory of governance. At its core, problem-oriented policing is about the application of science to problems faced by the police. In fact, one could argue that problem-oriented policing creates a group of "street scientists," police who are addressing problems.

There are two critical questions that need to be asked at this stage: how can the police implement such a strategy, and what is a problem? Some have suggested that there is a third question, "Does problem-solving produce better results than alternatives?" (Weisburd et al., 2010). As Gloria Laycock (2010) said, "Problem-Oriented Policing is the application of the scientific method to policing. So what is the alternative; non-science?" This third question, then, should be interpreted as a form of the first question.

The second question is far more interesting and important. Originally, Goldstein defined problems more by example than formal definition, and by what problems are not. Problems are not singular events. Problems are not concerns of interest solely to police administrators. Problems are not just about crime. Clarke and Eck (2003) codified a definition of problem into the CHEERS criteria: they occur within the Community, they involve Harms, there is a public Expectation of police involvement, and they are made up of Events that are Repeating and Similar. In essence, they are patterns of harmful behaviors occurring in the community that some within the public expect the police to handle.

In the police research literature, problem-oriented policing has become synonymous with a practical device used to aid implementation: the SARA process. This four stage procedure – Scanning or problem identification, Analysis or investigation, Response or solution implementation, and Assessment or evaluation – is merely a variant of planning processes used in many fields (Eck and Spelman, 1987). Sparrow (2000) has even proposed an interesting six-step alternative that has wide applicability. But because SARA is simple, and perhaps due to ignorance, many academics and police consider this to be the heart of problem-oriented policing.

This is where Goldstein's theory of problem-oriented policing ends: police are about handling problems and they should do so in a scientific manner. Problem-oriented policing does not have a theory of problems. It does not state how problems are created, how they can be classified, how they are distributed or what their vulnerabilities might be. It is completely silent on these questions. Imagine a theory of civil engineering that is silent on physical forces. Or a theory of economics that is silent on human decision-making. Or a science of medicine that is silent on physiology, chemistry and biology. But this is exactly what we have in policing. Like almost all police theories, problem-oriented policing has nothing to say about the very thing policing is to be oriented toward.

Enter Ronald V. Clarke. His situational crime prevention is a prescriptive theory about how to prevent crime. We will not explain it in detail, as this has been done by Clarke (1980, 1995, 1997, 2008) and by other authors in this volume. Rather we will stick to the basic features and how it informs the practice of problem-oriented policing. Situational crime prevention is based on the notion of offenders' bounded rationality (Cornish and Clarke, 2008). That is, offenders respond to their perceived effort and risk of committing a crime as well as the rewards they expect. Later, excuses and provocations were recognized as part of the decision calculus (Clarke, 2008). Importantly, situational crime prevention is based on the assumption that offenders make their final decisions about whether to commit a crime at times and places proximal to the crime target, so perceptions of risk, reward, effort, excuses and provocations that occur long before or in places distant from the possible crime have far less impact on decisions than those perceptions immediately around the crime site near the moment a crime could take place.

Along with routine activity theory (Felson, 2008), no other theory of crime has had such an important influence on policing. But this influence on policing is almost exclusively through a problem-oriented approach. Situational crime prevention is peculiarly useful to police problem-solvers. First, it does not involve psycho-babble or require police to become para-social workers: offender decision-making is not fundamentally different from non-offender decision-making, and the motivations are understandable (even when morally indefensible). Second, situational crime prevention focuses on interventions at the meso-level: above the level of the individual but below large-scale social institutions. At this level, the police can take action with the prospect of making a difference. Third, the process for undertaking situational crime prevention is fully compatible with problem-oriented policing: identify a crime problem, conduct an analysis of the situation, and then select an intervention that fits the facts of the matter. Finally, situational crime prevention does not require treating offenders with kid-gloves; it's highly pragmatic approach that is highly compatible with notions of deterrence.

Importantly, when combined with other crime science theories – routine activity theory (Felson, 2008) and crime pattern theory (Brantingham and Brantingham, 2008) – rational choice and situational crime prevention provide a basic theory of crime problems that problem-oriented policing lacks. However, these theories are crime theories, and problem-oriented policing involves far more than crime. A very large part of the police business involves various forms of disorder- and traffic-related concerns. Fortunately, situational crime prevention has applicability beyond standard street crimes.

Table 6.1 illustrates this. The data come from a systematic compilation of quantitative situational crime prevention evaluations (Center for Problem-Oriented Policing, 2010). While many of these evaluations examine policing initiatives, many others do not. Although crimes predominate in these evaluations, disorder- and vehicle-related problems are well represented. The central lesson from Table 6.1 is that situational crime prevention has been applied to a wide variety of problems, and these applications have used the full range of situational methods. That said, some problem types dominate – burglary most obviously – and some methods are used more than others – particularly increasing risk and effort. The database for this table is heavily influenced by what interests the evaluators, and what they can publish, so it may not be representative of the scope of situational crime prevention. Nevertheless, it does illustrate the diverse set of problems to which it has been applied and the range of situational measures that have been applied.

Another way of describing the broad scope of situational crime prevention is to look at the types of problems researchers have used the theory to address. Various forms of street disorder have been attacked with situational crime prevention, including graffiti (Weisel, 2002), bullying (Sampson, 2002), drinking-related disturbances (Homel et al., 1997) and noise (Scott, 2001). Drug dealing (Harocopos and Hough, 2005) and prostitution activity (Scott and Dedel, 2006), have also been addressed. Traffic has been the concern of a number of studies and policing applications (LaVigne, 2007; Scott and Maddox, 2010; Heinonen and Eck, 2007). Crowd-related disorder and violence has also been addressed (Madensen and Eck,

Table 6.1 Problem types and situational methods

		Violence	Robbery	Burglary	Fraud	Alcohol and drugs	Disorder	Vehicle-related	Various	Total
Increasing effort	Target harden	3	7	28	4		3	2	5	52
	Control access	8	3	17	4	8	4		8	52
	Screen exits			5						5
	Deflect offenders	1	1	5		3	2		3	15
	Control tools/weapons									0
Increasing risk	Extend guardianship	2	2	25	1	3		5	11	49
	Assist natural surveillance	5	2	22	1	1	5	1	25	62
	Reduce anonymity			1	4		1			6
	Use place managers	1		4	2	5	3	1		16
	Strengthen formal surveillance	6	7	35	2	5	10	3	28	96
Decreasing rewards	Conceal targets									0
	Remove targets		1	3	1		1			6
	Identify property		1	12				1		14
	Disrupt markets	1		1		3	1			6
	Deny benefits	1	2	6	1		4	2	1	17
Decreasing provocations	Reduce frustrations and stress	1								1
	Avoid disputes	2				1				3
	Reduce emotional arousal	1								1
	Neutralize peer pressure									0
	Discourage imitation									0
Decreasing excuses	Set rules	1			1		1			3
	Post instructions		1							1
	Alert conscience			6	1			1	1	9
	Assist compliance									0
	Control drugs and alcohol					1	1			2
	Total	33	27	170	22	30	36	16	82	416

Source: Center for Problem-Oriented Policing. http://www.popcenter.org/library/scp/index.cfm. Table was created by selecting "all" for problem type, and "type of situational crime prevention technique" for sorting method.

2008; Madensen and Knutsson, 2011). In addition to these problems, situational crime prevention has been applied to suicide (Clarke and Mayhew, 1988), terrorism (Freilich and Newman, 2009), domestic violence (Sampson, 2006), child abuse (Wortley and Smallbone, 2006b), child pornography (Wortley and Smallbone, 2006a), organized crime (van de Bunt and van der Schoot, 2003) and electronic crime (Newman and Clarke, 2003). In short, despite the fact that situational crime prevention (and other crime science theories) was developed with common crimes in mind, it has been applied to a much broader range of maladies. In fact, it seems probable that any problem the police deal with will be addressable, at least in part, through situational measures. The same cannot be said for any other criminological theory.

To sum up our argument so far, problem-oriented policing is a theory of policing but does not have a theory of problems. Situational crime prevention helps fill this gap. But to what extent do police use situational crime prevention in their problem-solving efforts?

Addressing problems with situational measures

The Herman Goldstein Award was established in 1993 to formally recognize police agencies that embrace problem-oriented policing. Each year, the Center for Problem-Oriented Policing solicits written submissions that document attempts to reduce community problems. These efforts must address specific recurring crime, disorder or public safety problems using all four stages of the SARA problem-solving model. Award finalists, who are deemed to have engaged in measureable, innovative and effective problem-solving, are selected from the general pool of submissions. Winners are selected from this subset at the annual Problem-Oriented Policing Conference based on a set of judging criteria related to each SARA phase (see www.popcenter.org/goldstein). As is the case with the systematic compilation of published studies examined above, these data do not provide a representative sample of all problem-oriented policing projects. Rather they show a range of experiences of some of the best projects.

Between the years 1993 and 2010, 126 Herman Goldstein Award submissions were selected as winners or finalists by the Center for Problem-Oriented Policing (www.popcenter.org/library/awards/goldstein). In an effort to determine the extent to which police rely on situational measures to effectively reduce community problems, we examined the interventions described in these submissions over the past ten years (2001–10: fifty-nine individual projects). For each project we documented the interventions described in the "response" phase of the SARA process and categorized them as either situational or non-situational. We defined situational measures as those that altered behavioral opportunity structures using one or more of the five major headings of Table 6.1.

For example, situational measures include interventions such as the placement of signs providing instructions, CCTV cameras, changes to lighting, directed police patrols, new locks/fencing, the setting of rules through behavioral contracts, or street closures. Non-situational measures include interventions such as community partnerships, general media campaigns to gain public acceptance for a police strategy (not to alter behaviors of specific victims or offenders), reorganization of police structures, new data collection strategies, or offerings of non-mandatory general social service programs.

Table 6.2 summarizes the results of this analysis. The table gives the number of projects (finalists and winners) selected, the total number of interventions used, and the percent of these interventions classified as situational, by year. Across all years, more situational interventions are used than non-situational interventions. There is some variability in the percent of situational measures used by year. Still, 86 percent the fifty-nine projects used at least one situational measure, and ten projects used only situational measures. Further, at least half of the interventions were situational in 73 percent of the projects.

We undertook a separate analysis to identify differences in the use of situational methods between the ten winning projects and the runner-up projects. We found no meaningful difference. The percent of situational interventions used by winning strategies (76.5) was almost identical to the total average (75.9). However, only one of the winning strategies did not include a situational intervention. So there is slight evidence that the winning projects made more use of situational crime prevention than the finalists who did not win.

By any measure, it is clear that situational crime prevention is heavily used in the more advanced problem-solving projects, and that this strategy for reducing police problems is used far more than any other strategy. These findings support our contention that situational crime prevention has helped problem-oriented policing to thrive, while problem-oriented policing has provided an institutional infrastructure for applying the crime-reduction principles of situational crime prevention.

Problems as a management function

Place-based problem-solving is a particularly common approach to reducing crime, disorder or safety problems. We know that crime is highly concentrated in

Table 6.2 Percentage of situational interventions

Year	No. of projects	Total interventions	Situational
2010	6	43	67.4
2009	6	42	61.9
2008	7	71	76.1
2007	5	26	76.9
2006	4	37	89.2
2005	8	40	77.5
2004	5	41	85.4
2003	6	40	67.5
2002	6	63	74.6
2001	6	40	82.5
Total/mean	**59**	**443**	**75.9**

specific locations (Sherman, Gartin and Buerger, 1989) and within a subset of particular types of places (Eck, Clarke and Guerette, 2007). Therefore, it was not surprising to find that many of the Herman Goldstein Award submission interventions focused on changing behavioral opportunity structures by changing places. Table 6.3 shows that while about 27 percent of interventions focused on offenders and about 15 percent focused on victims, just over 55 percent were place-based strategies. Furthermore, fourteen of the fifty-nine submissions (23.7 percent) reported using at least one intervention that focused specifically on holding managers and owners of locations accountable for problems at places.

Police have long attempted to address problems by holding place managers accountable for the activities that occur on their properties. Police attempts to coerce non-offending parties, and particularly place managers, to take actions to reduce crime and disorder is often referred to as "third-party policing" (Buerger and Mazzerole, 1998). Police, when engaged in efforts to change place manager behaviors, are considered "super controllers" (Sampson, Eck and Dunham, 2010). Super controllers can reduce crime by providing incentives for place managers to create environments that suppress, rather than facilitate, crime. It is presumed that place managers, like offenders (see Cornish and Clarke, 2008), engage in rational decision-making processes (see Madensen, 2007). Both parties weigh the cost and benefits associated with any course of action. Incentives toward appropriate behaviors can have a positive impact on both offenders and non-offenders. This similarity should not be surprising as the rational choice perspective is premised on the idea that offenders make decisions like everyone else (Cornish and Clarke, 2008).

Given that place managers are rational, it is useful to consider how situational crime prevention can be extended to encourage place managers to reduce crime in and around their properties. As super controllers, police may be able to use situational crime prevention principles to alter the incentive structure for place

Table 6.3 Percentage of offender-, victim- and place-based interventions*

Year	Offender-based	Victim-based	Place-based
2010	23.3	16.3	58.1
2009	45.2	14.3	28.6
2008	29.6	11.3	54.9
2007	11.5	0.0	84.6
2006	24.3	24.3	48.6
2005	25.0	17.5	55.0
2004	12.2	17.1	68.3
2003	47.5	15.0	35.0
2002	25.4	14.3	60.3
2001	20.0	17.5	62.5
Total/mean	**26.4**	**14.8**	**55.6**

Note
* Yearly percentages may not total to 100 percent; not all interventions could be classified as offender-, victim- or place-based.

managers. This incentive structure should persuade managers to create and maintain safe environments. For example, police should ask themselves the following questions:

1   How can we make it easier for managers to create safe environments?
2   How can we reduce the risks that managers may face in implementing change?
3   How can we increase the rewards associated with reducing crime and disorder at this location?
4   How can we reduce provocations associated with creating environments that encourage harmful behaviors?
5   How can we eliminate the rationalizations managers use to deny responsibility for crime facilitating conditions?

Useful answers to these questions can only come from a complete understanding of place manager functions in any given location, and how these functions create conditions associated with crime and disorder. Police must identify managers that create harmful environments, analyze the types of manager decisions and subsequent behaviors that promote unsafe conditions, implement interventions to change problematic manager behaviors (using situational crime prevention principles) and assess the effectiveness of these interventions. The complementary and symbiotic relationship between the theories of problem-oriented policing and situational crime prevention, again, appears unmistakable.

The lichen conjecture of policing strategies

We have argued that Goldstein's problem-oriented approach to policing is unique among police reforms in that it not only focused police on outcomes (ends) but redefined the unit of police work as "the problem." It brought the scientific method to standard police practices. However, this revolutionary approach would not have gained traction absent Clarke's situational crime prevention ideas. Though developed independently, the symbiotic relationship between these two theories began relatively early in the application of problem-oriented policing (Eck and Spelman, 1987) and accelerated throughout the 1990s. With the formation of the Center for Problem-Oriented Policing the connections between the theories became cemented, and Clarke and Goldstein conducted research together on two policing projects in Charlotte, North Carolina (2002, 2003).

It is important to recognize that there were no competitors to situational crime prevention for the attention of the police. Standard criminology had no useful theory of the problems police were called upon to address. That is still the case today. Situational crime prevention and its allies in crime science are the sole useful theories of crime.

Criminal justice and policing researchers have neglected the role of situational crime prevention in problem-oriented policing. Rather there seems to be an obsession with whether or not the SARA process has been used. This despite the existence of alternative problem-solving processes (Sparrow, 2000). This implies that there is an unstated assumption among academics who study police; one can understand police without understanding the nature of the problems police are called upon to address. If this approach to policing were used to study medicine, medical researchers would discuss hospital administration, ambulance deployment and physician misconduct, but not discuss the causes and processes of diseases and injuries, or the efficacy of various treatments. If this approach were used in civil engineering, then academic civil engineering professors would focus on the organization of public works organizations rather than how to measure stress in various materials. Police use of situational crime prevention would appear to be a better measure of the degree to which problem-oriented policing is being applied than the use of SARA or any other process.

The neglect of situational crime prevention and other crime science theories by academics and practitioners has also meant that almost all proposals for improving policing have been means-focused. Starting with community policing of the 1980s (Greene and Mastrofski, 1988) to COMPSTAT (Silverman, 1999) of the 1990s, there is no link to the science of crime. There are some exceptions. Broken windows theory is a theory of crime and policing that has influenced policing, and a large proportion of the debate surrounding this theory has to do whether the theory of crime is correct. Additionally, Jerry Ratcliffe's (2008) approach to intelligence-led policing (ILP) is firmly grounded in the same crime sciences theories as problem-oriented policing – which explains in large part why it is so compatible with Problem-oriented policing – though other expressions of ILP are devoid of a theory of crime that could make their administrative proposals effective.

Problem-oriented policing has been around for over three decades probably because it has formed a symbiotic relationship with situational crime prevention. The prevalence of situational crime prevention is probably due to its alliance with problem-oriented policing. We suggest that practitioners and researchers take a lesson from this experience. We propose what we call the *lichen conjecture*. Lichens are highly successful organisms that thrive in a wide variety of conditions. They are composed of a fungus and a plant capable of photosynthesis (Brodo, Sharnoff and Sharnoff, 2001). In artificial laboratory conditions, either component can survive and reproduce separate from the other. But in natural environments both need to work together to survive. Policing theories and crime theories are like this. They can look good in the artificial environments of academic journals and practitioner conferences. But to survive and flourish in the real world, any valid policing theory must form a symbiotic relationship with a valid theory of the work the police are called upon to address. Currently, the only valid theories of crime and disorder problems faced by the police come from crime science and environmental criminology.

References

Bittner, E. (1980) *The Functions of Police in Modern Society*, Rockville, MD: National Institute of Mental Health.

Brantingham, P.J. and Brantingham, P.L. (2008) "Crime pattern theory," in R. Wortley and L. Mazerolle (eds) *Environmental Criminology and Crime Analysis*, Cullompton: Willan Publishing.

Brodo, I.M., Sharnoff, S.D. and Sharnoff, S. (2001) *Lichens of North America*, New Haven: Yale University Press.

Buerger, M.E. and Mazzerole, L.G. (1998) "Third party policing: a theoretical analysis of an emerging trend," *Justice Quarterly*, 15(2): 301–27.

Center for Problem-Oriented Policing. (2010) Online. Available at: http://www.popcenter.org/library/scp/index.cfm (accessed July 23, 2010).

Clarke, R.V. (1980) "Situational crime prevention: theory and practice," *British Journal of Criminology*, 20(1): 136–47.

Clarke, R.V. (1995) "Situational crime prevention," in M. Tonry and D. Farrington (eds) *Building a Safer Society: Strategic Approaches to Crime Prevention*, Chicago: University of Chicago Press.

Clarke, R.V. (1997) *Situational Crime Prevention: Successful Case Studies*, Albany, NY: Harrow and Heston.

Clarke, R.V. (2008) "Situational crime prevention," in R. Wortley and L. Mazerolle (eds) *Environmental Criminology and Crime Analysis*, Cullompton: Willan Publishing.

Clarke, R.V. and Eck, J.E. (2003) *Become a Problem-solving Crime Analyst: In 55 Small Steps*, London: Jill Dando Institute for Crime Science.

Clarke, R.V. and Eck, J.E. (2005) *Crime Analysis for Problem Solvers: In 60 Small Steps*, Washington, DC: US Department of Justice, Office of Community Policing Services.

Clarke, R.V. and Goldstein, H. (2002) "Reducing theft at construction sites: lessons from a problem-oriented project," in N. Tilley (ed.) *Analysis for Crime Prevention, Crime Prevention Studies*, vol. 13, Monsey, NY: Criminal Justice Press.

Clarke, R.V. and Goldstein, H. (2003) "Thefts from cars in center-city parking facilities: a case study in implementing problem-oriented policing," in J. Knutsson (ed.) *Mainstreaming Problem-oriented Policing Crime Prevention Studies*, vol. 15, Monsey, NY: Criminal Justice Press.

Clarke, R.V. and Mayhew, P. (1988) "The British gas suicide story and its criminological implications," in M. Tonry and N. Morris (eds) *Crime and Justice: A Review of Research*, vol. 10, Chicago: University of Chicago Press.

Cornish, D.B. and Clarke, R.V. (2008) "The rational choice perspective," in R. Wortley and L. Mazerolle (eds) *Environmental Criminology and Crime Analysis*, Cullompton: Willan Publishing.

Eck, J.E. (2006) "Science, values and problem-oriented policing," in D. Weisburd and A. Braga (eds) *Prospects and Problems in an Era of Police Innovation: Contrasting Perspectives*, New York: Cambridge University Press.

Eck, J.E. and Spelman, W. (1987) *Problem-solving: Problem-oriented Policing in Newport News*, Washington, DC: Police Executive Research Forum.

Eck, J.E., Clarke, R.V. and Guerette, R.T. (2007) "Risky facilities: crime concentration in homogeneous sets of establishments and facilities," in G. Farrell, K. Bowers, K.D. Johnson and M. Townsley (eds) *Imagination for Crime Prevention: Essays in Honour of Ken Pease, Crime Prevention Studies*, vol. 21, Cullompton: Willan Publishing.

Felson, M. (2008) "Routine activity theory," in R. Wortley and L. Mazerolle (eds) *Environmental Criminology and Crime Analysis*, Cullompton: Willan Publishing.

Freilich, J.D. and Newman, G. (eds) (2009) *Reducing Terrorism through Situational Crime Prevention, Crime Prevention Studies*, vol. 25, Monsey, NY: Criminal Justice Press.

Goldstein, H. (1979) "Improving policing: a problem-oriented approach," *Crime and Delinquency*, 25(2): 236–58.

Greene, J.R. and Mastrofski, S.D. (1988) *Community Policing: Rhetoric or Reality*, New York: Praeger.

Harocopos, A. and Hough, M. (2005) *Drug Dealing in Open-air Markets, Problem-oriented Guides for Police, Problem-specific Guides Series*, no. 31, Washington, DC: US Department of Justice, Office of Community Policing Services.

Heinonen, J.A. and Eck, J.E. (2007) *Pedestrian Injuries and Fatalities, Problem-oriented Guides for Police, Problem-specific Guides Series*, no. 51, Washington, DC: US Department of Justice, Office of Community Policing Services.

Homel, R., Hauritz, M., McIlwain, G., Wortley, R. and Carvolth, R. (1997) "Preventing drunkenness and violence around nightclubs in a tourist resort," in R.V. Clarke (ed.) *Situational Crime Prevention: Successful Case Studies*, Albany, NY: Harrow and Heston.

La Vigne, N. (2007) *The Problem of Traffic Congestion Around Schools Problem-oriented Guides for Police, Problem-specific Guides Series*, no. 50, Washington, DC: US Department of Justice, Office of Community Policing Services.

Laycock, G. (2010) "Science and policing," presentation to the Royal New Zealand Police Research Symposium, Wellington, Royal New Zealand Police College, July.

Madensen, T.D. (2007) *Bar Management and Crime: Toward a Dynamic Theory of Place Management and Crime Hotspots*, Cincinnati: University of Cincinnati.

Madensen, T.D. and Eck, J.E. (2008) *Spectator Violence in Stadiums, Problem-oriented Guides for Police, Problem-specific Guides Series*, no. 54, Washington, DC: US Department of Justice, Office of Community Policing Services.

Madensen, T.D. and Knutsson, J. (eds) (2011) *Preventing Crowd Violence, Crime Prevention Studies*, vol. 26, Boulder, CO: Lynne Reinner.

Newman, G. and Clarke, R.V. (2003) *Superhighway Robbery: Preventing E-commerce Crime*, Cullompton: Willan Publishing.

Ratcliffe, J.H. (2008) *Intelligence-led Policing*, Cullompton: Willan Publishing.

Sampson, R. (2002) *Bullying in Schools, Problem-oriented Guides for Police, Problem-specific Guides Series*, no. 12, Washington, DC: US Department of Justice, Office of Community Policing Services.

Sampson, R. (2006) *Domestic Violence, Problem-oriented Guides for Police, Problem-specific Guides Series*, no. 45, Washington, DC: US Department of Justice, Office of Community Policing Services.

Sampson, R., Eck, J.E. and Dunham, J. (2010) "Super controllers and crime prevention: a routine activity explanation of crime prevention success and failure," *Security Journal*, 23(1): 37–51.

Scott, M.S. (2001) *Loud Car Stereos, Problem-oriented Guides for Police, Problem-specific Guides Series*, no. 7, Washington, DC: US Department of Justice, Office of Community Policing Services.

Scott, M.S. and Dedel, K. (2006) *Street Prostitution*, 2nd edn, *Problem-oriented Guides for Police, Problem-specific Guides Series*, no. 2, Washington, DC: US Department of Justice, Office of Community Policing Services.

Scott, M.S. and Maddox, D.K. (2010) *Speeding in Residential Areas*, 2nd edn, *Problem-oriented Guides for Police, Problem-specific Guides Series*, no. 3, Washington, DC: US Department of Justice, Office of Community Policing Services.

Sherman, L.W., Gartin, P.R. and Buerger, M.E. (1989) "Hot spots of predatory crime: routine activities and the criminology of place," *Criminology*, 27(1): 27–55.

Sparrow, M. (2000) *The Regulatory Craft: Controlling Risks, Solving Problems, and Managing Compliance*, Washington, DC: Brookings Institution Press.

Silverman, E.B. (1999) *NYPD Battles Crime: Innovative Strategies in Policing*, Boston: Northeastern University Press.

van de Bunt, H.G. and van der Schoot, C. (2003) *The Prevention of Organized Crime: A Situational Approach*, Amsterdam: Boom Juridische uitgevers.

Weisburd, D., Telep, C.W., Hinkel, J.C. and Eck, J.E. (2010) "Is problem-oriented policing effective in reducing crime and disorder? Findings from a Campbell systematic review," *Criminology and Public Policy*, 9(1) 139–72.

Weisel, D.L. (2002) *Graffiti, Problem-oriented Guides for Police, Problem-specific Guides Series*, no. 9, Washington, DC: US Department of Justice, Office of Community Policing Services.

Wortley, R. and Smallbone, S. (2006a) *Child Pornography on the Internet, Problem-oriented Guides for Police, Problem-specific Guides Series*, no. 41, Washington, DC: US Department of Justice, Office of Community Policing Services.

Wortley, R. and Smallbone, S. (eds) (2006b) *Situational Prevention of Sexual Offenses Against Children, Crime Prevention Studies*, vol. 19, Monsey, NY: Criminal Justice Press.

7 Ron Clarke's contribution to improving policing

A diffusion of benefits

Michael S. Scott and Herman Goldstein

Introduction

As a criminologist, Ron Clarke never set out to reform policing, yet his work in situational crime prevention has meshed so well with parallel work in problem-oriented policing that the effect has been to significantly improve the policing field, a true diffusion of benefits if we ever saw one.

Ron's principal objective has always been to improve crime prevention practice by whoever is in position to take effective action, whether criminologists, private security officials, manufacturers and designers, community organizations, private citizens, or government agencies. When Ron became better acquainted with the policing field, he astutely recognized that the police were well positioned to engage more deeply in situational crime prevention even though they had not been so engaged as yet. Having immersed himself in the body of work being done by police under the auspices of problem-oriented policing, he concluded that "[p]ooling of experience in [problem-oriented policing and situational crime prevention] would bring considerable benefits in the application of both concepts" (Clarke, 1997b: 67).

When Ron first began to examine problem-oriented policing, his foremost interest might have been in how situational crime prevention could improve and enhance problem-oriented policing. Alternatively, his foremost interest might have been in how situational crime prevention could benefit from connecting with problem-oriented policing. (This would be so because the police are the social institution bearing the greatest responsibility for addressing most crime problems, and because the police have an institutional orientation to pragmatic and effective action. If the police could be persuaded that situational crime prevention methods can yield substantial crime reductions, they would be likely to embrace the concept.)

However Ron himself may view the influence of situational crime prevention on problem-oriented policing, and vice versa, we have come to greatly value the contribution, however unintended, that Ron and his situational crime prevention approach have made to our central goal of improving the overall functioning of the police in society.

Ron has done so largely by reinforcing the value of careful analysis of discrete public safety problems, which can reveal more precisely and confidently what ought to be done – beyond merely arresting and prosecuting offenders – to ameliorate those problems, and by whom. In helping the police better understand what causes or facilitates crime and disorder, the police are put in a much firmer position to shift, share, and apportion responsibility for controlling crime and disorder. A more intelligent and equitable apportioning of responsibility for crime and disorder control, with more appropriate strategic responses, ultimately relieves much of the nearly impossible burden that the police have historically borne in trying to carry out their function, a burden that has rendered the police often ineffective, and occasionally brutal and corrupt. In short, smarter, evidence-based crime prevention contributes tremendously to fairer and more effective policing.

Early developments on both sides of the Atlantic Ocean

It was during the late 1970s and early 1980s that one of us (Herman) synthesized two decades' prior work into the overarching problem-oriented policing framework (Goldstein, 1979) and that Ron synthesized his prior work into the overarching situational crime prevention framework (Clarke, 1980). Problem-oriented policing and situational crime prevention proved, ultimately, to be remarkably compatible, but their early development was quite independent of one another.

On the American side of the Atlantic Ocean in the early 1970s some police scholars and police executives were raising serious questions about the effectiveness of conventional policing strategies. The research that emerged from this period of intense inquiry into longstanding police practices challenged core assumptions about the relative value of preventive patrol, rapid police response to citizen requests for service, and detectives' contributions to criminal investigations (see Eck and Spelman, 1987; Goldstein, 1990; and Bayley, 1998 for collections and summaries of this body of research). The growing realization that the broad strategies police were employing to achieve their objectives were not wholly satisfactory fueled one of our (Herman's) own ruminations about police effectiveness, which culminated in the proposal of a new problem-oriented approach to policing (Goldstein, 1979, 1990).

Simultaneously, on the British side of the Atlantic Ocean, researchers were also examining police effectiveness in dealing with crime generally, and in dealing with specific forms of crime. In the summer of 1979, Ron, then with the British Home Office, co-convened a workshop on police effectiveness at the Cambridge Institute of Criminology. The papers presented at that workshop (published as a collection edited by Clarke and Hough, 1980; see also Clarke and Heal, 1980) reflected a significant shift in the Home Office's research focus toward gauging the effectiveness of police policies and practices.

Problem-oriented policing emerged from a body of research that called into question the value of conventional policing strategies in achieving police objectives, yet left largely unanswered just what strategies might be more effective. The concept, rooted in organizational theory, sought not to dictate what strategies the police should adopt, but rather to better position the police to answer those questions for themselves.

Situational crime prevention emerged as an amalgamation of theories about how crime could effectively and efficiently be prevented by manipulating the physical and social environment and context within which it was occurring, principally by reducing the opportunities for easy offending. Ron's particular theoretical contribution to situational crime prevention was his work on rational choice theory (Clarke, 1980; Clarke and Cornish, 1985; Cornish and Clarke, 1986).

The cross fertilization of problem-oriented policing and situational crime prevention

Although some of the American research was undoubtedly informed by the British research, and vice versa, it is more accurate to say that American and British policing and crime scholars were proceeding along parallel, but not yet merged, paths.

American and British police scholars and practitioners were learning about one another's work through a variety of exchanges. Gary Hayes, an enthusiastic student of policing at the University of Wisconsin Law School and later the founding executive director of the Police Executive Research Forum (PERF), spent a year with the police in London in the early 1980s. John Eck, then a researcher at PERF with substantial expertise in problem-oriented policing, spent six months with the London Metropolitan Police in 1984. The London Metropolitan Police, under the command of Sir Kenneth Newman and in consultation with one of us (Herman), was among the first British police agencies (along with Surrey Police) to test the problem-oriented policing approach in the early 1980s (Hoare, Stewart, and Purcell, 1984; Leigh, Read, and Tilley, 1996). London Met and Surrey police officials were following closely the experimental problem-oriented work being undertaken in Madison, Wisconsin; Baltimore County, Maryland; and Newport News, Virginia. Other British police forces followed suit in the 1990s with various problem-oriented efforts being undertaken in Thames Valley, Northumbria, West Yorkshire, Merseyside, Leicestershire, and Cleveland during this period (Leigh, Read, and Tilley, 1996, 1998).

In turn, Ron was invited to the United States from the United Kingdom to give talks on situational crime prevention at Sam Houston State University in Texas in 1979; to be a visiting professor at the State University of New York at Albany in 1981–2; to join the faculty at Temple University in Philadelphia in 1984; and ultimately, to join the faculty at Rutgers University in New Jersey in 1987.

One of us (Herman) and Ron first became acquainted – personally and with one another's work – at the first Environmental Criminology and Crime Analysis (ECCA) meeting in Montreal in 1992. This was but the first of many subsequent meetings, correspondences, and collaborations. Herman visited Ron and gave a talk at Rutgers University in 1994. Ron and Herman both spoke at crime prevention conferences sponsored by the UK Home Office in 1995. Ron met with Herman in Madison, Wisconsin, the following year and, upon Herman's suggestion, Ron began to attend the annual Problem-Oriented Policing Conference in 1996. Ron subsequently was invited by PERF to become the chairperson of the Herman Goldstein Award for Excellence in Problem-Oriented Policing. Ron has had a strong and positive influence on the judging committee's work by emphasizing quality analysis as the essential criteria for determining award winners.

Ron and Herman's most extensive collaboration occurred in 1999–2001 when Chief Dennis Nowicki, and his successor, Darrel Stephens, of the Charlotte-Mecklenburg, North Carolina, Police Department (CMPD) secured government funding to support bringing Herman into the department as a loosely defined "professor in residence." To assist the CMPD in its ambitious problem-oriented policing efforts, Herman brought in Ron to sharpen the analytical rigor of the CMPD's problem-solving efforts, especially with regard to evaluating the impact those efforts had on the targeted problems. The most substantial of these problem-oriented projects culminated in reports on the police response to two large crime problems: thefts from construction sites (Clarke and Goldstein, 2002) and thefts from vehicles in parking facilities (Clarke and Goldstein, 2003). This was perhaps Ron's most extensive contact with the police up to that point in his career. It undoubtedly gave him greater insight into the culture, politics, and bureaucracy of the American police, shaping his understanding of what it will take to fully incorporate problem-oriented policing and situational crime prevention into the routine functioning of the police.

Commonalities between situational crime prevention and problem-oriented policing

Situational crime prevention and problem-oriented policing have much in common (Clarke, 1997b; Tilley, 1999; Scott, 2000). Both concepts emerged from an overriding concern about effectiveness: effectiveness in preventing crime and effectiveness in achieving lawful policing objectives, respectively.

Both concepts were precipitated by a recognition that conventional approaches to crime control and to policing – namely, the application of deterrence through enforcement of the criminal law and the physical presence of the police – are ultimately rather limited in their effectiveness.

Both concepts acknowledge that crime and disorder problems have causes and contributing factors that extend beyond offenders' deep-seated motivations and predilections to offend; that there are social and environmental conditions that make it relatively easy and tempting for offenders to offend, conditions that, if ameliorated, would at least shrink the sheer volume of crime and disorder.

Both concepts promote thinking beyond the measures that can be taken to directly intervene in offenders' and victims' behavior to thinking about the measures that third parties can take to alter the physical and social conditions that indirectly influence offenders' and victims' behavior.

Both concepts emphasize the need to examine crime and disorder in a highly specific, as opposed to a generic, fashion; to recognize that different forms of crime and disorder have different causes and contributing conditions and, therefore, call for carefully tailored responses.[1]

Both situational crime prevention and problem-oriented policing place high value on careful and close analysis of specific crime and disorder problems to understand their causes and to gauge the relative effectiveness of responses to them. Accordingly, both concepts highly value applying research methods to policing and crime prevention practice. Both concepts particularly value the action-research model by which researchers collaborate with practitioners to design, implement, and evaluate interventions rather than merely observe and assess practitioners' efforts or accept the practitioners' claims of impact.

Perhaps most significantly, situational crime prevention and problem-oriented policing have in common a practical bent: a preference for adopting realistic, pragmatic measures in lieu of advocating for more idealistic reforms that would have less certain effects and that are unlikely to be adopted due to political or logistical obstacles.

Differences between situational crime prevention and problem-oriented policing

Where situational crime prevention and problem-oriented policing diverged was in their academic origins. Situational crime prevention emerged from the criminology field whereas problem-oriented policing emerged from the public administration field. More to the point, situational crime prevention was principally interested in how to reduce crime; problem-oriented policing was principally interested in how to improve the functioning of police. This meant that situational crime prevention was less interested in the police as an institution – the scope of their mandate, their exercise and abuse of authority and force, their accountability to political and community authorities, and so forth. It was interested in crime prevention regardless of who was undertaking it. Problem-oriented policing was less interested in crime prevention that did not implicate police action. It was interested not just in crime, but in all matters for which police assumed some responsibility. Situational crime prevention is explicitly grounded in criminological theory, explaining why crime occurs and how it can be prevented. Problem-oriented policing is not explicitly wedded to any particular criminological theory, being open to any and all theories that lead police to practical and effective interventions.

The contribution of practical crime theory to effective policing

As Ron became more familiar with and interested in the problem-oriented approach to policing, he took special note that it is not explicitly committed to any specific criminological theory. He argued that the problem-oriented approach suffered from its disconnection with criminological theory; that, while the approach could exhort the police to study crime and disorder problems, it couldn't adequately guide them toward more effective solutions in the absence of explanations as to what caused crime and disorder (Clarke, 1997b: 25). He pressed for more rigorous analysis, informed by good theory, that would establish tighter linkages between causes and effects and explain the mechanisms by which interventions could be expected to effectively address problems. In sum, Ron argued for a stronger linkage between the work being done under the auspices of problem-oriented policing and the work being done under the auspices of situational crime prevention (Clarke, 1997b, 1998).

As a theoretical matter, the validity of problem-oriented policing does not depend upon the validity of any particular criminological theory. Indeed, some quite effective problem oriented interventions have been undertaken by application of criminological theories other than those encompassed by situational crime prevention. For example, the widely heralded project that reduced gun violence among Boston's youth gangs was attributed to a particularly effective application of deterrence theory rather than to situational crime prevention (Boston Police Department, 1998; Braga et al., 2001; Kennedy, 2008), even though the principal researchers on this project also firmly subscribe to situational crime prevention theories.

As a practical matter, though, Ron has been proven quite correct about the benefits of informing problem-oriented policing practice with situational crime prevention theories. Police, rather sensibly, don't pay much heed to criminological theories that have little or no practical application to police work. Because police view themselves as having little capacity to affect such distant causes of crime and disorder as genetics, prenatal care, parenting methods, mental disease and defects, substance abuse, relative economic deprivation, unemployment, and the like, they tend to concern themselves only with those few criminological theories that clearly implicate conventional police action, most notably and almost exclusively, deterrence theory. As David Kennedy (2008) has persuasively argued, there is much that police and other criminal justice actors can do to improve their application of deterrence theory, but it is equally true that there is much that police can do – either directly or, more often, indirectly by persuading third parties to take action – to alter the opportunities for crime and disorder.

Through our own experiences teaching and working with police, we find police to be extraordinarily receptive to situational crime prevention theories when they are clearly explained because they readily see how their application might be effective and, moreover, might help alleviate some of the undue burden placed upon police to control crime and disorder through the limited means of arrest and the physical presence of the police. Accordingly, whereas police do not seem eager to learn more about the distant causes of crime and disorder, they do seem eager to learn more about their more immediate causes. Introducing police officers to such theories and models as routine activity theory (and the so-called crime triangle), rational choice theory, crime pattern theory, the CRAVED[2] model pertaining to the relative attractiveness of theft targets, and the twenty-five techniques of situational crime prevention nearly always engages them and sparks their interest in learning how to apply these theories and models to their routine policing practices.

Like all academic theorists, Ron is interested in demonstrating that his theories have merit. Situational crime prevention theories compete with a wide array of other criminological theories – social disorganization, differential association, anomie, strain, control, labeling, life course, etc. – for the interest and engagement of criminologists and crime prevention practitioners. Theories must be tested to be validated and, with respect to crime prevention, this means testing them in the field rather than in a laboratory, and field testing requires the cooperation of field practitioners.

Because the police bear substantial responsibility for dealing with crime, control substantial resources that might be devoted to crime control and prevention, and command substantial political and public support, engaging the police in practicing situational crime prevention would greatly expand the practical application of the theories. Accordingly, Ron has come to recognize what useful allies the police can be in applying and testing situational crime prevention theories, and ultimately, promoting their practice. As Ron presaged in his second edition of *Situational Crime Prevention: Case Studies*, "police interest in situational crime prevention is likely to be subsumed under problem-oriented policing" (Clarke, 1997a: 41).

Moreover, since the government has increasingly channeled much of its crime control resources through the police (at least in the United States), integrating situational crime prevention with policing holds out the promise of bringing greater financial resources to its practice. While it is not given that police would choose to use extra government resources on applying situational crime prevention or problem-oriented policing, as opposed to, say, trying to arrest more offenders, the possibilities for doing so are greater than they would be without those additional resources. Indeed, much US federal funding for police was provided under the broad and rather loose expectation that it would be devoted to community policing, which, if nothing else, has recognized that police cannot remain exclusively dependent on the criminal justice system in order to achieve their broad objectives.

The contribution of crime analysis to effective policing and crime prevention

In addition to contributing sound, practical criminological theory to the practice of policing, Ron has contributed greatly to improving police capacity for and appreciation of sound, practical data analysis.

Much of the early work conducted under the auspices of situational crime prevention did not directly involve the police (Clarke, 1992). Many of the studies and subsequent situational crime prevention interventions were conducted nearly entirely without police involvement; in others, police cooperated in a limited way; and in only a few did police agencies take an active or lead role in studying the crime problem or implementing new responses to it. This undoubtedly reflected a general lack of analytical capacity and orientation within police agencies and a lack of familiarity with situational crime prevention, as well as insufficient efforts on the part of situational crime prevention theorists to try to connect with the police. Police were, however, actively undertaking problem-oriented policing projects that nominally called for them to engage in problem analysis and subsequent evaluation.

As a byproduct of Ron's work on the judging committee for the Herman Goldstein Award for Excellence in Problem-Oriented Policing, he began to delve more deeply into the body of work being undertaken by police agencies according to the problem-oriented policing model. He secured a research grant from the National Institute of Justice (NIJ) in 1995 to study the reports that were submitted to the Goldstein Award program. His report to NIJ predictably and appropriately highlighted the need – if POP were to achieve its stated objectives – to improve the quality of analysis to understand the causes of crime and disorder problems that police were seeking to address and to improve the quality of the analysis to gauge the effects of their interventions (Clarke, 1997b, 1998).

Although many police agencies in both the United States and the United Kingdom have undertaken crime analysis for many decades, the quality of much of that analysis has been spotty and rudimentary. Moreover, historically, much of what has constituted crime analysis in police agencies has been restricted to analyzing spatial and temporal crime patterns to anticipate where and when the next crime might occur and to analyzing offenders' methods of operation so as to identify and apprehend them. This type of crime analysis has little value for the sort of preventive, proactive policing and crime prevention contemplated by problem-oriented policing and situational crime prevention. Although there are notable exceptions, a great deal of the work done in problem-oriented policing could be strengthened by more rigorous and competent analysis of the problem's causes and assessment of the project's interventions (Clarke, 1997b; Scott, 2000; Goldstein, 2003).

Ron clearly demonstrated the value of employing sound, yet practical, research methods to policing during his aforementioned work with the CMPD. In the study of the two major problems cited above, Ron had a major role in cleaning up the data with which the police were working so that it became apparent which locations were at high or low risk for theft and what products were being targeted for theft. These analytical refinements greatly facilitated subsequent analyses of the factors that best explained theft risks and, in turn, pointed the way toward effective interventions to the problems. His later work with the Newark, New Jersey, Police Department examining a problem involving retail drug dealing in apartment complexes (Zanin and Clarke, 2004) similarly employed sound, practical analytical methods.

Ron has further contributed to improving police analysis capacity by helping to conceptualize and produce several guides and manuals written for a police audience. (Ron's work on developing the Problem-Oriented Guides for Police is described more fully below.) Independently, Ron and John Eck (1984) had extensive experience trying to bring the best of applied research methods to the practice of crime prevention and policing, respectively. When the two of them collaborated in producing a manual for crime analysts that explicitly incorporated the principles and methods of problem-oriented policing and situational crime prevention, the results were impressive indeed. Their manual, *Become a Problem-Solving Crime Analyst: In 55 Small Steps* has become an international "best-seller."[3] Ron also co-authored a guide for police on researching problems (Clarke and Schultze, 2005) and one on understanding the concept of risky facilities (Clarke and Eck, 2007), and is presently co-authoring another manual with John Eck on adapting intelligence analysis techniques to problem-oriented policing.

Crime analysis training is increasingly being infused with problem-oriented policing and situational crime prevention principles and methods. The Jill Dando Institute of Crime Science uses the Clarke and Eck crime analysis manual in its training courses and academic programs for crime analysts, many of whom are then placed in British police agencies. The International Association of Crime Analysts has increasingly incorporated situational crime prevention and problem-oriented policing into its organization's products and services and, in 2010, joined its annual conference with the annual problem-oriented policing conference on a pilot basis.

Among the numerous special contributions that Ron's work on analytical methods has made to policing, one of the most significant is his work examining crime displacement, and its corollary opposite, diffusion of benefits (Clarke and Weisburd, 1994). The upshot of Ron's work in this area has been to caution police against blind pessimism: against believing that the best result they can hope for from their crime prevention efforts is to displace crime – to another location, another time, another offender, another method, or another crime type. Moreover, he has helped police understand not only that their efforts might not displace crime, but also that they might have crime prevention benefits beyond what was anticipated. Overcoming irrational pessimism is proving crucial to encouraging police both to adopt crime prevention measures and to assess whether displacement or a diffusion of benefits has occurred.

Perhaps the most lasting of Ron's contributions to improving crime analysis in policing will prove to be through the work of his many colleagues and graduate students whom he has encouraged to work with the police studying crime problems, publish the work, and in turn, teach others similar skills and methods. Some luminaries of crime prevention, including Marcus Felson, Ken Pease, Nick Tilley, and Gloria Laycock, are now better known to the police in part because Ron introduced them, directly or indirectly, to problem-oriented policing. A growing number of Ron's graduate students, including David Weisburd, Anthony Braga, Nancy La Vigne, Martha Smith, Mangai Natarajan, Rob Guerette, Emmanuel Barthe, Sharon Chamard, and Gohar Petrossian, have contributed to experimenting with (or critiquing) problem-oriented policing, improving problem analysis, or writing publications for the Center for Problem-Oriented Policing. Ron's reputation has lent important credibility for other criminologists to work collaboratively with the police.[4]

Building a body of substantive knowledge for policing: the "POP Guides" and the Center for Problem-Oriented Policing

In 1999, one of us (Mike) held a visiting fellowship with the US Department of Justice Office of Community Oriented Policing Services (COPS) researching the state of progress that had been made up to that point in developing and adopting problem-oriented policing across the police profession. One stop of many Mike made during that year was to Charlotte, North Carolina, to observe Ron and Herman in their consulting work with the police. Mike had known Herman for twenty years then, but had only briefly met Ron some years prior at a problem-oriented policing conference. Observing Ron advise the police on the analysis of and response to specific crime problems gave Mike fresh insights into the value that such knowledge and expertise could have for improving real-world policing.

In Mike's final report to the COPS Office on this project he wrote:

> The police field continues to lack an organized and substantial body of knowledge about effective methods for addressing common community problems. [. . .] The police profession would do well to begin such a systematic compilation and digesting of relevant knowledge if problem-oriented policing is to become an even more viable approach. A systematic program to conduct applied research on substantive community problems, and to compile and disseminate the results of the research findings to the police, would begin to build a body of knowledge both about specific types of problems and about types of responses to address them.
>
> (Scott, 2000: 117)

Thus, when the opportunity arose to begin to build just this sort of body of knowledge, Mike welcomed the chance to include Ron in such an enterprise. Along with Herman and other long-time colleagues, John Eck, Rana Sampson, Deborah Weisel, and Karin Schmerler, Mike joined up with Ron to propose a federally funded programme of work now known as the Problem-Oriented Guides for Police (or "POP Guides" for short). This work began in earnest in 2000 and, from its inception, it sought to blend the best of situational crime prevention and problem-oriented policing into coherent and concise guidance for police to help them be more effective in crime and disorder control and prevention.

That modest pilot project has continued and grown over the past decade. Ron and Mike enlisted in this enterprise Graeme Newman, a renowned criminologist in his own right with valuable expertise in publishing and website development. They formally established the Center for Problem-Oriented Policing, a consortium of police and criminology scholars, police officials, and US government sponsors as a vehicle for building and disseminating the body of knowledge to promote effective policing and crime prevention. (See the Center for Problem-Oriented Policing website at www.popcenter.org.)

Ron's special contributions to the POP Center enterprise are several. He brings a vast knowledge about criminological theory and effective (and ineffective) crime prevention that few police scholars possess; an orientation toward practical interventions that comports well with the police's own orientation toward practicality; a reputation for high-caliber research and scholarship; a sophisticated understanding of practical research methods; and access to a growing network of criminologists who understand the situational crime prevention approach, many of whom have since been recruited as POP Guide authors. In addition, much of the situational crime prevention research that has been published in the *Crime Prevention Studies* series that Ron initiated has informed the writing of the POP Guides. Given the long history of trying to incorporate research into policing practice (Cordner and White, 2010), bringing the skills and research findings of situational crime prevention researchers to bear on policing has been especially welcome.

The police field has become progressively more sophisticated over the past four decades as its personnel have become better educated, its information technology improved, and its relationship with the public improved (National Research Council, 2004). Additionally, the police operate under periodic fiscal constraints that compel them to seek out more cost-effective strategies. This has better positioned the police field to take a more active role in crime prevention than it has historically, and it is better able to apply the principles and methods of problem-oriented policing and situational crime prevention. At no time in its history has the police field been more receptive to what thoughtful and practical criminologists such as Ron Clarke have to offer to improve policing.

Conclusion

The situational crime prevention and problem-oriented policing movements could well have proceeded along parallel and independent paths, but Ron Clarke's contributions to joining them up have greatly enhanced the prospects for fully realizing the benefits of both of these big ideas. Although Ron never set out to improve policing, his efforts to improve crime prevention practice, having now been firmly linked to policing, offer this diffusion of benefits.

Notes

1 Indeed, Ron had by this time in his career already given close and careful study to the problems of runaway youths (Clarke and Martin, 1971) and vandalism (Clarke, 1978, 1981; Clarke and Mayhew, 1982). He would thereafter continue to carefully study other specific crime and disorder problems such as burglary (Clarke and Hope, 1984); suicide (Clarke and Lester, 1986, 1989; Clarke and Poyner, 1994); motorcycle theft (Clarke et al., 1989; Clarke and Natarajan, 1994); robbery of betting parlors (Clarke and McGrath, 1990); obscene phone calls (Clarke, 1990); accidental shootings (Clarke and Lester, 1991); bank robbery (Clarke, McGrath, and Field, 1991; Clarke and McGrath, 1992); auto theft (Clarke and Harris, 1991, 1992a, 1992b; Clarke, Field, and Harris, 1991; Clarke and Brown, 2003); subway fare evasion (Clarke, 1993; Clarke, Natarajan, and Cody, 1994); ransom kidnapping (Clarke and Marongiu, 1993); theft of car radios (Clarke and Braga, 1994); drug dealing via pay telephones (Clarke, Natarajan, and Johnson, 1995; Clarke, Natarajan, and Belanger, 1997); shoplifting (Clarke and DiLonardo, 1996); payphone toll fraud (Clarke and Bichler, 1996); robbery in the subway system (Clarke, Belanger, and Eastman, 1996); crime in low-rent apartment buildings (Clarke and Bichler-Robertson, 1998); crime in parking lots (Clarke and Mayhew, 1998); cell phone fraud (Clarke, Kemper, and Wyckoff, 2001); theft from construction sites (Clarke and Goldstein, 2002); theft from vehicles in parking facilities (Clarke and Goldstein, 2003); and drug dealing in apartment complexes (Zanin, Shane, and Clarke, 2004).
2 CRAVED is an acronym for "concealable, removable, available, valuable, enjoyable, and disposable," characteristics of theft targets that research has demonstrated increase their appeal to thieves.
3 The manual was originally produced for and published by the Jill Dando Institute of Crime Science in London with funding from the British Home Office (Clarke and Eck, 2003) and subsequently, with funding from the US Department of Justice, rewritten

for an American readership (Clarke and Eck, 2005). Although the British edition of the manual is offered for sale, the American edition is distributed at no charge by the US Department of Justice. The manual has since been translated into the Chinese, Dutch, Estonian, Farsi, German, Italian, Japanese, Korean, Portuguese, Slovenian, Spanish, Swedish, and Turkish languages, and distributed throughout the relevant countries. See http://www.popcenter.org/library/crimeanalysis_translations.cfm for links to translated editions.

4 Coincidentally, George Kelling, another former student at the University of Wisconsin and a renowned police scholar in his own right, concluded his distinguished academic career as one of Ron's colleagues at Rutgers University. George undoubtedly reinforced for Ron the value of working in support of the policing function.

References

Bayley, D. (ed.) (1998) *What Works in Policing*. Oxford: Oxford University Press.

Boston Police Department. (1998) "Operation Cease-Fire." Submission for the Herman Goldstein Award for Excellence in Problem-Oriented Policing.

Braga, A., Kennedy, D., Piehl, A., and Waring, E. (2001) *Reducing Gun Violence: The Boston Gun Project's Operation Ceasefire*. Washington, DC: US Department of Justice, National Institute of Justice.

Clarke, R.V. (1978) *Tackling Vandalism*. Home Office Research Studies No. 47. London: HMSO.

Clarke, R.V. (1980) "Situational crime prevention: theory and practice," *British Journal of Criminology*, 20: 136–47.

Clarke, R.V. (1981) "Vandalism: causes and cures," in *Proceedings of Conference on Vandalism of Youth*. Messina, Italy: International Centre for Penal, Penitentiary and Sociological Research.

Clarke, R.V. (1990) "Deterring obscene phone callers: preliminary results of the New Jersey experience," *Security Journal*, 1: 143–8.

Clarke, R.V. (ed.) (1992) *Situational Crime Prevention: Successful Case Studies*. Guilderland, NY: Harrow and Heston.

Clarke, R.V. (1993) "Fare evasion and automatic ticket collection on the London Underground," in R.V. Clarke (ed.) *Crime Prevention Studies*, Vol. 1. Monsey, NY: Criminal Justice Press.

Clarke, R.V. (ed.) (1997a) *Situational Crime Prevention: Successful Case Studies. Second Edition*. Guilderland, NY: Harrow and Heston.

Clarke, R.V. (1997b) "Problem-oriented policing and the potential contribution of criminology." Report to the National Institute of Justice.

Clarke, R.V. (1998) "Defining police strategies: problem-solving, problem-oriented policing and community-oriented policing," in T. O'Connor Shelley and A. Grant (eds) *Problem-oriented Policing: Crime-specific Problems, Critical Issues and Making POP Work*. Washington, DC: Police Executive Research Forum.

Clarke, R.V., Belanger, M., and Eastman, J. (1996) "Where angel fears to tread: a test in the New York City subway of the robbery/density hypothesis," in R.V. Clarke (ed.) *Crime and Mass Transit. Crime Prevention Studies*, Vol. 6. Monsey, NY: Criminal Justice Press.

Clarke, R.V. and Bichler, G. (1996) "Eliminating payphone toll fraud at the Port Authority Bus Terminal in Manhattan," in R.V. Clarke (ed.) *Crime and Mass Transit. Crime Prevention Studies*, Vol. 6. Monsey, NY: Criminal Justice Press.

Clarke, R.V. and Bichler-Robertson, G. (1998) "Place managers, slumlords and crime in low rent apartment buildings," *Security Journal*, 11: 11–19.
Clarke, R.V. and Braga, A. (1994) "Improved radios and more stripped cars in Germany: a routine activity analysis," *Security Journal*, 5: 154–9.
Clarke, R.V. and Brown, R. (2003) "International trafficking in stolen vehicles," in M. Tonry (ed.) *Crime and Justice: A Review of Research*, Vol. 30. Chicago: University of Chicago Press.
Clarke, R.V. and Cornish, D.B. (1985) "Modelling offenders' decisions: a framework for policy and research," in M. Tonry and N. Morris (eds) *Crime and Justice*, Vol. 6. Chicago: University of Chicago Press.
Clarke, R.V. and DiLonardo, R. (1996) "Reducing the rewards of shoplifting: an evaluation of ink tags," *Security Journal*, 7: 11–14.
Clarke, R.V. and Eck, J. (2003) *Become a Problem Solving Crime Analyst: In 55 Small Steps*. London: Jill Dando Institute of Crime Science.
Clarke, R.V. and Eck, J. (2005) *Crime Analysis for Problem Solvers: In 60 Small Steps*. Washington, DC: US Department of Justice, Office of Community Oriented Policing Services.
Clarke, R.V. and Eck, J. (2007) *Understanding Risky Facilities*, Problem-oriented Guides for Police, Problem-solving Tools Series No. 6. Washington, DC: US Department of Justice, Office of Community Oriented Policing Services.
Clarke, R.V., Field, S., and Harris, P. (1991) "The Mexican vehicle market and auto theft in border areas of the United States," *Security Journal*, 2: 205–10.
Clarke, R.V. and Goldstein, H. (2002) "Reducing theft at construction sites: lessons from a problem-oriented project," in N. Tilley (ed.) *Analysis for Crime Prevention*, *Crime Prevention Studies*, Vol. 13. Monsey, NY: Criminal Justice Press.
Clarke, R.V. and Goldstein, H. (2003) "Thefts from cars in center-city parking facilities: a case study in implementing problem-oriented policing," in J. Knutsson (ed.) *Problem-oriented Policing: From Innovation to Mainstream*, *Crime Prevention Studies*, Vol. 15. Monsey, NY: Criminal Justice Press.
Clarke, R.V. and Harris, P. (1991) "Car chopping, parts marking and the Motor Vehicle Theft Law Enforcement Act of 1984," *Sociology and Social Research*, 75: 107–16.
Clarke, R.V. and Harris, P. (1992a) "A rational choice perspective on the targets of automobile theft," *Criminal Behaviour and Mental Health*, 2: 25–42.
Clarke, R.V. and Harris, P. (1992b) "Auto theft and its prevention," in M. Tonry (ed.) *Crime and Justice: A Review of Research*, Vol. 16. Chicago: University of Chicago Press.
Clarke, R.V. and Heal, K.H. (1980) "Police effectiveness in dealing with crime: some current British research," in P. Engstad and M. Lioy (eds) *Proceedings of Workshop on Police Productivity and Performance*. Ottawa: Research Division, Ministry of the Solicitor General.
Clarke, R.V. and Hope, T. (1984) *Coping with Burglary*. Boston: Kluwer-Nijhoff.
Clarke, R.V. and Hough, J.M. (1980) *The Effectiveness of Policing*. Farnborough: Gower.
Clarke, R.V., Kemper, R., and Wyckoff, L. (2001) "Controlling cell phone fraud in the US – lessons for the UK 'Foresight' prevention initiative," *Security Journal*, 14(1): 7–22.
Clarke, R.V. and Lester, D. (1986) "Detoxification of motor vehicle exhaust and suicide," *Psychological Reports*, 59: 1034.
Clarke, R.V. and Lester, D. (1991) "The influence of firearm ownership on accidental deaths," *Social Science and Medicine*, 32: 1311–13.
Clarke, R.V. and Lester, D. (1989) *Suicide: Closing the Exits*. New York: Springer-Verlag.

Clarke, R.V. and McGrath, G. (1990) "Cash reduction and robbery prevention in Australian betting shops," *Security Journal*, 1: 160–3.

Clarke, R.V. and McGrath, G. (1992) "Newspaper reports of bank robberies and the copycat phenomenon," *Australian and New Zealand Journal of Criminology*, 25: 83–8.

Clarke, R.V., McGrath, G., and Field, S. (1991) "Target hardening of banks in Australia and displacement of bank robberies," *Security Journal*, 2: 84–90.

Clarke, R.V. and Marongiu, P. (1993) "Ransom kidnapping in Sardinia, subcultural theory and rational choice," in R.V. Clarke and M. Felson (eds) *Routine Activity and Rational Choice, Advances in Criminological Theory*, Vol. 5. New Brunswick, NJ: Transaction Publishers.

Clarke, R.V. and Martin, D.N. (1971) *Absconding from Approved Schools*, Home Office Research Studies No. 12. London: HMSO.

Clarke, R.V. and Mayhew, P.M. (1982) "Vandalism and its prevention," in P. Feldman (ed.) *Developments in the Study of Criminal Behavior, Vol. II Violence*. London and New York: Wiley.

Clarke, R.V. and Mayhew, P. (1998) "Preventing crime in parking lots," in M. Felson and R. Peiser (eds) *Crime Prevention through Real Estate Management and Development*. Washington, DC: Urban Land Institute.

Clarke, R.V., and Natarajan, M. (1994) "The role of helmet laws in preventing motorcycle theft in Madras, India," *Indian Journal of Criminology*, 22: 22–6.

Clarke, R.V., Natarajan, M., and Belanger, M. (1997) "Drug dealing and pay phones: the scope for intervention," *Security Journal*, 7: 245–51. (Earlier version published in the *Japanese Journal of Crime and Delinquency*, 1997.)

Clarke, R.V., Natarajan, M., and Cody, R. (1994) "Subway slugs: tracking displacement on the London Underground," *British Journal of Criminology*, 34(2): 122–38.

Clarke, R.V., Natarajan, M., and Johnson, B. (1995) "Telephones as facilitators of drug dealing," *European Journal on Crime Policy and Research*, 3(3): 137–53.

Clarke, R.V. and Poyner, B. (1994) "Preventing suicide on the London Underground," *Social Science and Medicine*, 38(3): 443–6.

Clarke, R.V. and Schultze, P. (2005) *Researching a Problem*, Problem-oriented Guides for Police, Problem-solving Tools Series No. 2. Washington, DC: US Department of Justice, Office of Community Oriented Policing Services.

Clarke, R.V. and Weisburd, D. (1994) "Diffusion of crime control benefits: observations on the reverse of displacement," in R.V. Clarke (ed.) *Crime Prevention Studies*, Vol. 2. Monsey, NY: Criminal Justice Press.

Clarke, R.V. et al. (1989) "Motorcycle theft, helmet legislation and displacement," *Howard Journal of Criminal Justice*, 28: 1–8.

Cordner, G. and White, S. (eds) (2010) *The Evolving Relationship Between Police Research and Police Practice. Special Issue: Police Practice & Research: An International Journal*, 11(2): April.

Cornish, D.B. and Clarke, R.V. (eds) (1986) *The Reasoning Criminal: Rational Choice Perspectives on Offending*. New York: Springer-Verlag.

Eck, J. (1984) *Using Research: A Primer for Law Enforcement Managers*. Washington, DC: Police Executive Research Forum. [Published as a second edition as Eck, J. and N. La Vigne (1994). Washington, DC: Police Executive Research Forum.]

Eck, J. and Spelman, W. (1987) *Problem Solving: Problem-oriented Policing in Newport News*. Washington, DC: Police Executive Research Forum.

Goldstein, H. (1979) "Improving policing: a problem-oriented approach," *Crime and Delinquency*, April.

Goldstein, H. (1990) *Problem-oriented Policing*. New York: McGraw-Hill.
Goldstein, H. (2003) "On further developing problem-oriented policing: the most critical need, the major impediments, and a proposal," in J. Knutsson (ed.) *Problem-oriented Policing: From Innovation to Mainstream, Crime Prevention Studies*, Vol. 15. Monsey, NY: Criminal Justice Press.
Hoare, M., Stewart, G. and Purcell, C. (1984) *The Problem-oriented Approach: Four Pilot Studies*. London: Metropolitan Police, Management Services Department.
Kennedy, D. (2008) *Deterrence and Crime Prevention: Reconsidering the Prospect of Sanction*. London: Routledge.
Leigh, A., Read, T., and Tilley, N. (1996) *Problem-oriented Policing: Brit POP*, Crime Detection and Prevention Series, Paper 75. London: Home Office Police Research Group.
Leigh, A., Read, T., and Tilley, N. (1998) *Brit POP II: Problem-oriented Policing in Practice*, Police Research Series, Paper 93. London: Home Office Policing and Reducing Crime Unit.
National Research Council (2004) *Fairness and Effectiveness in Policing: The Evidence*, W. Skogan and K. Frydll (eds). Washington, DC: The National Academies Press.
Scott, M. (2000) *Problem-oriented Policing: Reflections on the First 20 Years*. Washington, DC: US Department of Justice, Office of Community Oriented Policing Services.
Tilley, N. (1999) "The relationship between crime prevention and problem-oriented policing," in C. Solé Brito and T. Allan (eds) *Problem-oriented Policing: Crime-specific Problems, Critical Issues and Making POP Work*, Vol. 2. Washington, DC: Police Executive Research Forum.
Zanin, N. and Clarke, R.V. (2004) "Reducing drug dealing in private apartment complexes in Newark, New Jersey. A final report to the US Department of Justice, Office of Community Oriented Policing Services on the field applications of the Problem-Oriented Guides for Police Project." Unpublished report available at http://www.popcenter.org/library/researcherprojects/DrugsApartment.pdf.
Zanin, N., Shane, J., and Clarke, R.V. (2004) "Reducing drug dealing in private apartment complexes in Newark, New Jersey," a final report to the US Department of Justice, Office of Community Oriented Policing Services on the Field Applications of the Problem-Oriented Guides for Police Project. Accessible at http://www.popcenter.org/Library/researcherprojects/DrugsApartment.pdf.

8 Vulnerability of evaluators of problem-oriented policing projects

Johannes Knutsson

Introduction

My first assignment as a young researcher was to evaluate crime prevention initiatives carried out by the Swedish police. It was in the mid-1970s and crime prevention was a totally new activity the police had embarked upon. As a scheme to prevent household burglaries the police launched Operation Identification. By marking property with a unique identifier and putting up a sticker (a decal) at the entrances, those living in the dwelling signalled to potential burglars that, since it was protected by Operation Identification, it would be a bad choice to burglarize that particular home.

This particular measure was deemed to be substantial enough to evaluate. For this purpose 3,500 dwellings in an area of detached and semi-detached houses on the outskirts of Stockholm were followed prospectively for four years. To establish which households took part in the scheme, three observation studies were carried out. By checking police complaint records it was possible to ascertain which households had been burglarized. To control for differences in vulnerability, homes in the protected and unprotected groups that had been victimized by burglars were retrospectively studied for a four-year period prior to the start of the study. The extent to which stolen goods could be returned to the rightful owners was examined by comparing the rate of returns of stolen goods from burglarized Operation Identification participants with that of non-participants. Eventual differences in clearance rate between Operation Identification households and non-participants were checked with police records. As part of the evaluation a group of burglars, operating in the Stockholm area, was interviewed.[1]

The results can be summarized as follows: the risk of victimization was not affected, the chance of getting back stolen property did not increase and the clearance rate was unaffected. The interviews indicated that, on the whole, burglars did not perceive Operation Identification as a credible threat to their activities. To summarize, it was a pretty solid zero-effect evaluation (Knutsson 1984).[2]

The evaluation was conducted in the early days of situational crime prevention and problem-oriented policing (Clarke and Mayhew 1980; Goldstein 1979). It was an early example of a situational crime prevention study.

How did those who had commissioned the study react to its findings? Predictably, they were not at all happy. The scheme was run by a newly established unit at the Swedish National Police Board. When the evaluation was commissioned those in charge of the unit were pretty clear, if not to say blunt: 'We want you to show that this is effective so we can get more resources.'

The results were leaked before the study was published. In order for the police to be prepared, the Commissioner of the Stockholm Police formally requested a copy of the study before it was published. The police could then launch a 'counter attack' with assistance from a journalist they had in their pockets. When the study appeared, he wrote an article in a major daily newspaper stressing the effectiveness of Operation Identification. At the National Police Board there was a plan to evaluate the evaluation – a plan that, however, never saw the light of day. Some of the affected police officers showed clear signs of disapproval when I met them. Investments in prestige, careers and in their mission made the police officers' reaction understandable.

Actually, the reaction did not come as a surprise. Nevertheless it prompted me to reflect on the usefulness of evaluations when negative outcomes seem to be dismissed, and on how to react and adapt to social pressures in these kinds of situations. Although the published study did not flatter the police, it did demonstrate integrity both to them and, even more so, to sceptical colleagues at the university.

In this chapter the somewhat frail situation of evaluators, especially those who are involved both in the implementation of preventive measures and the evaluation of their effects, will be discussed. Problem-oriented policing will be used as the backdrop since it illustrates many of the critical issues.

Evaluation in problem-oriented policing

Problem-oriented policing can be characterized as a philosophy enabling police to improve their function with a focus on crime prevention. The philosophy was created by an insightful member of academia – Herman Goldstein – and promoted an evidence-based approach to crime prevention (Tilley and Bullock 2009). It uses an action research model where the goal is to decrease problems of crime and social disorder. It has repeatedly been pointed out that, for problem-oriented policing to be carried out to its full potential, it needs to be supported by university-trained persons (Goldstein 1979, 1990, 2003). It is foremost a question of skills in methods from social science but also of knowledge of crime prevention.

What is involved in problem-oriented policing is summarized by the SARA acronym (scanning, analysis, response and assessment) (Eck and Spelman 1987). An open-ended iterative process is required, where feedback is repeatedly used to improve the work and generate further cycles of the SARA process. Assessment is an integral part of the procedure, to find out whether intended effects of the implemented measures have or have not come about. The rank order of preferred outcomes is as follows (Eck and Spelman 1987: 49):

1 eliminating the problem;
2 reducing it;
3 reducing its harmfulness;

110 *Johannes Knutsson*

4   deal with the problem in better ways;
5   get someone else to attend to it.

The challenge with a no-effect finding is the interpretation of and reaction to the result – should it be considered as preliminary or as definitive? A negative outcome could mean that the analysis was not correct and that the measures put into effect were not adequate, and the process should continue. It takes a high level of sophistication and trust in the philosophy from those involved in the project and from their superiors to do so (for examples see Lancashire Constabulary 2008; Chula Vista Police Department 2009; Plant and Scott 2011). Without support from leaders the effort could be halted.

The practice of problem-oriented policing

Since the concept is open ended, problem-oriented policing may organizationally and technically be executed in various ways. It might be useful to divide the practice of problem-oriented policing into two modes: *instrumental* and *conceptual*, where instrumental use signifies utilization of evidence relating to a specific problem in order to resolve it (Cherney 2009). Instrumental modes have, however, been criticized for being too shallow. An example would be an application of the SARA process with superficial or lacking analysis and an overemphasis on putting a response in effect – a response that very well might have been decided upon in advance.

Conceptual practice is, in contrast, characterized by depth and openness. Hypotheses might be checked in the process of defining the problem, creating a foundation for the most appropriate ways of solving the problem. There is an understanding of the core theoretical concepts underpinning the responses suggested (Cherney 2009: 246–7). It is more demanding, requiring a higher level of competence of those involved in the project, than in a pure instrumental mode. However, in reality, when conducting problem-oriented policing as it is intended, a mixture of conceptual and instrumental practice is needed, where the conceptual aspect (analysis) precedes the instrumental (putting measures into effect).

Problem-oriented policing projects have, in general, been run by practitioners without support from others. For instance, in the first efforts to implement problem-oriented policing in the UK during the 1980s, community police officers were given the task. In Sweden, as part of a major reform of the police in the mid-1990s, a considerable proportion of all front-line police officers were appointed to work as community police officers and were instructed to utilize problem-oriented policing in their efforts to prevent crimes. In none of these instances were the officers given proper preparation and support to fulfil their mission. It is no wonder, then, that examinations of problem-oriented policing projects in a number of countries have repeatedly documented a lack of rigor in their execution[3] (Leigh et al. 1998; Read and Tilley 2000; Scott 2000; Clarke 2002; Thomassen 2005; Hammerlich 2007; Sollund 2008). Many of these instances can in all likelihood be classified as instrumental. As might be expected, since evaluation is technically demanding, this particular part of the process has been found to be weak even in

Vulnerability of evaluators of problem-oriented policing projects 111

police forces known to be good at practising problem-oriented policing (Bullock et al. 2006).

There are, however, a fair number of spectacular examples of problem-oriented policing carried out by police officers to its full potential and with striking results. Many award-winning projects and runners-up in the Herman Goldstein Award and the Nick Tilley Award belong to this category.[4] Yet, even in projects considered to show best practice, with academics supporting the practitioners, the standard of assessments in most cases is not high (Knutsson 2009).

Contexts for conducting problem-oriented policing

This chapter examines the circumstances that may affect quality and objectivity of a particularly fragile part of the problem-solving process, namely the assessment. Rigour and objectivity can be expected to vary by formal competence of those engaged in the projects and also by the manner in which projects are carried out.

Figure 8.1 shows three broad contexts for conducting problem-oriented policing, where each might take different specific forms. To make the principles clear, only a few actors at different levels with interacting roles are included – policy-makers, administrators, practitioners and evaluators. An evaluator can sometimes also be a practitioner, thus having dual roles, and at other times be an academic. All can have different stakes in problem-oriented policing. Administrators, who often occupy leadership positions in organizations, might support it more or less enthusiastically and have different levels of familiarity with the philosophy. The same goes for practitioners.

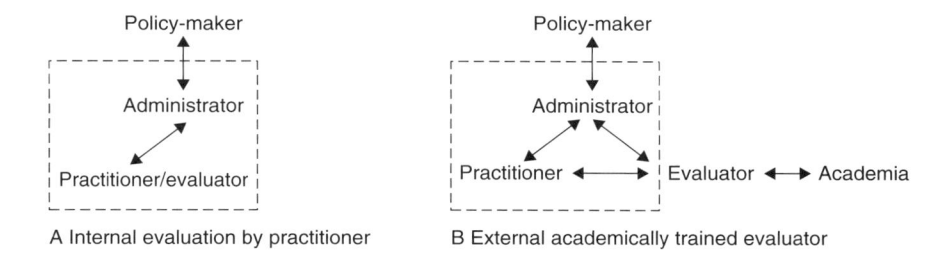

Figure 8.1 Contextual configurations for conducting problem-oriented policing.

Relationships that academically trained evaluators have formed with academia are vital. One part is their professional identity, notably an attitude of scepticism: in order to be convinced only 'hard facts' are, or should be, accepted. Another vital part is the basis on which judgements are made on the quality of their achievements: most formally this involves submitting journal articles for peer review; less formally it includes asking a qualified colleague to read and comment on a manuscript. These habits are not always found among practitioners and administrators.

Configuration A in Figure 8.1 might comprise a rather common situation where it is decided by a central governing body that the police shall work according to the principles of problem-oriented policing. Leaders in the organization, in order to comply, assign officers to perform the activity; officers who are more or less well prepared and/or supported. Problem-oriented policing seems to have been introduced in this fashion in a number of countries, most often with a weak implementation (Leigh et al. 1996, 1998; Read and Tilley 2000; Scott 2000; Clarke 2002; Thomassen 2005; Hammerlich 2007; Sollund 2008). However, this configuration could also include cases with energetic enthusiasts, burning to solve problems, trying hard to follow the principles of problem-oriented policing. These individuals might, or might not, be supported by their leaders. Many award-winning projects seem to belong to this particular category.

Configuration B represents cases where academically trained persons support the police in their endeavour, but are not part of the police organization. They could be drawn in on a consultant basis for especially tricky parts of the process, like the assessment. Another example is an undertaking in the form of a research project, where academics are interested in following the formula, enabling them to spread light on some more specific features (see e.g. Braga and Bond 2009; Knutsson and Søvik 2005). The latter cases cannot be considered as ordinary problem-oriented policing projects, but can nevertheless give rise to important results that may contribute to developing the philosophy by giving feedback to policy-makers and others.

Configuration C differs from B in the sense that the person with academic qualifications is part of the organization, e.g. as an analyst supporting practitioners in their efforts to perform problem-oriented policing. This means somewhat different relationships to the administrators and the practitioners compared to external evaluators. It provides more opportunities to form strong relationships and to obtain access to information. On the negative side is the possibility of increased susceptibility to different kinds of pressures.

Implications for standard and objectivity

What then are the implications for the standard and objectivity of the assessments? Table 8.1 compares the typical situation where assessment in a problem-oriented policing project is carried out by a practitioner or with an academically trained evaluator involved.

Table 8.1 undoubtedly characterizes the situation somewhat provocatively in the pursuit of simplicity and clarity, but the experience of the writer suggests these

Table 8.1 Assessments in problem-oriented policing projects by practitioner and academic respectively

	Practitioner	*Academic*
Technical competence	Weak	Strong
Design of evaluation	Frail	As strong as possible
Attitude	Personal involvement	Distanced
Aim	Show response to be effective	Determine eventual effectiveness
Accountable to	Leader	Assigner/colleagues
Consequence if outcome positive	Increased status	Positive from assigner but scepticism likely from colleagues
Consequence if outcome negative	Blamed	Negative from assigner but approval likely from colleagues

generalizations are often not far from the truth. At worst, the table can be interpreted as offering a series of hypotheses.

Practitioners do not usually have a high degree of competence for the technically demanding task of assessment. As for the academic this ought to be one of his or her strengths, with a commitment to do as strong an evaluation as possible. This should be part of their professionalism, sometimes reinforced by a wish to publish a paper in order to add another line to their CV. The practitioners' personal involvement in the project might jeopardize a neutral posture. The academic should be protected by a professional attitude, but may nonetheless be liable to different pressures.

A critical element is the practitioners' place in a hierarchical organization. Demands to deliver a positive result could be very strong from senior staff leaders, especially if the activity concerns a politically prioritized issue. The administrators can be under strong pressure to deliver politically correct results, which are passed on to the practitioner. Academics are less vulnerable. One reason is that they expect support from their colleagues if they experience difficulties in reporting a zero-effect result; another is their position relative to the organization. If external, they are less susceptible. The practitioner evaluator is left alone, surrounded by members of an organization with little acceptance of what might be considered a shortcoming of the one in charge of the project, and not the undertaking. There are, then again, instances with positive outcomes that are obvious and easy to observe. However, an administrator may have little understanding for the need to document such a positive outcome and be reluctant to set aside time and resources for the evaluation. This can frustrate academic evaluators with their emphasis on publishing findings on impact, whatever they may be.

Biased evaluations and assessments?

Eisner (2009) questions findings from a large portion of evaluations of crime preventive measures by reporting consistent differences of results in evaluations where the evaluators have had some stake in the outcomes – such as programme developers – compared to evaluations conducted by independent evaluators. The size of the treatment effect is considerably larger in the former cases. He proposes a model in which both intentional and unintentional factors might give rise to biased results.

Eisner's data consisted of evaluations of different types of programmes intended to bring about changes in dispositions by delivering standardized interventions to exposed groups. It represents quite another paradigm of evidence-based crime prevention than problem-oriented policing (Tilley 2006). Table 8.2 indicates the extensive differences – to evaluate a programme is a different undertaking than to make an assessment in a problem-oriented policing project. However, the open-ended character of problem-oriented policing makes it hard to exactly pinpoint some of its features. The principle has been to define it from 'standard' practice.

The preferred design when evaluating programmes is the randomized controlled trial. Checks are usually made to investigate whether the programme is instigated in the proscribed manner. Even if there is not a fixed preventive approach to be used in problem-oriented policing, it is clear that situational prevention, with its focus on proximate causes (Ekblom 1994), is the most suitable approach, with opportunity blocking as the main strategy (Clarke and Eck 2003). The response should be tailor-made to suit the particular context where it is supposed to work. In the majority of cases the projects are area-based with the consequence that, on the whole, the one-group or comparison group before-and-after design is the feasible one (Knutsson 2009); a design that furthermore usually is quite adequate (Eck 2002). Here, the need to measure crime displacement and the diffusion of

Table 8.2 Evaluations of treatment programmes and problem-oriented policing projects respectively

	Treatment programmes	*Problem-oriented policing*
Effect intended to come about by	Dispositional change	Blocking of opportunities
Variability of implemented measures	Strict standard	Adapted to specific problems and contexts
Unit	Individuals/aggregates of individuals	Commonly a geographical area
Design	Randomized controlled trial	One-group or comparison group before-and-after design
Methodological rigour in traditional experimental terms	High	Questionable
Time frame of effects	Long term	Immediate
Outcome variables	Complicated to observe	Often directly observable
Meta-analysis	Possible	Of uncertain utility
Evaluator	Researcher	Practitioner (analyst)
Role of evaluation	Try out programme	Check if intended effects come about
Social pressures	Can be present	Can be present
Economic interest	Can be present	Hardly present

prevention benefits often requires the inclusion of adjacent areas to capture spatial shifts in offending. The result is that meta-evaluation of problem-oriented policing appears of less utility since randomized controlled experiments are extremely atypical.[5]

Programmes are generally expected to achieve long-term effects, which are often complicated to measure. The chosen outcome variables can be more or less valid with varying degrees of biases. This creates options for more or less intentional manipulation. By choosing a particular outcome variable, known to have a bias favouring a certain result, the 'right' outcome may be attained.

For problem-oriented policing projects, especially where the physical environment is manipulated, the effects may be fairly easy to observe. Situational measures, if they are effective, also give rise to immediate effects. Absence of behaviour or consequences of behaviour can, of course, be measured in various ways. The main problem is, however, lack of competence, and hence the production of amateurish 'evaluations'. In an examination of projects reported to the Danish National Police, the most common classification of the evaluations was 'anecdotal', which signifies 'subjective impression of the result' (Hammerlich 2007). Even if not stated in the study, the obvious suspicion will be that 'hoped for' results were the reported ones. The targeted problem for the police was politically decided. Consequently there was, in all likelihood, strong pressure from both higher administration and leaders of the police to achieve 'positive' results.

To rigorously evaluate a programme often requires a professional evaluator, while practitioners in most cases have executed the assessments in problem-oriented policing projects. The role of the evaluations differ as well – to test and develop the effectiveness of a programme, or to assess to what extent a problem has been affected. Especially in cases where a programme developer has conducted the evaluation there is a considerable risk that economic interests may exert an influence. There are some very good reasons to make use of independent evaluators. It is, however, hard to see pure economic interests being implicated for those carrying out evaluations in problem-oriented policing projects.

Conclusion

It would be naive to believe that problem-oriented policing projects are not susceptible to biased results. A thorough examination would probably end up with a rather mixed result ranging from clear cases of 'overoptimistic' reported results to solid and truthful ones. On the negative side is the possibility of a lack of competence among many of those who conduct the evaluations, giving scope for more or less intentional bias. The risk increases considerably in instances where politically prioritized problems are addressed by the problem-oriented policing effort. In such instances, social pressures may exert a substantial influence.

A more positive issue is that the favoured preventive approach in problem-oriented policing projects is that of situational crime prevention. It has proven to be fairly robust and applicable for many types of problems (see Clarke 1997, 2008;

Guerette 2009). There is also the approach of the philosophy itself, with an iterative process and flexible criterions of success that, taken to its farthest, almost makes it infallible.[6]

Given the state of affairs in the execution of problem-oriented policing where projects fulfilling all criteria of high quality seem to be the exception, the challenge is in making the extraordinary ordinary. A major obstacle is lack of necessary skills. There may be only one way of improving this situation – increased interaction between the police and the section of academia that is well versed in both problem-oriented policing and evaluation methods. This remains a small, if growing, subsection of academia and one that has grown and learned significantly due to the contribution of Ronald Clarke. Further development of links between the police and academia will not mean that problem-oriented policing projects will become immune to distorted assessments where uncorroborated positive outcomes are reported, but will help in promoting more accurate evaluations.

Notes

1 The burglars were interviewed in a remand prison where they were investigated for having committed burglaries. It is hard to know whether they had been operating in the project area. Given the layout and demographics of Stockholm it is reasonable to assume that they at least had been active in similar areas.
2 It should be mentioned that this piece of work has been used as a 'good bad' example of a conventional evaluation study (Pawson and Tilley 1997). Thereby it represents an example of unintended but constructive and useful utilization of an evaluation.
3 However, part of what the police have accomplished cannot rightly be characterized as problem-oriented policing, but as problem-solving. It refers to acting against rather delimited problems that do not take a thoroughgoing application of all or some of the stages in the SARA process (Clarke 1998). Problem-solving is not as time-consuming and technically demanding to carry out as proper problem-oriented policing. It is nevertheless an important activity for the police service but seems to be performed only by a minority of highly motivated and skilled first-line police officers (Holgersson and Knutsson 2009).
4 See e.g. www.popcenter.org/library/awards/goldstein.
5 An examination of a meta-analysis of problem-oriented policing shows that only an extremely low number of projects fulfil the inclusion criteria (Weisburd et al. 2008). It is furthermore atypical that problem-oriented policing projects are executed as controlled experiments, with researchers in charge, and projects where the unit consists of individuals and not area.
6 Even cases with the problem still remaining, but where the police has managed to get someone else to attend to it, are considered a positive outcome.

References

Braga, A.A. and Bond, B.J. (2009) 'Community perceptions of police crime prevention efforts: using interviews in small areas to evaluate crime reduction strategies', in J. Knutsson and N. Tilley (eds) *Evaluating Crime Reduction Initiatives*, Crime Prevention Studies, vol. 24, Monsey, NY: Criminal Justice Press, pp. 87–119.
Bullock, K., Erol, R. and Tilley, N. (2006) *Problem-oriented Policing and Partnerships*.

Implementing an Evidence Based Approach to Crime Reduction, Cullompton: Willan Publishing.

Cherney, A. (2009) 'Exploring the concept of research utilization: implications for evidence-based crime prevention', *Crime Prevention and Community Safety*, 11(4): 243–57.

Chula Vista Police Department (2009) 'Reducing crime and disorder at motels and hotels in Chula Vista, California', http://www.popcenter.org/library/awards/goldstein.cfm?browse=abstracts&year=2009 (accessed 7 February 2011).

Clarke, R.V. (1997) *Situational Crime Prevention: Successful Case Studies*, New York: Harrow and Heston.

Clarke, R.V. (1998) 'Defining police strategies: problem-solving, problem-oriented policing and community-oriented policing', in T. O'Connor Shelley and A.C. Grant (eds) *Problem-oriented Policing: Crime-specific Problems, Critical Issues and Making POP Work*, Washington, DC: Police Executive Research Forum.

Clarke, R.V. (2002) *Problem-oriented Policing, Case Studies*. Report to the US Department of Justice. Document 193801, www.popcenter.org/library/reading/pdfs/POP-SCP-Clarke.pdf (accessed 7 February 2011).

Clarke, R.V. (2008) 'Situational crime prevention', in R. Wortley and L. Mazzerolle (eds) *Environmental Criminology and Crime Analysis*. Cullompton: Willan Publishing, pp. 178–94.

Clarke, R.V. and Eck, J. (2003) *Become a Problem-solving Crime Analyst: In 55 Small Steps*, London: Jill Dando Institute of Crime Science.

Clarke, R.V. and Mayhew, P. (1980) *Designing out Crime*, London: HMO.

Eck, J. (2002) 'Learning from experience in problem-oriented policing and situational prevention: the positive functions of weak evaluations and the negative functions of strong ones', in Tilley, N. (ed.) *Evaluation for Crime Prevention*, Crime Prevention Studies, vol. 14, Monsey, NY: Criminal Justice Press, pp. 93–117.

Eck, J. and Spelman, W. (1987) *Problem-solving. Problem-oriented Policing in Newport News*, Washington, DC: Police Executive Research Forum/National.

Eisner, M. (2009) 'No effects in independent prevention trials: can we reject the cynical view?', *Journal of Experimental Criminology*, 5: 163–83.

Ekblom, P. (1994) 'Proximal circumstances: a mechanism-based classification of crime prevention', in R.V. Clarke (ed.) *Crime Prevention Studies*, vol. 2, Monsey, NY: Criminal Justice Press, pp. 185–232.

Goldstein, H. (1979) 'Improving policing: a problem-oriented approach', *Crime and Delinquency*, 25(2): 234–58.

Goldstein, H. (1990) *Problem-oriented Policing*, New York: McGraw Hill.

Goldstein, H. (2003) 'On further developing problem-oriented policing: the most critical need, the major impediments and a proposal', in J. Knutsson (ed.) *Problem-oriented Policing: From Innovation to Mainstream*, Crime Prevention Studies, vol. 15, Monsey, NY: Criminal Justice Press, pp. 13–47.

Guerette, R.T. (2009) 'The pull, push, and expansion of situational crime prevention evaluation: an appraisal of thirty-seven years of research', in J. Knutsson and N. Tilley (eds) *Evaluating Crime Reduction Initiatives*, Crime Prevention Studies, vol. 24, Monsey, NY: Criminal Justice Press, pp. 29–58.

Hammerich, M. (2007) Problemorientert politiarbeide – når tjenesten tilladet det. Avgangsprojekt, Diplomuddannelsen i kriminologi, Københavns universitet.

Holgersson, S. and Knutsson, J. (2009) 'Differences in individual productivity among uniformed police officers', paper presented at Stockholm Symposium, June 22–24.

Knutsson, J. (1984) *Operation Identification? A Way to Prevent Burglaries?*, report no. 14, Stockholm: National Council for Crime Prevention.

Knutsson, J. (2009) 'Standard of evaluations in problem-oriented policing-projects. Good enough?', in J. Knutsson and N. Tilley (eds) *Evaluating Crime Reduction Initiatives.* Crime Prevention Studies, vol. 24, Monsey, NY: Criminal Justice Press, pp. 7–28.

Knutsson, J. and Søvik, K.-E. (2005) *Problemorienterat polisarbete i teori och praktik, rapport 2005:1*, Stockholm: Polishögskolan.

Lancashire Constabulary (2008) 'Operation Pasture – Reducing Road Casualties in the Rural Communities of Lancashire, United Kingdom', http://www.popcenter.org/library/awards/goldstein.cfm?browse=abstracts&year=2008 (accessed 7 February 2011).

Leigh, A., Read, T. and Tilley, N. (1996) *Problem-oriented Policing. Brit POP*, Crime Detection and Prevention Series, Paper 75, London: Home Office.

Leigh, A., Read, T. and Tilley, N. (1998) *Brit POP II. Problem-oriented Policing in Practice*, Police Research Series Paper 93, London: Home Office.

Pawson, R. and Tilley, N. (1997) *Realistic Evaluation*, London: Sage Publications.

Plant, J. and Scott, M. (2011) 'Trick or treat? Policing Halloween in Madison, Wisconsin', in T.D. Madensen and J. Knutsson (eds) *Preventing Crowd Violence*, Crime Prevention Studies, vol. 26, Boulder, CO: Lynne Rienner Publishers, pp. 159–89.

Read, T. and Tilley, N. (2000) *Not Rocket Science? Problem-solving and Crime Reduction*, Crime Reduction Research Series, Paper 6, London: Home Office.

Scott, M.S. (2000) *Problem-oriented Policing. Reflections on the First 20 Years*, Washington, DC: US Department of Justice, Office of Community Oriented Policing Services.

Sollund, R. (2008) 'The implementation of problem-oriented policing in Oslo, Norway: not without problems?', in K.T. Froeling (ed.) *Criminology Research Focus*, New York: Nova Science Publishers, pp. 175–93.

Thomassen, G. (2005) Implementering av problemorientert politiarbeid. Noen sentrale utfordringar, http://www.nsfk.org/downloads/seminarreports/researchsem_no47.pdf, pp. 218–23 (accessed 10 August 2010).

Tilley, N. (2006) 'Knowing and doing: guidance and good practice', in J. Knutsson and R.V. Clarke (eds) *Putting Theory to Work. Implementing Situational Prevention and Problem-oriented Policing*, Crime Prevention Studies, vol. 20, Monsey, NY: Criminal Justice Press, pp. 217–52.

Tilley, N. and Bullock, K. (2009) 'Evidenced-based policing and crime reduction', *Policing*, 3(4): 381–7.

Weisburd, D., Telep, C., Hinkle, J. and Eck, J. (2008) 'The effects of problem-oriented policing on crime and disorder', *Campbell Systematic Reviews*, 2008: 14.

9 Evaluation for everyday life

Mike Maxfield

Introduction

More than most other social scientists, criminologists are well situated and often involved in applied research and public policy. Such involvement assumes three general forms. First, applied research appears in specialized journals that publish articles on policy questions generally (*Criminology and Public Policy*; *Criminal Justice Policy Review*; *Crime Prevention and Community Safety*), or different policy domains (police, corrections, probation, offender therapy, crime prevention). Second, criminologists have participated in all types of applied field research that involves crime and justice agencies in many countries. Third, and something of a spin-off from applied field research generally, scholars have long conducted evaluation studies of justice policy. Evaluations have taken many forms, and approaches to evaluation have become something of a battleground of words among criminologists. In this chapter I focus not so much on joining the battle, but on calling attention to lessons learned from three sources: (1) previous efforts by social scientists, mostly those based in research universities, to advise public officials on social policy; (2) some of the writings of Donald Campbell who is cited as something close to an oracle of evaluation; and (3) a body of applied research that has produced major changes in crime and justice policy, reduced crime in several countries, but has either been overlooked or misrepresented in recent writings on evaluation in crime and justice.

Social scientists behaving badly

In a study of technical assistance to urban agencies in the 1960s and 1970s, Peter Szanton (1981) describes how researchers and local officials collaborated on the development, implementation, and evaluation of a broad array of programs to attack problems in US cities. Problems included poverty, crime, poor housing, and inequality, among others. It's significant that the problems tended to be vaguely defined and referred to collectively as the "urban crisis." Nonetheless, Szanton describes how mayors were able to make a successful case to state and national officials that substantial money was needed to fix an array of problems.

In much the same way that stated research grant priorities affect the behavior of university research generally, the availability of large sums for urban aid attracted social scientists. These efforts were supported by university presidents who saw benefits from involving their institutions in community problems, not to mention the availability of outside funds to support collaboration.

The title of Szanton's book, *Not Well Advised*, is significant, but obscures differences in how well consultants worked with urban officials. As federally supported social science research grew in universities, it also spawned consulting firms and think tanks. Szanton describes examples of the more successful experiences that local officials had when they worked with consulting firms, such as the RAND Corporation, compared to academic researchers. The principal reason for this is that research and consulting firms exist to provide services for clients. It's their business to address the problems presented to them by governmental clients and others.

In contrast, researchers based in colleges and universities are accustomed to answering questions that interest them using methods of research and communication approved by peers. The questions and types of answers favored by the academy were often at odds with those sought by public officials. These differences are summed up in a comparison of the different cultures of academic researchers and public officials. Table 9.1 is adapted from Szanton's comparison (1981, p. 64).

Largely because of academic traditions and the reward system in most universities, researchers are evaluated by their peers. Published research screened and read by peers is the most valued form of expression. Academics seek to produce original insights that are not limited to any particular problem or local setting. They usually focus on abstract elements of problems, not much concerned with feasibility of problem solutions. Academics tend to write detailed reports and qualify conclusions to reflect possible problems. The research programs of most academics in criminal justice have quite a long time horizon; in particular, years may elapse between a project's inception and the publication of results. Finally,

Table 9.1 Two cultures

Cultural traits	**Academic**	**Local officials**
Ultimate objective	Respect of academic peers; publication.	Serve public; attain policy goals; satisfy mandates.
Most valued outcome	Original insight; generalizable to other settings.	Reliable solution for specific problem.
Center of attention	Internal logic of problem; abstract.	External, contingent on setting, political feasibility.
Preferred mode of expression	Detailed written report; uncertainties emphasized.	Brief report, decisive; PowerPoint presentation.
Time horizon	Longer, few constraints.	Shorter, constrained by budget, related decision, political cycles.
Concern for feasibility	Low.	High.
Problem logic	Null hypothesis of no impact.	Assume interventions will work.

Source: Adapted from Szanton (1981, p. 64).

the principles of statistical analysis used by most justice researchers lead them to adopt a mien of skepticism, officially assuming that results are coincidental unless proven otherwise.

Justice professionals, and most other local officials, have different perspectives. Though not elected, most justice officials are ultimately responsible to officeholders who depend on the approval of voters. Political accountability is important. Local officials are most interested in reliable solutions to specific problems, and tend to focus on how these will work in specific settings. Generalizing to other settings is of little interest to officials bound to local constituencies. Busy officials require brief reports, decision memos, or even presentations. Justice professionals face acute time pressures unknown to most university researchers; their actions are inflexibly keyed to the preparation of annual budgets, reports, and periodic oversight. Feasible solutions are absolutely required. Public officials normally assume what they do will work.

National policies and local problems

Similar kinds of incompatibility are cited in how US federal and local officials approach many policy areas. As described in the classic study of federal aid (Pressman and Wildavsky 1984), the legislators, agency officials, and advisers who design federal programs routinely overlook the messy details of implementation. This is partly the consequence of a unitary, off-the-shelf bias inherent in many federal programs. Mears (2010, p. 28) refers to something like this in his description of enduring beliefs in "silver bullet" causes and responses to crime. Researchers often focus on single purported root causes of crime (e.g., drugs, inequality), while officials embrace single responses that are expected to solve the problem (e.g., incarceration, community policing). Environmental criminologists have long recognized the importance of local, contextual variation in crime problems. But this view of crime and disorder has not been uniformly embraced.

The potential effectiveness of large-scale federal programs in the US has been traditionally diluted even further by legislative requests to expand coverage of multi-site projects:

> Time and again, proposed multi-site demonstrations have been stretched thin in the legislative process, expanding to cover a large number of Congressional districts even as appropriation levels are pared down. Such inadequately funded experiments only reinforce skeptics' expectations when they fail to achieve the ambitious goals of federal policymakers.
> (O'Connor 1995, p. 51)

Big programs, big science, and big evaluation

Approaches to evaluating social policy initiatives in the 1960s and 1970s mirrored the administration of federal programs. Evaluation developed as a research field partly as a result of federal demand. It reflected a general social science tendency to mimic "hard sciences" with controlled experiments. Experiments were more scientific and required the special expertise of university researchers. This reinforces the academy's self-image of monopolizing technical and analytical skills.

Alice O'Connor (O'Connor 1995) describes how incompatible interests of national and local actors in the scope of urban policy affected evaluation approaches. Federal sponsors favored large demonstration programs accompanied by formal evaluations in the hope of identifying a standard intervention that could be applied in many settings. In contrast, local officials favor local problem solving and evaluation geared to improving program operations in specific cities. With respect to Model Cities initiatives, O'Connor reports that the different priorities of federal sponsors and local officials produces: "tensions [that] have been played out in the evaluation process, raising basic questions about who should have responsibility for evaluation, how criteria for success will be determined, and to what end evaluation results will be used" (1995, p. 51).

O'Connor presents the experience of Community Development Corporations (CDC) as a counterpart to more standardized federal programs such as Model Cities. Though funded by federal dollars, CDC projects involved more local planning to tailor investments to local needs. Evaluations of CDC initiatives used small case studies, but involved little effort to integrate and synthesize lessons learned (O'Connor 1995, p. 55). CDC required contextual evaluation, but little capacity for this existed given the programmatic forces that called for large-scale experimental approaches to evaluation.

An important component of all this is the peculiar federalist structure of US government, in which federal agencies exercise limited direct influence over what happens in state and local governments. Apart from regulation, federal agencies act as advocates who bankroll state and local projects. This is true for criminal justice as much as any other policy area. The federal role is largely reduced to one of cheerleading, back by bundles of cash. Federal funds are offered to state and local governments if they will try something new and agree to host an evaluation of the initiative.

All of this is convenient for researchers bent on large-scale evaluations. They can lobby federal program and research agencies in hopes of gaining favorable treatment of research proposals. Academic researchers are not that different from others, such as defense department contractors, who seek federal contracts for their work. For example, a builder of armor-coated office chairs for use in combat zones wishes to make a case that their chairs are superior to all others as a way of monopolizing access to contracts. In much the same way, university researchers can benefit from claiming special knowledge as a way to dominate access to research funds. Advocating experimentalism as an exclusive or dominant approach to evaluation is a possible example.

Several general lessons for US criminal justice evaluators are prominent in these reviews of social science attempts to affect and evaluate urban policy initiatives. The fit is not perfect and the days of large-scale demonstration projects are gone for now. But important lessons hinge on understanding the logic of federally sponsored initiatives traced by Szanton, Pressman and Wildavsky, O'Connor, and others:

- federally directed initiatives seek standard if not uniform solutions to problems;
- federally directed initiatives paid little attention to how programs would be implemented;
- variation in local problems and resources, together with political environments, precluded the potential effectiveness of one-size-fits-most solutions;
- failure to consider the details of implementation in varied local settings further undermined the already tenuous chances that federal initiatives would succeed.

A big-science derivative model of evaluation is well suited to this logic of federal initiatives, and vulnerable to problems that can result:

- uniform, stable interventions are assumed;
- implementation of interventions will be consistent;
- there will be little variation in the nature and scope of problems faced by different sites;
- random assignment of units to treatment conditions, or treatment conditions to units, will produce pre-intervention equivalence of treatment and non-treatment units/conditions;
- pre-intervention equivalence will not be undermined by any post-assignment changes, irregularities in implementation, or differences among experimental units.

The traditional model of evaluation fits the self-image and incentive structure of university-based researchers and administrators:

- big evaluation mimics big science;
- it applies models of science to social interventions;
- it seeks to discover or verify general causal relationships;
- special training, knowledge, and expertise are required to conduct such evaluations;
- the academy offers service to public officials, something that's especially desirable for public universities.

By the same token, public officials initially embrace these perspectives on social interventions and their evaluation:

- an off-the-shelf, best practice is attractive, especially if it's supported by outside funding;
- the involvement of experts lends credibility to interventions and evaluation;
- if things go wrong, accountability can be protected by shifting blame to the outsiders and experts whose advice was initially credible.

This summary of the logic underlying a potential train wreck is remarkably similar to problems listed by Donald Campbell in a seminal article on program evaluation (1979).

Clarifying Campbell: an alternative C2

Donald Campbell's name graces an international consortium of social scientists who appeal to his writings in support of experimentation as the most-desired approach to evidence-based social science in general, including crime and justice. Such views are often based on a narrow and dated interpretation of Campbell's work. His most cited work (Campbell and Stanley 1966) emphasizes the central role of reducing threats to internal validity of causal inference, and describes how randomized experiments are especially well-suited to doing that. Later writings focus more narrowly on evaluation, describing a broader variety of designs that can produce interpretable results.

Many writings on environmental criminology, situational crime prevention, and realistic evaluation have offered alternative approaches. These are well-known to likely readers of this volume. In most cases, alternative approaches stress the need to understand local problems in context. Pawson and Tilley (1997) come close to formalizing this in their models of mechanisms and contextual triggers. But in their descriptions, ranging from realistic evaluation to bologna (Eck 2006), environmental criminologists rarely cite Donald Campbell's work to support their more useful approach to evaluation. An exception is Knutsson and Tilley's introduction to a volume on evaluating crime reduction (2009). The authors summarize an example of later writings by Campbell that describe how government should pursue multiple approaches to measuring program effectiveness, a position substantially different from that described in the Campbell and Stanley monograph most often cited by experimentalists.

The most comprehensive treatment stemming from Campbell's work (Shadish, Cook, and Campbell 2002) describes a variety of approaches to causal inference. These approaches draw on different tools to strengthen our confidence in results. Shadish, Cook, and Campbell describe how tools are best viewed as design elements of research and evaluation, not as specific research designs:

- a key feature of experiments is "to deliberately vary something so as to discover what happens to something else later" (Shadish, Cook, and Campbell 2002, p. 3);
- theory that describes highly specific patterns of outcomes (Cook and Campbell 1979; Shadish, Cook, and Campbell 2002);
- pattern-matching by stating what results will support specified outcomes (Cook and Campbell 1979; Shadish, Cook, and Campbell 2002);
- large effect sizes – "cliff-edge effects" (Shadish, Cook, and Campbell 2002);
- case studies in small, specific settings that can be controlled and monitored (Campbell 1975, 1994);

- replication by conducting different versions of an experiment in different settings (Shadish, Cook, and Campbell 2002; Campbell 1975);
- "administrative experiments" incorporated into routine organization practice (Campbell 1979, p. 72).

These tools of evaluation are remarkably similar to those evident in different streams of environmental criminology. Each depends on exercising some type of control in the research setting. Not control in restricting which experimental units receive or do not receive a treatment, but control over evaluation settings in the sense that laboratory scientists can observe and restrict the potential impacts of outside variables. Deliberately varying something is an example especially common in problem-oriented policing.

Though they are not always labeled "theories," three theoretical frameworks central to environmental criminology underlie the analysis of crime patterns, selection of responses, and assessment of results. Crime pattern theory (Brantingham and Brantingham 1991), rational choice theory (Cornish and Clarke 1986), and routine activity theory (Cohen and Felson 1979) generally do a better job of accounting for regularities than other approaches embraced by other criminologists, so the label *theory* is appropriate. Looking back over publications produced in the last thirty years or so, it's remarkable how influential these theories have become. Most important, each has been used to describe highly specific patterns of outcomes in the manner described by Campbell and others.

Theory and pattern-matching produce control by tailoring interventions to highly specific outcomes, then determining whether those outcomes were obtained. In traditional language, Shadish, Cook, and Campbell describe how a "highly differentiated causal hypothesis" (2002, p. 124) leads to very specific predictions. If predicted outcomes are empirically observed, the findings have high internal validity. One of my favorite examples of this is the impact of laws requiring helmets on motorcycle theft (Mayhew, Clarke, and Elliott 1989). Whenever I mention this to students, their initial puzzlement quickly gives way to an intuitive understanding of the differentiated causal mechanism at work.

Large effect sizes that follow an intervention exercise control by obviating alternative explanations. When a "cliff-edge" follows an intervention, it's difficult to identify credible alternative causes. Clarke and associates (Clarke, Kemper, and Wyckoff 2001) describe how changes in technology virtually eliminated the cloning of cell phones in the US. Early results from the Boston gun project showed short-term reductions in gun killings of youth that could not possibly be associated with anything other than a comprehensive package of interventions (Braga et al. 2001).

Case studies, especially those described by Eck as "small-claim" interventions (2002), are a counterpart of laboratory settings where potential outside effects are either controlled or carefully monitored. Small-scale interventions in small settings are counterparts to isolating causal mechanisms in a laboratory. Applied environmental criminology is grounded in hundreds of case studies produced by academic researchers, and thousands by practitioners with and without collaboration from researchers. Successful case studies produced through variants of situational crime prevention were presented in two editions of a volume edited by Clarke, later presented in the serial *Crime Prevention Studies*, now continuing to accumulate on websites. Challenging a systematic review of problem-oriented policing (Weisburd et al. 2008), Guerette (2009) catalogs the continued success of case studies.

Replication is a version of Kuhn's "normal science" in which theories are subject to repeated tests with incremental variation in interventions and/or settings. Evidence and knowledge accumulate through an expanding body of case studies and other evaluations. Gloria Laycock describes the key role of replication in situational crime prevention and repeat victimization (Laycock 2001, 2002). Even with designs that might generally be considered to be weak, the large number of successful case studies contributes increasingly strong evidence of what works and what's promising.

It is interesting to note that the word "replication" was not much in evidence in a special issue of the *Journal of Experimental Criminology* (*JEC*) on evaluating criminal justice programs (Vol. 2, no. 3, 2006). "Replication" appeared twenty-six times in 143 pages across ten articles; it was used twelve times in one of the ten articles. The word was even less evident in the report, *Improving Evaluation of Anticrime Programs*, on which the *JEC* special issue was based – nine times (National Research Council 2005).

Replication is a natural consequence of other principles of environmental criminology, together with an important source of support for the validity of collective research. Most research centers on highly disaggregated crimes and very specific kinds of problems. Replication more generally is keyed to varying settings and interventions. Replication by tailoring intervention to specific problems in specific settings is consistent with general concept of control.

Finally, Campbell advocated that administrative experiments become a routine practice in public organizations, something that might be termed "evidence-based administration." Public organizations are non-market-oriented in lacking a bottom line to gauge success. Rather than deploying outside researchers to conduct large, costly, and rare evaluations, experimental interventions and evaluation should be routine for public organizations. Problem-oriented policing is a good example of what Campbell had in mind, and represents one of two general approaches to evaluation for everyday life that stem from the work of Ronald Clarke.

Ronald Clarke and evaluation for everyday life

The US federal officials described by Peter Szanton were poorly advised by social scientists who inappropriately applied a "big-science"-based evaluation model to inappropriately large-scale interventions. Their experience could hardly be more different than the countless people in public and private sectors throughout the world who have been influenced by Ronald Clarke's work. A formulaic model of problem analysis and evaluation often requires researchers with special expertise and costly projects. Clarke's work promotes evaluation for everyday life (EEL).

Though it is not likely to become one of his signature acronyms, EEL might just as well have been coined by Clarke. Its principles are simple and will be familiar to readers of this volume. EEL is evident in situational crime prevention, problem-oriented policing, and realistic evaluation. The numerous writings in each of those areas describe each approach in detail. Here I summarize brief principles, noting their application in the everyday life of justice agencies:

- The focus is on smaller-claim interventions in context, which is what public officials often do. In this way it's more realistic.
- An evaluation is tailored as a result of problem analysis. Experimental approaches may require that interventions be modified to suit the requirements of evaluation design.
- Knowledge about what works is accumulated from the varied evaluations that stem from the problem solving process. We keep track of what we learn from growing numbers of evaluations tailored to specific problems. This is different from applying a uniform standard to screen what can be learned from past research.
- The needs and interests of public officials are central in guiding the technical expertise of researchers.
- EEL can be incorporated into what justice agencies do with minimal disruption of routine operations.
- EEL is evidence-based. Public officials and researchers gather data to better understand the nature of local problems.

The label "evidence-based" is relatively recent and now seems an essential adjective for justice policy, medicine, education, and just about everything. Clarke's scholarship has always been evidence-based in the more general sense described here. Situational crime prevention (SCP) was described from the outset as an example of action research in which evidence is used to plan and implement preventative action. Over the years, accumulating evidence has produced the matrix of techniques for crime prevention. They numbered twenty-five in a recent summary of situational crime prevention (Clarke 2008), up from sixteen opportunity-reducing techniques described over ten years earlier (Clarke 1997). As evidence accumulates, the framework for considering appropriate responses grows accordingly.

Similarly, problem-oriented policing has built and built upon a foundation of evidence-based practice. It's not been evidence-based according to a standard scale devised by researchers. It's evidence-based according to a fast-growing body of small-claim studies of different types. Collectively these represent replications of an approach to solving local problems, rather than the replications of a one-size-fits-many intervention. The Center for Problem-Oriented Policing is home to a growing body of examples in different categories.

Most prominent is the series of guides to crime and disorder problems. Produced by researchers and practitioners, each problem guide is a kind of systematic review of what works, what doesn't, and what we're not sure about yet.

No methods strength score is offered. Instead, each guide follows a template to lay out what's known about a problem, how to gather data about local problems, and what evidence exists to recommend or not recommend different responses. Each guide concludes with a table summarizing responses, how they work, and what contexts should be considered. Not only are these guides evidence-based, they are singularly useful in everyday life.

Conclusion

This is not intended to join the growing number of voices raised against attempted experimental hegemony. Others have done that much more convincingly. It's especially interesting to see that prominent scholars not traditionally associated with environmental criminology have begun to challenge experimentalists (Sampson 2010; Sparrow 2011; Hough 2010).

Instead, the purpose has been to take a broader look at the tenets of experimentation and quasi-experimentation, and to reflect on long-past attempts by academics to use their version of science to advise public officials. Doing so reveals substantial compatibility between the types of evaluations produced in environmental criminology, and approaches to evaluation described by Donald Campbell. A look back also reminds us of earlier unsuccessful attempts to dominate evaluation through inflexible scientism. Though he supported randomized experimentation, Campbell recognized the many situations where that approach could not be used and described strategies for producing interpretable evaluations.

The concept of applying a gold standard for accumulating evidence-based interventions risks promoting an off-the-shelf approach to crime prevention and control. It's self-limiting and therefore unrealistic. Universals or even broadly applicable off-the-shelf principles are in short supply in criminal justice. This is even more true for evidence-based principles. In fact the most prominent evidence-based principle is to base interventions on evidence.

EEL offers evidence-based tools for developing, applying, and assessing innovative approaches to solving problems and preventing crime. Reasoning criminologists have used those tools to build an impressive body of knowledge for reducing crime. Most important, EEL is used by police and others in assessing what works and what doesn't.

References

Braga, Anthony A., David M. Kennedy, Elin J. Waring, and Anne Morrison Piehl. (2001) "Problem-oriented policing and youth violence: an evaluation of Boston's Operation Ceasefire." *Journal of Research in Crime and Delinquency* 38(3, August): 195–225.

Brantingham, Paul J. and Patricia L. Brantingham. (eds) (1991) *Environmental Criminology*. 2nd edn. Prospect Heights, IL: Waveland.

Campbell, Donald T. (1975) "'Degrees of freedom' and the case study." *Comparative Political Studies* 8: 178–193.

Campbell, Donald T. (1979) "Assessing the impact of planned social change." *Evaluation and Program Planning* 2: 67–90.

Campbell, Donald T. (1994) "Introduction." In Robert K. Yin *Case Study Research: Design and Methods*. 2nd edn. Thousand Oaks, CA: Sage Publications.
Campbell, Donald T. and Julian Stanley. (1966) *Experimental and Quasi-experimental Designs for Research*. Chicago: Rand McNally.
Clarke, Ronald V. (1997) "Introduction." In *Situational Crime Prevention: Successful Case Studies*. 2nd edn. New York: Harrow and Heston.
Clarke, Ronald V. (2008) "Situational Crime Prevention." In Richard Wortley, Lorraine Mazerolle, and Sacha Rombouts (eds) *Environmental Criminology and Crime Analysis*. Cullompton: Willan Publishing.
Clarke, Ronald V., Rick Kemper, and Laura Wyckoff. (2001) "Controlling cell phone fraud in the US: lessons for the UK 'Foresight' initiative." *Security Journal* 14(1, January): 7–22.
Cohen, Lawrence E. and Marcus Felson. (1979) "Social change and crime rate trends: a routine activity approach." *American Sociological Review* 44: 588–608.
Cook, Thomas D. and Donald T. Campbell. (1979) *Quasi-experimentation: Design and Analysis Issues for Field Settings*. Boston: Houghton Mifflin.
Cornish, D.B. and Ronald V. Clarke. (eds) (1986) *The Reasoning Criminal: Rational Choice Perspectives on Offending*. New York: Springer-Verlag.
Eck, John E. (2002) "Learning from experience in problem-oriented policing and situational prevention: the positive functions of weak evaluations and the negative functions of strong ones." In Nick Tilley (ed.) *Evaluation for Crime Prevention. Crime Prevention Studies*, vol. 14. Monsey, NY: Criminal Justice Press.
Eck, John. (2006) "When is a bologna sandwich better than sex? A defense of small-*n* case study evaluation." *Journal of Experimental Criminology* 2: 345–362.
Guerette, Rob T. (2009) "The pull, push, and expansion of situational crime prevention evaluation: an appraisal of thirty-seven years of research." In Johannes Knutsson and Nick Tilley (eds) *Evaluating Crime Reduction Initiatives. Crime Prevention Studies*, vol. 24. Monsey, NY: Criminal Justice Press.
Hough, Mike. (2010) "Gold standard or fool's gold? The pursuit of certainty in experimental criminology." *Criminology and Criminal Justice* 10: 11–21.
Knutsson, Johannes and Nick Tilley. (2009) "Introduction." In *Evaluating Crime Reduction Initiatives. Crime Prevention Studies*, vol. 24. Monsey, NY: Criminal Justice Press.
Laycock, Gloria. (2001) "Hypothesis-based research: the repeat victimization story." *Criminal Justice* 1(1, February): 59–82.
Laycock, Gloria. (2002) "Methodological issues in working with policy advisers and practitioners." In Nick Tilley (ed.) *Analysis for Crime Prevention. Crime Prevention Studies*, vol. 13. Monsey, NY: Criminal Justice Press.
Mayhew, Patricia, Ronald V. Clarke, and David Elliott. (1989) "Motorcycle theft, helmet legislation, and displacement." *Howard Journal* 28: 1–8.
Mears, Daniel P. (2010) *American Criminal Justice Policy: An Evaluation Approach to Accountability and Effectiveness*. New York: Cambridge University Press.
National Research Council. (2005) *Improving Evaluation of Anticrime Programs*. Committee on Improving Evaluation of Anti-Crime Programs. Committee on Law and Justice, Division of Behavioral and Social Sciences. Edited by Mark W. Lipsey. Washington, DC: National Academy Press.
O'Connor, Alice. (1995) "Evaluating comprehensive community initiatives: a view from history." In James P. Connell, Anne C. Kubisch, Lisbeth B. Schorr, and Carol H. Weiss (eds) *New Approaches to Evaluating Community Initiatives: Concepts, Methods, and Contexts*. Washington, DC: Aspen Institute.

Pawson, Ray and Nick Tilley. (1997) *Realistic Evaluation*. Thousand Oaks, CA: Sage.

Pressman, Jeffrey L. and Aaron Wildavsky. (1984) *Implementation*. 3rd edn. Berkeley, CA: University of California Press.

Sampson, Robert J. (2010) "Gold standard myths: observations on the experimental turn in quantitative criminology." *Journal of Quantitative Criminology* 26: 489–500.

Shadish, William R., Thomas D. Cook, and Donald T. Campbell. (2002) *Experimental and Quasi-experimental Designs for Generalized Causal Inference*. Boston: Houghton Mifflin.

Sparrow, Malcolm K. (2011) *Governing Science. New Perspectives on Policing*. Washington, DC: US Department of Justice, Office of Justice Programs, National Institute of Justice.

Szanton, Peter. (1981) *Not Well Advised*. New York: Russell Sage.

Weisburd, David, Cody W. Telep, Joshua C. Hinkle, and John E. Eck. (2008) *The Effects of Problem-oriented Policing on Crime and Disorder*. Campbell Systematic Reviews. Oslo: University of Oslo. Www.campbellcollaboration.org/lib/download/663/.

10 Using rational choice and situational crime prevention to inform, interpret, and enhance public surveillance efforts

A three-city study

Nancy La Vigne

Introduction

As a doctoral student at Rutgers School of Criminal Justice in the 1990s I had the honor of working as a research assistant for Ron Clarke. I was immediately taken with the deceptively simple yet tremendously powerful utility of Ron's theories and their applications for crime prevention. Ron's work harkened that of another great thinker and visionary, R. Buckminster Fuller, who argued persuasively to "reform the environment, not the man." This refreshing perspective attracted the pragmatists among us, who viewed it as more expedient and cost-effective to implement and evaluate crime prevention measures centered on physical structure and management practices – areas within the control of employees, businesses, and law enforcement – rather than to contemplate what makes some people criminals. Indeed, the scholarly community and practitioners alike have observed first-hand the utility of situational crime prevention (SCP) and its flexibility in guiding effective measures to reduce a wide array of crime types in all manner of environments.

One area in which rationale choice and SCP has been applied extensively is in the use of public surveillance cameras, often referred to as closed-circuit television (CCTV) cameras. The theory underlying the effectiveness of public surveillance technology as a crime control tool is based on the belief that if potential offenders know they are being watched, they will refrain from criminal activity. This belief is consistent with rational choice theory, which posits that offenders make purposeful, rational (albeit bounded[1]) decisions to commit crime after weighing the potential costs and benefits of the crime in question (Cornish and Clarke 2003). Practical applications of rational choice theory are typically embodied under the SCP rubric, which offers an array of means by which the cost–benefit ratio of offending opportunities can be altered, including the following: (1) increasing the risk of being apprehended; (2) increasing the effort involved in committing the crime; (3) decreasing the rewards of the crime; (4) increasing the shame and guilt expected to result from the crime or felt at the immediate moment of decision-making; and/or (5) reducing provocations that create criminal opportunities (Clarke 1997; Cornish and Clarke 2003).

Applying rational choice theory and SCP to public surveillance camera use, one would hypothesize that any impact of cameras on offenders' perceptions is likely to take the form of increasing the risk of apprehension (Ratcliffe 2006; Welsh and Farrington 2002). However, to increase perceived risk, an offender must be aware of the presence of the camera(s) and thus be deterred from committing crime. Overt camera systems accomplish this by placing cameras in public view and coupling them with signage and/or flashing lights advertising their presence (Ratcliffe 2006).

These systems often rely on media and publicity campaigns to communicate information to potential offenders (Mazerolle et al. 2002; Ratcliffe 2006). Yet, even when potential offenders are aware that a camera system exists, they may not know the extent of the system's capacity. This imperfect knowledge about what the cameras can see may actually magnify their deterrent impact. As is evident with other crime prevention measures, such as "hot spot policing" (see Weisburd et al. 2006), cameras may prevent crime in areas beyond the immediate area of intervention, a phenomenon known as diffusion of benefits (Clarke and Weisburd 1994; Gill 2006; Gill and Spriggs 2005; Ratcliffe 2006; Weisburd et al. 2006).

Ron Clarke routinely emphasized that in order to be effective, SCP strategies that are put in place should be crime-specific. That is, each crime has a different "opportunity structure" that would guide the selection of SCP measures to prevent it (Cornish and Clarke 1987). One might posit, on the one hand, that cases of domestic violence, for example, would be relatively immune to public surveillance cameras, as they typically occur behind closed doors. On the other hand, street crimes, such as robbery, drug marketing, assaults, and gun violence, would likely be responsive to the increased surveillance that cameras afford, as would car crimes in parking facilities. The middle ground is that of crimes that occur out of view of cameras but for which cameras could identify offenders entering and exiting that crime location. This could apply to business larcenies and auto thefts that take place indoors or in private, underground, or enclosed parking garages. In this case we might expect cameras to have a marginal crime prevention impact.

Public surveillance systems may also prevent crime by increasing perceptions of safety among legitimate users of the public areas monitored by cameras, thereby encouraging people to frequent places they may previously have been fearful of visiting (Gill 2006; Ratcliffe 2006). As more people use these spaces for pro-social purposes, their presence may serve as a further deterrent to crime, providing natural surveillance as informal guardians and potential witnesses (Welsh and Farrington 2002, 2004).

Advocates of public camera use also theorize that the technology's surveillance capabilities can enhance criminal justice system efficiency. Camera monitors can alert police of crimes and potentially dangerous situations as they occur, providing crucial information that can help police determine the safest, most effective response, including how many officers to deploy and how to respond on the scene (Goold 2004; Levesley and Martin 2005). Video footage documenting crimes that transpired and identifying perpetrators and witnesses may aid in investigations and prosecutions, increasing police and prosecutorial efficiency, benefiting victims of crimes whose cases are able to be closed through the use of video evidence, and incapacitating a greater number of offenders from committing future crimes (Chainey 2000; Gill and Hemming 2004; Ratcliffe 2006).

Detractors of the technology, however, point to the likelihood that potential criminals will "wise up" and simply move to locations beyond the cameras' viewsheds. This argument is based on the premise that criminals have an accurate perception of the extent of a camera's reach, and also assumes that cameras will not discourage opportunistic offenders from refraining from a particular criminal act altogether. Prior research, however, indicates that displacement is by no means a certainty and when it does occur, it is nowhere near 100 percent (i.e., only a fraction of the crime prevented is displaced) (Barr and Pease 1990; Hesseling 1994; Eck 1993; Guerette and Bowers 2009). This argument also fails to acknowledge the possibility that implementers of SCP strategies anticipate where and when crime is likely to displace and take measures to prevent it from occurring. Indeed, such measures could not only prevent potential displacement associated with camera use, but could also increase the likelihood of a diffusion of benefits.

Evaluations of public surveillance camera impact both in the United Kingdom and the United States have produced uneven support for the theories described above. One early study based in the United Kingdom produced promising results in reducing street crime with the absence of displacement (Chainey 2000), while another demonstrated consistent impacts on reduced fear of crime but scant evidence of crime decline, and differential impacts by crime type (Gill and Spriggs 2005). Welsh and Farrington (in 2002, 2004, and 2008) conducted studies of previous public surveillance evaluations worldwide, of which forty-one were identified as having sufficient methodological rigor to be included in a formal meta-analysis. Overall, the authors found that cameras reduce crime to a small degree, although impact varied based on location of cameras and country of intervention, with significant reductions in crime found in UK settings, but no effect in other countries.

A subsequent meta-analysis, combined with an evaluation of two public surveillance locations in Los Angeles (California), echoes the mixed findings of Welsh and Farrington (Cameron et al. 2007). Of the forty-four sites included in the meta-analysis (eleven of which were of sites in the US), almost 41 percent (eighteen) showed a statistically significant decrease in crime, with the remainder demonstrating either a rise in crime or null results. The impact was slightly more positive for camera systems implemented specifically in commercial areas, where just under half (twelve) of twenty-five sites experienced a positive impact. By contrast, cameras placed in residential areas typically failed to reduce crime. Of the nine sites included in this category, the vast majority (seven) had no significant impact, while a significant rise in crime was found in the remaining two sites. None of the eleven US sites showed a significant decrease in crime in any category.

Three recent studies have taken a closer look at public surveillance use and impact in US cities. In Los Angeles, neither crime nor arrest data changed significantly after the city's camera system was implemented (Cameron et al. 2007).

In the other two cities, however, results were more mixed. Philadelphia's camera evaluation found a significant reduction in crime within a month of camera installation at half of the camera locations (Ratcliffe and Taniguchi 2008). Four of the eight sites included in the study experienced a statistically significant decrease in disorder incidents in the target areas and witnessed a reduction of crime in the buffer area, which researchers deemed a diffusion of the benefits associated with the camera installation. The evaluation does not address the question of why some camera sites had an impact on crime while others did not.

A more comprehensive study of San Francisco's public surveillance system found similarly mixed results (King et al. 2008). The study examined nineteen camera sites, each with multiple cameras, from 209 days before installation to 264 days afterward. In that period, there were no statistically significant changes in drug offenses, vandalism, prostitution, or violent crime. Property crime rates, however, declined significantly (23 percent) within 100 feet of the cameras with no signs of displacement to areas adjacent to but not within the viewsheds of the cameras. The effect was driven entirely by declines in larceny theft.

This cursory review of the theories underlying the crime prevention impact of public surveillance cameras and prior evaluations of camera use raises questions about specific aspects of the technology that may bolster its effectiveness. The vast majority of evaluations reviewed above were conducted in the absence of a thorough process evaluation to consider variations in camera monitoring and use that might explain their differential impact on crime. Yet theoretically we would expect these factors to play a significant role in the technology's crime prevention impact. These hypotheses were explored by The Urban Institute (UI) through a rigorous process and impact evaluation of the implementation and use of public surveillance cameras for crime control purposes in three US cities: Baltimore, Maryland; Chicago, Illinois; and Washington, DC (see La Vigne et al., forthcoming). Researchers collected and synthesized qualitative data on the ways in which cameras are employed to support patrol, investigations, tactical unit activities, and prosecutions and conducted impact analyses using reported crime data and employing comparison areas that were matched on historical crime volume, geographic location, land use, and demographics of the surrounding area.

Evaluation findings

The process evaluation component of this study involved the synthesis of qualitative data obtained from interviews with forty-four stakeholders representing the planners and public officials involved in each city's decisions to acquire and employ this technology, as well as the law enforcement officers, civilians, and other local criminal justice practitioners engaged in camera use. UI evaluators supplemented these interviews with the collection and review of documents related to public surveillance camera implementation, monitoring, and use. In addition, the UI research team conducted site visits to each jurisdiction, observing monitoring practices and use of cameras by line officers, detectives, and supervisors. Findings on the implementation and use of public surveillance systems varied significantly by study site. Baltimore virtually saturated its downtown area with cameras and employed around-the-clock monitoring of the live video footage. Chicago employed an extensive wireless network of cameras that gave camera access to all sworn officers. Washington implemented the fewest cameras in specific high-crime areas while restricting live monitoring of cameras to a narrow set of actors and contexts in order to safeguard citizens' rights to privacy.

The process evaluation yielded critical contextual information with which to interpret results of the impact analysis. The impact analysis employed two categories of methods: (1) descriptive, time series, and difference-in-differences (DiD) analyses (employing comparison areas matched on historical crime, socio-economic factors, and land use) of pre- and post-intervention reported crimes in each camera area to detect the degree to which cameras had an impact on crime; and (2) analyses of potential displacement and diffusion effects in areas adjacent to the camera locations by conducting DiD analyses of intervention areas compared to diffusion and displacement buffers, employing the weighted displacement quotient (see Bowers and Johnson 2003), and examining pre- and post-implementation spatial means.

Baltimore, Maryland

Baltimore implemented cameras in both its downtown area and in select neighborhoods identified as high-crime areas. The city's greatest investment in cameras was in downtown Baltimore, referred to as the CitiStat area: cameras there are highly concentrated, with overlapping viewsheds throughout the fifty-block area, and are monitored around-the-clock by a team of retired sworn officers. The cameras are prominently advertised with signs and flashing blue lights. Officers use the CitiStat cameras for special events, routine patrol activities, and undercover investigations. The city later introduced cameras in several high-crime neighborhoods, although neither the degree of camera saturation nor monitoring level matches that of the downtown Baltimore area. In addition, interviews with law enforcement indicate that the technology in the downtown area was fully and strategically integrated into other police patrol, operations, and investigations efforts. For example, areas of potential displacement were identified and patrols were allocated to those locations, which actually facilitated the apprehension of offenders.

The impact analysis of Baltimore's camera system, employing structural break analysis, indicates a statistically significant reduction in crime in the downtown Baltimore area, where both property and violent crimes declined by large percentages in the months following camera implementation (see Table 10.1). Notably, the cameras had an impact on larcenies occurring behind closed doors. These reductions were identified without any signs of crime displacement to neighboring areas. Crime near the camera area but beyond the camera viewsheds also declined during the post-implementation period, suggesting a diffusion of benefits.

Impacts on crime in other Baltimore camera areas were mixed, with some areas demonstrating statistically significant drops in some types of crimes and one area

Table 10.1 Significant average monthly changes in crime, downtown Baltimore*

Crime	Time from installation	Pre-shift mean	Post-shift mean	% change
Larceny inside†	3 months	36.79	25.03	−31.97%
Larceny outside†	11 months	41.47	27.13	−34.58%
Violent†	6 months	21.17	16.36	−22.72%
Total	4 months	119.05	89.47	−24.85%
1000-ft buffer	5 months	82.83	58.38	−29.52%

Notes: * First set of cameras were installed in early May 2005; therefore, the intervention point was determined to be May 2005. The downtown extension cameras were not included in this analysis.
† Significant at $p < 0.05$.

yielding no measurable impact at all. Areas with significant reductions were neither accompanied by displacement, nor by a diffusion of benefits.

Chicago, Illinois

At the time the evaluation began, Chicago had approximately 8,000 cameras in operation, of which 2,000 were operated by the Chicago Police Department (CPD) and were the main focus of this evaluation.[2] Termed "PODs" (portable observation devices), the cameras are highly visible and are typically accompanied by both signage and blue flashing lights. Due to the wireless networking of Chicago's camera system, the city is unique in its ability to make live video feed accessible to as many authorized users as it chooses. In Chicago, this means that all sworn officers have the ability to monitor cameras from their desktop computers. However, while the camera system may be actively monitored at all times, the extent of monitoring varies by police district. Even in the districts that engage in the most proactive monitoring, relatively few individuals are charged solely with the task of viewing live camera footage.

Two Chicago areas with high concentrations of cameras were employed for the impact analysis, one located in the Humboldt Park neighborhood and the other in the West Garfield Park neighborhood. As depicted in Table 10.2, the DiD analysis

Table 10.2 Significant average monthly changes in crime, Humboldt Park, Chicago*

Crime type	Area	Before	After	Change	DiD
All crime	Treatment	301.39	243.53	−57.86	−38.30†
	Comparison	349.57	330.00	−19.57	
Violent	Treatment	33.00	23.19	−9.81	−5.87†
	Comparison	29.57	25.62	−3.95	
Drug	Treatment	115.22	77.31	−37.91	−33.49†
	Comparison	120.57	116.14	−4.43	
Robbery	Treatment	11.52	8.53	−2.99	−3.17†
	Comparison	11.43	11.61	+0.18	
Weapons	Treatment	3.96	2.58	−1.37	−2.15†
	Comparison	3.78	4.56	+0.77	

Notes: * First camera installation on July 31, 2003 and, therefore, intervention line inserted at August 2003. † Significant at $p < 0.05$.

revealed a significant decrease in average monthly total crime counts in the Humboldt Park area following camera installation. In addition, the average monthly crime counts for drug-related and robbery offenses were reduced by nearly one-third, with drug crime decreasing by more than thirty incidents and robbery by three incidents on average per month.

While weapons-related crimes in the camera target area declined by more than half – or roughly two fewer incidents per month, this finding should be interpreted with caution given the low base rate of this crime category. However, the violent crime category also declined significantly by approximately one-fifth, with six fewer incidents on average per month following camera installation. In summary, the decrease in crime in the treatment area, which was significantly greater than that experienced by the comparison area, suggests that the Humboldt Park area cameras accomplished their desired crime control impact. This impact was achieved with no signs of spatial displacement; initial evidence of a diffusion of benefits was not found to be statistically significant.

The second Chicago camera area evaluated, West Garfield Park, yielded little to report. When examining the mean change before and after camera installation using independent samples t-tests, only prostitution and robbery changed significantly, with prostitution increasing and robbery decreasing. However, these findings did not hold up when applying a more rigorous DiD analysis.

Given the strong crime prevention impact that cameras had in Humboldt Park, we explored in more detail differences between Humboldt Park and West Garfield Park that might explain why cameras had an impact in one area and not another. One possible explanation for the difference is that cameras were employed by law enforcement differently in the two sites. Both areas are housed in the same police district with the same leadership, suggesting that use of cameras was similar in the two areas. Perceptions of West Garfield Park residents, however, suggest differently; one community advocate shared that it is her perception and that of her neighbors that police do not watch the cameras in West Garfield Park. Another possible reason for the difference in impact between Humboldt Park and West Garfield Park is the concentration of cameras. The Humboldt Park area has a much higher concentration of cameras (approximately fifty-three per square mile) compared to West Garfield, at approximately thirty-six per square mile. This difference in camera saturation could have influenced the degree to which cameras are able to catch crimes in progress and thus officers to intervene, make arrests, and deter other potential offenders.

Washington, DC

The camera system that served as the focus of the Washington, DC component of this evaluation was designed to have a direct impact on crimes occurring in specific high-crime neighborhoods. All seventy-three of these neighborhood cameras are clearly visible, with signs posted near the cameras to alert passersby that a camera is present and recording. In addition, the location of each camera is published on the Metropolitan Police Department's (MPD) website. However, unlike Baltimore and Chicago, the cameras are not advertised with flashing blue lights.

At the outset, District residents were very vocal and forthright in expressing their concerns that the neighborhood cameras would be subject to misuse and pose a threat to privacy rights. The city council therefore passed guidelines to protect against misuse. While these regulations are often held up as a rare example of sound policy safeguarding camera use,[3] they severely limit the extent of active monitoring employed in DC. Active monitoring can only take place in a single location, the control center that is employed to monitor cameras and other alert technology. Monitoring procedures require that a sworn MPD staff person at the rank of lieutenant or higher be in the monitoring room at all times. This protocol was developed to minimize misuse of cameras by monitors and other MPD staff and to remind those viewing the footage to follow the guidelines set forth to protect citizens' privacy. Up to two staff persons serve as monitors on each shift. During a shift, one monitor will usually watch four to five cameras while the other works primarily with other crime-alert technology in the room.

With the limited number of cameras in DC, investigators reported that it is hit or miss in terms of whether a camera captures a crime. They do not typically have the ability to extract footage from multiple cameras in the area because it is unusual for more than one camera to exist in any given location. Stakeholders who were interviewed indicated that while they viewed cameras as useful tools in solving crime, they underscored that cameras are not consistently useful.

Given these limitations in camera saturation and use, it is perhaps not surprising that impact analyses failed to identify any statistically significant impact of cameras on crime in DC. Comparisons of means for crimes occurring before and after camera implementation found significant reductions in assault with a deadly weapon and violent crime, while larcenies increased significantly. However, none of these crime changes remained significant after controlling for competing effects that are not attributable to the cameras through the introduction of comparison areas. Indeed, the control areas followed the same pattern of change for each of the crime categories (i.e., assault with a deadly weapon and violent crime declined, while larceny increased). This suggests that other factors contributed to crime reduction throughout the city and that while cameras may have had some impact, they were not on their own a significant contributing factor to the crime decline.

Implications

The three-city evaluation conducted by UI researchers sheds new light on the potential crime prevention impact of public surveillance cameras due to the extensive process evaluations that accompanied the impact analyses in each site. The process evaluation enabled us to identify variations in the way cameras were deployed and used, and provides insights into how they can yield the greatest impact that are consistent with Ron Clarke's rational choice perspective and SCP principles. One would posit, for example, that cameras that are extremely well advertised through signage and lighting would have a greater deterrent impact on crime. Theory also suggests that cameras that are monitored around the clock by police staff are more likely to have an impact on criminal behavior because the monitors have the ability to detect crimes as they occur and radio patrols to intervene on the spot, thereby increasing the perceived risk of apprehension. Likewise, the presence of a high concentration of cameras would also increase the perceived risk of apprehension by aiding in investigative efforts that lead to the identification of suspects. Finally, theory suggests that full integration of camera technology into police patrol, operations, and investigations could be used strategically to minimize crime displacement and increase the prospects of diffusion of benefits.

The evaluation findings indicate that of the three study sites, the camera system in Baltimore's downtown CitiStat area comes closest to meeting these theoretical prerequisites for effectiveness. Cameras are highly concentrated, publicized through signs and flashing lights, actively monitored around the clock, and fully integrated into law enforcement activities. Thus, it might be expected that the system would achieve a crime prevention impact on both violent and property crimes, including larcenies occurring behind closed doors. These findings suggest that cameras, when deployed thoroughly and actively monitored, are not a crime-specific SCP intervention, yielding a far broader impact than most SCP measures. The fact that law enforcement anticipated and strategically planned for displacement may likely explain the diffusion of benefits that was identified.

The evaluation results from the other two cities are consistent with prior literature, which suggests that in some contexts and locations crime reduction benefits are not realized from the investment and use of surveillance cameras. Two possible explanations for the lack of the surveillance technology's impact on crime in certain study areas, which are guided by Ron Clarke's work, are that (1) the no-impact areas have relatively low concentrations of cameras with fewer overlapping viewsheds and thus a reduced ability to capture crimes in progress; and (2) the cameras are not actively monitored on a routine basis. Both explanations suggest that the impact of cameras on perceptions of risk were dampened due to the scarcity of cameras and the lack of human surveillance of them. These are critical factors that both current and future investors of surveillance technology should consider when expanding or implementing camera systems. It is equally important for jurisdictions to understand that public surveillance technology is only as good as the manner in which it is employed. If it is employed minimally or is not well-integrated into other policing functions, it is unlikely to yield a significant impact on crime.

Notes

1 Rational choice theory acknowledges that an offender's decision-making processes may not be truly rational, in that they could be influenced by intoxication or drug addiction, low intelligence levels, and/or an inclination to discount the future costs of one's actions.
2 In addition to the police camera system, Chicago has both overt and covert cameras that are monitored primarily for homeland security purposes.
3 The Constitution Project, *Guidelines for Public Video Surveillance: A Guide to Protecting Communities and Preserving Civil Liberties*, 2007.

References

Barr, Robert and Ken Pease. (1990) "Crime placement, displacement, and deflection." *Crime and Justice* 12: 277–318.

Bowers, Kate J. and Shane D. Johnson. (2003) "Measuring the geographical displacement and diffusion of benefit effects of crime prevention activity." *Journal of Quantitative Criminology* 19: 275–301.

Cameron, Aundreia, Elke Kolodinski, Heather May, and Nicholas Williams. (2007) *Measuring the Effects of Video Surveillance on Crime in Los Angeles*. CRB-08-007. Sacramento, CA: California Research Bureau.

Chainey, Spencer. (2000) "Optimizing closed-circuit television use." In Nancy La Vigne and Julie Wartell (eds) *Crime Mapping Case Studies: Successes In the Field*, Vol. 2, pp. 91–100. Washington, DC: Police Executive Research Forum.

Clarke, Ronald V. (1997) "Introduction." In Ronald V. Clarke (ed.) *Situational Crime Prevention: Successful Case Studies*, 2nd edition, pp. 1–43. Monsey, NY: Criminal Justice Press.

Clarke, Ronald and David Weisburd. (1994) "Diffusion of crime control benefits: observations on the reverse of displacement." In Ronald V. Clarke (ed.) *Crime Prevention Studies*, Vol. 2, pp. 165–183. Monsey, NY: Criminal Justice Press.

The Constitution Project. (2007) *Guidelines for Public Video Surveillance: A Guide to Protecting Communities and Preserving Civil Liberties*. Washington, DC: The Constitution Project.

Cornish, Derek B. and Ronald V. Clarke. (1987) "Understanding crime displacement: an application of rational choice theory." *Criminology* 25(4): 933–947.

Cornish, Derek B. and Ronald V. Clarke. (2003) "Opportunities, precipitators and criminal decisions: a reply to Wortley's critique of situational crime prevention." In Martha J. Smith and Derek B. Cornish (eds) *Theory for Practice in Situational Crime Prevention*, Crime Prevention Studies, Vol. 16, pp. 41–96. Monsey, NY: Criminal Justice Press.

Eck, John E. (1993) "The threat of crime displacement." *Criminal Justice Abstracts* 25: 527–546.

Gill, Martin. (2006) "CCTV: is it effective?" In Martin Gill (ed.) *The Handbook of Security*, pp. 438–461. New York: Palgrave Macmillan.

Gill, Martin and Martin Hemming. (2004) "The evaluation of CCTV in the London borough of Lewisham: a report." Leicester: Perpetuity Research and Consultancy International.

Gill, Martin and Angela Spriggs. (2005) "Assessing the impact of CCTV." Home Office Research Study 292. www.homeoffice.gov.uk/rds/pdfs05/hors292.pdf (accessed January 18, 2007).

Goold, Benjamin J. (2004) *CCTV and Policing: Public Area Surveillance and Police Practices in Britain*. New York: Oxford University Press.

Guerette, R.T. and Bowers, K.J. (2009) "Assessing the extent of crime displacement and diffusion of benefits: a review of situational crime prevention evaluations." *Criminology* 47: 1331–1368.

Hesseling, Rene B.P. (1994) "Displacement: a review of empirical literature." In Ronald V. Clarke (ed.) *Crime Prevention Studies*, Vol. 3, pp. 195–230. Monsey, NY: Criminal Justice Press.

King, Jennifer, Deidre K. Mulligan, and Steven Raphael. (2008) "CITRIS report: the San Francisco Community Safety Camera Program." Berkeley, CA: University of California Center for Information Technology Research in the Interest of Society.

La Vigne, Nancy G., Samantha S. Lowry, Joshua A. Markman, and Allison M. Dwyer.

(forthcoming) "The eyes have it: documenting the use of public surveillance cameras for crime control and prevention in three U.S. cities." Washington, DC: US Department of Justice, Office of Community Oriented Policing Services.

Levesley, Tom and Amanda Martin. (2005) "Police attitudes to and use of CCTV." Home Office Online Report. London: UK Home Office, Research, Development and Statistics Directorate.

Mazerolle, Lorraine, David Hurley, and Mitchell Chamlin. (2002) "Social behavior in public space: an analysis of behavioral adaptations to CCTV." *Security Journal* 15(3): 59–75.

Ratcliffe, Jerry. (2006) "Video surveillance of public places." Washington, DC: US Department of Justice, Office of Community Oriented Policing Services.

Ratcliffe, Jerry and Travis Taniguchi. (2008) "CCTV camera evaluation: the crime reduction effect of public CCTV cameras in the city of Philadelphia, PA Installed during 2006." Philadelphia: Temple University.

Weisburd, David, Laura A. Wyckoff, Justin Ready, John E. Eck, Joshua C. Hinkle, and Frank Gajewski. (2006) "Does crime just move around the corner? A controlled study of spatial displacement and diffusion of crime control benefits." *Criminology* 44: 549–591.

Welsh, Brandon C. and David P. Farrington. (2002) "Crime prevention effects of closed circuit television: a systematic review." Home Office Research Study 252. London: UK Home Office, Research, Development and Statistics Directorate.

Welsh, Brandon C. and David P. Farrington. (2004) "Surveillance for crime prevention in public space: results and policy choices in Britain and America." *Criminology and Public Policy* 3(3): 497–526.

Welsh, Brandon C. and David P. Farrington. (2008) "Effects of closed circuit television surveillance on crime." The Campbell Collaboration Crime and Justice Coordinating Group.

11 Spatial displacement and diffusion of crime control benefits revisited

New evidence on why crime doesn't just move around the corner

David Weisburd and Cody W. Telep

Introduction

More than fifteen years ago, Ronald Clarke and David Weisburd (1994) published a chapter that was to turn conventional thinking about crime prevention on its head. There was perhaps no more common assumption about crime prevention strategies than the idea that focused prevention efforts would simply "displace" crime to other "forms, times and locales" (Reppetto 1976: 167). According to this reasoning, focusing police, for example, on one place during a specific time period would simply encourage offenders to look for other ways or places to commit crime, or to shift their criminality to other times of day. Underlying the displacement hypothesis were specific assumptions about the nature of offenders and the nature of crime opportunities. In this model, which was predominant for much of the last century, criminal motivations were assumed to be very strong and the number of opportunities for crime in the urban landscape almost unlimited (Clarke and Felson 1993; Trasler 1993).

Clarke and Weisburd (1994) drew from a series of recently conducted situational prevention studies to argue that displacement was not an inevitable outcome of crime prevention, and that another phenomenon which indicated "the reverse of displacement" was a common outcome of focused crime prevention efforts. They defined this "diffusion of crime control benefits" as

> the spread of the beneficial influence of an intervention beyond the places which are directly targeted, the individuals who are the subject of control, the crimes which are the focus of intervention or the time period in which an intervention is brought.
>
> (Clarke and Weisburd 1994: 169)

While the idea of unintended benefits had been raised by others as the "multiplier" effect (Chaiken et al. 1974), the "halo" effect (Scherdin 1992), "free rider" effects (Miethe 1991) and "free bonus" effects (Sherman 1990), Clarke and Weisburd (1994) provided a more detailed explanation of the diffusion phenomenon and gave some possible reasons for why diffusion as opposed to displacement occurs.

The work has proven to be quite influential in the last decade and a half. A Google Scholar citation count search shows 140 cites of the Clarke and Weisburd (1994) article and a search of "diffusion of crime control benefits" comes up with 244 scholarly pieces that use the terminology. Thus, the terminology has fairly quickly entered the mainstream of criminology.

In this chapter, we revisit the issues raised by Clarke and Weisburd (1994), focusing in particular on theoretical gaps in the original paper. Much has been learned in the past fifteen years that can help us to expand and elaborate upon Clarke and Weisburd's original formulation. In particular we draw upon recent work on spatial displacement of crime that has been the focus of much research and theorizing over the last two decades (see reviews by Braga 2007; Guerette and Bowers 2009; Weisburd et al. 2006).[1] We introduce two new concepts to the displacement and diffusion literature. The first is linked to recent research on micro crime places that suggests a "tight coupling" of crime to place. In contrast to early assumptions about crime and displacement, which saw crime as easily moveable, this research suggests that crime is strongly connected to places and that this creates a natural resistance to spatial displacement. The second adds to Clarke and Weisburd's (1994) original propositions regarding the importance of deterrence and discouragement in encouraging diffusion (which as we note below are as well reinforced by recent research), by emphasizing the importance of other non-psychological explanations for the diffusion phenomenon. Finally, we raise questions about the ways in which recent scholars have understood the general displacement and diffusion processes, suggesting that it is important to distinguish what is happening in target areas from what is happening in buffer or catchment areas.

Crime displacement and diffusion of crime control benefits: a brief review of the evidence

Since 1990 there have been four main reviews of empirical studies that report on displacement: Barr and Pease (1990); Eck (1993); Hesseling (1994); and Guerette and Bowers (2009). All four reviews arrive at three basic conclusions.[2] First, there is little evidence of crime prevention strategies that displaced as much crime as was prevented. Second, displacement, when it occurs, is usually less than the amount of crime prevented. And third, for crime prevention evaluations that reported on displacement, the most common finding was that there was no evidence of displacement. In sum, most studies found no, or negligible, displacement of crime. Guerette and Bowers (2009) were the only to focus explicitly on the diffusion of crime control benefits, finding some displacement in 26 percent of the 574 observations from the 102 studies they examined,[3] and a diffusion of crime control benefits in 27 percent of the examined studies. Focusing only on spatial displacement and diffusion, they found that 37 percent of the observations showed evidence of spatial diffusion while only 23 percent showed evidence of spatial displacement.

One area where the evidence regarding displacement is particularly strong and consistent is spatial displacement as an outcome of hot spots policing. There is little evidence of displacement of crime to areas nearby targeted hot spots. Indeed, a series of studies suggest that there is likely to be a diffusion of crime prevention benefits to areas near to hot spots policing targets. In the Jersey City Drug Market Analysis Experiment (Weisburd and Green 1995a), for example, displacement within two block areas around each hot spot was measured. No significant displacement of crime or disorder calls was found. Importantly, however, the investigators found that drug-related and public-morals calls actually declined in the catchment areas. This diffusion of crime control benefits was also reported in the Jersey City Violent Crime Places experiment (Braga et al. 1999), the Beat Health study (Mazerolle and Roehl 1998) and the Kansas City Gun Project (Sherman and Rogan 1995). The Campbell systematic review on hot spots conducted by Braga (2001, 2005, 2007) examined displacement data for five of the nine eligible studies, finding that none reported substantial immediate spatial displacement of crime into areas surrounding the targeted locations and four of the five studies found evidence of a diffusion of crime control benefits.

These results must be taken with three important caveats. First, the amount of displacement depends, in part, on the type of intervention being used. Second, the amount of displacement also depends, in part, on the crime or disorder being prevented. Third, and most importantly, because most of the studies examined did not set out to examine displacement, it was rare that evaluators were able to use a methodologically sound research design for detecting it (see Weisburd and Green 1995b). This is the case in part because researchers must make decisions about the allocation of scarce research funds and resources. If, for example, a researcher is unsure about the direct crime control benefits of a program, it makes sense to invest in assessing the direct target effects rather than outcomes that are important only if a target effect is found.

More recently, a study by Weisburd et al. (2006) of hot spots policing interventions at drug and prostitution markets explicitly examined spatial displacement and diffusion as primary outcomes. The study employed analyses of more than 6,000 twenty-minute social observations at the research sites, supplemented by interviews with arrestees from the target areas and ethnographic field observations. Quantitative findings indicated that for the crime hot spots examined, crime did not simply move around the corner in response to intensive police crime prevention efforts at places. Indeed, the study supported the position that the most likely outcome of such focused crime prevention efforts is a diffusion of crime control benefits to nearby areas. We return to the arrestee interviews and ethnographic field work in this study below as they provide important insights into why place-based interventions may lead to a diffusion of crime control benefits as opposed to crime displacement.

Tight coupling of crime and place: why crime doesn't just move around the corner

What can help us to understand this growing body of literature that suggests that spatial displacement is most often inconsequential? In their 1994 article, Clarke and Weisburd focused in particular on the theoretical foundation for understanding diffusion of crime control benefits. That made sense in the context of their efforts to redirect thinking in this area, which was focused primarily on the idea of displacement. We think that more can be said on the processes discouraging spatial displacement, especially given recent research on crime hot spots, and crime places more generally. In particular, what we know about crime places suggests that crime is "tightly coupled" to place, and that the characteristics of places vary within small geographic areas. The terms "tight coupling" and "loose coupling" are used frequently in organizational studies of the criminal justice system (e.g., Hagan et al. 1979; Maguire and Katz 2002; Manning 1982; Thomas 1984). What we mean here is that specific characteristics of places and the development of human connections to place discourage the displacement of crime. The traditional displacement hypothesis assumes that offenders are not tightly coupled to places. Recent research suggests that offenders and crime are tightly linked to place. This tight coupling as we describe below is the key reason why spatial displacement does not represent a significant threat to place-based prevention programs.

Beginning in the late 1980s a series of studies suggest significant clustering of crime at micro levels of place, regardless of the specific unit of analysis defined (see Brantingham and Brantingham 1999; Crow and Bull 1975; Pierce et al. 1986; Sherman et al. 1989; Weisburd and Mazerolle 2000; Weisburd et al. 1992; Weisburd et al. 2004; Weisburd et al. 2009). Perhaps the most influential of these was Sherman et al.'s (1989) analysis of emergency calls to street addresses over a single year. They found that only 3.5 percent of the addresses in Minneapolis, Minnesota produced 50 percent of all calls to the police. Weisburd et al. (2004), using fourteen years of crime incident data in Seattle, found that only 4.5 percent of the street segments produced 50 percent of incidents, and less than 1 percent of the hottest street segments produced more than 20 percent of crime. Clearly, crime is not distributed randomly across place, and such concentrations suggest that there are factors that are linking or concentrating crime to place.

Concentration on its own, however, does not necessarily mean that crime is tightly coupled to places. For example, if hot spots of crime shift rapidly from place to place it would suggest a weak coupling of crime and place. However, a number of studies show that crime is not only concentrated at a small number of places, but also that these concentrations remain stable over time. Spelman (1995) for example, examined calls for service at schools, public housing projects, subway stations, and parks and playgrounds in Boston. He found evidence of a very high degree of stability of crime at the "worst" of these places over a three-year period. Taylor (1999) also reported evidence of a high degree of stability of crime at place over time examining crime and fear of crime at ninety street blocks in Baltimore, Maryland using a panel design with data collected in 1981 and 1994 (see also Taylor 2001).

A study conducted by Weisburd et al. (2004) not only confirms the concentration of crime at place, but also establishes that there is stability of such concentrations across a long time period. Using group-based trajectory analysis (Nagin 1999, 2005; Nagin and Land 1993) Weisburd et al. identified clusters of similar developmental trajectories in crime incidents over a fourteen-year period. They identified eighteen specific trajectory patterns in their data. The most important finding in their study was that crime remained fairly stable at places over time (see Figure 11.1). Indeed, while some trajectories indicate increasing or decreasing patterns, there is a remarkable amount of stability in the patterns especially for the most serious "hot spots" of crime in the city (see Figure 11.1, trajectory 17).

While crime is highly concentrated and these concentrations remain relatively stable over time, it is also important to examine the geographic distribution of crime across the city. If, for example, high crime locations were all clustered in the same area, then it would suggest that crime could easily displace within these larger areas. This is particularly important because recent hot spots policing and situational crime prevention efforts are generally focused on very small geographic areas. Groff et al. (2009) examined this issue by assessing the clustering of juvenile arrest hot spots in Seattle. Examining spatial dependence of street segments, they found tremendous street by street variability in the trajectory patterns of street segments. They conclude that "a great deal of the 'action' [of crime] is indeed at micro places such as street blocks" (Groff et al. 2009: 84), indicating not only that crime is strongly clustered but that serious crime locations are concentrated in specific places within neighborhoods or communities. Figure 11.2 illustrates this point, using the eighty-six most chronic juvenile crime street segments in Seattle as identified by Weisburd et al. (2009). While there is a clustering of these juvenile crime hot spots in the downtown area, the crime hot spots are

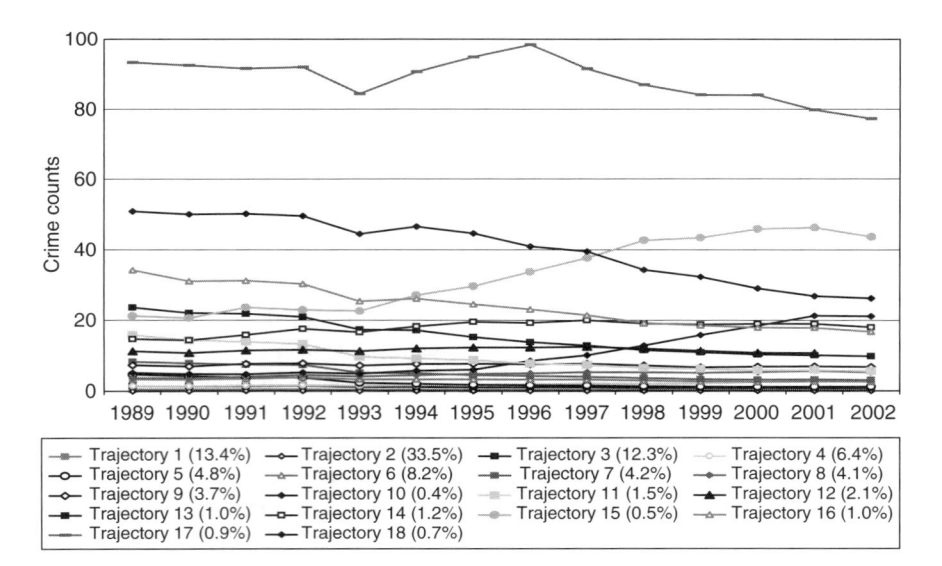

Figure 11.1 Eighteen trajectories of crime incidents in Seattle.

Source: Weisburd et al. (2004).

Note: The percentages in parentheses represent the proportion of street segments that each trajectory accounts for in the city of Seattle.

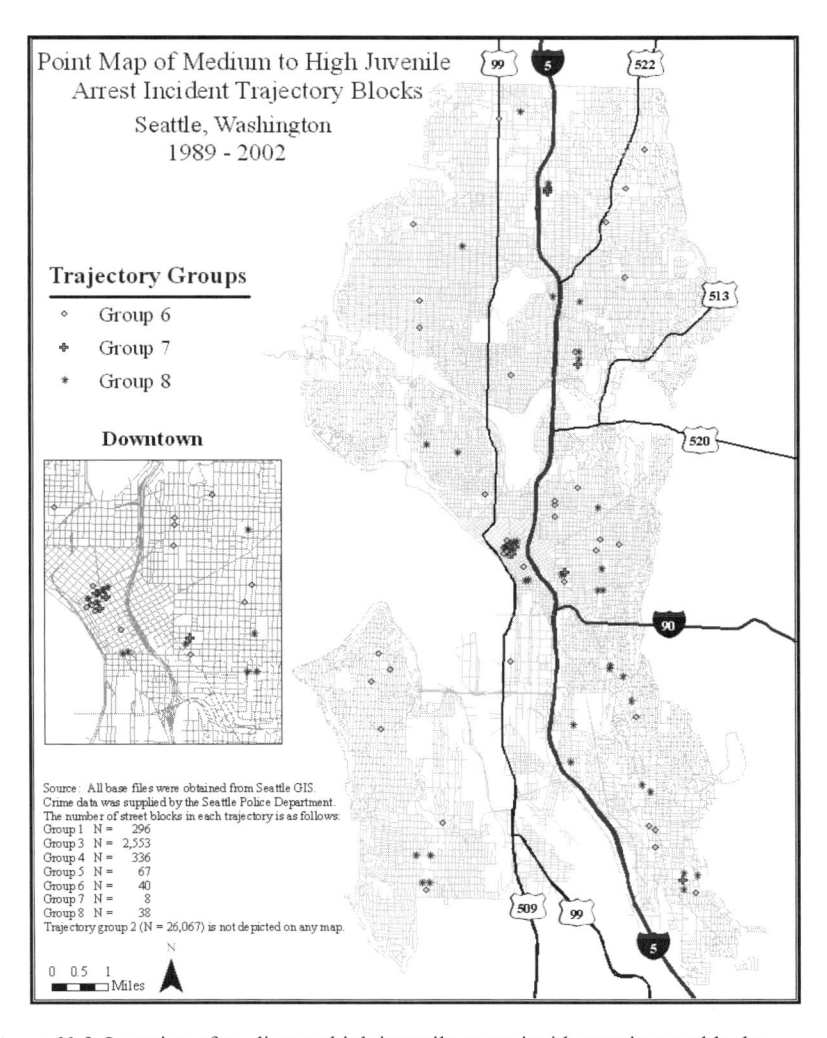

Figure 11.2 Location of medium to high juvenile arrest incident trajectory blocks.

Source: With kind permission from Springer Science+Business Media: *Journal of Quantitative Criminology*, Hot spots of juvenile crime: a longitudinal study of street segments in Seattle, Washington, vol. 25, 443–467, David Weisburd, Nancy Morris and Elizabeth R. Groff, Figure 4.

generally spread widely. And even in the central business district, there is significant street by street variability of crime.

Groff et al. (2010) explored this issue more comprehensively, examining temporal and spatial variation in all crime incidents across Seattle streets over a sixteen-year period. Groff et al. drew upon trajectory group patterns identified by Weisburd et al. (forthcoming). They then applied a variety of quantitative spatial statistics to the spatial arrangement of each pattern's members to establish whether streets having the same temporal trajectory pattern are collocated spatially or whether there is street to street variation in the temporal patterns of crime. Their analyses revealed a surprisingly high degree of heterogeneity in the temporal crime trajectory patterns of street segments. In other words, the temporal crime trajectory pattern often changes from street segment to street segment. This was apparent in both the descriptive map and in their finding that low stable street segments were "weakly attracted" to moderate stable, high increasing and high decreasing street segments, suggesting proximal places can have very divergent temporal crime trajectories. What varied from place to place was not the phenomenon of heterogeneity but rather the specific temporal trajectory pattern involved. Thus, it is often the case that high crime street blocks are in close proximity to street blocks with little crime.

The concentration and stability of crime at place, and the evidence of spatial heterogeneity, point to specific characteristics that couple crime to places. This evidence is reinforced by recent studies. For example, data from Weisburd et al.'s (2009) study of juvenile crime in Seattle provide strong confirmation of the relevance of juvenile activity spaces (Felson 2006) and routine activity theory (Cohen and Felson 1979; Felson 1994; Osgood et al. 1996) for understanding the very high concentration of juvenile arrest incidents at places. Weisburd et al. were able to identify where crime events occurred, and thus they were able to describe the activity spaces most associated with hot spots of juvenile crime. Incidents in the highest rate trajectories were most likely to be found at and around schools and youth centers, or shops, malls and restaurants. This means that hot spots of juvenile crime are likely to be located in places where juveniles congregate. Not surprisingly, given Weisburd et al.'s (2009) focus on juvenile crime, very few arrest incidents are found at bars, clubs and taverns, which are often hot spots of adult crime (see Roncek and Bell 1981; Roncek and Maier 1991).

Recent research by Weisburd et al. (forthcoming) that models trajectory patterns for crime incidents in Seattle over a sixteen-year period reinforces the strong links between situational and contextual opportunities for crime and crime patterns. The most important predictors of a street segment being a crime hot spot include the number of employees on the block, as well as the number of problem youth who live there. Weisburd et al. find that blocks with more employees (and assumedly places with more potential victims) and those with more problem youth (i.e. those with more potential "offenders") are much more likely to be in the most serious crime trajectory groupings. And they also find strong spatial heterogeneity of employment and problem youth patterns block to block.

Ecological theories of social disorganization used to explain crime patterns in communities (see Shaw and McKay 1969 [1942]) also link crime to place. For example, scholars have recently emphasized the importance of "collective efficacy" in communities as an indicator of a community's ability to realize common values and regulate behavior (see Sampson et al. 1997; Sampson 2004). Using voting behavior at the street segment level as an indicator of collective efficacy, Weisburd et al. find a direct relationship between collective efficacy and crime patterns.

As expected the chronic high crime trajectory segments have the lowest evidence of voting participation. And again, there is important heterogeneity in such characteristics at a very low level of geography (Weisburd et al. forthcoming).

These findings emphasize that there are strong links between the characteristics of places and crime at place. In this context, it is easy to understand resistance to displacement. For example, juvenile activity spaces are not found on every block but are located on a limited and specific number of street segments. Doing something about crime at a shopping mall is in this context unlikely to lead to spatial displacement because another shopping mall is not likely to be nearby. At the same time, knowledge about the tendency of offenders to stay close to home suggests that the problems at one specific place may not easily move to malls out of the neighborhood (Bernasco and Block 2009; Brantingham and Brantingham 1993; Wiles and Costello 2000). Potential victims for crime also vary block by block (Weisburd et al. forthcoming) suggesting that cracking down on a specific high crime block with a large number of employees will not simply shift crime to nearby blocks, which may be primarily residential. In turn, high collective efficacy on one street block that discourages crime would discourage crime movement from other blocks that are the focus of crime prevention efforts.

Returning to the Weisburd et al. (2006) study discussed earlier, we can identify not only characteristics of places that tightly couple crime to place, but also the specific nature of the human connections that are formed with place. In the case of market-based crimes, offenders have often worked for long periods to establish a specific place as a profitable area to carry out criminal activity. For example, a number of offenders complained in interviews about the time and effort it would take to reestablish their activities in other areas as a reaction to the police intervention. One respondent arrested at the drug crime site, for example, explained that it is difficult to move because the "money won't be the same," that he "would have to start from scratch," and that it "takes time to build up customers" (Weisburd et al. 2006: 578).

Weisburd et al. (2006) also show that one important explanation for the resistance to spatial displacement is simply that offenders, like non-offenders, come to feel comfortable with their home turf and the people that they encounter. In this case tight coupling is due to a very human desire for the familiar. As with non-offenders, where moving jobs or homes can be seen as an important and difficult change in life circumstances (see Holmes and Rahe 1967), moving crime locations is seen by offenders as uncomfortable. As one prostitute noted:

> I walked over (to the graveyard cemetery) . . . It was unfamiliar to me . . . I didn't know the guys (clients). On Cornelison you recognize the guys. I know from being out there every day (on Cornelison), the cars, the faces. It's different. In my area, I know the people. Up on "the hill" – I don't really know the people at that end of town.
>
> (Brisgone 2004: 199)

Moving to other places can also be dangerous, and offenders voiced fears of getting caught or being victimized in areas where for example, they don't know "who will call the police and who won't." One arrestee explained, "you really can't deal in areas you aren't living in, it ain't your turf, that's how people get themselves killed" (Weisburd et al. 2006: 578).

We think that the tight coupling of crime and place provides a straightforward explanation for why displacement is not a common outcome of place-based crime prevention. Simply put, crime does not move easily to other places because crime and offenders are "tightly coupled" to place. The displacement hypothesis is based on an assumption that people and crime are loosely coupled to place and will move easily to other places. The empirical literature on crime places suggests just the opposite. What is surprising in this context is displacement and not its absence.

But why diffusion of crime control benefits?

While the tight coupling of crime to place explains the resistance that has been found to spatial displacement, it does not provide a direct explanation for why a number of studies have observed a "diffusion of crime control benefits." Clarke and Weisburd (1994) suggest two processes that may be at work when a diffusion of crime control benefits occurs, deterrence and discouragement. Deterrence refers to situations where offenders overestimate the risk associated with a particular intervention, and accordingly avoid offending in areas not targeted by the initiative. Crime control benefits would therefore diffuse because of offender fear of arrest. Discouragement focuses more on costs and benefits and refers to situations where the police intervention makes the effort required to offend greater than the benefit acquired from the crime. This reward reduction can lead to a general benefit for a community that expands beyond the initial target.

An examination of the ethnographic field work and arrestee interviews conducted by Weisburd et al. (2006) reinforces the importance of deterrence in understanding the diffusion processes observed.[4] In interviews with offenders arrested in the target areas, Weisburd et al. found that they often did not have a clearly defined understanding of the geographic scope of police activities. Such understanding often improved in what might be termed a "learning curve" over time (Brisgone 2004). Nonetheless, the qualitative data suggest that offenders acted in a context of what rational choice theorists call "bounded rationality" (Johnson and Payne 1986) in which they made assumptions about police behavior that were based on limited or incorrect information. In this context, they often assumed that the crackdowns were not limited to the target areas but were part of a more general increase in police enforcement.

Support for this argument is found in a review of situational crime prevention studies conducted by Smith et al. (2002). Examining a phenomenon they describe as "anticipatory crime prevention benefits," they find that in about 40 percent of studies reviewed, crime declined before the intervention had begun. Smith and her colleagues argue that the crime prevention benefit in such cases can be traced primarily to "publicity" or "disinformation." They speculate that such factors as pre-program media reports about interventions, the visibility of preparations for interventions (e.g. the installation of CCTV), or "hearsay" regarding impending police actions, lead potential offenders to assume that the risks or efforts associated with offending have increased.

While Weisburd et al. (2006) focused more on deterrence than discouragement as an explanation for diffusion, Green (1995) suggests discouragement may provide an important explanation for the diffusion of crime control benefits she found in her examination of the Oakland Specialized Multi-Agency Response Team (SMART) intervention. It is important to note that Green's (1995) assessment (along with the arguments of Weisburd et al. 2006), is only speculative, because there has not been research on how to properly differentiate between deterrence and discouragement in understanding the diffusion processes. Green (1995) suggests that efforts in the SMART project sites to clean up physical disorder and change the appearance of drug crime areas may have led customers (and possibly sellers) to think their old buying location was no longer open. Improving the appearance of one part of a larger drug market may have sent a signal that drug dealing would no longer be tolerated in this area, leading to a diffusion of benefits beyond the targeted locations.

Similarly Clarke and Goldstein (2002) report the possibility of discouragement effects in their study of appliance theft in construction sites in Charlotte. After a group of builders began delaying the installation of appliances until just before home occupancy, appliance thefts dropped sharply among this group of builders, but also more generally among all home builders in the target police sector. Even though a large proportion of homes still had the appliances installed, Clarke and Goldstein (2002) suggest burglars may have been discouraged by the amount of effort needed to find opportunities for appliance theft.

Both discouragement and deterrence operate at the level of the individual offender. These psychologically based explanations derive from rational choice theory (e.g., see Clarke and Cornish 1985, 2001; Cornish and Clarke 1986). But we think it important to consider how crime prevention efforts affect the places and ordinary people in areas nearby those targeted. In this context, recent research and theorizing suggests other possible explanations for diffusion of crime control benefits.

In the 1994 paper, Clarke and Weisburd argued that diffusion of crime control benefits was not the same thing as the long-term developmental processes that led to crime control gains in "broken windows" theory (Wilson and Kelling 1982). In that case the crime prevention intervention (order maintenance policing) was meant to have a direct effect in the long run on more serious crime. This was not a case of diffusion of crime control benefits. Nonetheless, aspects of broken windows theory may be relevant for understanding how and why diffusion occurs. In particular, broken windows theory argues that intensive efforts by police to reduce social and physical disorder can reverse the breakdown of community social controls that accompanies untended and unrestrained violations of social order. Thus, crime is reduced in part because of efforts by the police and in part because of increased vigilance by community members.

Kleiman and Smith (1990: 88) describe the potential benefits of an intensive police effort to reduce drug crime and disorder by noting "a dramatic police effort may call forth increased neighborhood efforts at self-protection against drug dealing activity; given police resources such self-defense may be essential to long-run control of drug dealing." Although there is little empirical evidence on the topic, it is possible that this sense of community empowerment could spread beyond areas directly targeted by the police. In this case, a more widespread increase in neighborhood self-control could lead to a more widespread decrease in crime, and hence a diffusion of crime control benefits.

Mears and Bhati (2006) examined how resource deprivation in one community affects violence in neighboring areas (and socially similar but not geographically proximate neighborhoods). Although their unit of analysis is larger than our conception of place, their results suggest that neighboring communities can indeed influence one another. They do, however, explicitly mention the benefits of hot spots approaches and note, "the influence of an initiative aimed at reducing community disadvantage may have positive ripple effects that extend to other communities in geographic and social space, especially insofar as social networks and ties are not constrained by neighborhood boundaries" (Mears and Bhati 2006: 537). Thus a diffusion of crime control benefits could occur as residents in one small area communicate with those in nearby areas through existing social networks and ties about their positive experiences, potentially enhancing levels of social organization and collective efficacy in both places (although see Browning et al., 2004).

Taniguchi et al. (2009) explore why targeting illegal drug markets may lead to a diffusion of crime control benefits rather than displacement. Importantly, they also take a non-psychological approach to the issue, relying on the economic theory of "agglomeration economies." Applying this to Philadelphia they find that removing the largest and most profitable site from an illegal drug market will reduce the size of the overall market by making drug dealing in the surrounding area less profitable. The logic here is similar to the economics of the legitimate retail sector where closing a major department store in a mall may negatively impact the profits of smaller surrounding stores. As Taniguchi et al. (2009: 691) note

> eliminating an especially active drug dealing location is expected to have benefits for surrounding areas as well since the agglomeration economies of the place being known as the location to buy drugs is changed to being known as the location *not* to buy drugs.

While this has a similar outcome to the notion of discouragement, the specific mechanism explaining diffusion is more market-based.

Additionally, recent research in urban affairs and public administration is relevant to understanding why a diffusion of crime control benefits occurs. In a sense, this work brings together the ideas of community empowerment in an economic framework. Zielenbach and Voith (2010), for example, examine how the redevelopment of public housing projects in Boston and Washington, DC affected crime and property values in the surrounding neighborhoods. They find evidence suggestive of a diffusion of crime control benefits, although they were unable to assess whether the movement of some former residents led to displacement in other parts of the city. They frame these findings in the context of overall economic spillover benefits resulting from improved housing markets surrounding the newly developed public housing sites.

Thomson (2008) does not focus explicitly on crime reduction in his review of community development programs, but he summarizes a series of studies demonstrating that public investment to improve a small number of homes or buildings in an area, under certain circumstances, can spark more private investment that leads to a widespread improvement in the community overall – a phenomenon he refers to as the "multiplier effect" (e.g., see Galster 1987; Rothenberg et al. 1991). The idea here is that when residents see some public investment in their community they are motivated to invest their own resources into repairs as a result of this positive externality for the neighborhood. The multiplier effect refers to this occurring within a single neighborhood while the spillover effect refers to improvements occurring across neighborhoods. While these multiplier and spillover effects are traditionally measured using increased property values, they suggest similar processes might be at work in crime control. An initial allocation of public (i.e. police) resources may inspire residents to take greater ownership and control over their block or area. While a full review of the community development literature is beyond the scope of this chapter, research in this area is suggestive of processes that could be occurring in the area of crime prevention.

Distinguishing displacement and diffusion from target area impacts

These perspectives more generally focus not on offenders but on the contexts in which crime occurs in the areas near to intervention sites. This reflects an important distinction from traditional understandings of displacement and diffusion, which refer directly to the "movement" of offenders. For example, displacement is traditionally thought of as a process that results from offenders in the target area moving crime activities to other areas. Diffusion, in turn, is often linked to the notion that offenders who might ordinarily commit crimes in the target area and catchment area are discouraged or deterred from committing crimes in the areas near crime prevention targets. In one commonly used measure of displacement and diffusion for example, the "weighted displacement quotient," the amount of displacement is weighted against the overall changes in crime in the target areas (Bowers and Johnson 2003; Guerette and Bowers 2009). However, our discussion here suggests the importance of separating out what is happening in the target areas from what is happening in the catchment areas.

In their important review of displacement and diffusion in situational crime prevention, Guerette and Bowers argue that "it makes no sense to consider displacement or diffusion where there has been no scheme [i.e., direct effect on the targets of crime prevention] effect" (2009: 1349). However, following our argument it is possible to imagine displacement and diffusion effects when there are not direct crime prevention benefits in the target areas. This could happen for example, when the police bring an environmental or community intervention to an area that does not have the desired impact in the targeted sites but nonetheless impacts upon the dynamics or conditions in areas nearby. It may be in this context that those areas are more amenable to crime prevention outcomes because crime is common but not as chronic as the target areas. In this regard, Weisburd and Green (1995a) did not find a consistent and significant reduction of drug crime in the drug markets, but did find a diffusion of crime control benefits in areas surrounding those sites. Displacement moreover could occur even if there is no crime prevention benefit, similarly because the dynamics of nearby areas are affected. Certainly it is not reasonable to assume that changes in the numbers of crimes or offenders in areas around targeted sites are due simply to the "movement" of offenders after crime prevention initiatives. In this sense diffusion or displacement should be measured without reference to the specific effect of the intervention at the target sites.

Conclusions

Since the publication of Clarke and Weisburd's (1994) chapter on the diffusion of crime control benefits, we have witnessed an increased focus on issues surrounding crime displacement and diffusion and new research evidence further reinforcing the importance of diffusion as an outcome of place-based crime prevention efforts. Here we have provided an update on our knowledge base and explored reasons why spatial displacement is not inevitable and why spatial diffusion effects are found frequently. We have tried to expand upon Clarke and Weisburd's (1994) original article on diffusion of crime control benefits in two ways. First, we have argued that recent research on micro crime places provides a strong explanation for the resistance found to spatial displacement in existing studies. Crime does not just "move around the corner" because crime is tightly coupled to place. This coupling means both that it is difficult to move the site of criminal behavior, and that areas nearby often do not provide the same opportunities but often provide new dangers to offenders. We also show that explanations for diffusion of crime control benefits should expand beyond the offender-based psychological causes that were the focus of Clarke and Weisburd's (1994) original paper. Areas near to the targets of intervention may change as a result of crime prevention, and these changes can result in diffusion of crime control benefits or displacement, irrespective of the impacts of the crime prevention initiative on offenders at the targeted sites. This means as well, that scholars need to reconsider notions that see displacement and diffusion as simply an outcome of the effects of an intervention at target sites. We suggest that there can in this sense be displacement or diffusion with no evidence of direct crime prevention effects.

Notes

1 Our focus in part develops from the growing body of high-quality studies of interventions at crime places, often termed hot spots, reviewed below. But it is interesting to note more generally that spatial displacement has been the primary focus of research more generally in situational crime prevention. Guerette and Bowers (2009), for example,

found that of the 574 total observations of displacement in their review, fully 47 percent examined spatial displacement. The next most common focus of study was "offense" displacement, which accounted for less than a quarter of their observations. In turn, almost every study that they examined that looked at displacement included measures of spatial displacement.
2 A Campbell systematic review on displacement and diffusion in police interventions was completed too late for us to detail in our chapter. However, the overall findings follow closely those reported in earlier reviews (see Bowers et al. 2011).
3 Though it is important to note that in none of these cases was the amount of displacement greater than the direct crime prevention benefits of the program (see Guerette and Bowers 2009: 1346, note 12).
4 Another possible explanation for diffusion of crime control benefits in the catchment areas discussed by Weisburd et al. (2006) is "incapacitation." Many offenders were arrested in the target areas, and if these individuals were also responsible for crime in the catchment areas, we might expect observed crime and disorder to have declined in the catchment areas. However, despite the intensive enforcement activities at the target sites, many offenders remained active in these areas throughout the study period.

References

Barr, R. and Pease, K. (1990) "Crime placement, displacement, and deflection," in M. Tonry and N. Morris (eds), *Crime and Justice: A Review of Research*, vol. 12. Chicago: University of Chicago Press.

Bernasco, W. and Block, R. (2009) "Where offenders choose to attack: a discrete choice model of robberies in Chicago," *Criminology*, 47: 93–130.

Bowers, K.J. and Johnson, S.D. (2003) "Measuring the geographical displacement and diffusion of benefit effects of crime prevention activity," *Journal of Quantitative Criminology*, 19: 275–301.

Bowers, K., Johnson, S., Guerette, R.T., Summers, L. and Poynton, S. (2011) "Spatial displacement and diffusion of benefits among geographically focused policing interventions," a Campbell Collaboration systematic review. Available online at: http://www.campbellcollaboration.org/lib/download/1171/.

Braga, A.A. (2001) "The effects of hot spots policing on crime," *The Annals of the American Academy of Political and Social Science*, 578: 104–115.

Braga, A.A. (2005) "Hot spots policing and crime prevention: a systematic review of randomized controlled trials," *Journal of Experimental Criminology*, 1: 317–342.

Braga, A.A. (2007) *Effects of Hot Spots Policing on Crime*. A Campbell Collaboration systematic review. Available online at: http://www.campbellcollaboration.org/lib/download/117/.

Braga, A.A., Weisburd, D., Waring, E.J., Mazerolle, L.G., Spelman, W. and Gajewski, F. (1999) "Problem-oriented policing in violent crime places: a randomized controlled experiment," *Criminology*, 37: 541–580.

Brantingham, P.L. and Brantingham, P.J. (1993) "Environment, routine, and situation: toward a pattern theory of crime," in R.V. Clarke and M. Felson (eds), *Routine Activity and Rational Choice. Crime Prevention Studies*, vol. 5. New Brunswick, NJ: Transaction Publishers.

Brantingham, P.L. and Brantingham, P.J. (1999) "Theoretical model of crime hot spot generation," *Studies on Crime and Crime Prevention*, 8: 7–26.

Brisgone, R. (2004) "Report on qualitative analysis of displacement in a prostitution site," in D. Weisburd, L.A. Wyckoff, J. Ready, J.E. Eck, J.C. Hinkle and F. Gajewski (eds),

Does Crime Just Move Around the Corner? A Study of Displacement and Diffusion in Jersey City, NJ. Report submitted to National Institute of Justice. Grant No. 97-IJ-CX-0055. Washington, DC: US Department of Justice.

Browning, C.R., Feinberg, S.L. and Dietz, R.D. (2004) "The paradox of social organization: networks, collective efficacy, and violent crime in urban neighborhoods," *Social Forces*, 83: 503–534.

Chaiken, J., Lawless, M. and Stevenson, K. (1974) *The Impact of Police Activity on Crime: Robberies on the New York City Subway System*. Santa Monica, CA: Rand Corporation.

Clarke, R.V. and Cornish, D.B. (1985) "Modeling offender's decisions: a framework for research and policy," in M. Tonry and N. Morris (eds), *Crime and Justice: A Review of Research*, vol. 6. Chicago: University of Chicago Press.

Clarke, R.V. and Cornish, D.B. (2001) "Rational choice," in R. Paternoster and R. Bachman (eds), *Explaining Criminals and Crime*. Los Angeles: Roxbury Publishing.

Clarke, R.V. and Felson, M. (1993) "Introduction: criminology, routine activity, and rational choice," in R.V. Clarke and M. Felson (eds), *Routine Activity and Rational Choice. Advances in Criminological Theory*, vol. 5. New Brunswick, NJ: Transaction Press.

Clarke, R.V. and Goldstein, H. (2002) "Reducing theft at construction sites: lessons from a problem-oriented project," in N. Tilley (ed.), *Analysis for Crime Prevention. Crime Prevention Studies*, vol. 13. Monsey, NY: Criminal Justice Press.

Clarke, R.V. and Weisburd, D. (1994) "Diffusion of crime control benefits: observations on the reverse of displacement," in R.V. Clarke (ed.), *Crime Prevention Studies*, vol. 2. Monsey, NY: Criminal Justice Press.

Cohen, L.E. and Felson, M. (1979) "Social change and crime rate trends: a routine activity approach," *American Sociological Review*, 44: 588–605.

Cornish, D. and Clarke, R.V. (eds) (1986) *The Reasoning Criminal: Rational Choice Perspectives on Offending*. New York: Springer-Verlag.

Crow, W. and Bull, J. (1975) *Robbery Deterrence: An Applied Behavioral Science Demonstration – Final Report*. La Jolla, CA: Western Behavioral Science Institute.

Eck, J.E. (1993) "The threat of crime displacement," *Criminal Justice Abstracts*, 25: 527–546.

Felson, M. (1994) *Crime and Everyday Life: Insight and Implications for Society*. Thousand Oaks, CA: Pine Forge Press.

Felson, M. (2006) *Crime and Nature*. Thousand Oaks, CA: Sage Publications.

Galster, G.C. (1987) *Homeowners and Neighborhood Reinvestment*. Durham, NC: Duke University Press.

Green, L. (1995) "Cleaning up drug hot spots in Oakland, California: the displacement and diffusion effects," *Justice Quarterly*, 12: 737–754.

Groff, E.R., Weisburd, D. and Morris, N. (2009) "Where the action is at places: examining spatio-temporal patterns of juvenile crime at places using trajectory analysis and GIS," in D. Weisburd, W. Bernasco and G.J.N. Bruinsma (eds), *Putting Crime in its Place: Units of Analysis in Geographic Criminology*. New York: Springer-Verlag.

Groff, E.R., Weisburd, D. and Yang, S.-M. (2010) "Is it important to examine crime trends at a local 'micro' level? A longitudinal analysis of street to street variability in crime trajectories," *Journal of Quantitative Criminology*, 26: 7–32.

Guerette, R.T. and Bowers, K.J. (2009) "Assessing the extent of crime displacement and diffusion of benefits: a review of situational crime prevention evaluations," *Criminology*, 47: 1331–1368.

Hagan, J., Hewitt, J.D. and Alwin, D.F. (1979) "Ceremonial justice: crime and punishment in a loosely coupled system," *Social Forces*, 58: 506–527.

Hesseling, R.B.P. (1994) "Displacement: a review of the empirical literature," in R.V. Clarke (ed.), *Crime Prevention Studies*, vol. 3. Monsey, NY: Criminal Justice Press.

Holmes, T.H. and Rahe, R.H. (1967) "The social readjustment rating scale," Journal of Psychosomatic Research, 11: 213–221.

Johnson, E. and Payne, J. (1986) "The decision to commit a crime: an information-processing analysis," in D.B. Cornish and R.V. Clarke (eds), *The Reasoning Criminal: Rational Choice Perspectives on Offending*. New York. Springer-Verlag.

Kleiman, M.A.R. and Smith, K.D. (1990) "State and local drug enforcement: in search of a strategy," in M. Tonry and J.Q. Wilson (eds), *Drugs and Crime. Crime and Justice: A Review of Research*, vol. 13. Chicago: University of Chicago Press.

Maguire, E.R. and Katz, C.M. (2002) "Community policing, loose coupling, and sense-making in American police agencies," *Justice Quarterly*, 19: 503–536.

Manning, P.K. (1982) "Producing drama: symbolic communication and the police," *Symbolic Interaction*, 5: 223–242.

Mazerolle, L. and Roehl, J. (1998) "Civil remedies and crime prevention," in L. Mazerolle and J. Roehl (eds), *Civil Remedies and Crime Prevention, Crime Prevention Studies*, vol. 9. Monsey, NY: Criminal Justice Press.

Mears, D.P. and Bhati, A.S. (2006) "No community is an island: the effects of resource deprivation on urban violence in spatially and socially proximate communities," *Criminology*, 44: 509–548.

Miethe, T.D. (1991) "Citizen based crime control activity and victimization risks: an examination of displacement and free-rider effects," *Criminology*, 29: 419–440.

Nagin, D.S. (1999) "Analyzing developmental trajectories: a semiparametric group-based approach," *Psychological Methods*, 4: 139–157.

Nagin, D.S. (2005) *Group-Based Modeling of Development over the Life Course*. Cambridge, MA: Harvard University Press.

Nagin, D.S. and Land, K.C. (1993) "Age, criminal careers, and population heterogeneity: specification and estimation of a nonparametric, mixed Poisson model," *Criminology*, 31: 327–362.

Osgood D.W., Wilson, J.K., O'Malley, P.M., Bachman, J.G. and Johnston, L.D. (1996) "Routine activities and individual deviant behavior," *American Sociological Review*, 61: 635–655.

Pierce, G., Spaar, S. and Briggs, L.R. (1986) *The Character of Police Work: Strategic and Tactical Implications*. Boston, MA: Center for Applied Social Research, Northeastern University.

Reppetto, T. (1976) "Crime prevention and the displacement phenomenon," *Crime and Delinquency*, 22: 166–177.

Roncek, D.W. and Bell, R. (1981) "Bars, blocks and crimes," *Journal of Environmental Systems*, 11: 35–47.

Roncek, D.W. and Maier, P.A. (1991) "Bars, blocks, and crimes revisited: linking the theory of routine activities to the empiricism of 'hot spots'," *Criminology*, 29: 725–753.

Rothenberg, J., Galster, G.C., Butler, R.V. and Pitkin, J.R. (1991) *The Maze of Urban Housing Markets: Theory, Evidence, and Policy*. Chicago: University of Chicago Press.

Sampson, R.J. (2004) "Neighborhood and community: collective efficacy and community safety," *New Economy*, 11: 106–113.

Sampson, R.J., Raudenbush, S.W. and Earls, F. (1997) "Neighborhoods and violent crime: a multilevel study of collective efficacy," *Science*, 277: 918–924.

Scherdin, M.J. (1992) "The halo effect: psychological deterrence of electronic security systems," in R.V. Clarke (ed.), *Situational Crime Prevention: Successful Case Studies*. Albany, NY: Harrow and Heston.

Shaw, C. R. and McKay, H.D. (1969) [1942] *Juvenile Delinquency and Urban Areas. A Study of Rates of Delinquency in Relation to Differential Characteristics of Local Communities in American Cities* (revised edn). Chicago: University of Chicago Press.

Sherman, L.W. (1990) "Police crackdowns: initial and residual deterrence," in M. Tonry and N. Morris (eds), *Crime and Justice: A Review of Research*, vol. 12. Chicago: University of Chicago Press.

Sherman, L.W. and Rogan, D.P. (1995) "Effects of gun seizures on gun violence: 'hot spots' patrol in Kansas City," *Justice Quarterly*, 12: 673–694.

Sherman, L.W., Gartin, P.R. and Buerger, M.E. (1989) "Hot spots of predatory crime: routine activities and the criminology of place," *Criminology*, 27: 27–56.

Smith, M.J., Clarke, R.V. and Pease, K. (2002) "Anticipatory benefits in crime prevention," in N. Tilley (ed.), *Analysis for Crime Prevention, Crime Prevention Studies*, vol. 13. Monsey, NY: Criminal Justice Press.

Spelman, W. (1995) "Criminal careers of public places," in J.E. Eck and D. Weisburd (eds), *Crime and Place, Crime Prevention Studies*, vol. 4. Monsey, NY: Willow Tree Press.

Taniguchi, T.A., Rengert, G.F. and McCord, E.S. (2009) "Where size matters: agglomeration economies of illegal drug markets in Philadelphia," *Justice Quarterly*, 26: 670–694.

Taylor, R.B. (1999) *Crime, Grime, Fear, and Decline: A Longitudinal Look*. Research in Brief. Washington, DC: National Institute of Justice, US Department of Justice.

Taylor, R.B. (2001) *Breaking Away from Broken Windows: Baltimore Neighborhoods and the Nationwide Fight against Crime, Grime, Fear, and Decline*. Boulder, CO: Westview Press.

Thomas, J. (1984) "Some aspects of negotiated order, loose coupling, and mesostructure in maximum security prisons," *Symbolic Interaction*, 7: 213–231.

Thomson, D.E. (2008) "Strategic, geographic targeting of housing and community development resources," *Urban Affairs Review*, 43: 629–662.

Trasler, G. (1993) "Conscience, opportunity, rational choice, and crime," in R.V. Clarke and M. Felson (eds), *Routine Activity and Rational Choice. Advances in Criminological Theory*, vol. 5. New Brunswick, NJ: Transaction Publishers.

Weisburd, D. and Green, L. (1995a) "Policing drug hot spots: the Jersey City Drug Market Analysis Experiment," *Justice Quarterly*, 12: 711–736.

Weisburd, D. and Green, L. (1995b) "Measuring immediate spatial displacement: methodological issues and problems," in J.E. Eck and D. Weisburd (eds), *Crime and Place, Crime Prevention Studies*, vol. 4. Monsey, NY: Willow Tree Press.

Weisburd, D. and Mazerolle, L.G. (2000) "Crime and disorder in drug hot spots: implications for theory and practice in policing," *Police Quarterly*, 3: 331–349.

Weisburd, D., Maher, L. and Sherman, L. (1992) "Contrasting crime general and crime specific theory: the case of hot spots of crime", in F. Adler and W. Laufer (eds), *New Directions in Criminological Theory, Advances in Criminological Theory*, vol. 4 (pp. 45–69). New Brunswick, NJ: Transaction Press.

Weisburd, D., Groff, E.R. and Yang, S.-M. (forthcoming) *The Criminology of Place: Street Segments and Our Understanding of the Crime Problem*. New York: Oxford University Press.

Weisburd, D., Morris, N. and Groff, E.R. (2009) "Hot spots of juvenile crime: a longitudinal study of street segments in Seattle, Washington," *Journal of Quantitative Criminology*, 25: 443–467.

Weisburd, D., Bushway, S., Lum, C. and Yang, S-M. (2004) "Trajectories of crime at places: a longitudinal study of street segments in the city of Seattle," *Criminology*, 42: 283–321.

Weisburd, D., Wyckoff, L.A., Ready, J., Eck, J.E., Hinkle, J.C. and Gajewski, F. (2006) "Does crime just move around the corner? A controlled study of spatial displacement and diffusion of crime control benefits," *Criminology*, 44: 549–592.

Wiles, P. and Costello, A. (2000) *The "Road to Nowhere": The Evidence for Traveling Criminals*. London: Home Office; Research, Development, and Statistics Directorate.

Wilson, J.W. and Kelling, G. (1982) "The police and neighborhood safety: broken windows," *Atlantic Monthly*, 127: 29–38.

Zielenbach, S. and Voith, R. (2010) "HOPE VI and neighborhood economic development: the importance of local market dynamics," *Cityscape: A Journal of Policy Development and Research*, 12: 99–132.

12 Suicide and opportunity
Implications for the rationality of suicide

David Lester

Ronald Clarke's interest in this topic began with studies of criminal behavior, such as research on the impact of helmet laws for motorcyclists on motorcycle theft (Mayhew, Clarke and Elliott, 1989) and the impact of Caller ID on obscene telephone calls (Clarke, 1990), but he saw that the impact of the detoxification of domestic gas in England on suicide rates would provide additional research evidence in support of his position (Clarke and Mayhew, 1988). My interest in this topic stemmed from my involvement in suicide prevention and the role of strict gun control laws on the use of guns for suicide (and homicide) in the American states (Lester and Murrell, 1980).

Ron contacted me about collaborating on research on the topic, and we produced a series of studies on the impact on suicide rates and accidental death rates from reducing the toxicity of car exhaust and restricting access to firearms. We published these studies, as well as our individual research, in a book, *Suicide: Closing the Exits* (Clarke and Lester, 1989).

From the point of view of suicide prevention, the first question is whether restricting access to lethal methods for committing suicide, or reducing the lethality of available methods for suicide, will have an impact on the use of these methods for suicide and on the total suicide rate. It is difficult to prevent total access to a particular method for suicide. For example, the introduction of emission controls for car exhaust makes the exhaust gas less toxic by removing much of the carbon monoxide. People using car exhaust to kill themselves, therefore, require a longer time to die from inhaling the exhaust and may die from suffocation (that is, from a lack of oxygen as the air in the car is displaced by the car exhaust) rather than carbon monoxide poisoning. The longer time involved increases the probability that someone will come upon the suicide attempt and rescue the would-be suicide.

In rare circumstances, it is possible to make a particular method for suicide less available, as when the viewing deck at the top of the Empire State Building in New York City was enclosed in the 1940s (Douglas, 1996).[1] More recently, in some locations, bridges that have become popular sites for suicidal individuals to jump to their deaths have been fenced in to eliminate this opportunity. However, there are typically bridges nearby that have not been fenced in, and from which would-be suicides can jump.

The second issue in this tactic for suicide prevention is whether people prevented from using their preferred method for suicide will switch to an alternative method. This is called *displacement* or *substitution*. Clarke and Lester (1989) noted that this issue can be studied at the individual level and at the population level. On the one hand, at the population level, it seems likely that a population exploits or develops an alternative method for committing suicide when one method becomes less available. For example, although suicide using domestic gas declined in England after the detoxification of domestic gas, after a few years the use of car exhaust for suicide began to increase (Clarke and Lester, 1989). This can be seen as an example of *delayed displacement* at the population level. However, even this delayed displacement may have saved hundreds (or even thousands) of lives in the years spanning this delayed displacement.

On the other hand, individuals, if prevented from killing themselves at one point in time, may find other solutions to their problems and abandon their plan to commit suicide. For example, if a person who wants to commit suicide using a gun goes to obtain a license to purchase a handgun and has to wait a week for the license to be approved and issued, much may happen in that week to change the person's life circumstances so that he or she becomes less suicidal. After all, this is the rationale behind crisis intervention using telephone services. Getting the caller through a difficult night or couple of days may result in a reduction in the suicidal impulse. Putting a psychiatric patient or jailed inmate in a suicide-proof room prevents that person from committing suicide there and then.

A recent review of the research

Lester (2010) reviewed the research conducted on reducing access to lethal methods for suicide in order to see whether reliable conclusions could be drawn after thirty years of study. He reviewed research on the detoxification of domestic gas, the detoxification of car exhaust, fencing in bridges and other venues from which people jump, restricting access for would-be subway and train suicides, restrictions on medication, poisons and pesticides, and, in Canada, Australia and New Zealand, restrictions on gun ownership. He concluded that *severely restricting* access to a lethal method for suicide reduces its use for suicide. The research on the impact of the switch from toxic coal gas (with a high level of carbon monoxide) to natural gas eliminated the use of domestic gas as a method for suicide. Fencing in a suicide venue from which people jump to their death (such as a bridge or a subway station) removes that venue as an option for suicides. There can be no dispute about this.

What is the impact of *limiting* access to a lethal method for suicide? If car exhaust is made less toxic (through the use of catalytic converters that lower the level of carbon monoxide in the gas), but not completely non-toxic, does this have an impact on the use of car exhaust for suicide? If a strict gun control law is passed that does not greatly impact the level of ownership of guns in a society, does this reduce the use of guns for suicide?

Here the evidence was less clear. With regard to car exhaust, some countries experienced a decline in the use of that method for suicide as a greater proportion of cars were fitted with catalytic converters (such as the United States), while others did not (such as Australia). The evidence for the impact of a stricter gun control law is even more inconsistent, with researchers drawing different conclusions from the same data set. In general, the research suggested that, overall, limiting access to a lethal method for suicide (rather than eliminating it) usually reduces the use of that method for suicide.

The evidence regarding switching methods for suicide is also unclear. For some methods, such as the impact of gun control laws, the research is inconsistent. For other methods, such as the detoxification of domestic gas, the increasing use of car exhaust seems to have occurred in some countries. For a method such as medication or pesticide, restricting the availability of one substance often leads to an alternative substance (medication or pesticide) taking its place. This switch does not always occur immediately (as, for example, in the case of domestic gas and car exhaust in England), but it may occur eventually.

Law et al. (2009) used a natural quasi-experiment in the subways in Hong Kong where one system (MTR) installed platform screen doors (in order to reduce air-conditioning costs, as in Singapore) while the other system (KCR) did not. The doors were installed during the period 2002–2005. On the MTR system, there were thirty-eight suicides in the five-year period 1997–2001 but only seven in the five-year period 2003–2007. In contrast, the corresponding numbers for the KCR system were thirteen and fifteen, respectively. The reduction in suicides on the MTR system seemed to be present both for those with a psychiatric history and those without such a history. Suicide on the railway did not constitute a large proportion of the suicides in Hong Kong, and so the installation of platform doors did not impact on the total Hong Kong suicide rate. In addition, during this time, suicide by using the gas emitted from burning charcoal became very popular for suicide, and the total suicide rate rose in Hong Kong (Liu et al., 2007).

In order to explore this problem more thoroughly, it is important that research is conducted on individuals. How many people do switch methods as they make a series of non-fatal attempts at suicide? What are the most common switches in method, that is, if domestic gas or car exhaust is not available, do those whose who switch have a preferred alternative method? What distinguishes those who switch methods from those who do not? This research has not yet been carried out.

The answers to these questions are important when we consider whether restricting access to a lethal method for suicide has an impact on the overall suicide rate (using all methods combined). The research on the detoxification of domestic gas provided an interesting answer to this. Lester (1995a) found that, when domestic gas was a very popular method for suicide in a country (Northern Ireland, Scotland and Switzerland), then detoxification of domestic gas was accompanied by a reduction in the overall suicide rate. When domestic gas was an uncommon method for suicide in a country (Japan, the Netherlands and the United States), the detoxification of domestic gas had no impact on the overall suicide rate.

A broader view of making the environment safe

Wortley (2002) explored an environmental point of view, but he construed it broadly, focusing on any aspect of the environment that affects the behavior of individuals. Wortley was interesting in controlling the behavior of prisoners in jails and prisons, and so many of his examples came from that context. If the design of a prison makes it easy for a prisoner to break a glass object (such as a light bulb or a drinking glass) and to produce a glass shard with which to cut himself, then removing access to glass objects is an obvious way of reducing the risk of suicide by this method. But Wortley also considered the possibility that overcrowding in prisons may increase the level of stress and, in turn, increase the risk of suicide. Whereas the prisoners and the prison staff are conscious of the role of glass in the prisoners' suicidal behavior, they may not be aware of the role of overcrowding.[2]

Wortley noted that situational tactics are not long-term solutions for suicidal individuals. For example, once the prisoner is released from prison, the situational tactics for preventing suicide in prison are no longer relevant in the outside world. In Wortley's words, "situational intervention is about creating safe situations rather than creating safe individuals" (2002, p. 4).

There are theories of suicide that are based on an environmental perspective. For example, Lester (1987) proposed a learning theory of suicide in which he examined the roles of such factors as the punishment experiences of childhood, the failure of socialization, the positive and negative reinforcers for suicidal behaviors, contagion, modeling the suicidal behavior on that of relatives and significant others, cultural and subcultural factors, societal expectations about when suicide is appropriate, and societal attitudes toward suicide (acceptance versus condemnation). All of these factors would fall into the broad definition of situational factors consider by Wortley in his study of prisoner behavior, but they clearly move far beyond controlling access to lethal methods for suicide. Wortley also considered such situational factors as social influence (including conforming to, obeying and complying with the demands of others), atmospheric conditions and crowding. For prisons, the focus of his concern, he also included factors such as inmate composition and the turnover of the inmate population.

Wortley made a distinction between situational factors that precipitate or initiate a behavior and those that regulate (that is, inhibit or encourage) the behavior. Situational factors can present stimuli (or cues) that prompt individuals to perform a behavior, exert pressure on individuals to behave in that way, permit individuals to engage in the behavior, and produce emotional arousal that provokes the behavior. Controlling precipitators involves:

- controlling prompts;
- controlling pressures;
- reducing permissibility;
- reducing provocations.

Controlling regulators involves:

- increasing the perceived effort;
- increasing the perceived risk;
- reducing anticipated rewards;
- increasing anticipated punishments.

Wortley gave examples relevant to controlling violent acts by prisoners. However, examples can be found for suicide prevention. For example, the current discussion of suicide bombers focuses on how the indoctrination period of training exerts social pressure on the individual to go through with the act, a component relevant to controlling precipitators. The religious prohibitions against suicide and, in the past, laws prohibiting suicide, are examples of ways to increase the anticipated punishment for committing suicide, a component relevant to controlling regulators.

What if the tactic has no impact?

If restricting access to a lethal method for suicide were to have no impact on the overall suicide rate, is it worth restricting access to that method? I have always found this question odd because it is never asked in other areas of public health. Government agencies concerned with occupational health and safety remove all hazards from the workplace regardless of whether they save a few lives or many. A medication can be withdrawn if only a few people die from the side-effects regardless of how many people are saved from illness or death for which the medication was designed. In these areas, saving one life is considered to be important. For suicide, saving one life is rarely considered to be as important.

This point is illustrated by the objection to fencing in bridges from which suicides jump to their death because of esthetic reasons! I put an exclamation point at the end of that sentence because it is amazing to me that those who object on esthetic grounds put so little value on saving lives.

As we have seen, some critics of situational suicide prevention often bring up the possibility that people will switch methods for suicide as an argument for not fencing in the bridge (or restricting other methods for suicide). In the United States, the requirement that backyard swimming pools be fenced in to prevent accidents is not affected by the possibility that people may drown themselves accidentally in lakes, rivers and oceans. Making the environment safe is a worthy goal even if it cannot be made absolutely safe.

It is noteworthy that the major movements to restrict access to lethal methods for suicide have typically been made on cost or environmental grounds. The use of emission controls on cars was motivated by efforts to reduce pollution. The change from toxic coal gas to less toxic natural gas for domestic use was prompted by cost and pollution considerations. Preventing suicide was not a primary consideration. In contrast, efforts to reduce the widespread availability of pesticides have been motivated by efforts to prevent their use for suicide and accidental deaths.

Implications for a theory of suicide

Many years ago, Nilson (1970) published a book of cartoons about people hanging themselves. In one, a man is on his way to hang himself from a tree, but a black cat crosses his path on the way there, and he decides to abandon the plan since this is bad luck. In real life, would a person intent on suicide really be deterred by such an incident? The research on situational suicide prevention raises a similar question. Would a person seriously intent on committing suicide be deterred by having to wait a few days before buying a gun? Or would a person intending to use acetominophen (paracetamol in England) be deterred by having to go to several drug stores (chemists) in order to buy enough or by having to tear the pills out of blister packs (tactics used in England to reduce the use of paracetamol for suicide)? If the answer is "yes," then this has implications for a theory of suicide.

If some individuals would not switch methods for suicide if their preferred method for suicide was not available, what does this say about their intent to die? Would different variables precipitate suicide in those who would switch and those who would not? Would different theories of suicide be applicable to these two groups? If some individuals have a preferred method for suicide, what determines this preference? There is a great deal of research on simple demographic differences (by age and sex, for example) in those using different methods for suicide, but almost no research on the psychodynamics and personality of those choosing different methods.

At the aggregate level, Lester (1990) factor analyzed suicide rates by method over the states of America in 1980 and identified three clusters: (1) hanging, cutting and jumping; (2) gas and drowning; and (3) solids/liquids and firearms. A measure of social disintegration correlated only with suicide rates by solids/liquids and firearms, limiting the generality of Durkheim's (1897) classic theory of suicide. Thus, suicide by different methods may constitute different sociological phenomena. Might this be true also at the individual level?

The decision to commit suicide

Clarke and Lester (1989) discussed this issue. They noted that it is common to view "suicide as a desperate act, committed by seriously dysfunctional people at their wit's end" (p. 97). However, the research conducted by Clarke and Lester indicates that situational factors play a role in the decision to commit suicide. They argued that suicide was the result of a dynamic interplay between intrapsychic processes, including wishes (such as the desire to die), cognitions (such as hopelessness) and emotions (such as depression and despair), and facilitating situational conditions (such as access to lethal methods for suicide). Suicidality may, for some individuals, be a transitory state, and the risk of a person acting upon suicidal ideation may vary over time, although for others, suicidality may be a long-term (even permanent) and intense state.

> The judgment that life is no longer worth living, the decision to end it, and the choice of method may be interactive rather than sequential. For example,

despairing or depressed individuals for whom suicide is prohibited on religious grounds may gradually redefine their situations or find other solutions. Others may support their plan for suicide with thoughts about people who have found it the only way out, and may only give up the idea when they cannot find an acceptable method. Those who do identify a method may go on to develop realistic plans, including a detailed scenario of the place and time of their deaths . . . . [T]hey may carefully plan their funeral and the disposal of their belongings. Elaborate fantasies about the effects of their deaths on others may also be constructed. This mental preparation helps reinforce feelings of hopelessness and the belief that there is no other way out . . . . From this perspective, suicide is seen as an intentional act . . ., the outcome of a decision made with varying degrees of rationality and determination to end a life without hope.

(Clarke and Lester, 1989, p. 98)

In setting up telephone crisis intervention services, part of the rationale was that suicidal crises are often time-limited. Helping individuals in crisis to get through the night or the next few days may find them in a less suicidal mood later and, thereby, save their lives. Many suicidal actions (fatal and non-fatal) are made impulsively.[3] Let me give a few examples of research on this issue.

On the one hand, Kaplan et al. (1992) found that clinically rated suicidal risk was associated with impulsivity, as well as anger, depression, hopelessness, attraction to death and attraction to life (negatively) in patients seen at a military mental health clinic. For Israeli soldiers given psychiatric examinations, Koslowsky et al. (1992) found that suicidal risk was predicted by impulsivity, anger, violence and depression. Kashden et al. (1993) found that suicidal adolescent psychiatric inpatients had higher depression and hopelessness scores, and higher impulsiveness scores on one of three tests of the construct. They did not differ in problem-solving ability.

On the other hand, Schmidtke and Schaller (1994a, 1994b) found no differences between suicide attempters and psychiatric controls on measures of impulsivity (or on verbal or performance intelligence test scores). Female attempters were more impulsive than male attempters, and repeaters more than one-timers. Attempters did not differ from controls in rigidity, field dependence, dichotomous thinking, depression, hopelessness, anxiety or locus of control.

Psychiatric research indicates that impulsive suicide attempts are more common in individuals with borderline personality disorder (Keilp et al., 2006) and with post-traumatic stress disorder (Kotler et al., 2001) and in those who abuse alcohol (Suominen et al., 1997). Weyrauch et al. (2001) found that the number of stressful life experiences in the prior year predicted the impulsiveness of medically serious suicide attempts.[4]

There are many more studies like these examples, and this research has used a variety of measures of impulsivity as a stable persistent trait, including clinical judgment, self-report questionnaires and cognitive performance involving inhibiting initial responses, and this makes it difficult to draw a firm conclusion from the research.

Other research studies, however, have obtained data on the impulsivity of the suicidal act itself. Cheah, Schmitt and Pridmore (2008) reported the case of a young man who had misappropriated some money and lost it gambling, who was crossing a bridge one day. One-third of the way across, he began to worry about his crime. At the top of the bridge (forty-nine meters high), he decided to commit suicide and jumped. The planning process, therefore, took only a few seconds. As soon as he jumped, he regretted his decision. He assumed the "pin-drop" position, legs straight and toes pointed, and survived the jump. (Only three jumpers out of thirty-two had survived the jump in the past.) On examination, the psychiatrists could find no Axis I or Axis II psychiatric disorder. This serious suicide attempt, therefore, should have resulted in death and was clearly impulsive.

In a study of eighty-two individuals who had just made a suicide attempt, Deisenhammer et al. (2009) found that nearly half (48 percent) reported that the time between first *thinking* about suicide and their actual suicide attempt was ten minutes or less, while 74 percent said that the time between the *decision* to commit suicide and the attempt was less than ten minutes. Interestingly, the "impulsive" attempters did not differ from the "non-impulsive" attempters in a measure of trait impulsivity, indicating the irrelevance of paper-and-pencil self-report trait measures of impulsivity to actual behavioral impulsivity in the suicidal act.[5]

Simon et al. (2001) found that only 24 percent of their sample of attempted suicides were impulsive, but they defined impulsive as having five minutes or less between the decision to commit suicide and the actual act (rather than ten minutes as in the Deisenhammer et al. study). However, 5 percent spent just one second. The impulsive attempters in this study were more likely to be men, attempting suicide at night (between 7 pm and 7 am), using a violent method and not depressed.

In contrast, using a criterion of five minutes premeditation, Williams, Davidson and Montgomery (1980) found that 40 percent of attempted suicides were impulsive. The impulsive attempters were more often observed performing the suicidal act, thought they would survive, had a low depression score and experienced reduced tension as a result of the act. The two groups did not differ in the number of prior attempts, sex, alcohol ingestion, use of bottled as opposed to foil-packaged tablets, or modeling behavior.

It is important to note that methods for suicide differ in the impulsivity possible when using the methods. It takes time to die from inhaling car exhaust or from an overdose of medication. Many people change their mind about dying and call for help, or passers-by intervene and save them from death. In contrast a suicidal individual who has a loaded gun in their home can find it quickly and use it impulsively for a suicidal act, with a high risk of fatality.

Although this research on impulsivity in suicidal actions is interesting, the samples studied have been attempted suicides rather than completed suicides, and we need similar data for completed suicides, hard though it may be to obtain (since, obviously, they cannot be interviewed after their suicidal act).

The role of serotonin

The neurotransmitter serotonin has been implicated in suicidal behavior. Lester (1995b) found, after a meta-analysis of research studies, that attempted suicides, especially those using violent methods, had lower levels of the breakdown product of serotonin in their cerebrospinal fluid, as did those making subsequent suicidal attempts.

Research has shown that higher level of serotonin inhibit impulsive responding while lower levels are associated with increased impulsivity, disinhibited behavior, impaired learning and insensitivity to punishment cues (Cools et al., 2005; Manuck et al., 2003; Rogers et al., 2003). It would be of great interest to explore the levels of serotonin in those engaging in impulsive suicidal behavior versus those engaging in non-impulsive suicidal behavior and whether those taking serotonin-reuptake inhibitors (SSRIs) make less impulsive suicidal acts. Mishra and Mishra (2010) have argued that diet can enhance the levels of serotonin and, thereby, affect impulsivity, and they demonstrated this in people who had consumed a tryptophan-rich meal.[6]

Discussion

Becker (1962), an economist, suggested two ways in which people might behave irrationally. The first type involves random, erratic, impulsive behavior subject to whim. The second type of irrational behavior is inert, habitual and sluggish and a repetition of previous behavior. Lester and Yang (1991) noted that this matches a dichotomy in suicidal behavior. One view of suicidal individuals conceptualizes the suicidal process as an impulsive and acute episode (but not necessarily random). The other view is that suicidal individuals have a long-standing history of psychiatric disturbance, with deep-rooted psychological problems, a chronic series of external stressors and a history of multiple suicide attempts.

The existence of impulsive suicidal behavior raises the possibility that a large proportion of suicidal actions are carried out on a whim and, therefore, not subject to rational decision-making. The same conclusion seems to be warranted if the temporary absence of a method with which to commit suicide leads to the reduction in the desire to commit suicide. This has implications for the civil liability of third parties who may be found responsible for a suicide if they failed in their duty to prevent the suicide from occurring (Smith et al., 2008).[7] To the extent that some suicides are impulsive, and not foreseeable, this may make winning some liability suits more difficult for those who sue.

As Clarke and Lester concluded in 1989, suicide may truly be "the outcome of a decision made with varying degrees of rationality," and the research on the impact of restricting access to methods for committing suicide supports the proposition that, for many individuals, the decision to commit suicide is impulsive and irrational.

Notes

1 Despite the enclosure, a spiked ten-foot-high fence, a Yale university student jumped to his death on March 30, 2010, from the observation deck on the eighty-sixth floor.
2 Wortley's broadened perspective would encompass tactics such as taxes on alcohol, liquor outlet density, and a zero-tolerance law for drivers, all of which have been found to be associated with suicide rates (Lester, 1993; Carpenter, 2004), and especially youth suicide rates (Markowitz et al., 2003).
3 It should be noted that many non-fatal suicide attempts often result in serious and permanent physical harm to the person.
4 The impulsiveness of the suicide attempt was assessed using three items of Beck's Suicide Intent Scale (Beck, Morris and Beck, 1974): amount of planning for the attempt, final acts in preparation for the attempt and writing a suicide note. An absence of these three characteristics indicated an impulsive suicide attempt.
5 Eighty-three percent were alone when the idea to commit suicide occurred, and 87 percent were alone when they made the decision to commit suicide.
6 Tryptophan is a precursor to serotonin.
7 Smith et al. (2008) argue that most suicides are *not* impulsive.

References

Beck, R.W., Morris, J. and Beck, A.T. (1974) "Cross-validation of the Suicide Intent Scale," *Psychological Reports*, 34, 445–446.
Becker, G.S. (1962) "Irrational behavior and economic theory," *Journal of Political Economy*, 70, 1–13.
Carpenter, C. (2004) "Heavy alcohol use and youth suicide," *Journal of Policy Analysis and Management*, 23, 831–842.
Cheah, D., Schmitt, G. and Pridmore, S. (2008) "Suicide, misappropriation and impulsivity," *Australian and New Zealand Journal of Psychiatry*, 42, 544–546.
Clarke, R.V. (1990) "Deterring obscene phone callers," *Security Journal*, 1(3), 143–148.
Clarke, R.V. and Lester, D. (1989) *Suicide: Closing the Exits*. New York: Springer-Verlag.
Clarke, R.V. and Mayhew, P.M. (1988) "The British gas story and its criminological implications," in M. Tonry and N. Morris (eds) *Crime and Justice*, 10, 79–116. Chicago: University of Chicago Press.
Cools, R., Blackwell, A., Clark, L., Menzies, L. Cox, S. and Robbins, T.W. (2005) "Tryptophan depletion disrupts the motivational guidance of goal-directed behavior as a function of trait impulsivity," *Neuropsychopharmacology*, 30, 1362–1373.
Deisenhammer, E.A., Ing, C. M., Strauss, R., Kemmler, G., Hinterhuber, H. and Weiss, E.M. (2009) "The duration of the suicidal process," *Journal of Clinical Psychiatry*, 70, 19–24.
Douglas, G.H. (1996) *Skyscrapers*. Jefferson, NC: McFarland.
Durkheim, E. (1897) *Le suicide*. Paris: Felix Alcan.
Kaplan, Z., Bennebishty, R., Waysman, M., Solomon, Z. and Bleich, A. (1992) "Clinician's assessments of suicide risk," *Israel Journal of Psychiatry*, 29, 159–166.
Kashden, J., Fremouw, W.J., Callahan, T.S. and Franzen, M.D. (1993) "Impulsivity in suicidal and nonsuicidal adolescents," *Journal of Abnormal Child Psychology*, 21, 339–353.
Keilp, J.G., Gorlyn, M., Oquendo, M.A., Brodsky, B., Ellis, S.P., Stanley, B. and Mann, J.J. (2006) "Aggressiveness, not impulsiveness or hostility, distinguishes suicide attempters with major depression," *Psychological Medicine*, 36, 1779–1788.

Koslowsky, M., Bleich, A., Apter, A., Solomon, Z., Wagner, B. and Greenspoon, A. (1992) "Structural equation modelling of some of the determinants of suicide risk," *British Journal of Medical Psychology*, 65, 157–165.

Kotler, M., Iancu, I., Efroni, R. and Amir, M. (2001) "Anger, impulsivity, social support, and suicide risk in patients with posttraumatic stress disorder," *Journal of Nervous and Mental Disease*, 189, 162–167.

Law, C.K., Yip, P.S.F., Chan, W.S.C., Fu, K.W., Wong, P.W.C. and Law, Y.W. (2009) "Evaluating the effectiveness of barrier installation for preventing railway suicides in Hong Kong," *Journal of Affective Disorders*, 114, 254–262.

Lester, D. (1987) *Suicide as a Learned Behavior*. Springfield, IL: Charles C. Thomas.

Lester, D. (1990) "The regional variation of suicide by different methods," *Crisis*, 11, 32–37.

Lester, D. (1993) "Restricting the availability of alcohol and rates of personal violence (suicide and homicide)," *Drug and Alcohol Dependence*, 31, 215–217.

Lester, D. (1995a) "Effects of the detoxification of domestic gas on suicide rates in six nations," *Psychological Reports*, 77, 294.

Lester, D. (1995b) "The concentration of neurotransmitter metabolites in the cerebrospinal fluid of suicidal individuals," *Pharmacopsychiatry*, 28, 45–50.

Lester, D. (2010) *Preventing Suicide: Closing the Exits Revisited*. Hauppauge, NY: Nova Science.

Lester, D. and Murrell, M.E. (1980) "The influence of gun control laws on suicidal behavior," *American Journal of Psychiatry*, 137, 121–122.

Lester, D. and Yang, B. (1991) "Suicidal behavior and Becker's definition of irrationality," *Psychological Reports*, 68, 655–656.

Liu, K.Y., Beautrais, A., Caine, E., Chan, C., Chao, A., Conwell, Y., Law, C., Lee, D., Li, P. and Yip, P.S.F. (2007) "Charcoal burning suicides in Hong Kong and urban Taiwan," *Journal of Epidemiology and Community Health*, 61, 248–253.

Manuck, S.B., Flory, J.D., Muldoon, M.F. and Ferrell, R.E. (2003) "Neurobiology of intertemporal choice," in G. Loewenstein, D. Read and R. Baumeister (eds) *Time and decision*, pp. 139–172. New York: Russell Sage Foundation.

Markowitz, S., Chatterji, P. and Kaestner, R. (2003) "Estimating the impact of alcohol policies on youth suicides," *Journal of Mental Health Policies and Economics*, 6, 37–46.

Mayhew, P., Clarke, R.V. and Elliott, D. (1989) "Motorcycle theft, helmet legislation and displacement," *Howard Journal of Criminal Justice*, 28(1), 1–8.

Mishra, A. and Mishra, H. (2010) "We are what we consume: the influence of food consumption on impulsive choice," *Journal of Marketing Research*, 47, 1129–1137.

Nilson, B. (1970) *The Hanging Book*. New York: Holt, Rinehart and Winston.

Rogers, R.D., Tunbridge, E.M., Bhagwagar, Z., Drevets, W.C., Sahakian, B. and Carter, C.S. (2003) "Tryptophan depletion alters the decision-making of healthy volunteers through altered processing of reward cues," *Neuropsychopharmacology*, 28, 153–162.

Schmidtke, A. and Schaller, S. (1994a) "Impulsivity and suicidal behavior," in D. Lester (ed.) *Suicide '94*, pp. 142–144. Denver: American Association of Suicidology.

Schmidtke, A. and Schaller, S. (1994b) "The role of cognitive factors in suicidal behavior," in U. Bille-Brahe and H. Schiodt (eds) *Intervention and Prevention*, pp. 104–124. Odense: Odense University Press.

Simon, T.R., Swann, A.C., Powell, K.E., Potter, L.P., Kresnow, M. and O'Carroll, W.W. (2001) "Characteristics of impulsive suicide attempts and attempters," *Suicide and Life-threatening Behavior*, 32 (Supplement), 49–59.

Smith, A.R., Witte, T.K., Teale, N.E., King, S.L., Bender, T.W. and Joiner, T.E. (2008)

"Revisiting impulsivity in suicide: implications for civil liability of third parties," *Behavioral Sciences and the Law*, 26, 779–797.

Suominen, K., Isometsa, E., Henriksson, M., Ostamo, A. and Lonnqvist, J. (1997) "Hopelessness, impulsiveness and intent among suicide attempters with major depression, alcohol dependence, or both," *Acta Psychiatrica Scandinavica*, 96, 142–149.

Weyrauch, K.F., Roy-Byrne, P., Katon, W. and Wilson, L. (2001) "Stressful life events and impulsiveness in failed suicide," *Suicide and Life-threatening Behavior*, 31, 311–319.

Williams, C.L., Davidson, J.A. and Montgomery, I. (1980) "Impulsive suicidal behavior," *Journal of Clinical Psychology*, 36, 90–94.

Wortley, R. (2002) *Situational Prison Control*. Cambridge: Cambridge University Press.

13 Ron and the Schiphol fly

Ken Pease and Gloria Laycock

In this chapter we seek to locate Ron Clarke's contribution within the context of psychological understanding at the outset of his career, to illustrate how research since has buttressed the position he developed in the late 1960s, and diffidently to suggest a theoretical home for the prevention of crime committed by quasi-rational offenders by means of manipulating the situations in which crime is liable to occur. We take at least quasi-rationality on the part of an offender as a necessary condition of situational crime prevention (hereinafter SCP) efficacy. Without such an assumption, burglars would be as likely to enter the Pentagon as an unguarded warehouse, and as likely to attempt to rob a boxing champion as a seven stone weakling, and to rape in a public as a private setting. Whatever motivational state underlies crime, failing to match the act to the opportunity is unthinkable. Were such failures common, attempts at crime would be mostly capricious, typically unsuccessful and occasionally risible.

The first article authored by R.V.G. Clarke (the 'G' has been used and discarded apparently at random) published in a criminology journal appeared in 1966, the second, third and fourth (in the same journal) over the course of the next three years. The journal was the *British Journal of Criminology*. It is in the second, dealing with absconding from an approved school (Clarke 1967) that we discern the first stirring of SCP ideas. The summary reads as follows:

> The previous literature on absconding has concentrated on its deeper psychological motivation. . . . [T]he present research has demonstrated that absconding is also subject to environmental influences, which include daylight hours and sunshine. Other relationships between absconding and temperature, absconding and distance of the home, and also absconding and variables of the school regime were suggested by the figures.
>
> (Clarke 1967, p. 202)

This was the first public Clarkeian toe in the water of situationalism. Four years later we find Ron splashing around happily in the deep end of the pool, the topic again being, absconding (Clarke and Martin 1971). We read: 'The main finding of this research is that environmental factors seem to predominate in the causation of offending. Most of the variation in absconding rates between schools and between individuals is probably due to the influence of environment' (p. 95).

The environmental factors associated with high rates of offending included

1 recency of admission;
2 recency of holiday periods;
3 dark winter evenings;
4 unseasonal weather;
5 admission at busy periods.

One sentence is especially noteworthy: 'It is clear from all the research undertaken on absconding from approved schools that environment is of great importance in its *aetiology*' (Clarke and Martin 1971, p. 72, emphasis added). It is thus evident that Ron was, by this stage in his career, sceptical of the search for 'root causes' of problem behaviour. Describing environmental causes in terms of aetiology – as signal rather than noise – and not as incidental and unimportant sources of variance, was a crucial step in SCP thinking.

What happened between 1967 and 1971 leading to the much more fully formed statement of the importance of immediate environment? The first factor is a matter of record, the second speculative. Ron Clarke accords generous credit to a seminar given by Iain Sinclair on his work on the factors associated with the varying success of probation hostels in the desistance from crime and troublesome behaviour. Subsequently published as Sinclair (1971) this criminological classic identified the social climate of probation hostels engineered by hostel wardens and matrons (as they were then known) as crucial factors in resident avoidance of criminality. This work, cited by Clarke and Martin (1971), chimed perfectly with their own work on absconders. Clarke's subsequent collaborations with Sinclair and Jack Tizard (Clarke and Sinclair 1973, 1981, 1982, 1991; Tizard, Sinclair and Clarke 1975) attest to the similarity of their thinking and the degree of mutual influence.

The second significant shaping event of the period was the award of Ron's doctorate. His research was unsupervised, as was then permitted at the University of London for those who already had a Masters degree from the same university (how times have changed). Successfully defending the unusual prominence given to environmental factors in the causation of absconding was a defining experience. One of Ron's external examiners was the late Gordon Trasler, a man both saintly and conscientious, the emphasis of whose own work was on enduring personal differences as explanatory variables. McGuire's (1961) inoculation theory holds that the susceptibility of beliefs to change is reduced after they have been defended from attack. Gordon Trasler as interrogator of Ron's doctoral work thus holds an honourable position in the development of his thinking.

Work on absconding continued, with Laycock building on Ron's insights in her doctoral studies of absconding from Borstal (Laycock 1977), and others at the Home Office Research Unit looking at escapes from open prisons (Banks, Mayhew and Sapsford 1975). Neither of these sets of studies was then explicit about the situational emphasis that characterized their work, but with hindsight it was clearly there.

The next major landmark in Ron Clarke's development of SCP came in 1976, with the publication of *Crime as Opportunity*, a collection of three studies carried out under Clarke's supervision in the Home Office Research Unit. This would generally come to be regarded as the publication that launched the movement towards crime reduction by changing environments rather than people. While the conduct of the original research reported in *Crime as Opportunity* obviously accounts for the somewhat lengthy time gap after the absconding work, two circumstances made the Zeitgeist in 1976 particularly favourable to the message of *Crime as Opportunity*. First, the mid-1970s marked the zenith of the notion that 'Nothing Works' by way of rehabilitation. Lipton, Martinson and Wilks (1975) advanced a version of this argument in a book whose impact was increased by its publication being initially suppressed. In the Home Office Research series, a report conveying the same message (Brody 1976) was published as Home Office Research Study 35, *Crime as Opportunity* (Mayhew et al. 1976) being no. 34. Thus, received wisdom at the time was 'Put not your faith in penal sanctions.' SCP emerged at a time when it was most likely to be received with enthusiasm. Second, Clarke's research in the 1972–76 period had included detailed consideration of obstacles to the measurement of the efficacy of penal sanctions. The publications resulting from that (Cornish and Clarke 1972, 1975) give pause for thought about conventional evaluation approaches. Taking the two elements together, in 1976 there was pessimism both about how to measure penal efficacy, and (in so far as measurement had been attempted) pessimism about the efficacy achieved. Intervening in pre-offending situations offered a way of cutting evaluation's Gaudian knot.

Crime as Opportunity, besides being a landmark in SCP research, also marked the point at which Ron Clarke first engaged with the psychological literature on situational determination of behaviour that predated his career. Here we find his first citation of the Character Education Inquiry (Hartshorne and May 1928) and the more recent research and writings of Albert Mischel (see Mischel and Gilligan 1964). The Character Education Inquiry is described thus:

> Although underdeveloped within criminology, a situational view of crime has respectable antecedents in the work of Hartshorne and May . . . The results showed that a supposedly stable trait such as honesty was not consistent across situations but was influenced by immediate situational factors such as the teacher in charge of the tests or the amount of supervision given. Those who behaved dishonestly in one situation did not necessarily do so in situations which are even slightly different, and only a very small minority of children behaved honestly all the time.
>
> (Mayhew et al. 1976, p. 2)

In fact, the support that Ron gleaned from mainstream psychology in *Crime as Opportunity* represents the bare minimum of what was available. A full account of the debate about the balance between personal and situational determinants of delinquent or other behaviour would have to take in the early twentieth-century borrowing from Binet intelligence testing to develop 'defective delinquent differentiating tests' (Fernald 1912), and the persistence of such testing beyond, and in spite of, the Hartshorne and May work. It would also have to incorporate Burton's (1963) re-analysis of the Hartshorne and May data, which showed a very modest level of individual consistency across situations. Looking more widely, when *Crime as Opportunity* was written, the classic Robber's Cave experiment had been published for twenty-two years (see Sherif 1966 for the most readily currently available account, the original having been published in 1954). This showed the ease with which inter-group violence could be engineered by changing aspects of the situation. Stanley Milgram's demonstration that men from the New Haven community, aged 20–50, could be induced to administer severe electric shocks to others by simply being ordered to do so by an authority figure had been available since 1963. Solomon Asch's demonstration that people could be induced to make judgements that were palpably wrong had been made some twenty years before (Asch 1952, 1958). The first published account of the Stanford Prison Experiment had appeared three years before *Crime as Opportunity* (Haney, Banks and Zimbardo 1973).

So why did Ron Clarke not draw more widely on the social psychological literature that would have buttressed his emphasis on situational determinants of behaviour? Three reasons suggest themselves:

1. He did not know the literature. This is inconceivable.
2. He knew the literature but did not see it as underpinning the crime as opportunity work. This is almost inconceivable, given Ron's psychological background, his customary thoroughness, and the explicit parallels already drawn between the Milgram work and Nazi atrocities, and between the Zimbardo (2007) work and what would now be thought of as institutional violence. He knew the literature and appreciated its relevance, but discerned a gap yet to be filled, namely inducements provided *asocially*. The psychology literature to that point was overwhelmingly about influence exerted by people, not by places and things. The concept of affordance, which filled that gap, was still three years from appearance in the public domain. More of this later.
3. He knew the literature and appreciated its relevance, but saw its use as being at odds with both Home Office and mainstream academic criminology perspectives of the time. This is readily conceivable. Burdening the clear demonstrations contained in *Crime as Opportunity* with a review of academic work, however relevant, would lose the 'commonsense' feel of the work that particularly appealed to the police and to his Home Office colleagues.

These are the crudely stated alternatives. The writers think there are elements of the second and third of the reasons listed that contributed to the selective use of the available psychological research. We believe Ron had come to the recognition of the power of the situation through his absconding work, and only subsequently incorporated extant psychology in his argument for SCP as fundamentally important. Tactically, he was probably right in giving it only fleeting attention, the danger being that it would be perceived as overly academic and risked alienating the criminological community, which was happily aligning itself with sociology rather than psychology. This would have been a distracting battle not to be entertained. But crucially, it was about defining situations primarily in terms of the influence of people rather than places or things, and hence not of primary concern.

Opportunity is not a word that is used in the parallel psychology literature. Milgram's students were not looking for an *opportunity* to shock their fellows, nor Zimbardo's for an *opportunity* to bully theirs. Opportunity is a word that becomes relevant only after one assumes motivation. For Milgram, Zimbardo, Asch and Sherif, the issue concerned how many people could be induced to behave in unpleasant and/or incorrect ways. For crime reduction, the distribution of such acts across people matters less than how one can engineer situations that minimize the incidence of wrongdoing. From the perspective of crime reduction, it is simply realistic to assume that some of those entering a setting will be inclined or can be induced to offend. Crime reduction can also set aside the conventional distinction in the psychology literature between conformity (when someone is induced to do something they *didn't* want to do by manipulation of situational features) and behavioural contagion (when someone is induced to do something they *did* want to do by manipulation of situational features) and coaction (when people didn't care one way or another). Whether opportunistic crime is conceived as conformity, coaction or behavioural contagion or a mixture of the three is not something with which crime reduction practitioners need concern themselves. A rough analogy can be drawn with vaccination programmes. It may be of interest to know what proportion of people already have immunity to a pathogen, but a vaccination programme can proceed on the usually safe assumption that many people do not have immunity. The opportunity for a pathogen to make people ill can for most purposes be minimized by vaccination without ever knowing what proportion of people were vulnerable pre-vaccination. By assuming that which the earlier psychology had set out to demonstrate, by making the concept of opportunity central, SCP came as a 'plug and play' kind of crime prevention that required strong situational influences to be present, but that did not require detailed review of the earlier work.

After *Crime as Opportunity*

Ron Clarke's stellar career following *Crime as Opportunity* taken as a whole constitutes a remorseless demonstration of the range and power of the applicability of situational change in the cause of crime reduction. This is interspersed with brilliant excursions outside crime, primarily into the susceptibility of rates of suicide to the ready availability of means of killing oneself. These excursions (e.g. Clarke and Lester 1987; Clarke and Mayhew 1989; Clarke and Poyner 1994) could as readily have been published in psychology journals as in the criminology and medical journals where they appeared.[1] The consequence is that his work is not widely cited in mainstream psychology and economics even where it would significantly buttress arguments advanced. For example, consider the central argument of Zimbardo's best-selling (2007) book *The Lucifer Effect: How Good People Turn Evil:*

> Changing or preventing undesirable behaviour of individuals or groups requires an understanding of what strengths, virtues and vulnerabilities they bring into a given situation. Then, we need to recognize more fully the complex of situational forces that are operative in given behavioural settings. Modifying them, or learning to avoid them, can have a greater impact on reducing undesirable individual reactions directed only at changing the people in the situation.
>
> (Zimbardo 2007, pp. x–xi)

This is the vineyard in which Ron Clarke had been labouring for close on three decades. Clarke's work is not cited by Zimbardo. Psychology has neglected Ron Clarke. Is this because Ron has neglected psychology? Looking at his published work, 'psychol . . .' has not appeared in the title of something he has written or in the journal title where his work has appeared since 1987. His citations of psychological work have also been infrequent. So the buds of integration of SCP and experimental social psychology that appeared in *Crime as Opportunity* have not flowered. Does this matter? The present writers think it does, for two reasons. First, as noted above, it has resulted in the neglect of the Clarke opus in mainstream psychology. Second, it reinforces the insularity of crime research that has recently evoked the attempt at integration which has come to be badged as 'crime science'.

In what remains of this chapter, we will deal superficially with some developments since 1976 that can be drawn upon in situational crime prevention, and seek to identify promising routes for progress, incidentally defusing the criticism of SCP as atheoretical. Part of what follows is a development of a prescient chapter written by Richard Wortley some fourteen years ago (Wortley 1997).

Why SCP is a hard sell

The fundamental attribution error is, well, fundamental. Sometimes known as the correspondence bias, it would be impossible to demonstrate if situational determinants were not powerful, and furthermore it provides the reason why SCP is so often derided. Originally demonstrated by Jones and Harris (1967), a later elegant demonstration went roughly as follows. Ross, Amabile and Steinmetz (1977) recruited students in groups of three. They were randomly assigned roles. They knew and observed that the allocation was random. One person was assigned the role of questioner (Q), one the role of answerer (A), and the third the role of observer (O). Q had to make up some general knowledge questions that A had to try to answer. O was subsequently, and in confidence, asked to assess the relative intelligence of Q and A. A moment's reflection is enough to conclude that there is no way rationally to assign different intelligence ratings to Q and A. The situation was set up so that Q was in a position to display his/her knowledge but not his/her ignorance.

Q was not about to ask A questions to which Q did not know the answer! By contrast, A would show both knowledge (in the form of right answers) and ignorance (in the form of wrong answers). So it was exclusively the *situation* that dictated performance differences. Yet typically people assigned higher intelligence to Q. The tendency to overstate the role of the person and understate the role of the situation in determining performance is the fundamental attribution error. The sting in the tail of the fundamental attribution error is that its existence will serve to mask recognition of its existence. That is to say, because people attribute performance to attributes of the person, they will be sceptical about the scope for manipulation of the situation to have much impact on performance. In so far as this is so, SCP is doomed to inhabit the margins of criminological thought, kept there by a well-understood and pervasive but erroneous habit of thought, the fundamental attribution error. Ashworth et al. (1984) suggest how this plays out in the courtroom. They found most judges believe that the factors that predominantly inhibit most people from committing crimes are moral beliefs and fear of social stigma, both personal rather than situational factors. A study on which the first author has just embarked concerns the expression of judicial causal thinking manifest in guideline judgements. This strongly supports the notion that dispositions are seen as central, situations as peripheral in assigning blame. Some debiasing suggestions have been made, but as yet without empirical support of which the writers are aware.

To restate the central reason for citing the fundamental attribution error as an important aspect of SCP promulgation: acceptance of SCP goes against the cognitive grain. To persuade policy-makers of the merits of SCP, ways must be found to neutralize the fundamental attribution error in their (and our) thinking. One promising route towards this lies in the fact that the fundamental attribution error is absent when we consider our own behaviour. We are happy to acknowledge situational determinants of our own peccadilloes! I am bad-tempered because I slept badly. He is bad-tempered because he is that sort of person.

The call of the baseball bat

Just too late for citation in *Crime as Opportunity* came J.J. Gibson's classic statement of the concept of affordance (Gibson 1977). Affordance refers to the perceived interactive possibilities of an object. The baseball bat is perceived as an assaultive weapon even in countries where baseball is seldom played, and is a commonly used weapon in the USA, causing severe injuries (Groleau et al. 1993). The first writer initially mused on notions of affordance when doing participant observation in a probation hostel. A disagreement escalated, and one resident picked up a heavy glass ashtray and used it as a weapon. The shock was not that violence had arisen. That was common. It was that the ashtray afforded use as a weapon. In the wake of the Dunblane massacre of schoolchildren, Prince Philip was sceptical of the call to ban certain firearms, opining 'If a cricketer, for instance, suddenly decided to go into a school and batter a lot of people to death with a cricket bat, which he could do very easily, I mean, are you going to ban cricket bats?'[2] Setting aside the lack of equivalence of the weapon comparison (cricket bats and guns), there is a serious affordance point to be made.[3] This is sometimes known as the weapon priming effect (Bartholemew et al. 2004).

While the fact that opportunity is a perception has always been implicit in Ron Clarke's writings, the explicit use of the affordance concept has only recently featured in the writings of those influenced by Clarke (Garwood 2011; Ekblom and Sidebottom 2008). In mainstream design it has featured more prominently (see e.g. Norman 1998, 1999). There is surely rich promise in crime-reductive design approaches that address affordance in both crime and prosocial behaviour (see e.g. Liljenquist, Zhong and Galinsky 2010).

Nudgeability

The discussion so far has established the extent to which situational factors determine behaviour, and the psychological obstacles to general recognition of that fact. Neither of these directly demonstrates behaviour change. Ron's work certainly does. What other recent work illustrates that behaviour can be changed by modest situational changes? What degree of leverage can one exert on a behaviour of concern by changing aspects of the immediate environment that are susceptible to change? On this point, the evidence is clear that modest changes can have significant effects. This is most lucidly expressed in the recent popular book *Nudge* (Thaler and Sunstein 2008).

The poster boy for the nudgeability thesis is the Schiphol fly. An image of a fly in the urinals of Schiphol airport led to spillage reductions of some 80 per cent. The bane of so many women's lives, the inaccuracy of urinary aim of the males in their home, was largely remedied not by admonition, but by the irresistibility of aiming for the fly. The Schiphol fly nudges. In contexts as diverse as the choice of retirement plans and the selection of healthy foods in self-service restaurants, they show how trivial changes in the presenting environment can yield substantial changes in behaviour. Thaler and Sunstein are economists. The word crime does not appear in the index among the topics, nor Ron Clarke among the names, but Thaler and Sunstein do provide a theoretical frame for situational crime prevention, to which Ron Clarke could subscribe. Paul Knapper (2009) has also recognized the relevant potential linkages between SCP and social policy.

Thaler and Sunstein speak of choice architects. We are all choice architects, recognized or otherwise, when we organize the context in which people make decisions. By making domestic gas supplies non-toxic or mandating catalytic converters, we change the self-harm choices available. By introducing Caller-ID systems, we shape the decisions of those making obscene or nuisance calls. By delaying the delivery of white goods to new homes, we change the decision-making of those who might steal them. Thaler and Sunstein justify the purposive use of choice architecture by reference to what they term libertarian paternalism. They summarize the perspective as follows:

> The libertarian aspect lies in the straightforward insistence that, in general, people should be free to do what they like. . . . The paternalistic aspect lies in

the claim that it is legitimate for choice architects to try and influence people's behaviour in order to make their lives longer, healthier, and better. . . . Drawing on some well-established findings in social science, we show that in many cases, individuals make pretty bad decisions.

(Thaler and Sunstein 2008, pp. 5–6)

An example given by Thaler and Sunstein serves to establish the point. Their friendly choice architect directs food services for a large city school system. She found that by placing healthy foods at eye level in self-service displays, she could increase their consumption by up to 25 per cent. The options she was thereby faced with as choice architect was to:

1 display for optimum health;
2 display for maximum profit;
3 display to mirror existing student choice (itself of course shaped by layout);
4 display randomly.

Readers of Naomi Klein's *No Logo* (2000) will already be familiar with the commercial pressures on school food services. We are not told what the service provider described by Thaler and Sunstein chose to do, but having described her as honourable and honest, we can at least guess what she did not do.

So we have a theoretical home into which to place SCP. It has the advantage of fitting comfortably, and promising to be influential. (Cass Sunstein is currently seconded to a job in the Obama administration, and those observing President Obama's health reform agenda will discern the influence of nudge thinking.)

What are the well-established findings in social science to which Thaler and Sunstein refer? They concern research on the fundamental attribution error, and related cognitive biases whose common feature is the manipulability of human decision-making by subtle variations in how situations are framed.[4] This completes the circle of scholarship and influence to which SCP is currently and regrettably marginal, despite the huge, admirable, original and often elegant research of Ron Clarke. The demonstration that legally restricting the number of tablets in paracetamol packets reduces their use in suicide (Hawton et al. 2001) is quintessentially Clarkeian, but lacks references to Ron's work on suicide.

A rapprochement between his own body of work and parallel advances in other disciplines seems the best way of ensuring that Ron Clarke's work is accorded its rightful place in both scholarship and crime policy. The examples chosen in the foregoing as potential points of contact scratch the surface of what is available and heuristically tempting. Braver writers might have included examples of situational control of threats by non-human species, and compared the typologies of risk and responses to risk in Ron Clarke's work and in that of Geerat Vermeij (2009). E.M. Forster's injunction in *Howards End* was 'Only Connect'. This should be taken seriously in the burgeoning discipline of crime science, to advance understanding and to acknowledge Ron Clarke's role in that advance.

Notes

1 The sole publication on the topic placed in a psychology journal is Clarke and Lester (1986).
2 See http://listverse.com/2007/09/11/top-15-quotes-of-prince-philip/ accessed 3 November 2009.
3 Cricket bats do not evoke violent images in the way that baseball bats do. Cricket bats are used in assaults, but rarely. Googling 'cricket bat assaults' and 'baseball bat assaults' will support the point.
4 We hope the reader forgives the burst of hubris that follows. The first author, with Catherine Fitzmaurice (Fitzmaurice and Pease 1986), sought and failed to introduce discussion of these effects to criminology some thirty years ago.

References

Asch, S.E. (1952) *Social Psychology*. Englewood Cliffs, NJ: Prentice-Hall.
Asch, S.E. (1958) 'Effects of group pressures upon modification and distortion of judgements'. In Maccoby, E.J., Newcomb, T.M. and Hartley, E.L. (eds) *Readings in Social Psychology* (3rd edn). New York: Holt.
Ashworth, A., Genders, E., Mansfield, G., Peay, J. and Player, A. (1984) *Sentencing in the Crown Court: Report of an Exploratory Study*. Oxford: Centre for Criminological Research Occasional Paper 10.
Banks, C., Mayhew, P. and Sapsford, R. (1975) *Absconding from Open Prisons*. Home Office Research Study 26. London: HMSO.
Bartholemew, B.D., Anderson, C.A., Carnagey, N.L. and Benjamin, A.J. Jr (2004) 'Interactive effects of life experience and situational cues on aggression: the weapons priming effect on hunters and non-hunters'. *Journal of Experimental Social Psychology*, 41, 48–60.
Brody, S.R. (1976) *The Effectiveness of Sentencing*. Home Office Research Study 35. London: HMSO.
Burton, R.V. (1963) 'Generality of honesty reconsidered'. *Psychological Review*, 70, 481–99.
Clarke, R.V.G. (1967) 'Seasonal and other environmental aspects of absconding by Approved School Boys'. *British Journal of Criminology*, 7, 195–202.
Clarke, R.V. and Lester, D. (1986) 'Detoxification of motor vehicle exhaust and suicide'. *Psychological Reports*, 59, 1034.
Clarke, R.V. and Lester, D. (1987) 'Toxicity of car exhausts and opportunity for suicide: comparison between Britain and the United States'. *Journal of Epidemiology and Community Health*, 41, 114–20.
Clarke, R.V. and Martin, D.N. (1971) *Absconding from Approved Schools*. Home Office Research Study No. 12. London: HMSO.
Clarke, R.V. and Mayhew, P. (1989) 'Crime as opportunity: a note on domestic gas suicide in Britain and the Netherlands'. *British Journal of Criminology*, 29, 35–46.
Clarke, R.V. and Poyner, B. (1994) 'Preventing suicide on the London Underground'. *Social Science and Medicine*, 38(3), 443–6.
Clarke, R.V.G. and Sinclair, I.A.C. (1973) 'Acting-out behavior and its significance for the residential treatment of delinquents'. *Journal of Child Psychology and Psychiatry*, 14, 283–91.
Clarke, R.V.G. and Sinclair, I.A.C. (1981) 'Cross-institutional designs'. In Goldberg, T. (ed.) *Evaluation Research*. London: Heinemann.

Clarke, R.V.G. and Sinclair, I.A.C. (1982) 'Predicting, treating and explaining delinquency: the lessons from research on institutions'. In Feldman, P. (ed.) *Developments in the Study of Criminal Behavior*. Vol. I. The Prevention and Control of Offending. London and New York: Wiley.

Clarke, R.V.G. and Sinclair, I.A.C. (1991) 'Studies of residential environments: lessons from the past and pointers to the future'. In Bebbington, P. E. (ed.) *Social Psychiatry: Theory, Methodology and Practice*. New Brunswick, NJ: Transaction Publishers.

Cornish, D.B. and Clarke, R.V.G. (1972) *The Controlled Trial in Institutional Research*. Home Office Research Studies No. 15. London: HMSO.

Cornish, D.B. and Clarke, R.V.G. (1975) *Residential Treatment and its Effects on Delinquency*. Home Office Research Studies No. 32. London: HMSO.

Ekblom, P. and Sidebottom, A. (2008) 'What do you mean "is it secure"? Redesigning language to be fit for the task of assessing the security of domestic and personal electronic goods'. *European Journal of Criminal Policy Research*, 14, 61–87.

Fernald, G.G. (1912) 'The defective delinquent class differentiating tests'. *American Journal of Insanity*, 68, 523–94.

Fitzmaurice, C. and Pease, K. (1986) *The Psychology of Judicial Sentencing*. Manchester: Manchester University Press.

Garwood, J. (2011) 'A quasi-experimental investigation of self-reported offending and perception of criminal opportunity in undergraduate students'. *Security Journal*, 24, 37–51.

Gibson, J.J. (1977) 'The theory of affordances'. In Shaw, R. and Bransford, J. (eds) *Perceiving, Acting and Knowing: Toward an Ecological Psychology*. Hillsdale, NJ: Lawrence Erlbaum.

Groleau, G.A., Tso, E.L., Olshaker, J.S., Barish, R.A. and Leaston, D.J. (1993) 'Baseball bat assault injuries'. *The Journal of Trauma*, 34, 110–23.

Haney, C., Banks, C. and Zimbardo, P. (1973) 'Interpersonal dynamics in a simulated prison'. *International Journal of Criminology and Penology*, 1, 69–97.

Hartshorne, H. and May, M.A. (1928) *Studies in Deceit*. New York: Macmillan.

Hawton, K., Townsend, E., Deeks, J., Appleby, L., Gunnell, D., Bennewith, O. and Cooper, J. (2001) 'Effects of legislation restricting pack sizes of paracetamol and salicylate on self-poisoning in the United Kingdom: before and after study'. *British Medical Journal*, 322, 1–7.

Jones, E.E. and Harris, V.A. (1967) 'The attribution of attitudes'. *Journal of Experimental Social Psychology*, 3, 1–24.

Klein, N. (2000) *No Logo: Taking Aim at the Brand Bullies*. Toronto: A.A. Knopf.

Knapper, P. (2009) 'How situational crime prevention contributes to social welfare'. *Liverpool Law Review*, 30, 57–75.

Laycock, G.K. (1977) *Absconding from Borstals*. Home Office Research Study 41. London: HMSO.

Liljenquist, K., Zhong, C.-B. and Galinsky, A. (2010) 'The smell of virtue: clean scents promote reciprocity and charity.' *Psychological Science*, 1–3.

Lipton, D., Martinson, R. and Wilks, J. (1975) *Effectiveness of Correctional Treatment – A Survey of Treatment Evaluation Studies*. Springfield, MA: Praeger.

Mayhew, P., Clarke, R.V.G., Sturman, A. and Hough, J.M. (1976) *Crime as Opportunity*. Home Office Research Study 34. London: HMSO.

McGuire, W. (1961) 'Resistance to persuasion conferred by active and passive prior refutation of the same and alternative counterarguments'. *Journal of Abnormal and Social Psychology*, 63, 326–32.

Milgram, S. (1963) 'Behavioural study of obedience'. *Journal of Abnormal and Social Psychology*, 67, 371–8.
Mischel, W. and Gilligan, C. (1964) 'Delay of gratification, motivation for the prohibited gratification, and responses to temptation'. *Journal of Abnormal and Social Psychology*, 69, 411–17.
Norman, D.A. (1998) *The Design of Everyday Things*. London: MIT Press.
Norman, D.A. (1999) 'Affordance, conventions and design'. *Interaction*, 6, 38–43.
Ross, L., Amabile, T.M. and Steinmetz, J.L. (1977) 'Social roles, social control and biases in social perception processes'. *Journal of Personality and Social Psychology*, 35, 485–94.
Sherif, M. (1966) *In Common Predicament: Social Psychology of Intergroup Conflict and Cooperation*. Boston: Houghton-Mifflin.
Sinclair, I.A.C. (1971) *Hostels for Probationers*. Home Office Research Study No. 6. London: HMSO.
Thaler, R. and Sunstein, C.R. (2008) *Nudge*. London: Penguin.
Tizard, J., Sinclair, I.A.C. and Clarke, R.V.G. (1975) *Varieties of Residential Experience*. London: Routledge and Kegan Paul.
Vermeij, G. (2009) 'Security, unpredictability and evolution'. In Sagarin, R.D. and Taylor, T. (eds) *Natural Security*. London: University of California Press.
Wortley, R. (1997) 'Reconsidering the Role of opportunity in situational crime prevention'. In Newman, G. et al. (eds) *Rational Choice and Situational Crime Prevention*. Aldershot: Ashgate.
Zimbardo, P. (2007) *The Lucifer Effect: How Good People Turn Evil*. London: Rider.

14 Exploring the person–situation interaction in situational crime prevention

Richard Wortley

The enduring contribution that Ron Clarke has made to the field of crime prevention is to highlight the role of the immediate micro-environment in the performance of criminal behaviour. He was one of the first to see the potential that the manipulation of situational factors offered for intervention at the level of environmental design. Better than anyone else, Clarke was able to translate the logic of situational prevention into a comprehensive set of concrete, practical and effective interventions that were accessible to in-the-field practitioners.

Clarke's model of prevention is built on a solid psychological principle. During the 1960s, the decade before Clarke's first writings on situational prevention appeared (Clarke and Martin 1975), one of the most vigorous debates in psychology concerned the cross-situational consistency of personality traits. Traditional dispositional personality theorists conceptualised traits as generalised behavioural tendencies that predicted how individuals behaved across different areas of their life. Someone who was aggressive in one situation was seen to be likely to be aggressive in many other situations as well. A person performs aggressive acts because he/she has an aggressive trait. Behavioural theorists, notably Walter Mischel (1968), argued instead that behaviour is highly variable and is a response to different situational demands and expectations. A person can be aggressive in one circumstance and not in others depending upon the context. It is the situation that causes the behaviour not the person. The variability of behaviour makes the very notion of a trait unsustainable. This theoretical position is known as situationalism.

As is the case with many debates, it soon became apparent that the truth lay somewhere in the middle. The correlation between measures of personality traits and their related behaviours is typically found to be in the order of .4 (Nisbett 1980), a strength of association that can be described as medium. The size of this correlation suggests that behavioural patterns develop around stable trait cores, while the level of unexplained variance is evidence for the role of situations in the behavioural expression of traits. Most personality theorists now agree that the performance of behaviour is best understood as the result of an interaction between dispositional and situational factors.

It is the person–situation interaction that ultimately explains the efficacy of situational interventions in crime prevention (Cornish and Clarke 2008; Clarke

Exploring the person–situation interaction in situational crime prevention 185

2008). If crime is the product of both the characteristics of offenders and the locations in which they commit their crimes, then addressing the situational side of the equation is at least as valid as is the traditional focus on attempting to change offenders' dispositions. Moreover, given a choice there are distinct advantages in preferring to focus prevention efforts on the situational characteristics of the crime event rather than on the psychological characteristics of the offender. As a general principle proximal causes exert more direct and modifiable effects on behaviour than do distal causes (Clarke 2008; Ekblom 1994).

The focus of this chapter is not on the relative importance of the person and the situation in behaviour, but on the word 'interaction'. An interaction means more than that dispositions and situations are both important in the commission of crime. The *Penguin Dictionary of Psychology* gives two possible meanings for interaction as it relates to behaviour (Reber, Allen and Reber 2009). An interaction may refer to a 'reciprocal effect or influence' or to instances in which 'the effect of two (or more) variables are interdependent'. Confusingly, both of these definitions have been used with respect to person–situation interactions in situational crime prevention, typically without the difference between the two meanings being made clear.

Interactions as reciprocal relationships

An interaction as a reciprocal relationship is the most common usage of the term in everyday language. Central to this concept of interaction is the idea of bidirectional causation. According to this definition, in a person–situation interaction the environment affects the individual and the individual in turn affects the environment (Figure 14.1). The morning alarm rings and the waking person fumbles to press the snooze button. Immediate environments can include other people such that the behaviour of one person acts as the stimulus for the behaviour of another.

Applying this definition in its broadest sense, virtually all criminal behaviour (indeed, all operant behaviour) can be said to arise through a person–situation interaction. Looking at situational effects on the person, the impact may occur at the motivational, cognitive and behavioural level. First, the very impetus to offend may be created by situational pressures and provocations. A crowded, airless nightclub may induce stress that increases the probability of aggression (Homel and Clark 1994). Next, the decision of the motivated offender to proceed with an offence is governed by an assessment of the opportunities offered by the situation. A burglar will select a house showing signs that the owner is away over a house showing signs of occupancy (Macintyre 2002). Finally, the precise modus

Figure 14.1 Reciprocal relationship between person and situation.

operandi adopted by the offender is a direct response to the particular situational contingencies encountered. The type of sex acts performed on victims by child sex offenders depends upon the age and gender of the child (Leclerc, Proulx, Lussiere and Allaire 2009). Looking at the other side of the equation, an interaction then requires that there is an overt response to these situational influences that acts in some way upon the immediate environment. The consequences of crime can almost always be measured in terms of situational impacts – a victim is harmed, property is damaged or removed, an illegal pornographic image is downloaded, a syringe is emptied and so on.

More interestingly, interactions defined by reciprocity are typically not single events but are iterative processes in which the outcome of one action affects the next action, the outcome of which affects the next action and so on. Thus, a conversation between friends is an iterative interaction – each response is a reaction to the previous response (assuming the participants are listening to each other). So too is the playing of a computer game where the actions of the player determines the playing strategy adopted by the computer program and vice-versa. Cornish (1994) makes the point that the crime event is a multi-staged process comprising a beginning, middle and end. Crime does not involve a single decision by the offender, but instead there is a connected chain of decisions based on an ongoing evaluation of the available options. The crime event unfolds as a dynamic process and may take many different paths depending upon the nature of the environmental feedback.

Iterative person–situations interactions can be fitted within a multi-staged crime-event framework. Indermaur (1996), for example, examined the interactions between robbers and their victims. He interviewed eighty-eight perpetrators and ten victims of violent property crime about the progression of the offence from beginning to end. The behaviour of the perpetrator depended upon the reactions of the victim. In particular, signs of resistance from the victim were pivotal points in the transaction inducing in perpetrators a sense of 'righteous indignation'. Indermaur advised victims of violent crime to adopt non-confrontational responses to the robber's actions in order to reduce the violence of the offence.

I suspect that for most writers and practitioners in the situational crime prevention field, the reciprocal relationship that an offender has with his/her immediate environment is the main way that the person–situation interaction is interpreted. While I have no issue with the validity of this interpretation, it needs to be recognised that this is just another way of describing the situationalism proposed by Mischel (1968) and other behaviourists. The person–situation interaction in this sense is a within-individual phenomenon – the nature of the individual changes according to the situation he/she is in. This process takes no account of the role that stable individual differences play in behaviour. As Figure 14.1 suggests, behaviourists make no distinction between the person and their behaviour. Incorporating a role for personal traits into the person–situation interaction is a necessary step in the resolution of the debate between dispositionalists and situationalists. This brings us to the concept of interaction as the interdependence of variables.

Exploring the person–situation interaction in situational crime prevention 187

Interactions as interdependent relationships

Interactions as interdependent relationships occur when the effect of one factor on an outcome variable is dependent upon the effect of another factor. In terms of the person and situation, there is a non-interactive relationship when each exerts an independent influence on behaviour (Figure 14.2). A person–situation interaction occurs when the effect of the situation on behaviour depends upon the nature of the particular person in question (Figure 14.3). That is, different individuals react differently to the same situation, with some individuals dispositionally more susceptible to criminogenic environments than others.

Interaction used in this way is the same sense that the term is used in statistics. According to this usage, behaviour is a function of person and situation (behaviour = f[person, situation]) rather than merely the sum of their independent effects (behaviour = person + situation). To illustrate the point, imagine that the function describing the interaction between person and situation is a simple product (behaviour = person × situation). Imagine, too, that it is possible to accurately calibrate the criminal propensity of an individual and the criminogenic nature of a situation. Let us assign some arbitrary values to these two variables: individuals

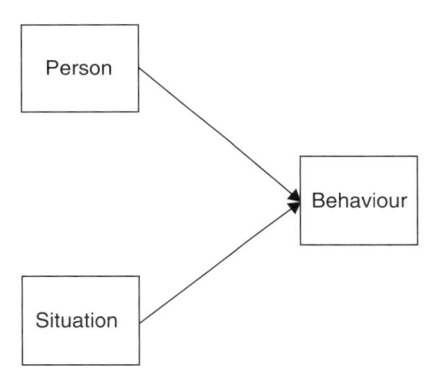

Figure 14.2 Relationship between the person, situation and behaviour in the non-interactive model.

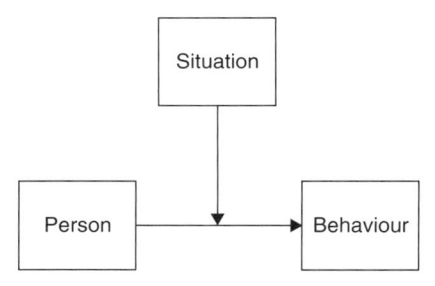

Figure 14.3 Relationship between the person, situation and behaviour in the interactive model.

who are low on criminality are rated as one and individuals who are high on criminality are rated as five; likewise, situations that have low-criminogenic features are rated one and situations that have high-criminogenic features are rated five. The outcome of additive and multiplicative combinations of person and situation are shown in Figures 14.4 and 14.5. In the additive, non-interactive condition an increase in the criminogenic nature of the environment has a uniform effect on both low- and high-criminality individuals. High-criminality individuals are always more likely to commit crime than are low-criminality individuals and the difference between the two remains constant across situations. In the multiplicative, interactive condition high-criminality individuals are marginally more likely than low-criminality individuals to commit crime in low-criminogenic environments, and low-criminality individuals are marginally more likely to commit crime in high-criminogenic situations than in low-criminogenic situations. However, when high-criminality individuals enter high-criminogenic situations the conditions are created for the 'perfect storm'. (Of course the exact shape of the lines in Figures 14.4 and 14.5 depends on the initial values used to measure criminality and criminogenic situations, and the mathematical function describing the interactive relationship between them.)

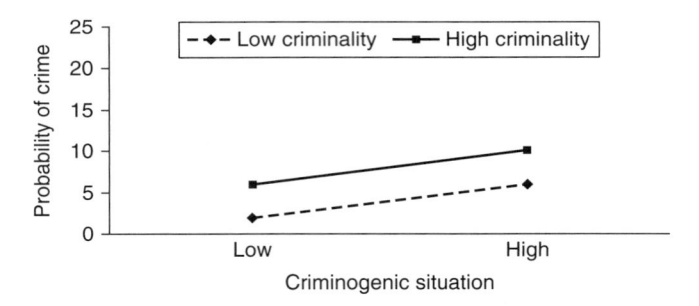

Figure 14.4 Probability of crime for a hypothetical person + situation model.

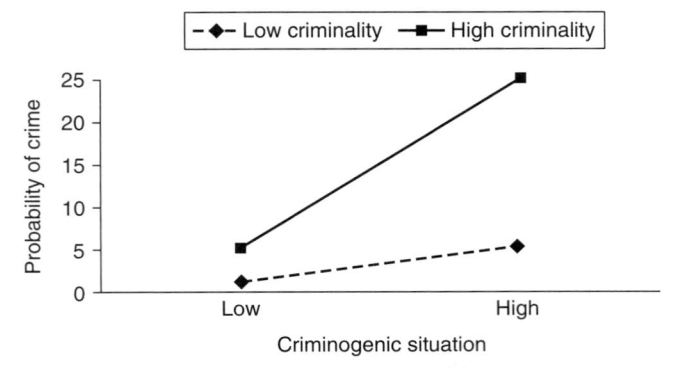

Figure 14.5 Probability of crime for a hypothetical person × situation model.

Person × situation effects for crime have been demonstrated by Lynam et al. (2000). They took measures of impulsivity and self-reported delinquency from a sample of 508 inner-city boys aged twelve to thirteen years. The researchers compared the relationship between these two measures as a function of the socio-economic characteristics of the neighbourhoods in which the boys lived. They found that the relationship between impulsivity and delinquency was stronger in poor neighbourhoods than in better-off neighbourhoods, but that there was little difference in delinquency between non-impulsive adolescents in the poor and better-off neighbourhoods. A follow-up longitudinal study when the boys were seventeen years confirmed these findings. Thus there is an interaction between impulsivity and adverse situational factors, and delinquency is especially likely when both are present.

Not all behaviour involves a person–situation interaction. Psychologists use the term *strong situations* to refer to conditions in which the environmental forces are so powerful as to induce uniformity of behaviour among individuals (Cooper and Withey 2009). There are many situations in which most people behave in a law-abiding way irrespective of their dispositions. For example, almost everybody acts in the same reverential way at a funeral. However some situations can be overwhelming and induce ordinary people to commit crimes they would otherwise not contemplate committing. For example, the breakdown of order following natural disasters may lead to widespread looting that involves both antisocial and normally law-abiding individuals.

The person × situation effect is explained by the *specificity* model of personality. According to the specificity model, while people do possess traits, trait differences between people only become meaningful in certain circumstances. Moreover, in some cases those circumstances can be very specific and encountered only occasionally. Consider the case of two friends, one with a high level of dispositional aggression and the other with a low level. They are chatting peaceably at a bar when they are accosted by a drunken patron. All other things being equal, the probability of an overtly aggressive response to this provocation will be higher for the aggressive friend than for the non-aggressive friend. The non-aggressive friend can probably also be induced to retaliate at some point, but it will take much stronger situational pressure for this to occur. At the same time, prior to the provocation, there was little outward difference in the behaviour of the two friends. The specificity model can help explain why individuals with criminal dispositions do not offend all of the time – and why they do offend when they do – as well as why normally law-abiding people can sometimes commit crimes that are apparently out of character.

Implications for situational crime prevention

Person–situation interactions as reciprocal relationships have from the start formed a conceptual basis for situational crime prevention and little more needs to be said about them here. Person–situation interactions as interdependent relationships, however, have been examined in less detail and, if taken seriously, suggest that some account needs to be taken in situational crime prevention of offender dispositions. Going down this road represents a new direction for situational crime prevention, and has been something that Ron Clarke has consistently resisted.

Of course, the interdependence of the person and situation in the commission of crime has not escaped situational crime prevention theorists. Cohen and Felson (1979) in their routine activity approach implicitly recognise the person × situation interaction in their description of the three necessary elements of a crime – a likely offender, a suitable target and the absence of a capable guardian. Felson (2002) describes the best candidate for a 'likely' offender as 'a young male with a big mouth who gets into many accidents, does poorly in school, loses jobs, and makes many visits to the emergency room' (p. 21). That is, whether crime occurs depends upon the convergence of a criminogenic situation (a suitable, unguarded target) and an individual with a predisposition to antisocial behaviour. In a similar vein, Ekblom (1994) discusses the 'conjunction' of proximal criminogenic elements that leads to crime. He notes that individuals do not encounter situations randomly and that high-criminality individuals may actively seek out high-criminogenic environments. For example, young people attracted to excitement are likely to place themselves in inner-city bars and discos where there is a relatively high potential to become an offender (or victim).

More recently, Cornish and Clarke (2003) delineated three types of offenders based on the strength of their criminal dispositions and the different roles played in their crimes by the immediate environment. The first type is the antisocial predator. These offenders possess ingrained criminal dispositions and actively seek out or create criminal opportunities. They utilise situational data to make rational choices about the relative costs and benefits of criminal involvement. The second type is the mundane offender. These offenders are less criminally committed than are antisocial predators, and engage in occasional, low-level crime. They may be defined by their inability to exercise self-restraint. They are opportunistic in their offending patterns, succumbing easily to the temptations offered in the situation. The third type is the provoked offender. Provoked offenders are conventional in their value-systems, and probably do not have a criminal record. Provoked offenders are reacting to a particular set of situational conditions – frustration, irritation, social pressures and so forth – that induce them to commit crimes that they would otherwise not commit. Their crimes include 'crimes of violence that erupt in the heat of the moment; or impulsive ones committed by offenders overcome by temptation, or a temporary failure of self control' (Cornish and Clarke 2003, p. 70).

Cornish and Clarke's typology can be interpreted in terms of the person–situation interaction by unpacking the dispositional and situational elements. Offenders vary in the strength of their criminality, from provoked offenders, through opportunists, to predators; situations vary in their criminogenic qualities, from those that challenge offenders by requiring them to create opportunities, through those that provide easy temptations, to those that actively provoke crime. The hypothetical interaction is shown in Figure 14.6. Notice that when interpreted in this way, offender types are not restricted to offending in the situational condition by which

Exploring the person–situation interaction in situational crime prevention 191

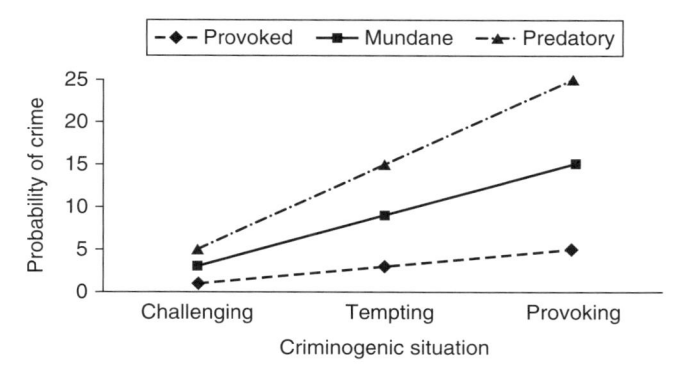

Figure 14.6 Hypothetical interaction between provoked, mundane and predatory offenders and the situation.

they are defined. Predatory offenders are most likely of the three types to offend in all three conditions. This brings to mind the case of one of Australia's most notorious criminals, Neddy Smith, who was ultimately convicted of murdering a stranger in a road-rage incident.

The question from a situational crime prevention point of view is not so much whether or not a person × situation interaction occurs but what is to be done about it. Cornish and Clarke are clearly reluctant to take the matter much further than the typology described above. They have had this to say:

> The rational choice perspective has had rather little to say about the nature of the offender. In accordance with good-enough theorising the original depiction of the offender was of an individual bereft of moral scruples – and without any defects such as lack of self-control that might get in the way of rational action. He (or she) was assumed to arrive at the crime setting already motivated and somewhat experienced in committing the crime in question, and to evaluate criminal opportunities on the basis of the likely rewards they offered, the effort they required, and the risks that were likely to involve. Although this picture has been modified over the years (Cornish and Clarke, 2003) the offender as antisocial predator has remained the perspective's default view. There is a practical reason for this reluctance to qualify this bleak picture. In many cases situational crime prevention knows little or nothing about the offenders whose activities it is trying to stop, reduce or disrupt. Under these circumstances the most effective measures may be those that credit the as yet identified offender with few qualities other than rationality.
> (Cornish and Clarke 2008, pp. 39–40)

Cornish and Clarke are arguing for parsimony and pragmatism, and they have a point. Ron Clarke in particular has always been suspicious of traditional criminological approaches that treat the problem of crime as an academic exercise and that ultimately sink under the weight of their own theorising. His main goal has always been to produce a crime prevention model that above all is useful. And for a model to be useful it needs to be in a form that is easily communicated to the end-users who actually implement crime prevention strategies. There has been good reason not to complicate situational crime prevention with unnecessary theoretical baggage and there is no doubt that Clarke's single-minded focus on utility has served his cause well. However, as Ken Pease and Gloria Laycock point out elsewhere in this volume, this approach also comes at a price. They argue that it has inhibited the integration of situational crime prevention into mainstream psychology and criminology and thus has limited the take-up of the ideas advanced. For my part I believe that situational crime prevention is now sufficiently well-established that it is safe to move beyond 'good-enough theorising' without compromising Clarke's original mission. To this end, exploring the person–situation interaction in more depth can provide a more sophisticated rendering of the intimate relationship between offenders and their crime scenes. My guess is that Ron Clarke would be happy enough for researchers to take up this line of enquiry as long as he does not have to be one of them.

References

Clarke, R.V. (2008) 'Situational crime prevention', in R. Wortley and L. Mazerolle (eds) *Environmental Criminology and Crime Analysis*. Cullompton: Willan Publishing.

Clarke, R.V. and Martin, D.N. (1975) 'A study of absconding and its implications for the residential treatment of deliinquents', in J. Tizard, I.A. Sinclair and R.V. Clarke (eds) *Varieties of Residential Experience*. London: Routledge and Keegan Paul.

Cohen, L.E. and Felson, M. (1979) 'Social change and crime rate trends: a routine activity approach'. *American Sociological Review*, 44, 588–608.

Cooper, W.H. and Withey, M.J. (2009) 'The strong situation hypothesis'. *Personality and Social Psychology Review*, 13, 62–72.

Cornish, D. (1994) 'The procedural analysis of offending and its relevance for situational prevention', in R. V. Clarke (ed.) *Crime Prevention Studies*, vol. 3. Monsey, NY: Criminal Justice Press.

Cornish, D.B. and Clarke, R.V. (2003) 'Opportunities, precipitators and criminal dispositions: a reply to Wortley's critique of situational crime prevention', in M.J. Smith and D.B. Cornish (eds) *Theory for Practice in Situational Crime prevention. Crime Prevention Studies*, vol. 16. Monsey, NY: Criminal Justice Press.

Cornish, D. B. and Clarke, R.V. (2008) 'Rational choice perspective', in R. Wortley and L. Mazerolle (eds) *Environmental Criminology and Crime Analysis*. Cullompton: Willan Publishing.

Ekblom, P. (1994) 'Proximal circumstances: a mechanism-based classification of crime prevention', in R. V. Clarke (ed.) *Crime Prevention Studies*, vol. 3. Monsey, NY: Criminal Justice Press.

Felson, M. (2002) *Crime and Everyday Life*. Thousand Oaks, CA: Sage.

Homel, R. and Clark, J. (1994) 'The prediction and prevention of violence in pubs and clubs', in R. V. Clarke (ed.) *Crime Prevention Studies*, vol. 3. Monsey, NY: Criminal Justice Press.

Indermaur, D. (1996) 'Reducing opportunities for violence in robbery and property crime:

the perspectives of offenders and victims', in R. Homel (ed.) *The Politics and Practice of Situational Crime Prevention. Crime Prevention Studies*, vol 5. Monsey, NY: Criminal Justice Press

Leclerc, B., Proulx, J., Lussiere, P. and Allaire, J. (2009) 'Offender–victim interaction and crime event outcomes: modus operandi and victim effects on the risk of intrusive sexual offenses against children', *Criminology*, 47, 595–618.

Lynam, D.R., Caspi, A., Moffitt, T.E., Wikström, P.H., Loeber, R. and Novak, S. (2000) 'The interaction between impulsivity and neighborhood context on offending: The effects of impulsivity are stronger in poorer neighborhoods', *Journal of Abnormal Psychology*, 109, 563–74.

Macintyre, S. (2002) 'Burglar decision making'. Unpublished doctoral thesis. Griffith University.

Mischel, W. (1968) *Personality and Assessment*. New York: Wiley.

Nisbett, R.E. (1980) 'The trait construct in lay and professional psychology', in L. Festinger (ed.) *Retrospections on Social Psychology*. New York: Oxford University Press.

Reber, A.S., Allen, R. and Reber, E.S. (2009) *The Penguin Dictionary of Psychology* (3rd edn). London: Penguin.

15 A rational choice analysis of organized crime and trafficked goods

Mangai Natarajan[1]

Introduction

When I recently quizzed two young colleagues about their dreams, both said they would love to create a concept or model that would immediately enter the criminological lexicon and remain there. Perhaps because all three of us know Prof. Clarke, one of them mentioned as an example the mnemonic, CRAVED (Concealable, Removable, Available, Valuable, Enjoyable and Disposable) that he coined to explain the objects sought by thieves (Clarke 1999). She said this was not only instantly memorable, but also it called attention to an important but neglected area of research.

I too like this concept and so do my students in environmental criminology who always apply it well in examinations. I was interested to find that Prof. Clarke and his graduate student, Stephen Pires, had recently used CRAVED to explain parrot poaching in Mexico (Pires and Clarke in press).[2] They argued that studying which species appeared in records of the illegal parrot trade could provide insight into who were the poachers. Thus, if the most frequently poached species were those that were easily captured (i.e. "removable") and widely available, this would suggest that they were being opportunistically taken from their nests by villagers looking for a few dollars to supplement their incomes. If the poached birds were disproportionately from among the most prized species (i.e. enjoyable and valuable birds) that require considerable time and effort to find, then this would suggest that professional poachers were involved. In fact, the results supported the idea that the poachers were predominantly opportunistic villagers, rather than professional, organized poachers.

To extend the application of CRAVED to birds illegally taken from the wild required considerable inventiveness in developing measures of the CRAVED variables suitable for the new context. The model proved to be robust; the only modification suggested by Pires and Clarke was that, when applied to poaching, it would be useful to divide "available" into *abundance* and *accessibility*. (They comment that this would not destroy the mnemonic, since it would become CRAAVED.)

Apart from its intrinsic interest, this study illustrates the evolution of Prof. Clarke's research agenda (this is after all his Festschrift!). In recent years, he has been taking an increasing interest in transnational crimes, in organized crimes and,

A rational choice analysis of organized crime and trafficked goods 195

most recently, in wildlife crimes, while all the time retaining his focus on prevention.[3] These topics do not fit the supposed interests of an "administrative" criminologist, as he has been labeled. Nobody in government or positions of power asked him to research these topics. Instead, he seems to be exploring whether his "situational" take on criminology, which has been of great value in reducing everyday crimes of theft and violence, can also be valuable in explaining and preventing more exotic and sometimes more complex crimes.

As it happens, his new research agenda fits well with my own interests in trafficking and organized crime, and the application of CRAVED to the illegal trade in parrots has led me to the subject of the present chapter: Can fresh insights about trafficking (in drugs, guns and cars, as well as in endangered species) result from studying the goods that are trafficked and how this is done?

I began to explore this question by asking Prof. Clarke what he thought were the key themes of the recent book that he had jointly edited on the application of situational prevention to organized crimes (Bullock et al. 2010). I asked him how the situational approach to the study of organized crime differs from the traditional approach. He told me to read the book and draw my own conclusions, which is typical of the way he always forces me to think. However, he relented because a few days later I received an email with a list of what he called the key principles of the situational prevention approach to organized crime:[4]

1 Focus first on the crimes committed and only afterwards on the organization.
2 Be aware that most organized crime groups are networks of criminal entrepreneurs not "the mafia."
3 Adopt a modified rationality theoretical perspective.
4 Ask how the crimes are committed not why (which is usually obvious).
5 Analyze the opportunity structure (OS) for specific kinds of organized crimes.
6 Analyze the modus operandi (MO), step by step.
7 Do not assume a Mr. Big or kingpin is co-ordinating the steps.
8 Always assume less organization at every stage rather than more.
9 Identify the promising pinch-points for intervention in the OS and MO.
10 Value prevention more than arrest.

Prof. Clarke's list was mostly consistent with my own experience of studying drug trafficking (Natarajan and Belanger 1998; Natarajan 2000, 2006), though I would not agree completely with the first point. It is true that most organized crime groups are not "the mafia"; indeed I have written a paper jointly with Prof. Clarke making just this point (Natarajan and Clarke 2004). However I do not think that the nature of the crimes committed can be separated from the nature of the organization. Instead, as Mike Levi (1998) has written: "different forms of crime may require different levels of organization" (p. 458) – a point anticipated by Cornish and Clarke (1987) in their discussion of the organizational needs for residential and commercial burglaries.

Apart from this, I felt that the list – especially items 4–7 – gave enough encouragement to proceed with answering the question I had raised. I thought I would try to use CRAVED to analyze different kinds of trafficked "goods" and this chapter, which is entirely theoretical, presents the results of my explorations. I begin by discussing the origins of CRAVED in routine activity theory and its affinities with the rational choice concept of "choice structuring properties" described by Cornish and Clarke (1987). I go on to explain why in answering my question about the value of analyzing goods that are trafficked it is important to extend CRAVED by using choice structuring properties and crime scripts (Cornish 1994).

Background to CRAVED

Prof. Clarke (1999) has described how CRAVED developed from the work of his close colleague, Marcus Felson, on suitable targets of crime. In their initial account of the routine activity approach, Cohen and Felson (1979) had briefly described the essential elements of a suitable target for predatory crime, which they encapsulated by VIVA – Value, Inertia, Visibility and Accessibility. They intended VIVA to apply to any target of predatory crime, whether people or property, whereas CRAVED was confined to objects of theft. This narrowed focus on theft allowed the elements of "suitability" to be more tightly specified.

Clarke (1999) also noted that CRAVED was influenced by work he undertook with another close colleague, Derek Cornish, on the "choice structuring properties" of different forms of crime, which they defined as

> those *properties* of offenses (such as type and amount of payoff, perceived risk, skills needed, and so on) which are perceived by the offender as being especially salient to his or her goals, motives, experience, abilities, expertise, and preferences. Such properties provide a basis for selecting among alternative courses of action and, hence, effectively *structure* the offender's *choice.*
> (Cornish and Clarke 1987, p. 935)

They developed this concept in an effort to explain the limits of displacement. They argued that blocked from committing particular kinds of crime, say residential burglary, offenders would not necessarily displace their efforts to another form of crime, even one that at first sight seemed to be similar, say commercial burglary. This is because these two kinds of crime might in fact differ considerably in their choice structuring properties. Thus residential burglary might often be highly opportunistic and require little planning. The goods sought might primarily be cash or easily fenced items of jewelry or electronics. Successful commercial burglaries, however, might rely upon detailed planning, team work and the use of cars or vans, and might need suitable contacts to fence the stolen goods. All this might be beyond the resources and skills of the average, opportunistic residential burglar. The more general point made by Cornish and Clarke was that even apparently similar forms of crime might differ considerably in their choice structuring properties when seen from the offender's perspective.

Applying CRAVED

This last point suggested to me that in using CRAVED to study different forms of trafficking it would be necessary to assign ratings to the CRAVED variables on

A rational choice analysis of organized crime and trafficked goods 197

some kind of scale rather than simply to determine whether the trafficked goods were, say *valuable*, or *available*. Table 15.1 shows the results of my attempt to rate each CRAVED component on a five-point scale for five kinds of trafficked goods: heroin, small arms, elephant ivory, cars and endangered parrots (high scores indicate favorable for trafficking). When making the ratings, I had specifically in mind the need to transport the goods across an international border (Natarajan 2011; Clarke and Brown 2011; Leggett 2011; Schneider 2011). While these ratings are entirely subjective and unscientific, the following were the criteria I used:

Concealable – Because all these goods are smuggled, they must be concealed to evade detection. The difficulties of concealment vary considerably with the goods. Trafficked heroin is often concealed in hidden compartments in vehicles and sometimes in the body cavities of couriers, or "mules." Small arms are often shipped in containers labeled as "used household appliances" or similar. The same is true of stolen cars, but, for those driven across land borders, it may not be necessary to alter their identities. This is because close inspection of vehicle documents would result in intolerable delays at the border. In any case, border agents can be bribed or they may lack the language skills or knowledge to interpret identifying documents. It is much easier to conceal ivory than it is to conceal endangered parrots. Ivory can be fashioned into crude representations of birds and animals, painted to look like wood and shipped in crates. Parrots can be tranquillized and stuffed in plastic tubes to constrict movement, but they cannot be left unattended for long periods in warehouses.

Removable – It is much easier to drive a stolen car across a land border than to ship it overseas from a port. Because a gun is much smaller than a car, it is easier to ship than a car. Cars can be disassembled for export, but this is costly, while a consignment of heroin can be divided up into small packages and ivory can be cut into small pieces for smuggling one-by-one. Smuggled parrots must be provided regularly with food and water or they will die.

Available – Only a few countries produce heroin, but they produce it in large quantities. Of the other goods considered in Table 15.1, cars might be the most readily accessible and abundant. There might be more ivory-bearing elephants in Africa than endangered parrots in South America. They might be equally inaccessible in remote areas, but having reached those areas it would be easier for poachers to find elephants in open bush land than parrots in the jungle. It might therefore be easier to secure a supply of elephant tusks in Africa than endangered parrots in the neo-tropics.

Valuable – To make sufficient money, traffickers must be able to obtain either a reliable, even if limited supply of high-value goods, or a continuous flow of lower-value goods. Traffickers in cars and heroin have the best of both worlds since heroin[5] and cars are valuable and can be obtained in large quantities. Ivory is valuable but the supply is probably less reliable as elephants have to be hunted and

Table 15.1 Hypothetical CRAVED scores for selected goods that are internationally trafficked*

CRAVED variables	Heroin	Small arms	Stolen cars	Elephant ivory	Endangered parrots
Concealable	5	3	2	4	1
Removable	5	3	3	3	1
Available	3	2	5	1	1
Valuable	5	3	5	5	3
Enjoyable	5	2	3	4	4
Disposable	5	1	4	2	1
	28	14	22	19	11

Note: * Higher scores indicate greater suitability for trafficking.

killed in remote areas. Some species of endangered parrots are valuable (Scarlet macaws, for example, can be sold to collectors for $15,000 or more) but the supply is very limited as relatively few of these birds are left in the wild. Weapons are relatively inexpensive, but supplies seem easy to obtain for those with the required contacts.

Enjoyable – All trafficked goods bring personal enjoyment to the buyers, but the enjoyment is probably most intense for heroin. It is probably least intense for small arms and possibly for cars, which, with the exception of luxury vehicles, may be purchased mostly for their usefulness to the new owners. Elephant ivory is fashioned into luxury items, such as bangles and necklaces, which would be widely prized. Endangered parrots would also be highly prized, but only by a small number of collectors.

Disposable – Heroin might be easier to sell than any of the other trafficked goods. Although expensive, users need buy only a small amount at any one time so that the drug would be within the financial reach of a large proportion of the population. Many people in developing countries (which are the main destinations of trafficked vehicles) might want to buy a stolen car, but few would have the money to do so. The market for ivory would be more constricted than for stolen cars, while that for parrots would be even more confined. Small arms would be sought only by guerrillas and those planning military action.

Discussion

While the ratings shown in Table 15.1 were entirely subjective they suggest that some goods are likely to be much more suitable for trafficking than others. For example, heroin scores more highly on all six of the CRAVED variables than endangered parrots, despite the fact that both goods are "produced" in South America, in the one case cultivated by villagers and in the other captured by them. They both gain their greatest value when they reach the developed world, but getting them, say, from rural Colombia or Bolivia to New York may involve more difficulties and less certain rewards for parrots than for heroin.[6] The limited availability of endangered parrots, the difficulties of concealing them and caring for them during transportation, and the relatively few potential buyers, all provide reasons why they would be less attractive to traffickers. Perhaps the only viable way to traffic these parrots would be as part of a legitimate wildlife export business that would have the necessary skills to care for the birds and the necessary contacts to sell them at a worthwhile profit. The traffickers would therefore be networks of criminal entrepreneurs, not the kind of traditional organized crime syndicates that might commit any profitable form of trafficking. This example reinforces my point about the need to examine the crimes and the organizations involved at the same time, not sequentially as suggested by the first item in Clarke's list.

These differences between heroin and parrots show that the systematic application of CRAVED could lead to important insights about trafficking. However, CRAVED did not prove easy to use. First, I soon found that its elements would be rated differently depending on the stage of trafficking. To take the example of trafficking in cars, *removable* and *available* might be of greatest importance when first stealing the car for export, but *concealable* might be of greater importance at the later stage of shipping it from a port. *Concealable* might also be important when driving the car across a land border, but not in the sense of concealing the car from view, but concealing that it was stolen. *Enjoyable* would presumably be of greatest importance for the end consumer while it would be mostly irrelevant at earlier trafficking stages. To deal with this problem I tried to focus my thinking on just one stage – that of getting the car across an international border, which is perhaps the defining feature of trafficking. The alternative of separately rating each stage of trafficking for each of its forms seemed of doubtful value given the subjectivity involved.

The second problem I experienced is that CRAVED fails to capture some important aspects of trafficking that could help determine the choice by organized criminals of particular kinds of goods to traffic. It ignores, in particular, some costs of trafficking in particular goods, such as the physical dangers involved in acquiring them (it may be more dangerous to hunt elephants than parrots), the risks of violent competition (especially in the drugs trade) and the punishments if caught (drug traffickers face much longer prison terms than parrot traders). Again, as these examples suggest, the elements neglected by CRAVED will also vary in importance with the stage of trafficking.

Others who have used CRAVED to study specific categories of stolen goods have also found that it is a useful starting point, but have concluded that the range of attributes it covers is too narrow. In at least two cases, the researchers have expanded the attributes and captured them in clever acronyms of their own. Thus, Whitehead et al. (2008) have proposed "IN SAFE HANDS"[7] as a summary of the features of mobile phones that protect them from theft, while Gill and Clarke (in press) have claimed that "AT CUT PRICES"[8] summarizes the features of fast moving consumer goods (such as grocery store and drug store items) that promote their theft.

Based on these examples and my own attempt to apply CRAVED, I would now argue that, instead of using CRAVED to compare different forms of trafficking at each stage of the trafficking process, more would be learned by undertaking a detailed comparison of the wider "choice structuring properties" of trafficking offences. Table 15.2 is my attempt to lay out these properties in the form of questions that potential traffickers would be likely to consider before becoming involved in any specific form of trafficking. The final column shows that CRAVED covers less than half the choice structuring properties that are listed – a not unexpected result given that CRAVED deals only with the attributes of the trafficked goods, not the wider considerations of involvement in trafficking.

Rather than pursue either of the alternatives it might be better to undertake a comparison among the choice structuring properties of each form of trafficking at each trafficking stage, beginning with the initial procurement of the goods to be trafficked, smuggling them into the destination country, and finally finding a buyer. To have any validity, the ratings of the choice structuring properties would most likely have to be made from the perspective of the person or group responsible for accomplishing each stage. So, for example, at the first stage of acquiring the product to be trafficked, the choice structuring properties would have to be evaluated, say, from the point of view of a farmer growing coca or opium for sale, or a car thief stealing a car from a parking lot or street.

Table 15.2 Choice structuring properties of trafficking offenses

Questions that confront traffickers	Relevant CRAVED elements
How available are the goods? (rare vs. widespread)	Available
How accessible are they (remote location?)	Available
How easy to procure? (stolen or purchased?)	Available
How dangerous to obtain? (ivory vs. parrots)	
How easy to move? (size and weight of goods)	Removable
How far must the goods travel from origin to destination?	Removable
How many international borders must the goods cross?	Concealable
How easy to conceal?	Concealable
How easy to identify if stolen?	Concealable
How much enjoyment do the goods bring to the traffickers?	Enjoyable
How easily can the goods be sold?	Disposable
How many stages of trafficking are involved?	
How many individuals or groups are involved?	
How much capital is needed?	
How big are the profits?	Valuable
How can the profits be laundered?	
How much technical knowledge is needed and at which stages?	
How vulnerable are the goods to confiscation, theft or damage?	
How large are the penalties for trafficking?	
What are the risks of informants?	
Who are the competitors? How many? How dangerous?	
How much violence must be used?	
How morally reprehensible is the trade? (parrots vs. heroin)	

This requirement to evaluate choice structuring properties from the person or group responsible for each stage could by itself shed new light on the organization of trafficking. It is often assumed, without much evidence (see point 7 in Clarke's list), that there is a "Mr Big" in charge of the whole operation and that the operation follows, to use Derek Cornish's term, some kind of "master-script." However, Bullock, Clarke and Tilley (2010, p. 10) are surely correct when they write as follows:

> There may sometimes be a "Mr Big" pulling the strings of those involved in complex crimes as they act out their parts in the performance of the extended master-script. In other instances, as with the legitimate market, those involved in the different stages in the production of the crime may know or care little about one another. The importer of stolen cars, for example, may have little interest or involvement with those who steal the cars from the streets in a distant country and the scripts they follow. Parts of the master-script may, thus, be owned and orchestrated by different directors.

Thus, it is possible that the kinds of groups and organizations involved could vary greatly at each stage of the operation. Consistent with this, I found in my analysis of seventy-nine drug trafficking cases prosecuted in the Federal courts in New York City from 1984 to 2007 (Natarajan, Zanella and Yu, 2010) that four main kinds of organizations were involved (family-based businesses, communal businesses, corporations and freelancers). These were to be found at all stages of trafficking (production/manufacture, smuggling/import, wholesale distribution and regional distribution). Larger organizations tended to be involved in several, but not all of the distribution stages. Smaller, freelance enterprises generally operated higher up, at the smuggling/importing stage in the drug distribution chain.

A second implication of the quotation above is that each of the people or groups working at particular stages might have little contact with each other and even less contact with those further up or down the line. For example, a South American peasant who takes a young parrot from the nest may need little contact with other villagers doing the same thing. He knows that if he waits a few days or weeks a parrot trader will come by and purchase the bird for few dollars. The trader makes his money by selling the birds to a pet market (operating illegally but openly) in the distant city. Another person might make his living by cruising the pet markets looking for valuable birds to buy and re-sell to those with the necessary contacts to get them out of the country and into the hands of wealthy buyers. It may be only at this point that more "organized" criminals enter the process. They would have spared themselves the difficulty and risks of catching the parrots and collecting sufficient of them together to make reasonable profit on their sale.

Taken together with item 8 in Clarke's list ("Always assume less organization at every stage rather than more") this scenario opens up a more nuanced and more interesting view of trafficking than normally portrayed in the literature, one that gives a greater part to autonomous networks of criminal entrepreneurs, or even to autonomous individuals, than to mafia-type criminal organizations. Again, this is consistent with my own experience of analyzing a heroin trafficking case prosecuted in a New York City court in the early 1990s (Natarajan 2006). Wiretap data showed that the thirty-five prosecuted individuals were only a fraction of the 294 people who showed up in the wiretap database, most of whom had limited contacts with others in the organization and it was unclear whether the prosecution had identified a large, loosely structured drug trafficking organization with a very wide span of operations or merely a segment of the drug market in New York City. Indeed, many of the individuals and small cliques identified in the analysis could have been independent operators, owing no particular allegiance to other individuals or cliques. They might simply have been exploiting what they regarded as opportunities that came their way in the ordinary course of business or opportunities that they created to make some money. I commented: "When law enforcement dips its ladle into this bubbling broth of entrepreneurial activity it might scoop out a random collection of small groups and individuals that, by its network of contacts, is defined as a criminal organization" (Natarajan 2006, p. 190).

Summary and conclusions

This chapter has explored the question of whether new insights about trafficking might result from focusing upon the goods that are trafficked. CRAVED ratings of a variety of trafficked goods (heroin, small arms, elephant ivory, cars and endangered parrots) suggested that the costs, risks and rewards of trafficking in these goods would vary considerably when viewed from the perspectives of traffickers. However, it became clear that CRAVED did not encompass all the important "choice structuring properties" of these different kinds of trafficking. It was also difficult to rate the goods because the importance of CRAVED elements would vary with the different stages of trafficking and the different perspectives of those engaged at each stage. It was therefore suggested that, rather than focusing exclusively on CRAVED, more would be learned by comparing the choice structuring properties of the different forms of trafficking at each stage in the trafficking process. The net result of such an approach could be a more nuanced and varied view of the traffickers involved and the tasks they must accomplish, as well as of the organization and co-ordination of their activities. This supports the claims made by Bullock, Clarke and Tilley (2010) about the scope offered by situational prevention for producing new knowledge about organized crime. Unfortunately, this short chapter could not comment upon a second and more important claim these authors make – that situational analysis could lead to many viable suggestions for preventing trafficking.

Notes

1 It was intimidating to produce a contribution to this Festschrift for my mentor, or as I prefer to call him, my guru, so I showed Professor Clarke the chapter in draft. As always, he made many helpful suggestions for which I am grateful.
2 They presented the paper at the eighteenth annual meeting of the ECCA (Environmental Criminology and Crime Analysis) Symposium in 2009 in Brasilia. Their paper was

entitled "Are Mexican parrots CRAVED?", but funnily the Portuguese version of the program translated this as "Are Mexican parrots drugged?" This resulted in much jollity about the possible contents of a paper with such a title.

3 For example, much of the discussion of the results of the parrot study is taken up with the preventive implications of the finding that most poaching seemed to be undertaken by *camposinos*.
4 Clarke acknowledged that the list was influenced by Marcus Felson's (2006) earlier list.
5 According to the World Drug Report 2009, heroin prices ranged from US$10,000 per kg in Colombia to US$45,000–70,000 per kg (for heroin of South American origin) in the United States and US$119,000 per kg in Canada.
6 On the other hand, those trafficking in heroin can expect much harsher penalties if caught than those trafficking in endangered parrots.
7 **I**dentifiable, **N**eutral, **S**een, **A**ttached, **F**indable, **E**xecutable, **H**idden, **A**utomatic, **N**ecessary, **D**etectable, **S**ecure.
8 **A**ffordable, **T**ransportable, **C**oncealable, **U**ntraceable, **T**radeable, **P**rofitable, **R**eputable, **I**mperishable, **C**onsumable, **E**valuable, **S**hiftable.

References

Bullock, K., Clarke, R.V. and Tilley, N. (eds) (2010) *Situational Prevention of Organized Crimes*. Cullompton: Willan Publishing.

Clarke, R.V. (1999) *Hot Products: Understanding, Anticipating and Reducing Demand for Stolen Goods*. Police Research Series, Paper 112. Policing and Reducing Crime Unit, Research Development and Statistics Directorate. London: Home Office.

Clarke, R.V. and Brown, R. (2011) "International trafficking of stolen vehicles." In Natarajan, M. (ed.) *International Crime and Justice*. New York: Cambridge University Press.

Cohen, L.E. and Felson, M. (1979) "Social change and crime rate trends: a routine activity approach." *American Sociological Review*, 44: 588–608.

Cornish, D. (1994) "The Procedural Analysis of Offending and Its Relevance for Situational Prevention." In Clarke, R.V. (ed.) *Crime Prevention Studies*, volume 3. Monsey, NY: Criminal Justice Press (accessible at www.popcenter.org).

Cornish, D. and Clarke, R.V. (1987) "Understanding crime displacement: an application of rational choice theory." *Criminology*, 25: 933–947.

Felson, M. (2006) *The Ecosystem for Organized Crime*, HEUNI Paper No. 26. Helsinki: HEUNI (accessible at http://www.heuni.fi/uploads/2rreolo2h.pdf).

Gill, M. and Clarke, R.V. (in press) "Differential theft risks of fast moving consumer goods." In Ekblom, P. (ed.) Crime Prevention and Product Design, *Crime Prevention Studies*. Boulder, CO: Lynne Reinner.

Levi, M. (1998) "Perspectives on organized crime: an overview." *The Howard Journal*, 37 (4): 335–345.

Leggett, T. (2011) "Small arms trafficking." In Natarajan, M. (ed.) *International Crime and Justice*. New York: Cambridge University Press.

Natarajan, M. (2000) "Understanding the structure of a drug trafficking organization: a conversational analysis." In Natarajan, M. and Hough, M. (eds) *Illegal Drug Markets: From Research to Policy*, *Crime Prevention Studies*, volume 11. Monsey, NY: Criminal Justice Press.

Natarajan, M. (2006) "Understanding the structure of a large heroin distribution network: a quantitative analysis of qualitative data." *Quantitative Journal of Criminology*, 22 (2): 171–192.

Natarajan, M. (2011) "Drug trafficking." In Natarajan, M. (ed.) *International Crime and Justice*. New York: Cambridge University Press.

Natarajan, M. and Belanger, M. (1998) "Varieties of upper-level drug dealing organizations: a typology of cases prosecuted in New York City." *Journal of Drug Issues*, 28 (4): 1005–1026.

Natarajan, M. and Clarke, R.V. (2004) "Understanding and controlling organized crime: the feasibility of a situational approach." Paper presented at the annual Environmental Criminology and Crime Analysis Seminar, Wellington, New Zealand, July.

Natarajan, M., Zanella, M. and Yu, C. (2010) "Typology of drug trafficking organizations in New York City." Paper presented at the nineteenth annual ECCA Seminar, Brisbane, Australia, July 5–8.

Pires, S. and Clarke, R.V. (in press) "Are parrots CRAVED? An analysis of parrot poaching in Mexico." *Journal of Research in Crime and Delinquency*.

Schneider, J. (2011) "Endangered species markets: a focus for criminology?" In Natarajan, M. (ed.) *International Crime and Justice*. New York: Cambridge University Press.

Whitehead, S., Mailley, J., Storer, I., McCardle, J., Torrens, G. and Farrell, G. (2008) "IN SAFE HANDS: a review of mobile phone anti-theft designs." *European Journal on Criminal Policy and Research*, 14: 39–60.

16 The structure of angry violence

Marcus Felson

In his oration defending Roscio Amerino, Cicero (BC 80) proclaimed: "*Sic vita hominum est ut ad maleficium nemo conetur sine spe atque emolumento accedere.* [Such is the life of man that no one commits crimes without a hope of gain.]" Similar thinking has guided Ronald V. Clarke in his pursuit of situational crime prevention and his incessant explorations of how diverse types of offenders think in many different contexts. Clarke and colleagues have applied this approach not only to theft and burglary (e.g., Clarke, 1999), but also to terrorism (Clarke and Newman, 2006, 2009), absconding juveniles (Clarke and Martin, 1971), electronic commerce (Newman and Clarke, 2003), suicide (Clarke and Lester, 1989), vandalism (Clarke, 1978), elephant poaching (Lemieux and Clarke, 2009), cellphone fraud (Clarke, Kemper and Wyckoff, 2001), exceeding the speed limit (Clarke, 1996) and many other topics.

Clarke's approach to the offender's calculation of gain is broad. It includes not only monetary gain but also reputation enhancement, revenge, fun and anything else that an offender might consider as a reason to commit a crime. He emphasizes the specific motive for a particular criminal act, *not* the generalized motivation for "being a criminal" over a longer period of time.

The current chapter applies situational and rational analysis to angry violent crime. Before proceeding, take note that personal anger against another person can also motivate property crime. The other Felson explains that many offenders engage in vandalism or even theft in order to get back at someone (Richard Felson, 2004). Nor is all violent crime the result of personal anger – ordinary robbery is a case in point.

We also should allow for the possibility that situations can provide order within which individuals exhibit disorderly decision processes. For example, drinking situations could conceivably trigger irrational responses. If so, situational prevention could conceivably reduce crime by altering the drinking situation, even without relying on rational choice theory. A literature on design and management of bars and bar situations takes such ideas into account. (See Homel et al., 1997, 2004; Felson, Baccaglini and Gmelch, 1986.) It is at least conceivable that irrationality can be manipulated to keep people from becoming disorderly, or to make disorderly people become peaceful. Thus even without rational offenders, situational prevention might find a way to remove the triggers for irrational violence. This possibility is left for future analysis.

The current chapter instead looks at how violent offenders make decisions with a modicum of rationality and order. The great irony is that angry violence involves *decisions* by those who do it.

Clearly, this chapter rejects the conventional dichotomy between expressive and instrumental violence. When an offender uses violence with no clear material gain, harming other people for its own sake, that does not justify the labels "irrational" or "expressive." Nor does it require inventing an indirect psychological, social or social psychological process to explain how the offender gets to that point.

This chapter argues the contrary. As explained by Tedeschi and Felson (1994), there is no expressive violence. There is no post-decisional period. Anger is not antithetical to decision-making. Angry decisions are still decisions. Situational prevention might apply at any stage in the violence process, even after people are angry and dangerous. Thus the current chapter follows a more difficult route, focusing on angry violence *chosen* by the offender and hence occurring within a rational choice framework.

Unfortunately "rational" creates more problems than solutions. The word sometimes implies wisdom, sagacity and a forward looking tendency that does not apply to most violent situations. Offenders in general and violent offenders in particular are oriented toward short-run thinking, ignoring the longer term consequences. Thus the offender makes a decision that might not be wise, and that he might himself realize later to have been erroneous. Yet so long as he made a violent decision at the time of the crime, it fits the perspective (see Tedeschi and Felson, 1994). Thus the term "rational choice" includes confusing connotations that pollute the discussion. Ronald Clarke's work does not assume that the offender has a long or thorough reasoning process, or looks far into the future. He merely assumes that the offender considers a few things. Limited rationality can be quick. The offender thinks, but not too much.

Clarke employed the term "rational choice" in order to link his ideas to a larger cross-disciplinary perspective. Unfortunately, he was therefore burdened to explain anew that this was not an incarceration-based approach to crime control and that he did not mean to say that all offenders are wise and forward-looking. It is unfortunate that we lack a good vocabulary to describe these acts.

In order to understand angry violence we must dispense with an over-idealized version of rationality. Under ideal conditions a person makes careful decisions that are good for him in the long run according to his well considered goals and means. Getting into a bar fight and ending up in the hospital does not fit these ideal conditions. We need to avoid a false dichotomy: that people either make good, careful and wise decisions, or they are not making decisions at all. To avoid semantic problems, perhaps we should refer to offenders as "decisional" (not as "rational").

A quick and narrow-minded decision is still a decision. A foolish decision is still a decision. Quick gain leading to unforeseen harm is still a decision. An uninformed decision is still a decision. Watching people play basketball or hockey we can see split-second decisions one after the other. Crime decisions often take no more than a fraction of a second. Someone perceiving an insult might respond with very quick revenge. A thief might see something and grab it right away.

A major mistake in crime analysis is to become too focused on financial gains, while neglecting other offender motives. In his work on situational crime prevention, Ronald Clarke has explored a vast variety of offender goals and has encouraged others to do the same. Graffiti painters may seek to spread their fame. Young offenders may display their prowess through vandalism or shoplifting. Offenders may steal for revenge. Gains are not necessarily financial. Thus gains include saving face and punishing others for misdeeds, if the offender thinks that should be done. Here we find a major convergence between Clarke's work and that of Tedeschi and Felson (1994).

The problem is to understand violence with no material gain, non-acquisitive violence that appears to be irrational, expressive, senseless and inexplicable save by indirect references to strains in society or individual. These indirect theories are highly obtuse and unfalsifiable. But many scholars and students need them anyway, for they offer a way to comprehend non-material violence that seems otherwise incomprehensible.

A few scholars take a different tack, arguing that non-acquisitive violence can still be purposive, instrumental, decisional and ultimately understood. They argue that anger is not necessarily irrational or undirected. And they offer a way to think about decisions to commit non-acquisitive acts of violence for a purpose. Certain social psychologists have helped us understand violence as a structured process always involving decision-making. This tradition began with David Luckenbill (1977), who analyzed "irrational" violence as the outcome of a situated transaction involving interpersonal conflicts. In practical terms, this means a quarrel got out of hand and escalated to the point of violence. This situated transaction helps us understand in social psychological terms that violent acts that seem to be irrational, at least to an outsider, in fact have a structure and logic in terms of the small numbers of people involved in a dispute. The leading theoretical and empirical work in this area was produced by my brother, Richard Felson (2000, 2004). He states that all violence is instrumental, and that expressive violence does not exist. The three types of instrumental violence begin with the classic instrumental category: using violence to gain something from somebody else – such as money or compliance. The second type of instrumental violence is social-psychological in origin – using violence against another to restore your own identity after it was attacked, at least in your own mind. This is the classic case of saving face after you feel insulted. Whether your perception is correct or not is entirely beside the point. The mind of the offender is central, and if that mind perceives insults, responds to the insults and produces escalation in oneself or others, then violence is a possible outcome. The third type of instrumental violence is employed to punish someone for doing something wrong to a third party or for violating rules. This is violence against somebody else for doing some sort of wrong, not necessarily to you.

To illustrate these three types of instrumental violence, think of how people driving cars honk their horns. A driver might honk at you to keep you from cutting in front – instrumental. If the driver keeps honking loudly, that's to punish you for cutting in front and getting back at you for the insult he perceives, thus in his mind saving face. Perhaps another driver honks for a third reason, taking it upon himself to correct you for doing something bad.

What if someone angry after a bad drive home then yells at his wife or kicks his dog. This is called displacement – a social-psychological process not to be confused with crime displacement evoked by crime prevention efforts. Such displacement is the essence of expressive violence. If people kick the dog to get back at the other drivers, expressive violence makes some sense. Unfortunately for quick scientific progress, researchers have verified that tensions and strains in fact can lead to more aggression. Thus laboratory experiments that increase aversive stimuli have demonstrated impact on subsequent aggression. This fits our commonsense notion that people are more difficult to deal with after a bad day at the office.

The other Felson explains this as an enhancement process rather than a causal process. When you get home after a bad day, you are more sensitive to insults and more likely to answer them in kind, and perhaps to escalate. And you are more likely to respond badly in an uncomfortable room. But this does not mean that aversive stimuli are the *cause* of your aggression.

People are more likely to respond to insults and escalate when they are too hot or otherwise annoyed. They are less likely to do that when more relaxed and comfortable. These facts are usually cited as proof that expressive aggression exists. It does not take too much analogizing to conclude that those on the bottom of society have more aversive stimuli and therefore must commit more crime because they are displaced.

An instrumentalist interprets these same facts differently. People have grievances. They usually suppress their annoyance at somebody or keep it in check, but sometimes they let their anger flow. And sometimes the recipient pays them back in kind. Thus the perceived grievance is the real source of aggression; the object of aggression is the person producing the grievance; and the aversive stimuli interfere with self-control. That means that stresses and strains work only indirectly to enhance aggressive escalations, by making it harder for people to suppress their annoyances at other people. The focus on the perceived grievance is much in tune with Clarke's emphasis on the offender's viewpoint. If the offender perceives a grievance, that perception influences his tendency to escalate towards violence.

Words vary, but interpretations of violence often are based on paired opposites: irrationality vs. rationality; out of control vs. under control; anger vs. calm. These dichotomies fit well with expressive vs. instrumental aggression. For an instrumentalist the dichotomy differs. Now there is no expressive, no irrationality, no "totally out of control." There may be anger, but it is not entirely devoid of direction. Rather, the anger is directed against the person or persons who displeased you, whether you are justified or not to think that.

From this viewpoint, an angry person still can make a very quick decision. That decision may be regretted later, but it is still a decision and still reflects what

The structure of angry violence 209

the decider wanted at the moment of truth. If you insult me, I give you double the insult back, you give me triple the first insult, and then one of us punches the other. We don't kick the dog or punch a third party. Our fight has a logic to it and involves decisions. Our anger is directed at the source of annoyance, at least in our mind at the time.

The instrumentalist social psychologists also emphasize third parties, such as bystanders, provokers, peacemakers and audiences (see Felson, Ribner and Siegel, 1984). Laboratory research can offer a very interesting approach to this question, for it varies these circumstances to see what happens. A confederate of the researcher insults the subject. The research question is whether the subject insults back and/or escalates the aggression. If a young male insults another young male, a response is more likely than when a middle-aged female insults a young male. If an audience is present during the insult, the subject is more likely to respond aggressively than when there is no audience except the insulter. If a peacemaker is present, instructed to calm the subject down, that often works. If a provoker is present to encourage a nasty response, that also tends to succeed. If a young male insults another young male in front of several other young males, then a response and escalation of aggression is especially likely. If we add alcohol and a variety of aversive stimuli, aggressive responses can be enhanced further.

Now we come to the most important point of this chapter. Each of the conditions generating aggression depends on routine activities. Likely insulters are not randomly distributed in time and space. Young males and other demographic groups are also non-random in their timing and spacing. Group sizes and compositions shift across the day and evening. The presence of alcohol, levels of intoxication, noise, presence of peacemakers – all of these conditions are subject to routine activity patterns, including leisure, work, school and home life. Convergences of family, friends, casual acquaintances and total strangers vary as well. And so the conditions for violence are highly contextual and situational, as well as very likely to be structured in the course of daily life.

Perhaps most important lesson is that self-control is not strictly an individual trait, a personal disposition. Self-control is itself an event that occurs in a context. Some contexts help an individual control himself while other contexts make that harder to do. This is not to deny that an individual may have an average ability to control himself, and that your average self-controllability may differ from mine. But each of us also has a variance within ourselves in our ability to control our emotions and to check our immediate decisions. The within-person variation may be as great as the between person variation, especially for the more frequent offenders.

Decisions vs. non-decisions – that is not the real battle inside each of us. Rather it is a battle of one decision process against another decision process. We have quick decision processes and reactions vs. slow decision processes. We have angry decision processes and calmer ones. We make decisions alone or influenced by others. Sometimes the others are nicer, sometimes, meaner, sometimes calmer, sometimes more agitated. Some decisions are under the influence of alcohol. Some decisions are inhibited and some are uninhibited.

The various situational measures that reduce or increase violence often operate through these mechanisms. Alcohol policy, pub and bar-room design, sports events, nightlife, school design, all of these influence where people are, what they are doing, how they converge and how criminal violence emerges. The audiences, provokers, peacemakers, encounters, alcohol levels, drinking contexts – all of these situational variations are very significant for crime, and many of them subject to situational crime prevention measures. And so we need to see angry violence as subject to structure and situation, sometimes amenable to policy containment.

References

Cicero, Marcus Tullius. (BC 80) *Pro Roscio Amerino Oratio 84*, available from http://www.thelatinlibrary.com. Accessed December 20, 2010.

Clarke, R.V. (1978) *Tackling Vandalism*. Home Office Research Studies No. 47. London: HMSO.

Clarke, R.V. (1996) "The distribution of deviance and exceeding the speed limit." *British Journal of Criminology* 36(2): 169–181.

Clarke, R.V. (1999) "Hot products: understanding, anticipating and reducing demand for stolen goods." Police Research Series, Paper 112. London: Home Office.

Clarke, R.V. and David Lester. (1989) *Suicide: Closing the Exits*. New York: Springer-Verlag.

Clarke, R.V. and D.N. Martin. (1971) *Absconding from Approved Schools*. Home Office Research Studies No. 12. London: HMSO.

Clarke, R.V. and Graeme Newman. (2006) *Outsmarting the Terrorists*. Portsmouth, NH: Praeger Security International.

Clarke, R.V. and Graeme Newman. (2009) *Policing Terrorism: An Executive's Guide. Office of Community Oriented Policing Services*. Washington, DC: US Department of Justice.

Clarke, R.V., R. Kemper and L. Wyckoff. (2001) "Controlling cell phone fraud in the US – lessons for the UK 'Foresight' prevention initiative." *Security Journal* 14(1): 7–22.

Felson, Richard B. (2000) "A social psychological approach to interpersonal aggression." In Vincent B. Van Hasselt and Michel Hersen (eds) *Aggression and Violence*. Boston: Allyn & Bacon.

Felson, Richard B. (2004) "A rational choice approach to violence." In Margaret A. Zahn, Henry H. Brownstein and Shelly L. Jackson (eds) *Violence: From Theory to Research*. Newark, NJ: LexisNexis/Anderson.

Felson, Richard B., Steven Ribner and Merrill Siegel. (1984) "Age and the effect of third parties during criminal violence." *Sociology and Social Research* 68: 452–462.

Felson, Richard B., William Baccaglini and George Gmelch. (1986) "Bar-room brawls: aggression and violence in Irish and American bars." In Anne Campbell and John J. Gibbs (eds) *Violent Transactions: The Limits of Personality*. New York: Basil Blackwell.

Homel, R., M. Hauritz, R. Wortley, G. McIlwain and R. Carvolth. (1997) "Preventing alcohol-related crime through community action: the Surfers-Paradise Safety Action Project." In R. Homel (ed.) *Policing for Prevention: Reducing Crime, Public Intoxication, and Injury*. Crime Prevention Studies, vol. 7. Monsey, NY: Criminal Justice Press.

Homel, R., R. Carvolth, M. Hauritz, G. McIlwain and R. Teague. (2004) "Making licensed venues safer for patrols: what environmental factors should be the focus of interventions?" *Drug and Alcohol Review* 23(1): 19–29.

Lemieux, Andrew M. and R.V. Clarke. (2009) "The international ban on ivory sales and its effect on elephant poaching in Africa." *British Journal of Criminology* 49: 451–471.

Luckenbill, David F. (1977) "Criminal homicide as a situated transaction." *Social Problems* 25(2): 176–186.

Newman, Graeme and R.V. Clarke. (2003) *Superhighway Robbery. Preventing Ecommerce Crime*. Cullompton: Willan Publishing.

Tedeschi, James and Richard B. Felson. (1994) *Violence, Aggression, and Coercive Actions*. Washington, DC: American Psychological Association (APA) Books.

17 Extending the reach of situational crime prevention

Graeme R. Newman and
Joshua D. Freilich

This chapter begins by demonstrating that the theoretical structure of situational crime prevention (SCP) set the foundation for its expansion and application to many different kinds of crimes that are largely ignored by mainstream criminology. Having begun with studies of car theft from parking lots, SCP now encompasses suicide, terrorism, cybercrime, child sexual abuse, corruption, and a range of organized crimes. The chapter ends by asking whether its rapid recent expansion may also spell its demise.

The theoretical evolution of SCP

The core concept of SCP is "opportunity reduction." First elaborated in a Home Office paper (Mayhew et al. 1976), the concept of opportunity was rescued from the then dominant paradigm of social opportunity (or lack of it) (Cloward and Ohlin 1960; Cohen 1955). The paper re-formed the concept by emphasizing (1) the immediate physical environment which made particular crimes possible and (2) the situational conditions that were "stimulus conditions, including opportunities for action presented by the immediate environment, . . . to provide – in a variety of ways – the inducements for criminality" (Mayhew et al. 1976: 2). The paper described other studies that demonstrated this aspect of opportunity in a variety of settings:

- steering locks that prevented car theft;
- changes in the physical environment that reduced boys absconding from borstal;
- reductions in the toxicity of coal gas that resulted in the decline of suicide by inhaling coal gas, a common method of suicide at the time;
- carelessness of victims that made stealing cars and burglary easier;
- the poor design of housing estates that reduced surveillance by neighbors thus increasing opportunities for crime and vandalism; and
- damage on busses resulting from poor supervision.

Thus, opportunity explained a variety of crimes, even suicide, which has traditionally been studied by psychiatrists because of its "obvious" deep psychological motivation. The general applicability of "opportunity" and the situational environment are built into the origins of SCP. The same 1976 paper outlines the essential components of opportunity:

1   offender based opportunities such as lifestyle, experience, age, and sex;
2   patterns of daily activity (clearly a precursor to routine activity theory);
3   the abundance of products that are available for theft (e.g., cars or items displayed in retail stores) or that may cause injury (e.g., guns);
4   environments where there is reduced security, such as dark streets, lack of surveillance or supervision in public places such as busses, housing estates, or retail stores.

These four types of opportunity were connected to eight opportunity reducing techniques (Clarke and Mayhew 1980) classified into three types: target hardening, target removal, and various forms of surveillance. Subsequent research on routine activity theory (Cohen and Felson 1979), inducements to crime and issues of access control and defensible space (Poyner 1991; Hough, Clarke, and Mayhew 1980) resulted in twelve techniques, organized under three headings: increasing the effort, increasing the risks, and reducing rewards of offending (Clarke 1992: 11). Clarke and Homel (1997) added a column of "removing excuses" for crime to incorporate "folk crimes" that "everybody does" (e.g., traffic offenses) unlike the predatory crimes of "hardened criminals" (Clarke 1997: 16). Finally, in response to criticism by Wortley (2001), who argued that situational aspects of the social and physical environments may precipitate criminal acts, Clarke and Cornish (2003) added another column, "reducing provocations" to make twenty-five techniques (see Table 17.1 – a more complete and interactive version is available at http://www.popcenter.org/25techniques/).

Table 17.1 summarizes the expansion of SCP from its simple beginnings to a complex social psychological theory of human behavior. Significantly, Cornish and Clarke's reply to Wortley initially emphasized commonality, but subsequently demonstrated how their approach differed. They showed that the first three columns were primary in a causal sequence of behaviors that led to criminal offending and that Wortley's precipitators were secondary. Wortley had argued the opposite (see Figure 17.1), that characteristics of the environment provoked internal dispositions in the offender and that without such conditions, offenders would not have the motivation to commit the crime. Wortley identified the controlling conditions that invoked these behaviors and implied that certain conditions were embedded within the psychology of individuals that may remain dormant, unless the external (situational) conditions of provocation or invocation were in place. The ways to control these external situational factors ("cues") are summarized in Table 17.2.

The difference in Cornish and Clarke's model of causation rests on the primacy given to "rational choice" and its relationship to motivation. The essential differences in their models are as follows.

Table 17.1 Twenty-five techniques of SCP

Increase the effort	Increase the risks	Reduce the rewards	Reduce provocations	Remove excuses
1 *Target harden* • Steering column locks and immobilizers • Anti-robbery screens • Tamper-proof packaging	6 *Extend guardianship* • Take routine precautions: go out in group at night, leave signs of occupancy, carry phone • "Cocoon" neighborhood watch	11 *Conceal targets* • Off-street parking • Gender-neutral phone directories • Unmarked bullion trucks	16 *Reduce frustrations and stress* • Efficient queues and polite service • Expanded seating • Soothing music/ muted lights	21 *Set rules* • Rental agreements • Harassment codes • Hotel registration
2 *Control access to facilities* • Entry phones • Electronic card access • Baggage screening	7 *Assist natural surveillance* • Improved street lighting • Defensible space design • Support whistleblowers	12 *Remove targets* • Removable car radios • Women's refuges • Pre-paid cards for pay phones	17 *Avoid disputes* • Separate enclosures for rival soccer fans • Reduce crowding in pubs • Fixed cab fares	22 *Post instructions* • "No parking" • "Private property" • "Extinguish camp fires"
3 *Screen exits* • Ticket needed for exit • Export documents • Electronic merchandise tags	8 *Reduce anonymity* • Taxi driver IDs • "How's my driving?" decals • School uniforms	13 *Identify property* • Property marking • Vehicle licensing and parts marking • Cattle branding	18 *Reduce emotional arousal* • Controls on violent pornography • Enforce good behavior on soccer field • Prohibit racial slurs	23 *Alert conscience* • Roadside speed display boards • Signatures for customs declarations • "Shoplifting is stealing"
4 *Deflect offenders* • Street closures • Separate bathrooms for women • Disperse pubs	9 *Utilize place managers* • CCTV for double-deck buses • Two clerks for convenience stores • Reward vigilance	14 *Disrupt markets* • Monitor pawn shops • Controls on classified ads • License street vendors	19 *Neutralize peer pressure* • "Idiots drink and drive" • "It's OK to say no" • Disperse troublemakers at school	24 *Assist compliance* • Easy library checkout • Public lavatories • Litter bins
5 *Control tools/weapons* • "Smart" guns • Disabling stolen cell phones • Restrict spray paint sales to juveniles	10 *Strengthen formal surveillance* • Red light cameras • Burglar alarms • Security guards	15 *Deny benefits* • Ink merchandise tags • Graffiti cleaning • Speed humps	20 *Discourage imitation* • Rapid repair of vandalism • V-chips in TVs • Censor details of modus operandi	25 *Control drugs and alcohol* • Breathalyzers in pubs • Server intervention • Alcohol-free events

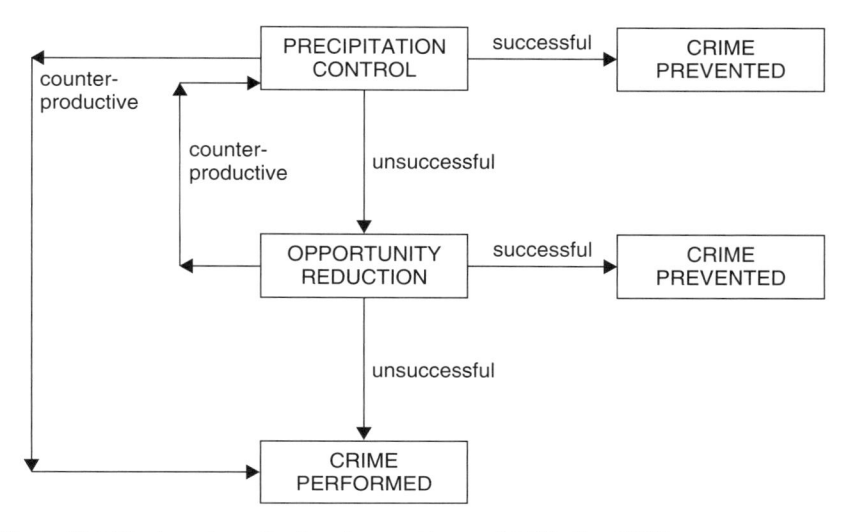

Extending the reach of situational crime prevention 215

Figure 17.1 The two-stage situational prevention model (Wortley 1998).

Table 17.2 Classification of precipitation-control strategies

Controlling Prompts	Controlling Pressures	Reducing Permissibility	Reducing Provocations
Controlling triggers	Reducing inappropriate conformity	Rule setting	Reducing frustration
Providing reminders	Reducing inappropriate obedience	Clarifying responsibility	Reducing crowding
Reducing inappropriate imitation	Encouraging compliance	Clarifying consequences	Respecting territory
Setting positive expectations	Reducing anonymity	Personalizing victims	Controlling environmental irritants

Source: Adapted from Wortley (2001).

Clarke and Cornish

Assumed motivated offender → rational choice → situational environment → choice structuring properties → offender "ready" → offense committed

Here the situational cues including provocations and precipitators modify rational choice, or feed into the choice structuring properties.

Wortley

Internal states awaiting provocation → situational environment → motivated offender → choice structuring properties → offender "ready" → offense committed

This summary simplifies the different models, but to delve further takes us beyond the present chapter. It is sufficient to note that, even though Clarke and Cornish devoted most of their paper responding to Wortley's critique, the table of twenty-five techniques ultimately incorporated most of Wortley's controlling techniques. Regardless, therefore, of Cornish and Clarke's protestations, they incorporated Wortley's complex theoretical assumptions about human motivation and the role of rational choice (or lack of it). The fourth and fifth columns of the twenty-five techniques are "soft" on rational choice. Indeed, they open the door for applying SCP techniques without the assumption of rational choice, but instead invoking psychological (or even biological) states. This is potentially a big door, since it engages the traditional preoccupations of criminology against which SCP originally claimed exception – offender dispositions and types of offenders, etc. In fact, Cornish and Clarke devote considerable space to types of offenders (though limited to opportunistic as against experienced offenders), and highlighted "individual differences," the hallmark of dispositional approaches. The theoretical expansion therefore, while integrating Wortley's criticisms, and making SCP more adaptable to all kinds of situations and offenders, could also spell its theoretical demise, should its unique perspective on the situational environment of crimes (as opposed to the offender) be undermined. This is unlikely however, because both models unswervingly focus on intervention, analyzing *behaviors at the crime scene*, i.e., the actual *product* of the causal sequences and working backward from there. The theoretical differences as to how these models operate must be inferred from their tables for the control of offending behavior and situational environments. In fact, a number of Wortley's intervention techniques had already been included in Clarke's sixteen techniques. As Clarke and Cornish (2003: 66) note:

> "[W]hatever the issues that "prompts," first-time offenders, and telescoped decision-making processes may pose for theory, as issues for crime prevention practice they are typically dealt with by the same techniques that regulate the basic opportunity cues (those of risk, effort, and reward) themselves.

The primacy of intervention therefore, remains. Wortley argues that it is enhanced by adding his "soft" interventions compared to the "hard" interventions typified in the first three columns of the twenty-five techniques. However, this is slightly misleading, and potentially troubling. There are at least two ways in which traditional SCP is hard. First, originally interventions were applied to the situational environment without regard to offender motivation or behavior. For example, Clarke's research (1999) on the inherent properties of targets that make them attractive to offenders (CRAVED), has little to do with offender characteristics (though these are implied). The construction of physical barriers has nothing to do with the internal psychology of offenders. If it works, it works and we know from countless studies that such hardening techniques work.

The second issue concerning "hard" and "soft" SCP is that of policy or, perhaps ideology. As Wortley observes, target hardening often involves visible and intrusive interventions such as physical barriers that sometimes may provoke rather than prevent (see for example Figure 17.1 above). Wortley counters that his "soft" interventions are less obvious or intrusive. For example, in a prison setting, physical barriers that separate inmates from guards may provoke inmates into retaliations. In contrast, the soft approach seeks to avoid such provocations by constructing social settings in which guard–inmate relations are more "amicable" and the prison environment is more inviting (Wortley 2002). Yet it is the quiet control of human behavior, less seen and not even noticed (hidden cameras, collection of information to track financial transactions, tracking routes taken on a freeway), that is currently attacked as undermining individual privacy rights (see for e.g., Garland 2001; Staples 1997, and for a reply, Newman and Clarke 2003: 178–206). Thus, from the ideological point of view, there is no distinction between SCP that is "hard" or "soft." Rather, the question is how much intrusion is acceptable for how much prevention (Felson and Clarke 1997). As SCP extends its reach it is difficult to know where that line will be drawn. Finding that line will be easier when "hard" interventions are applied however, since they are presumptively more visible so that we know at least when we are being controlled. With Wortley's soft control, we may not know until it is too late.

The genius of specificity

Let us return to the table of twenty-five techniques. Cornish and Clarke (1986) have repeatedly stated that SCP focuses interventions to reduce very specific crimes (e.g., reduction of car theft in parking lots, not reduction of crime or even car crime). They (1986: 2) note that "a crime-specific focus was adopted . . . because the situational context of decision making and the information being handled will vary greatly among offenses." This focus on the specificity of the crime was important to later research that evaluated the success of situational interventions (see for e.g., the many case studies in Clarke (1997) and in the SCP case studies database now available at http://www.popcenter.org/library/scp/). It also paved the way for the expansion of SCP into problem-oriented policing where the focus on solving specific problems dominates (see Eck and Madensen, Chapter 6, this volume and the extensive collection of Problem-Specific Guides for Police published by the Center for Problem-oriented Policing, many of which are heavily indebted to SCP). In sum, it is a matter for the SCP analyst to break down crime problems into their most specific forms, noting the specific environments in which they occur. Subsequently, he/she must scan the twenty-five techniques to craft the appropriate interventions. What works will depend on many factors, including the cost and practicality of implementation. There are so many techniques available that it is hard to imagine any problem to which one or more of them would not apply.

The specificity, therefore, tends toward the infinite and often there will be multiple techniques from which to choose. Felson and Clarke (1997) note that individual communities may differ in the type of policy they choose to prevent the very same problem. Rather than a "fortress society" invariably resulting from SCP techniques, each community will have the type of situational prevention with which it is most comfortable.

Extending the reach

SCP's theoretical structure and its emphasis on reducing opportunities to commit crime have formed an approach that is adaptable to different environments in which motivated offenders operate. The following is an incomplete listing of SCP's reach into crime problems that have resided beyond the bounds of traditional criminology, but which are easily encompassed by the twenty-five techniques.

Suicide

Paradoxically, this example exemplifies the complexity of crossing the traditional boundaries of any discipline. This is because the suicide studies (Clarke and Mayhew 1988, 1989) actually formed the early basis of SCP by daring to suggest that fluctuations in suicide could be explained as much by the opportunities present to carry it out as by deep internal psychological trauma. The study was based on a simple observation: suicides had unexpectedly decreased in England and Wales between 1963 and 1975, from 5,714 to 3,693, when suicide was increasing in most European countries. Much of this reduction resulted from the progressive decrease in the amount of toxic carbon monoxide in the coal gas used for cooking and heating in most homes. Clarke and Mayhew (1989: 2) concluded: "This view of suicide has implications for its [suicide] prevention and, by analogy, for the prevention of crime." The study was quickly followed by a book (Clarke and Lester 1989) that drew on studies from other disciplines and extended the observation to other forms of suicide including the availability of guns and the toxicity of automobile emissions.

Auto theft

Clarke and Harris' (1992a, 1992b) scientific study of car theft in the United States identified two types of car theft: permanent and temporary, and evaluated the effectiveness of parts marking on the reduction of car theft (it was not effective). Subsequently, a study of reducing car theft from parking lots (it depended on how the lots were designed and operated) (Clarke and Mayhew 1998), led to many studies that used SCP as a starting point (see for e.g., Maxfield and Clarke 2004; Farrell et al. 2008).

Cybercrime

The simple idea of opportunity applied obviously to cybercrime just as it did to car crime. The Internet, through its "superhighway" of communication and storage of valuable information, provided new opportunities for crime, especially access to valuable information, including money in bank accounts. Newman and Clarke (2003) surveyed these new opportunities for crime and focused on strategies for corporations and individuals to use in countering these "new" crimes. Many of the techniques that could be employed did not depend on high-tech solutions (though these were important) but on the analysis of how specific crimes were perpetrated and on constructing environments where human error was minimized. This work was followed by an analysis of the "new" crime of identity theft (McNally and Newman 2008).

Terrorism

After 9/11 it seemed obvious that, since much of the operational point of terrorists was to attack specific targets, SCP could prevent such attacks by reducing opportunities for terrorists to reach their targets. Clarke and Newman (2006) developed this thesis, identifying the four pillars of terrorist opportunity: targets, weapons, tools, and facilitating conditions, each of which provided unique opportunities for terrorists to successfully select their targets and carry out their attacks. The book challenged the presumption that eradicating terrorism's "root causes" was the only way to eliminate terrorism (Freilich and Chermak 2009). By linking the four pillars of terrorist opportunity to techniques from the table of twenty-five techniques, the authors constructed guidelines for governments to develop a coherent strategy for fighting terrorism. This was followed by a manual for policing terrorism at the local level (Newman and Clarke 2008) that used a problem solving approach. Recently, Freilich and Newman (2009) demonstrated how SCP's approach to terrorism was consistent and supported by work from a variety of disciplines, including military science, biology, public health, and epidemiology.

Child sexual abuse

Wortley and Smallbone (Smallbone and Wortley 2001; Wortley and Smallbone 2006a) examined the specific social psychological environments in which child sexual abuse occurred. They constructed a list of twenty-eight different strategies employed by child sex offenders, usually the use or construction of opportunities by offenders to gain access to children for sexual encounters. They adopted a tripartite classification of types of child sex abusers (situational, opportunistic, and predatory) – an acknowledgement of the "dispositional" approach to the causes of crime – and linked these to particular situations they described as challenging, tempting, and precipitating. As with most crimes, they found that location was supreme, that offenders sexually abused children most often in the child's home, institutional setting, or locations where access was easy (see also Terry 2008). However, their approach to actual techniques to be employed in prevention hinged on keeping children out of reach of offenders. They identified the familiar techniques of increasing the effort, increasing the risk, and controlling prompts as the most likely effective techniques of intervention. Wortley and Smallbone (2006b) also identified Internet child pornography as an important environmental condition that provided prompts, temptation, and access to possible victims, and offered a range of techniques of intervention.

Migration and border control

Guerette (2007) used the "Haddon matrix" that analyzed car crashes as a sequence of events (pre-crash, crash, and post-crash) to study border control at the Mexican border south of San Diego. The similarity of the Haddon matrix to SCP's requirement of careful analysis of the environmental conditions and specific nature of the offense guided Guerette's work in following the sequence of events for individuals to illegally cross the border into the US. Guerette and Clarke (2005) found that the erection of fences (increasing the effort) along the border accompanied by increased surveillance and border patrol (increasing the risk) reduced the amount of illegal immigration. However, it also shifted the problem to one of human smuggling, when organized criminal gangs began to charge money to guide illegals through hazardous terrain where fences had not been erected. Guerette (2006) also found that applying SCP to the study of border control could also help in reducing migrant deaths resulting from attempts to cross the border illegally.

Organized crime

SCP's emphasis on studying how crimes are carried out rather than why (Cornish 1994) led to analysis of organized crime, until recently viewed as the province of the mysterious, monolithic mafia-type of organization. As Cornish and Clarke (2001) began to demonstrate, organized crime could be analyzed as a series of scripts for specific types of criminal activity, each activity requiring its own type of organization (Levi 1998). It became apparent that, unsurprisingly, organized crime displayed many of the attributes of ordinary crime: it was facilitated by local conditions, particularly in respect to auto theft (Brown and Clarke 2004), composed typically of small networks of criminal entrepreneurs (Natarajan and Clarke 2004), and a step-by-step approach (of how cars were stolen and disposed of for example), revealed points where SCP techniques could be applied (Bullock et al. 2010a). Many studies have now applied SCP to organized crime (Bouloukos et al. 2003; Ekblom 2000; Felson 2006; Van de Bunt and van der Schoot 2003; van der Schoot 2006), culminating in the groundbreaking volume (Bullock et al. 2010b) that brought together papers covering a range of organized crimes, such as auto theft, timber theft, human trafficking, and contraband cigarettes.

Endangered species and market reduction

Organized crime invariably requires markets to exploit supply and satisfy demand for illegal goods and services. Disrupting markets in stolen goods is listed as technique number fourteen of the twenty-five techniques, first identified by Sutton (1998). Schneider (2008) has recently demonstrated the promising approach of market reduction to preserving endangered species, and Lemieux and Clarke (2009) have taken this further in their study of elephant poaching in Africa. They demonstrated how regulated markets reduced poaching, unregulated markets increased it, and weak border controls and local official corruption exacerbated the problem. Much of the effectiveness of market reduction depends on how regulations are enforced, which has led to an analysis of the ways of gaining compliance, such as "cap-and-trade," a technique of market manipulation that motivates compliance (Newman 2011).

Tax evasion

Research has demonstrated that antecedent events, including certain nonviolent activities, may act as a gateway to "escalating" illegal behavior that includes violent acts such as hate crime and terrorism (Damphousse and Smith 2004). Belli and Freilich (2009) applied SCP to a nonviolent crime common in the American far-right, i.e., the failure or refusal to file an income return for ideological reasons. Conceptually, ideologically motivated tax refusal presented an interesting challenge for SCP because it falls under the legal category of "crimes of omission." SCP has commonly been applied to criminal offenses requiring proactive behavior by offender (e.g., burglary, traffic offenses, etc.). However, this specific crime is one in which individuals are held criminally responsible as a result of their failure to act. They examined factors that contribute to the occurrence of tax refusal among far-right extremists, such as its passive nature and the offenders' decision-making process and resources, to highlight the opportunity structure and key points for intervention. Belli and Freilich suggested the use of a "soft" approach – as defined by Wortley – through eight situational techniques that promote compliance, remove excuses, and induce pro-social behaviors. Since tax refusal can be considered a *nonviolent crime with a political motive*, their study opens up the possibility that such incidents might be identified as precursors to violent ideologically motivated action, such as hate crime and terrorism, and therefore further highlights the potential of SCP as an effective counter-terrorism strategy.

Concluding remarks

This chapter, briefly, summarized SCP's history and reviewed its theoretical structure. It demonstrated that SCP has expanded greatly by increasing the number of its prevention techniques (from eight to twenty-five), allowing its application to new crime types that are mostly ignored by orthodox criminology. Significantly, SCP has not wavered from Ronald Clarke's lifelong commitment to crime reduction. Indeed, Clarke has worked with scores of collaborators and inspired legions of others to work for this same end (Freilich and Natarajan 2009). In doing so, SCP has prospered, evolved conceptually and been applied to the ever-changing face of new crime problems as well as the standard property and street crimes it long focused on. Consequently, its theoretical structure and assumptions about human behavior have expanded and even begun to encompass aspects of "mainstream" criminology, particularly its acknowledgment of dispositional characteristics of offenders – an orthodoxy of traditional criminology against which it originally rebelled. Will the undifferentiated mass of traditional criminology absorb SCP into its textbooks and journals, as it has in fact done to "rational choice?" We think not. Regardless of the growing commonality of the assumptions about human behavior between SCP and traditional criminology, SCP remains far apart because of its prime directive of solving practical problems – the prevention of crime – regardless of the theoretical constructs that drive it. Until mainstream criminology adopts an interventionist orientation to the study of crime, it is likely that SCP will remain in exile, and even evolve into areas of public security that move it far from the postmodern preoccupations of criminology today.

References

Belli, R. and J.D. Freilich. (2009). "Situational crime prevention and non-violent terrorism: a 'soft' approach against ideologically motivated tax-refusal." *Crime Prevention Studies*, 25, 173–206.

Bouloukos, A.C., G. Farrell, and G. Laycock. (2003). *Transnational Organised Crime in Europe and North America: The Need for Situational Crime Prevention Efforts.* HEUNI. http://www.heuni.fi/uploads/0gyxd5c8.pdf.

Brown, R. and R.V. Clarke. (2004). "Police intelligence and theft of vehicles for export: recent UK experience," in M.G. Maxwell and Clarke, R.V. (eds), *Understanding and Preventing Car Theft. Crime Prevention Studies*, volume 17. Monsey, NY: Criminal Justice Press.

Bullock, Karen, Ronald V. Clarke, and Nick Tilley. (2010a). "Introduction," in *Situational Prevention of Organised Crimes*. Jill Dando Institute of Crime Science. Cullompton: Willan Publishing.

Bullock, Karen, Ronald V. Clarke, and Nick Tilley (eds). (2010b). *Situational Prevention of Organised Crimes*. Jill Dando Institute of Crime Science. Cullompton: Willan Publishing.

Clarke, R.V. (1992). *Situational Crime Prevention: Successful Case Studies*. 1st edn. New York: Harrow and Heston.

Clarke, R.V. (1997). *Situational Crime Prevention: Successful Case Studies*. 2nd edn. New York: Harrow and Heston.

Clarke, R.V. (1999). *Hot Products: Understanding, Anticipating and Reducing Demand for Stolen Goods*. Police Research Series, Paper 112. London: Home Office.

Clarke, R.V. and D.B Cornish. (2003). "Opportunities, precipitators and criminal decisions: a reply to Wortley's critique of situational crime prevention," in M. Smith and D.B. Cornish (eds), *Theory for Situational Crime Prevention. Crime Prevention Studies*, volume 16. Monsey, NY: Criminal Justice Press.

Clarke, R.V. and P.M. Harris. (1992a). "Auto theft and its prevention," in M. Tonry (ed.), *Crime and Justice: A Review of Research*, volume 16. Chicago: University of Chicago Press.

Clarke, R.V. and P.M. Harris. (1992b). "A rational choice perspective on the targets of automobile theft." *Criminal Behaviour and Mental Health*, 2, 25–42.

Clarke, R.V. and R. Homel. (1997). "A revised classification of situational crime prevention techniques," in S.P. Lab (ed.), *Crime Prevention at a Crossroads*. Cincinnati: Anderson Publishing.

Clarke, R.V. and David Lester. (1989). *Suicide: Closing the Exits*. New York: Springer-Verlag.

Clarke, R.V. and P.M. Mayhew. (1980). *Designing out Crime*. London: HMSO.

Clarke, R.V. and P.M. Mayhew. (1988). "Crime as opportunity: a note on domestic gas suicide in Britain and the Netherlands." *British Journal of Criminology*, 29, 35–46.

Clarke, R.V. and P.M. Mayhew. (1989). "The British gas suicide story and its criminological implications," in M. Tonry and N. Morris (eds), *Crime and Justice*, volume 10. Chicago: University of Chicago Press.
Clarke, R.V. and P. Mayhew. (1998). "Preventing crime in parking lots: what we know and need to know," in M. Felson and R. Peiser (eds), *Crime Prevention Through Real Estate Management and Development*. Washington, DC: Urban Land Institute.
Clarke, R.V. and Graeme R. Newman. (2006). *Outsmarting the Terrorists*. Westport, CT: Praeger.
Cloward, R.A. and L.E. Ohlin. (1960). *Delinquency and Opportunity*. London: Routledge & Kegan Paul.
Cohen, A. (1955). *Delinquent Boys: The Culture of the Gang*. Glencoe, IL: Free Press.
Cohen, A. and M. Felson. (1979). "Social change and crime rate trends: a routine activity approach." *American Sociological Review*, 44(4), 558–601.
Cornish, D.B. (1994). 'The procedural analysis of offending and its relevance for situational prevention,' in R.V. Clarke (ed.), *Crime Prevention Studies*, volume 3. Monsey, NY: Criminal Justice Press (accessible at www.popcenter.org).
Cornish, Derek B. and Ronald V. Clarke. (1986). "Introduction," in *The Reasoning Criminal*. New York: Springer-Verlag.
Cornish, D.B. and R.V. Clarke. (2001). "Analyzing organised crimes," in A.R. Piquero and S.G. Tibbetts (eds), *Rational Choice and Criminal Behaviour: Recent Research and Future Challenges*. Hamden, CT: Garland Science.
Damphousse, K.R. and B.L. Smith. (2004). "Terrorism and empirical testing: using indictment data to assess changes in terrorist conduct." *Sociology of Crime, Law and Deviance*, 5, 75–90.
Ekblom, P. (2000). "Preventing organized crime: a conceptual framework." Presentation at Europol workshop on Organized Crime, The Hague, May 2000 (available from p.ekblom@csm.arts.ac.uk).
Farrell, G., N. Tilley, A. Tseloni, and J. Mailley. (2008). "The crime drop and the security hypothesis." *British Society of Criminology Newsletter*, 62, 17–21.
Felson, M. (2006). "The ecosystem for organized crime." HEUNI 25th Anniversary Lecture (Paper No. 26). Helsinki: The European Institute for Crime Prevention and Control, United Nations.
Felson, M. and R.V. Clarke. (1997). "The ethics of situational crime prevention," in G. Newman, R.V. Clarke, and S.G. Shoham (eds), *Rational Choice and Situational Crime Prevention*. Brookfield, VT: Ashgate.
Freilich, J.D. and S.M. Chermak. (2009). "Preventing deadly encounters between law enforcement and American far-rightists." *Crime Prevention Studies*, volume 25. Monsey, NY: Criminal Justice Press.
Freilich, J.D. and M. Natarajan. (2009). "Ronald Clarke," in K. Haywood, S. Maruna, and J. Mooney (eds), *Fifty Key Thinkers in Criminology*. New York: Routledge Press.
Freilich, Joshua D. and Graeme R. Newman. (eds) (2009). *Reducing Terrorism through Situational Crime Prevention. Crime Prevention Studies*, volume 25. Monsey, NY: Criminal Justice Press.
Garland, David. (2001). *The Culture of Control: Crime and Social Order in Contemporary Society*. Chicago: University of Chicago Press.
Guerette, Rob T. (2006). "Preventing deaths of illegal migrants: a possible role for situational crime prevention," in J. Freilich and R.T. Guerette (eds), *Migration, Culture Conflict, Crime and Terrorism*. Burlington, VT: Ashgate Publishing.
Guerette, Rob T. (2007). "Immigration policy, border security and migrant deaths: an

impact evaluation of life saving efforts under the border safety initiative." *Criminology & Public Policy*, 6(2), 201–222.
Guerette, Rob T. and Ronald V. Clarke. (2005). "Border enforcement, organized crime, and deaths of smuggled migrants on the United States–Mexico border." *European Journal on Criminal Policy and Research*, 11(2), 159–174.
Hough, J.M., R.V. Clarke, and P. Mayhew. (1980). "Introduction," in R.V. Clarke and P. Mayhew (eds), *Designing Out Crime*. London: HMSO.
Lemieux, Andrew M. and Ronald V. Clarke. (2009). "The international ban on ivory sales and its effects on elephant poaching in Africa." *British Journal of Criminology*, 49, 451–471.
Levi, M. (1998). "Perspectives on organised crime: an overview." *The Howard Journal*, 37(4), 335–345.
McNally, Megan and Graeme Newman. (eds). (2008). *Perspectives on Identity Theft. Crime Prevention Studies*, volume 23. Monsey, NY: Criminal Justice Press.
Maxfield, M.G. and R.V. Clarke (eds). (2004). *Understanding and Preventing Car Theft. Crime Prevention Studies*, volume 17. Monsey, NY: Criminal Justice Press.
Mayhew, P., R.V. Clarke, A. Sturman, and M. Hough. (1976). "Crime as opportunity." Home Office Research Study No. 34. London: HMSO.
Natarajan, M. and R.V. Clarke. (2004). "Understanding and controlling organised crime: the feasibility of a situational approach." Paper presented at the annual Environmental Criminology and Crime Analysis Seminar, Wellington, New Zealand, July (electronic copy available from rvgclarke@aol.com).
Newman, Graeme R. (2011). "A market approach to crime prevention," in P. Ekblom (ed.), *Design Against Crime: Crime Proofing Everyday Objects. Crime Prevention Studies*, volume 27. Boulder, CO: Lynne Rienner Publishers (in press).
Newman, Graeme R. and R.V. Clarke. (2003). *Superhighway Robbery. Preventing Ecommerce Crime*. Cullompton: Willan Publishing.
Newman, Graeme R. and R.V. Clarke. (2008). *Policing Terrorism: An Executive's Guide*. Washington, DC: US Department of Justice.
Poyner, B. (1991). "Situational crime prevention in two parking facilities." *Security Journal*, 2, 96–101.
Schneider, J.L. (2008). "Reducing the illicit trade in wildlife: the market reduction approach." *Journal of Contemporary Criminal Justice*, 24, 274–295.
Smallbone, S.W. and R.K. Wortley. (2001). "Child sexual abuse: offender characteristics and modus operandi." *Trends and Issues in Crime and Criminal Justice* #193. Canberra: Australian Institute of Criminology.
Staples, Willam G. (1997). *The Culture of Surveillance: Discipline and Social Control in the United States*. New York: St. Martin's Press.
Sutton, M. (1998). *Handling Stolen Goods and Theft: A Market Reduction Approach*. Home Office Research Study 178. London: Home Office.
Terry, K.J. (2008). "Stained glass: the nature and scope of sexual abuse crisis in the Catholic Church." *Criminal Justice & Behavior*, 35(5), 549–569.
Van de Bunt, H. and van der Schoot, C. (2003). *Prevention of Organised Crime*. The Hague: WODC 215. http://english.wodc.nl/onderzoeksdatabase/traceren-van-mogelijkheden-voor-preventie-die-zich-bij-lopende-opsporingsonderzoeken-aandienen.aspx.
van der Schoot, C. (2006). "Organised crime prevention in the Netherlands." Ph.D. thesis, Erasmus University, Amsterdam.
Wortley, R.K. (1998). "A two-stage model of situational crime prevention." *Studies on Crime and Crime Prevention*, 7, 173–188.

Wortley, R.K. (2001). "A classification of techniques for controlling situational precipitators of crime." *Security Journal*, 14, 63–82.

Wortley, R.K. (2002). *Situational Prison Control: Crime Prevention in Correctional Institutions*. Cambridge: Cambridge University Press.

Wortley, R.K. and S.W. Smallbone. (2006a). *Applying Situational Principles to Sexual Offenses against Children. Crime Prevention Studies*, volume 19. Monsey, NY: Criminal Justice Press.

Wortley, R.K. and S.W. Smallbone. (2006b). "Child pornography on the Internet guide No. 41 (2006)." Center for Problem-oriented Policing. Washington, DC: US Department of Justice.

18 Contrasting hotspots
Did the opportunists make the heat?

Kate Bowers and Shane Johnson

Introduction

Two of the many inspiring contributions made by Ron Clarke are his work on rational choice theory and his conceptual analysis of the likelihood of crime displacement (e.g. Clarke and Cornish 1985; Cornish and Clarke 1986, 1987; Clarke and Weisburd 1994). With respect to displacement, a prevailing concern for some has been that where interventions affect situations rather than people, offenders (their dispositions unchanged) will simply displace their activity in one way or another. The idea of the reasoning offender who weighs up the costs and benefits of committing crime (however brief this calculation might be) challenges this view and informs the way we think about the potential for crime and crime displacement. From this perspective, displacement is just one possible consequence of situational crime prevention. That is, such reasoning emphasises the possibility of the reverse of crime displacement – a diffusion of crime control benefit – whereby offenders not only decrease their offending against those in receipt of an intervention but also against those nearby or that (say) share similar characteristics. This is an important theoretical contribution but, perhaps more importantly to Ron, has clear implications for crime reduction policy. Our intention here is to consider crime displacement from a complementary but slightly different perspective, in this case using crime analysis and crime mapping techniques to explore differences between the locations of choice of *distinct groups* of offenders.

It is well established that crime risk varies geographically, with some areas representing hotspots of crime (e.g. Sherman et al. 1989). Just as crime risk varies across space, it is evident that the population of offenders is not homogeneous and offenders may be classified in a variety of ways. For example, Cornish and Clarke (2003) propose an offender typology that differentiates between antisocial predators, mundane offenders and provoked offenders. The exact details of the typology are not critical for present purposes, but the three groups might be thought of as varying along a continuum of those who routinely manipulate situations to facilitate unambiguous illegal activity, to ordinarily law-abiding citizens who are provoked into criminal action on rare occasions because (for example) they are forced to react to an encountered situation (see Wortley 1996).

A more general differentiation with which most readers will be familiar, but which is much less subtle than the Cornish and Clarke typology, contrasts those offenders who might be considered 'prolific' or 'career criminals' with those who could be described as more 'opportunistic' or 'occasional' offenders. Different groups of one kind or another are useful to consider as crime prevention effort might be expected to affect them differently (for a more thorough discussion, see Cornish and Clarke 2003). For example, while efforts to prevent crime might drastically reduce offending rates for opportunistic offenders, they might have little effect on prolific offenders or may merely displace their offending activity. If this is the case and the population of prolific offenders (however defined) is the dominant one then this would be problematic for crime control policy. If they are not, then such concerns will be assuaged. Of course, this is an oversimplification, but hopefully we have not moved too far from the core issues.

Considering crime hotspots, despite an acknowledgement that offenders do not represent a homogeneous group, there is relatively little empirical investigation (of which the authors are aware) of the spatial patterns of crime generated by those who might be classified into different groups using the kinds of typologies discussed. This is not to say that offender spatial decision-making has not been considered in the research literature. In fact, for some time there has existed a large body of research concerned with the journey to crime – the distance offenders travel from the home – to crime-site locations (for a recent treatment, see Townsley and Sidebottom 2010). Typically, such research suggests that most crime trips are short (e.g. Rengert and Wasilchick 1985).

Moreover, and inspired by rational choice theory, pioneering work by Bernasco and colleagues (Bernasco and Nieuwbeerta 2005; see also Clare et al. 2009) has employed a type of statistical technique known as the random utility model to try to identify variables – other than distance from the home location – that most strongly influence offender decision-making about where to offend. For burglary, such factors include the ethnic heterogeneity of areas and the percentage of single-family dwellings (Bernasco and Nieuwbeerta 2005). However, what these types of study tend to examine are the characteristics of the types of areas that offenders select, not the precise areas themselves. In the current chapter, we adopt the reverse approach and take some initial steps in exploring the utility of so doing. That is, our unit of analysis is the *hotspot*, and our goal is to examine if and how hotspots generated by different types of offenders vary.

Different types of hotspot have, of course, received attention in the literature before. For example, Brantingham and Brantingham (1995) differentiate between two theoretical types: crime attractors and generators. Crime generators are conceptualised as areas in which abundant criminal opportunities are uncovered (and exploited) as a consequence of offenders frequently using them while engaging in legitimate routine activities. Such opportunities may be exploited by any type of offender, and areas may emerge as hotspots even if they are rarely targeted by those who are most prolific.

Crime attractors, however, are those high-crime locales that are *known* to provide good opportunities for crime and generally attract offenders (presumably prolifics) for the sole purpose of offending. Thus, in these two types of area, crime pattern formation occurs as a result of two different types of process. In many cases, hotspots will be generated by a combination of the two processes, but one may be dominant. However, despite this theoretical development, as far as we are aware, little or no empirical research has examined crime hotspot configuration from the perspective of the types of offenders who target them, how far they travel to do so and so on.

In a recent paper, Short et al. (2010) describe a mathematical model of crime pattern formation which advances this avenue of enquiry. Put simply, their model encapsulates both time-stable and dynamic mechanisms and predicts that two types of crime hotspot likely exist: those that are *subcritical* or largely time-stable, and those that are *supercritical* or that are more influenced by dynamic factors, such as offender foraging strategies (see Johnson et al. 2009). The implications of their work are important and in particular generate different predictions for whether crime prevention will suppress or displace criminal activity in different types of hotspot. In particular, the model suggests that crime reduction strategies should suppress subcritical but not supercritical hotspots.

The Short et al. model is, of course, purely mathematical and has not been tested empirically. To do so is not the aim of the current chapter. Our aim is much more modest. Rather, given that there is a paucity – or possibly a complete absence – of research that has examined how hotspots vary in terms of the offenders who commit the crimes that take place within them, the aim of the current study is to take some initial steps in this direction using data for the crime of burglary in one county of the UK. The sorts of question we seek to explore are:

- Do prolific offenders travel further to commit crime?
- Do hotspots generated by prolific offenders overlap with those generated by more occasional offenders, or do they represent distinctly different spatial distributions?
- If differences exist, are these in line with theoretical expectation?
- Do observed patterns have implications for crime prevention, the likelihood of crime displacement and how one might plan interventions to minimise its likelihood?

Co-offending

One issue with the analysis of crimes detected by the police concerns co-offending. It has been acknowledged for some time that co-offending occurs, and crimes committed by more than one offender likely account for a substantial proportion of all crime committed (e.g. Zimring 1981). In a recent study, Andresen and Felson (2010) show that co-offending varies over the life course, being most prominent in the early teens, but declining rapidly during the teenage years (and beyond). Moreover, that rates of co-offending vary across crime types to the extent that – based on their sample of data at least – rates of co-offending are lower for residential burglary than they are for commercial burglary or residential burglary offences that occur outside of the victims' home. However, as far as we are aware there exists no examination of whether rates of co-offending vary spatially.

Accordingly, and to inform what follows, we examine how rates of co-offending vary across different hotspots and other areas.

Data

Crimes detected by the police

Two types of police data are analysed. The first concerns all incidents of residential burglary detected by the police in the county of Dorset (UK) for the period 1 January 2000 to 31 December 2005. It is important to acknowledge that such events represent only a sample of all those committed. For the area considered the rate of detection of 24 percent was good relative to other studies.[1] For example, in the studies by Bernasco and Niewbeerta (2005) and Clare et al. (2009), the detection rates were 7 percent and 5.5 percent respectively

These data comprise 2,988 burglaries, which, when account is taken of co-offending, represents 3,620 participation events (Andreson and Felson 2010). That is, some crimes involved more than one offender and hence there are more participations than detected offences. For each event, the time and location of the offence are known, with the latter accurate to a resolution of one metre. Some details are also provided about the offender such as a unique identifier, their occupation, nationality, age, gender and the full unit postcode for their address (as recorded at the time of an offence). The latter, which will be accurate to a resolution of around (say) 100–200m was used to generate x and y co-ordinates for the offender home locations. While this level of resolution is imperfect it is more than adequate for the types of analysis that follow.

Recorded victim data

Police recorded crime data concerning victimisation (whether detected or not) were used to allow a comparison between hotspots of detected offences and those for recorded crime. The victim data were available for the geographic area discussed above and for the same period of time. There were a total of 14,236 crimes and for each crime the timing and location of the event was known.

Census and Ordnance Survey data

Further data were used to contextualise the hotspot areas. These were extracted from the 2001 Census of Population and Ordnance Survey (OS) data sets. The census information provided area-level estimates of socio-demographic variables such as the age structure of residents, employment status, owner occupation, ethnic mix and household structure. Data were extracted at the census output area level, which is the lowest level of resolution at which it is available; output areas typically have a population of around 125 homes. The OS data were used to examine the physical structure of the types of areas within which hotspots were identified.

Data preparation and analysis

To prepare the data for analysis, it was necessary to create a new variable that identified how many times each offender had participated in crime over the five-year period for which data were available. It is acknowledged that because most crime goes undetected, the data most likely reflect only a sample of each offender's activity for the period of interest. However, because the data include TICs (i.e. those taken into consideration), we think that this issue is less problematic than in other research for which TICs are not available. Nevertheless, the point remains.

Having calculated how many events each offender participated in, offenders were categorised either as 'prolific' or 'occasional' offenders. Any criterion used to do this will be subject to debate but in the current study, to be coded as a prolific, they had to have undertaken five or more burglaries in the five-year period. This equates to roughly one offence per year. Those who committed fewer than five were categorised as 'occasional' offenders. Of course, one limitation of this approach is that if an offender was imprisoned for much of the five-year period they would be unable to commit further offences and hence some prolific offenders may have been incorrectly assigned to the 'occasional' offender group as a result of this.

Of the 3,621 participations, the home location of the offender was known for 2,481 (69 percent) events. The location of the crime was known for all events. Thus, for the hotspot analyses that concerned where crimes occurred, all crimes were available for analysis, but for those analyses that consider the journey to crime, only a subset could be analysed. As well as assigning offenders to one of the two groups, the crime *events* were categorised as having involved a prolific offender or not. That is, crimes were identified as the work of a prolific if *at least one* of the offenders involved in the crime had committed five or more crimes over the five-year interval.

Results

Descriptive statistics

Overall the offenders committed an average of 12.8 (median 5, range 1 to 180, SD = 17.9) offences over the five-year period, which equates to roughly 2.6 offences per year. However, the standard deviation of 17.9 indicates that there was considerable variation within the sample. Moreover, the skewness statistic of 2.1 (s.e.= 0.41) indicates that the distribution was far from normal (i.e. it did not conform to the Gaussian distribution) but was instead positively skewed, indicating that while the majority of offenders committed around five offences (the median indicates that 50 percent committed five or fewer) a good proportion committed substantially more (up to 180). There was also variation in terms of the distance travelled to commit offences, with the average being 7.5km (median 2.1km, range 4m to 67km, SD = 12.5km). Again, the skewness statistic 2.1 (s.e. = 0.05) indicates that the distribution of crime trips was positively skewed, demonstrating that most trips were (relatively) short but a good proportion of journeys were much longer than the measures of central tendency might suggest. Considering co-offending, an average of 1.2 (median 1, range 1 to 8, SD = 0.6) offenders were involved in each crime. Again, the distribution was positively skewed (skewness = 3.97, s.e. = 0.45) indicating that a meaningful number of crimes involved more than one offender.

Table 18.1 summarises the same information for the two groups of offender separately. It is apparent that that the prolific group generally travels further to commit crimes – in fact the mean distance travelled for this group was almost twice that for the other. The difference in the two distributions was statistically significant (Kolmogorov-Smirnov $Z = 3.430, p < 0.0001$). In terms of the number of offences committed, while it was anticipated that the average number of crimes for the prolific group would be higher it was substantially so (Kolmogorov-Smirnov $Z = 29.987, p < 0.0001$). Finally, it is apparent from the co-offending data that there was a tendency for the prolific group to operate on their own more often than the occasional offenders (Kolmogorov-Smirnov $Z = 2.973, p < 0.0001$).

A further analysis was conducted to examine in more detail the journey to crime patterns for the two groups. Figure 18.1 shows the number of participations per group that involved a journey of d metres or more. Thus, the left-most point on the graph indicates the total number of participations for each group. It is clear from this graph that most crime trips are short for both groups. However, it is also apparent that for the prolifics, a substantial proportion of crime trips are several orders of magnitude longer than the average journey. On the basis of this finding alone, it would not be unreasonable to speculate that the prolific offenders are attracted to some areas that are far from local with respect to where they resided at the time of the offence. Reasons for this might include an awareness of opportunities in such areas, or some areas may be known as a result of past experience (see Bernasco 2010).

Table 18.1 Summary statistics for the occasional and prolific groups

		Mean	Min	Max	SD	Median	Skewness	Kurtosis
Occasional group	Number of crimes committed	1.96	1	5	1.29	1	1.16 (0.06)	0.09 (0.11)
	Number of co-offenders	1.29	1	8	0.67	1	3.64 (0.07)	21.57 (0.13)
	Distance travelled to undertake crime	5,452m	4m	67,166m	9,751m	1,769m	2.93 (0.06)	8.32 (0.13)
Prolific group	Number of crimes committed	25.50	6	80	19.84	20	1.36 (0.06)	1.22 (0.12)
	Number of co-offenders	1.14	1	5	0.47	1	4.04 (0.61)	19.31 (0.12)
	Distance travelled to undertake crime	10,506m	12m	53,520m	15,145m	2,991m	1.44 (0.08)	0.36 (0.15)

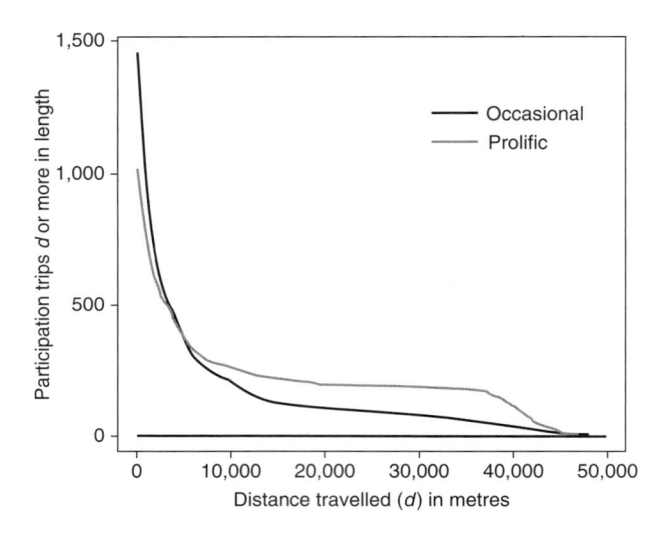

Figure 18.1 Journey to crime distribution for prolific and occasional offender groups.

For the purposes of the current analysis, crime hotspots could be identified and examined in a number of ways. For example, one could generate hotspot maps using data concerning victim locations and these spaces could then be examined to see what fraction of events were the work of prolific or occasional offenders. In the current chapter however, we take a different approach. Specifically, standard deviational hotspots (STAC hotspots)[2] were created using CrimeStatIII (Levine 2010) *separately* for those incidents committed by the group of offenders categorised as prolific and those categorised as occasional offenders. Briefly, the method is an iterative one that identifies ellipses that contain a density of crime per unit area that differs from expectation, assuming a uniform distribution in risk. This means that discrete areas are identified as hotspots, which is an advantage over other approaches such as kernel density estimation (KDE). A further advantage is that it produces tightly defined areas, represented as vector rather than raster data (i.e. are solid 'areas' and not just 'pictures' of where the hot areas are), which can be cross-referenced with other data using a Geographical Information System (GIS). The results are shown as Figure 18.2.

In some cases the hotspots identified for each group overlap. However, there are also some interesting differences. First, five hotspots were identified for the crimes committed by those categorised as occasional offenders (O1–O5), while six were identified for the crimes committed by those defined as prolific (P1–P6). There were two prolific hotspots that were not occasional ones (P4 and P6), and one occasional hotspot that was not a prolific one (O5).

To examine how the different hotspots differ, we first examine the characteristics of the offenders that committed crime within them, and then consider how the

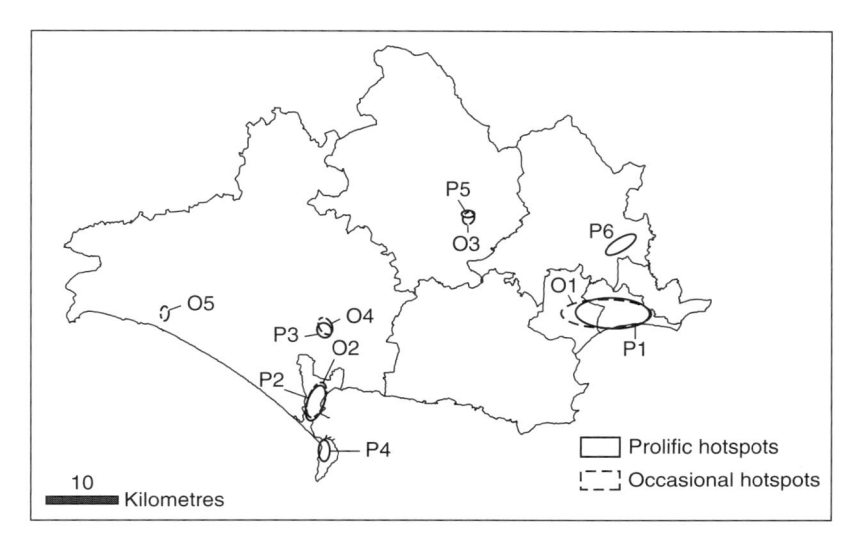

Figure 18.2 Occasional offender and prolific offender hotspots in the county of Dorset, UK.

areas vary in terms of socio-demographic factors. Table 18.2 shows descriptive statistics about the crimes committed within each of the hotspots identified. The final row of the table shows the density of crime per unit area in each hotspot. A comparison of the density estimates for each hotspot confirms that they are much higher than the mean density for the rest of the county.

With respect to the journey to crime, in this table we consider the journey to hotspots. That is, instead of considering all origin–destination trips, we focus only

Table 18.2 Offence data summaries for prolific-generated and occasional-generated hotspots (skewness statistics shown in parentheses)

Prolific hotspots	P1	P2	P3	P4	P5	P6	Outside
Number of crimes	1,309	256	48	32	21	22	1,300
Number of co-offenders	1.15	1.34	1.21	1.16	1.11	1.06	1.25
Distance travelled to undertake crime	7.66 (2.04)	3.21 (4.42)	4.64 (2.85)	1.44 (2.16)	5.01 (2.39)	27.71 (−0.46)	8.81 (12.35)
Area (square km)	34.6	9.8	3.0	3.5	1.5	6.6	2,633
Crime density	37.8	26.1	16.0	9.1	14.0	3.3	0.5

Occasional hotspots	O1	O2	O3	O4	O5	Outside
Number of crimes	1,413	251	47	40	18	1,219
Number of co-offenders	1.16	1.34	1.13	1.15	1.17	1.25
Distance travelled to undertake crime	7.47 (2.10)	3.23 (4.42)	4.22 (4.23)	5.82 (2.54)	5.74 (1.51)	9.21 (12.07)
Area (square km)	41.9	10.3	2.4	3.8	1.7	2,632
Crime density	33.7	24.4	19.6	10.5	10.6	0.5

on those for which the destination is a hotspot of detected crime*. In a recent study that considered all crime trips, Townsley and Sidebottom (2010) show that while the overall pattern of crime trips conforms to a distance decay function, when the distributions for each offender are considered, it is apparent that, while this relationship is largely evident for the most prolific offenders, it is not the case for all of them. In the current chapter, our interest is in disaggregating the data in a different way that allows us to see if the journey to crime varies across different hotspots. Such variation (for example) may imply different reasons for why an area is a hotspot and consequently have implications for crime prevention.

Considering the journey to hotspots, the mean distance varied across hotspots, and in all but one case the skewness statistics were statistically significant and positively skewed. For hotspot P6 (prolific only) the average journey to crime is much longer than that for all of the other hotspots and the skewness statistic for this hotspot was non-significant suggesting that the mean value was quite typical; most crime trips to this area were quite long. On the face of it, this could indicate that offenders are attracted to, and commute to area P6 for particular reasons. The number of co-offenders is also less than average for this hotspot indicating that trips to this area tend to be completed by offenders who work alone.

Interestingly, hotspot P4, which is also generated by the group of prolific offenders, has an average journey to crime trip that is much lower than is typical elsewhere. In this case, visual inspection of the map is instructive. This particular hotspot is situated on a peninsula where travel is potentially impeded by the physical structure of the area.

Table 18.3 summarises some of the census data for the hotspots generated by the offenders defined as occasional and prolific. Prolific hotspot P6 – for which offenders appear to travel the furthest to offend (see earlier) – has a particularly high owner occupation rate and a particularly low level of unemployment and

Table 18.3 Census data for the prolific and occasional hotspots

Hotspot no.	Owner occupation (%)	Unemployment	Long-term unemployment	Percentage of population white
Prolific-generated				
P1	68	3.02	1.02	96.9
P2	70	2.97	0.98	99.2
P3	72	1.98	0.41	98.0
P4	70	3.31	0.96	97.3
P5	72	1.79	0.63	98.5
P6	91	1.18	0.34	99.0
Occasional-generated				
O1	70	2.90	0.97	97.1
O2	70	3.11	0.98	99.2
O3	67	2.06	0.71	98.5
O4	71	2.06	0.37	98.2
O5	63	2.57	1.17	99.2

* The outside category gives details of all other journeys for comparison.

Contrasting hotspots 235

long-term unemployment. This indicates that it is an affluent suburb, which may make it an intended target of professional burglars looking to maximise benefits, even at the expense of having to travel further from their home location. If true, this would be an example of offenders balancing the rewards and costs associated with their activity.

In contrast, hotspot P4 – located on the peninsula and for which crime trips are the shortest for any of the hotspots – shows particularly high levels of unemployment and a fairly low level of owner occupation. It is possible that in this area, despite the evident deprivation, offenders who reside there commit at least some of their offences locally, rather than in alternative suburbs, due to the effort that would likely be involved in travelling further afield. However, this is not to say that they commit the majority of their offences within the hotspot. In fact, an examination of the crime trips for those offenders that live within hotspot P4 indicated that the median distance travelled of 5km was larger than that for offenders who lived within the other prolific hotspots (the range in the median values being 1km to 4.5km).

Figure 18.3 examines prolific hotspot P6 in more detail. The lines shown connect the home and offence locations for each offender who participated in a crime. The points with circles indicate the offence locations while the end of the line without a symbol indicates the home locations. It is evident that many offences occur around the ellipse as well as within it. It is also evident that while the hotspot is isolated, it is connected to other places by the major network of roads, being bisected by an A road. Moreover, the ellipse encapsulates two areas with

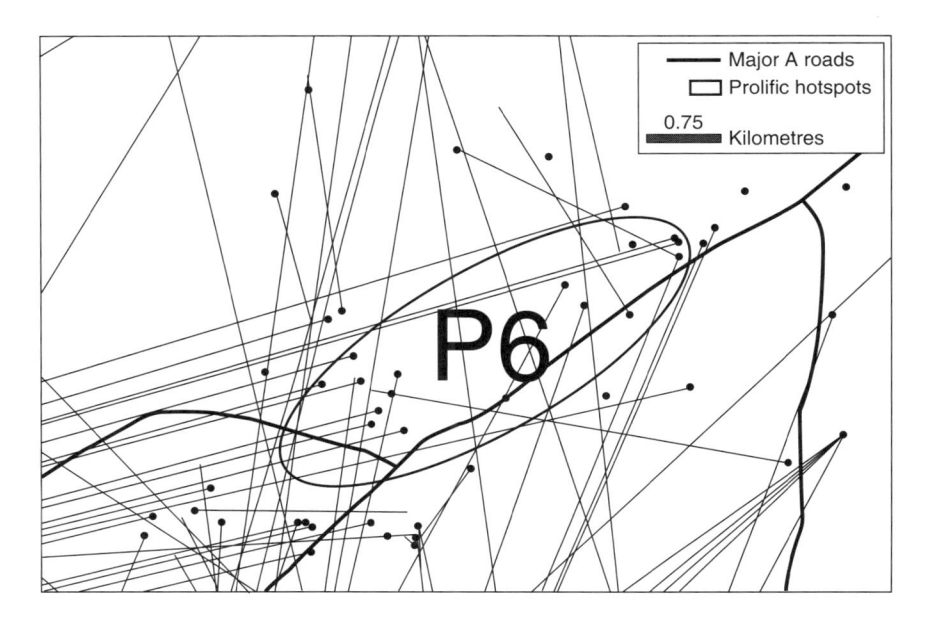

Figure 18.3 Journey to crime for prolific hotspot P6.

Source: Crown Copyright 2011. An Ordnance Survey/EDINA supplied service.

236 *Kate Bowers and Shane Johnson*

(relatively) high densities of crime. The two places are connected by a major road, but the area between them includes open space and is also bisected by a river (not shown). This is one explanation for why hotspot P6 has a lower crime density than any of the others; a large fraction of the area encapsulated simply does not contain homes and hence the opportunity for burglary to occur.

Visual inspection of the crime trips (crudely represented as the crow flies) indicates that many of these begin in the south-west region of the map. This follows the geometry of an A road that connects the hotspot and other built-up areas of the county. It would appear that offenders make use of this connectivity (see Johnson and Bowers 2010).

What is also apparent is that it is not the case that all the offences committed in and around this area are the work of the same offender. In particular, there appears to be a distinction between the left- and the right-hand regions of hotspot P6 with the river through the middle acting as a natural divide. To the right of the river the crime trips seem more varied, with offenders travelling from the north and the south as well as the south-west. This contrasts with the more consistent vector of travel identified for the other half of this hotspot.

Figure 18.4 compares the pattern of hotspots for detected burglaries with that of *all* recorded burglary incidents in the Dorset region for the same time period. Here we use maps generated using KDE[3] to allow us to overlay the two types of hotspot map in a way that is easy to inspect.

The salient points that can be taken from Figure 18.4 are that all the detected burglary hotspots appear to be general hotspots for burglary. This is particularly

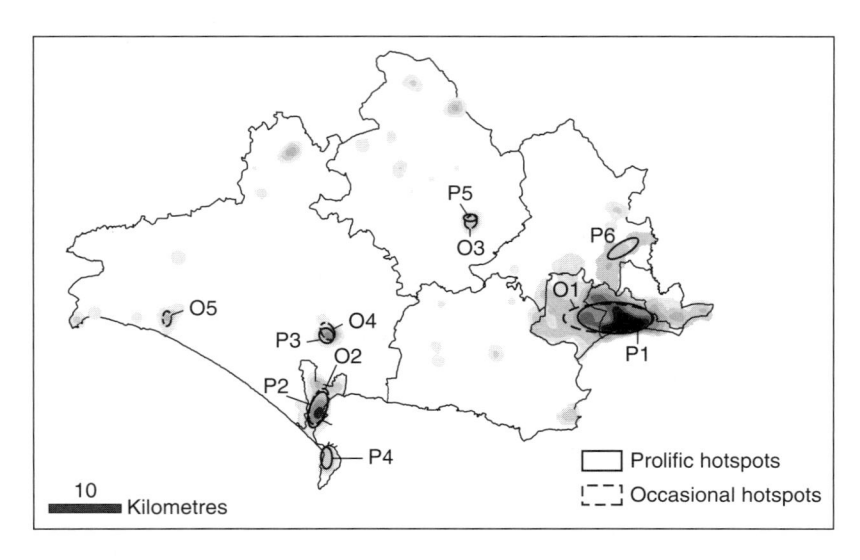

Figure 18.4 Occasional offender and prolific offender hotspots, and burglary density in the county of Dorset, UK.

Source: Crown Copyright 2011. An Ordnance Survey/EDINA supplied service.

true for the two larger STAC hotspots that were identified for both the prolific and occasional groups of offenders (P1 and O1). However, the prolific-generated hotspots (P4 and P6) were also located in areas defined as hot by the general KDE surface. This could be seen as an indication that the general risk in these areas disproportionately reflects the work of more prolific offenders who are attracted to these locations. A further observation is that there are some areas that are identified as hot using KDE that are not identified as hot spots using the detected data. Why these differences exist is an interesting question. This may indicate that detection is more common, and policing might be better resourced, in some areas in comparison to others, but answering this question in full is outside the scope of this chapter. It does, of course, indicate a limitation of the data concerned with crimes detected by the police in so far as they do not perfectly reflect the distribution of crimes recorded by them.

Discussion

According to the categorisation used here, 53 percent of all detected crimes were by those who, on the basis of the available data, would not be considered to be particularly active offenders. If this group *is* more likely to commit crime as a consequence of opportunity and is easily deterred from committing crime by the blocking of opportunity, then this suggests that situational interventions could reduce crime by a substantial amount. Moreover, that if these types of offender do not seek out criminal opportunity in the same way as might those who are more prolific, there is no reason to believe that their activity would be displaced.

Obviously, the criterion used to categorise offenders was determined subjectively, and some may argue we have been overly generous in defining those who committed up to five offences over the five-year period as 'occasional' offenders. However, others may argue that occasional or opportunistic offenders, depending upon their environment, could easily undertake larger numbers of crime. There is no suggestion by the authors that the criterion used was perfect, but we suggest that it was a useful one for the purpose of illustrating the types of analysis that might be conducted and as a starting point.

Despite this issue, the spatial analyses presented suggest that the criterion used led to the identification of groups of offenders for which variation exists in their spatial decision-making. There do appear to be some hotspots that are generated by the activities of the separate groups. For example, two hotspots seem to be more or less exclusively produced by more prolific offenders. Importantly, these areas are identified as hotspots using the victim data alone – so their identification is not purely an artefact of the detection data. Such hotspots may well be harder to suppress than others if they *are* committed by motivated offenders who are prepared to travel considerable distances to find and offend within them. That is, it is possible that crime reduction activity within these areas would be more likely to lead to displacement than other areas simply because with the opportunities removed the types of offenders that were attracted to them would simply seek out new opportunities.

However, a counterpoint discussed by Cornish and Clarke (1987) is that if offenders travel to these types of area *because* there is something particular about them that is attractive to them – their choice structuring properties as Cornish and Clarke put it – then if other areas do not represent substitutes for them, then even in these areas the likelihood of displacement may be minimal.

Notwithstanding the possibility of displacement discussed above, the analyses presented overall paint an optimistic picture. That is, while some hotspots may be the work of prolific offenders alone, others appear to be mainly the result of more occasional or opportunistic offenders. Increasing the effort associated with committing crime in such areas could well result in the total suppression of the hotspot, with little risk of crime displacement.

Furthermore, there were also many cases where there was geographic overlap in the hotspots generated by the two types of offender. These tended to be the 'hottest' areas according to the victim data. Thus, it would appear that in the areas most affected by crime, offences are not committed exclusively by the most active offenders; that is, those who would be most expected to find ways around attempts to block opportunities. In fact, in these areas more offences were committed by those offenders who were classified as occasional offenders. Accordingly, it is reasonable to argue that from a theoretical perspective, displacement will be far from inevitable in these locations.

Perhaps the most valuable implication for crime prevention practice from this study is that these types of analysis suggest ways of unpicking the particular processes that are likely to generate different hotspots. From a crime prevention perspective, it is perhaps more valuable to concentrate on hotspots generated by more occasional offenders or those created by a mixture of the two types of offender. With those hotspots that are likely to be disproportionately generated by prolific offenders, investigative effort might be prioritised in these areas and used to compliment crime prevention activity. Where crime prevention is implemented in such areas, thought should be given to the likelihood of displacement, and possible ways in which a diffusion of crime control benefit might be achieved.

Notes

1 Note that the data available for analysis includes those crimes that are taken into consideration (TICs) at the point of arrest. That is, offences that offenders admit to having committed as opposed to those detected through investigative effort. It is important to note that there is a requirement in UK policing to demonstrate that such offences *were* committed by the offender who admitted to them.
2 These were generated in CrimeStatIII using the same parameters to identify the two sets of hotspot. In both cases the boundary was defined by the same projected co-ordinates, the scan type used was rectangular and the search radius was 800 metres.
3 The KDE maps were generated in CrimeStatIII using a fixed bandwidth of 1,500 metres and a cell spacing of 100 metres.

References

Andresen, M.A. and Felson, M. (2010) 'The impact of co-offending', *British Journal of Criminology* 50 (1): 66–81.

Bernasco, W. (2010) 'A sentimental journey to crime: effects of residential history on crime location choice', *Criminology* 48 (2): 389–416.

Bernasco, W. and Nieuwbeerta, P. (2005) 'How do residential burglars select target areas?', *British Journal of Criminology* 44: 296–315.

Brantingham, P. and Brantingham, P. (1995) 'Criminality of place: crime generators and crime attractors', *European Journal on Criminal Policy and Research* 3: 5–26.

Clare, J., Fernandez, J. and Morgan, F. (2009) 'Formal evaluation of the impact of barriers and connectors on residential burglars' macro-level offending location choices', *Australian and New Zealand Journal of Criminology* 42: 139–58.

Clarke, R.V. and Cornish, D.B. (1985) 'Modelling Offenders' Decisions: A Framework for Policy and Research' in *Crime and Justice*. Vol. 6. Tonry, M. & Morris, N. (eds). Chicago: University of Chicago Press.

Clarke, R.V. and Weisburd, D. (1994) 'Diffusion of crime control benefits: observations on the reverse of displacement'. In Ronald V. Clarke (ed.), *Crime Prevention Studies*, Vol. 2. Monsey, NY: Criminal Justice Press.

Cornish, D.B. and Clarke. R.V. (eds) (1986) *The Reasoning Criminal*. New York: Springer-Verlag.

Cornish, D.B. and Clarke, R.V. (1987) 'Understanding crime displacement: an application of rational choice theory'. In Stuart Henry and Werner Einstader (eds), *The Criminology Theory Reader*. New York: New York University Press.

Cornish, D.B. and Clarke, R.V. (2003) 'Opportunities, precipitators and criminal decisions: a reply to Wortley's critique of situational crime prevention'. In M. Smith and D.B. Cornish (eds), *Theory for Situational Crime Prevention. Crime Prevention Studies*, Vol. 16. Monsey, NY: Criminal Justice Press.

Johnson, S.D. and Bowers, K.J. (2010) 'Permeability and crime risk: are cul-de-sacs safer?', *Journal of Quantitative Criminology* 26: 113–38.

Johnson, S.D., Summers, L. and Pease, K. (2009) 'Offender as forager? A direct test of the boost account of victimization', *Journal of Quantitative Criminology* 25: 181–200.

Levine, N. (2010) *CrimeStat: A Spatial Statistics Program for the Analysis of Crime Incident Locations* (v3.3), July. Houston, TX and Washington, DC: Ned Levine and Associates and the National Institute of Justice.

Rengert, G. and Wasilchick, J. (1985) *Suburban Burglary. A Time and Place for Everything*. Springfield, IL: Charles Thomas.

Sherman, L.W., Gartin, P.R. and Buerger, M.E. (1989) 'Hot spots of predatory crime: routine activities and the criminology of place', *Criminology* 27: 27–55.

Short, M., Brantingham, J., Bertozzi, A. and Tita, G. (2010) 'Dissipation and displacement of hotspots in reaction-diffusion models of crime', *PNAS* 107 (9): 3961–5.

Townsley, M. and Sidebottom, A. (2010) 'All offenders are equal, but some are more equal than others: variation in journeys to crime between offenders', *Criminology* 48(3): 897–917.

Wortley, R. (1996) 'Guilt, shame and situational crime prevention', *Crime Prevention Studies* 5: 115–32.

Zimring, F.E. (1981) 'Kids, groups and crime: some implications of a well-known secret', *Journal of Criminal Law and Criminology* 3: 867–85.

19 Situating situational crime prevention
Anchoring a politically palatable crime reduction strategy

*Paul J. Brantingham and
Patricia L. Brantingham*

Introduction – the broad meanings of crime prevention

Crime prevention is a broad term that carries many different meanings. It is claimed as a principal goal or objective by every criminal justice agency. Law makers, schools, social agencies, medical services and community groups see their activities as fundamental to the prevention of crime (Brantingham and Faust, 1976; Sherman, Gottfredson, MacKenzie and Eck, 1998). Businesses and homeowners spend large sums and engage in many different activities intended to effect crime prevention. Crime prevention claims are made for all manner of things: electronic merchandise tags; prenatal interventions in expectant mothers' consumption habits; burglar alarms (Winchester and Jackson, 1982); remedial reading programmes; street lighting (Cozens, Neale and Whittaker, 2003; Welsh and Farrington, 2004); high school vocational training courses; prison counselling programmes; recreation programmes (CCJA, 1989: 385; Lutzin and Orem, 1967; US House of Representatives, 1994); police street checks; neighbourhood organizing activities (CCJA, 1989: 385; Mazerolle, Wickes and McBroom, 2010; Shaw and McKay, 1969); control of sightlines in new construction; safe injection sites for illegal drug users (Löbmann and Verthein, 2009); particular management styles in bars pubs; subsidized day care programmes (CCJA, 1989: 283; Gottfredson, 1987; Lösel, Stemmler, Jaursch and Beelmann, 2009).

The very large spread of ideas about what types of activities constitute crime prevention flows from a continuing admixture of the domains of prevention and the levels of action at which crime prevention might occur (Brantingham, 2010). Understanding these domains of prevention and levels of action is critical to building effective crime prevention programmes.

Crime and criminality

Crime prevention programmes address two related but very different domains: crime and criminality. The domain of crime is focused on the criminal event itself and requires understanding all of its elements. An actual criminal action requires convergence of at least four elements in space-time: a law prohibiting or commanding some behaviour on pain of punishment; an offender ready to do the prohibited act; a target or object or victim of the offender's behaviour; and a situation (a set of physical and social conditions making the criminal act appealing to the offender). If you can prevent convergence of these elements you can prevent criminal events. The domain of criminality is focused on the individual's propensity to commit crimes. Crime prevention efforts as understood within the domain of criminality are intended to change an individual's fundamental character – criminal propensity – so that he or she will not want to commit a criminal act when a provocation or temptation or appealing situation is encountered. To prevent crime you must change the person.

Crime prevention and criminality prevention

The domain of crime prevention tends to assume the existence of people who will readily give in to any provocation or temptation to do a crime. It looks at the other elements of the criminal event in search of interventions that will: prevent the provocation or temptation from occurring; or separate potential offenders, in space and time, from those provocations and temptations that cannot be prevented. It operates on the assumptions that most offenders are not pathological and that their criminal behaviours will be grounded on non-pathological activity patterns similar to those of non-offenders. Situational prevention strategies are, in this view, paramount in reducing the levels of crime in society. Situational prevention strategies, when they work, tend to provide effective crime reductions quite quickly following their implementation and thus provide efficient feedback to both the operational and policy-making levels of government.

Traditional crime prevention strategies fall within the domain of criminality. They are grounded on the assumption that criminals are somehow pathologically different from the vast majority of people who are fundamentally non-criminal.[1] These traditional strategies tend to prescribe interventions aimed at changing individual propensity or enhancing community control capacity over the long run. They draw on a variety of biological, psychological and social assumptions and research findings about the development of personality and sociality as well as assumptions about the capacity of neighbourhood residents (communities) to exercise effective informal control over the criminal impulses of individuals.

Contemporary criminal career research strongly suggests that both stable individual personality differences and differential circumstances and situations contribute to the onset, duration, patterning and termination of criminal careers. In their comparative study of Dutch organized crime offenders and general criminals, for instance, van Koppen, de Poot and Blokland (2010) find that organized crime offenders differ from general criminals on both dimensions, although it appears that situational differences may be most critical. This suggests that comprehensive crime reduction programmes should include both crime prevention elements and criminality prevention elements.

Primary, secondary and tertiary crime and criminality prevention

Primary crime prevention identifies and seeks to change conditions in the social and physical environment that facilitate the development of criminality or provide opportunities for or precipitate criminal events. Secondary crime prevention identifies specific at-risk situations and places, groups and individuals before they develop persistent crime problems or engage in criminal activity and seeks to intervene to reduce the risk. Tertiary crime prevention deals with places that have established crime problems and with actual offenders. It provides interventions aimed at changing the physical site and social situations found at crime generators, crime attractors and other crime hot spots in ways that minimize the criminal opportunities found at them. It also provides interventions aimed at incapacitating, reforming and rehabilitating actual offenders so that they commit no further offences (Brantingham and Faust, 1976).

In general, crime prevention programmes and strategies provide focused, near-term crime reduction at the primary and secondary levels while criminality prevention programmes operate more at the secondary and tertiary levels and often require much more time before their benefits are likely to be realized. As Steven Lab has observed (2004), this typical long delay between programme initiation and crime reduction payoff often makes even the most promising and scientifically well-grounded criminality prevention programmes subject to confusion in objective, operation and effect, and renders them politically vulnerable.[2]

Situational crime prevention

Situational crime prevention theory and practice as invented by Dr Ronald V.G. Clarke (1980) and expanded by him and many co-authors and contributors since (e.g. Clarke, 1992, 1997; Clark and Homel, 1997; Cornish and Clarke, 1986, 2003; see, generally the more than 200 studies and manuals at www.popcenter.org) provides both a basis for delivery of immediate crime reduction and a basis for the construction of a politically palatable, comprehensive crime and criminality reduction programme that can both deliver immediate crime reduction and buy sufficient time for long-term programmes to mature and begin delivering crime reduction results as well.

Situational prevention can operate at and is implemented at the primary, secondary and tertiary levels, but focuses on the primary and secondary levels most of the time. Criminal events are considered in site- and situation-specific context and treated as the result of human decision sequences (some routine, some anomalous, some emotional or irrational, some highly rational). It is tightly bound to crime analysis and to evidence-based approaches to construction of specific crime reduction interventions (Clarke and Eck, 2005). The Center for Problem Oriented Policing provides examples of crime reduction interventions supported by research and the situational crime prevention crime analysis process (www.popcenter.org).

As developed by Ron Clarke, the situational crime prevention model advances five strategic sets of intervention possibilities that practitioners should consider.

Each strategic set provides five classes of techniques that could be used to prevent crimes being committed at specific places in specific situations. These strategic intervention sets include: techniques that increase the effort required to commit a crime; techniques that increase the risks of committing a crime; techniques that reduce the reward derived from crime; techniques that reduce provocations; and techniques that remove excuses for doing crime.

The genius of situational prevention is that it focuses on changing circumstances immediately proximate to criminal acts in ways so that criminal action is an unattractive behavioural choice at that time and place. A situational intervention begins to work immediately and is addressed to any and all potential criminal actors who encounter that site and situation. It does *not* require any permanent change in potential offenders' personality, morality or continuing criminality. Because of this, it is politically palatable in itself and, when bundled with criminality prevention programmes in a comprehensive package, can provide the near-term results needed to overcome the temporal and political problems faced by long-term criminality reduction interventions (Lab, 2004).

Political palatability

Political palatability is essential to both the initiation and the continuation of crime and criminality prevention programmes. By the term 'political palatability' we mean that a programme must seem fair and reasonable to a large proportion of the voters in the jurisdiction in which it is proposed. It must seem fair, reasonable and likely to produce demonstrably beneficial results to a working majority of the politicians who must find funds for it and deal with its consequences at the next election. Some crime and criminality prevention programmes fail because they are not based on adequate analysis of the problem and provide interventions targeted at the wrong things: more street lights will do little to deal with a daytime burglary problem; subsidized school lunches are unlikely to prevent youth from developing gambling addictions. Some prevention programmes fail because the theory underlying them is simply wrong. But many prevention programmes fail because they are implemented poorly.

Lack of political palatability ensures an implementation failure. Implementation depends on political feasibility within a democratic society. Politicians must be on side: they provide prevention programmes with both their legal authority and their operational funding. Professionals must be on side: they use legal authority and spend operational funding to install the item or define the procedure or deliver the service that constitutes the intended intervention. Voters must be on side: they can kill a programme that they think is unfair or too costly.

Keys to palatability

In designing a politically palatable crime reduction programme a series of questions needs to be asked. The fundamental question is: *what is the problem?* Careful analysis and understanding of the crime problem is a prerequisite for design of a programme of primary, secondary and tertiary interventions to reduce it. Understanding of the problem should indicate specific situational and developmental techniques that could be applied.

Once an intervention technique has been identified a series of subsidiary questions comes into play. The analyst should ask whether the proposed intervention actually relates to the problem as analysed. Does programme actually target some element of the problem? Is there a logical connection between what is proposed and some change in how the targeted element relates to the problem?

Although this group of questions would appear to be both trivially obvious and a clear requirement of good practice (Clarke and Eck, 2005), it is remarkable how often crime and criminality prevention programmes are adopted without these questions being asked just because they are fashionable or because they have been done elsewhere or because there is a simple cookbook formula for setting them up. It is surprising that in adopting particular crime or criminality prevention programmes the programme designers seem not to ask themselves: *what does the evaluation literature suggest?* What is really being asked is: *Could it work?* Until the preventive intervention has been implemented it is impossible to know whether it actually works to deal with the targeted crime problem.

Once the problem has been analysed and an intervention to address it has been selected additional considerations of feasibility and political acceptability must be addressed in order to implement the intervention and sustain it for the time it needs to deliver results. Feasibility questions relate to cost, time and human cooperation. The questions funders will necessarily ask will include: what will it cost?; where will the funds come from?; how long will it take?; how long must we continue to pay for this programme?; what will we save, in crimes and in money, if this works? Politically palatable interventions should be able to explain why the intervention will need to run for a specific period of time before it begins to deliver crime reduction results and to show that the benefits in money saved and crimes prevention can be expected to outweigh the costs.

The additional feasibility question that should be asked by programme designers and must be asked by programme implementers is: *who else must cooperate to make the programme work?* Many crime and criminality reduction interventions require the cooperation of diverse government agencies, private organizations and individuals that may have very different priorities. In addition to criminal justice professionals and personnel from agencies responsible, for instance, for schools, municipal planning or public health, cooperation from non-government organizations and private businesses as well as parents and prior or potential victims of crime may well be needed to accomplish a particular intervention or apply a particular preventive technique.

Understanding who all of the required partners are and finding ways to convince them that they should participate is often critical to both the practical feasibility and the political acceptability of the prevention programme (Scott and Goldstein, 2005).

The political palatability of a crime prevention programme inevitably involves understanding of the political ideology of the government in power.

Programmes that are entirely sensible on their merits may not be acceptable if they are incompatible with the government's ideology; programmes that make little or no scientific sense may be funded if they are compatible with the ideology of the government of the day. This poses major problems for long-time-to-payoff crime prevention programmes. The political cycle tends to be short: politicians must run for re-election within a few years. On the one hand, current politicians will want to support programmes that provide crime reduction payoffs before the next election; on the other hand, a change in governing party as the result of an election can undercut political support for long-time-payoff programmes initiated by the prior government. Examples of this political vulnerability would include the de-emphasis or termination of a series of long-time-payoff social development programmes initiated during the early 1960s in the United States following election of a new president from a different political party in 1968 or the de-emphasis or termination of a series of long-time-payoff programmes in England and Wales following a change of government in 2010. Encapsulating some of the long-time-payoff prevention programmes within a more comprehensive programme that coupled them with situational prevention strategies might well have insulated them.

Voter reaction to different crime and criminality prevention strategies and tactics is an important consideration in thinking about the political palatability of specific interventions. In particular, voters are likely to be angered by programmes that appear to punish victims on behalf of offenders or that appear to give criminals benefits denied to the law abiding. Situational interventions do neither while many scientifically worthy social development programmes appear to do one or the other or both. A comprehensive crime reduction programme that combines situational interventions with social interventions can, again, be structured so as to condition the benefits offenders derive in ways that limit the likelihood of voter anger. Consider the highly effective prolific offender management programmes operating in England and Wales. On the one hand, these programmes provide targeted prolific offenders with superior government services ranging from better job placement services to better housing placement to better access to drug and alcohol addiction treatment facilities than those available to non-offenders. On the other hand, these better services are coupled with strengthened formal surveillance, removal of excuses, both in terms of rule setting and compliance assistance, and an increase in the effort needed to meet with old friends and find old temptations by housing the prolifics in new neighbourhoods well away from their old haunts. The situational interventions offset the presumed special benefits of the programme.

Political palatability also involves adherence to national and international standards of human rights. In Canada, for instance, the analyst must, at a minimum, pay attention to rights protected by the constitutionally embedded Charter of rights and freedoms, to federal human rights and privacy acts, to provincial human rights and privacy acts, to international human rights treaties, and to the case law applying and interpreting them. Many primary and secondary criminality prevention programmes target parents and their children before any of them have committed any crime. Some programmes, Head Start for instance, are beneficial but require parents to engage in affirmative actions that are not always forthcoming. Other programmes may call for much more extensive, forced interventions in the lives of people and violate human rights. Social presumptions about parental rights, which may sometimes be at variance with some specific statutory rules, also play a role in public perceptions of the political acceptability of specific intervention programmes. Situational prevention programmes typically avoid most of these palatability issues by modifying conditions in the environment rather than doing things to individuals.

Using situational prevention to build better comprehensive crime reduction programmes

Crime and criminality prevention operating at the primary, secondary and tertiary levels can be made more effective, more evaluable (Brantingham, Brantingham and Taylor, 2005) and more politically palatable if different but related intervention programmes are bundled together to enhance the political palatability of the bundle. Most social and developmental programmes target individuals in order to reduce their future criminality. Such programmes operate at the secondary and tertiary levels of prevention while promising crime reduction payoffs in the middle and long terms.

Situational prevention programmes target the circumstances that create criminal opportunities rather than the personalities of individuals who might commit crime. Situational programmes operate at the primary and secondary levels while providing crime reduction payoffs in the near and medium terms. Situational prevention strategies are politically palatable because they do not create human rights issues and they can provide crime reduction payoffs to politicians before the next election. (For hundreds of examples of concrete situational prevention projects that fit this assertion see Clarke, 1992, 1997; www.popcenter.org.)

Criminality prevention interventions are politically palatable because they often involve delivery of a variety of services that are politically praiseworthy and socially beneficial in their own right: e.g. delivery of better pre- and post-natal care; improving children's school readiness; delivery of remedial education to early school leavers; provision of social services to dysfunctional families; drug and alcohol rehabilitation services; neighbourhood organization and development of community social efficacy. They can become politically vulnerable because they often must operate on time horizons that stretch beyond the next several political cycles and sometime prescribe actions that can be characterised as government intrusion or even violations of individual human rights. Moreover, eventual public and political impatience and dissatisfaction with the crime reduction delivered by criminality prevention programmes can lead to problems for the broader social programmes to which have been attached (see Lab, 2004; Marris and Rein, 1967; Moynihan, 1969; Poyner, 1993; Sherman, Gottfredson, MacKenzie and Eck, 1998).

Bundling interventions with different time scales together

Longer term interventions, especially those aimed at criminality prevention, must be funded and operated for years before the crime reduction payoffs can begin. Situational interventions often deliver very effective crime near-term reduction results. Situational prevention programmes can be designed, implemented and sustained on their own, without the need for accompanying longer term criminality prevention programmes. Longer term prevention programmes should be coupled with situational prevention programmes. Good near-term results can buy funder patience while waiting for medium- and long-term project results.[3]

Auto theft interventions – a temporal bundling example

Auto theft is a serious, high-volume crime in much of the world. It typically afflicts middle-income households and disproportionately impacts single-parent and blended families (Dauvergne, 2008; Perreault and Brennan, 2010; Tseloni, Mailley, Farrell and Tilley, 2010).

Car theft is dominated by young offenders (e.g. Dauvergne, 2008; Fleming, Brantingham and Brantingham, 1994) who indicate that their principal goals in stealing cars are joyriding, transportation and thrill-seeking. Stealing cars or car parts for sale and stealing cars to use in committing other crimes are important but secondary goals among most young, active car thieves. Most persistent young car thieves indicate that most of their thefts are opportunistic and rely on simple techniques. Most are put off by technical challenges and by the likelihood that they might be caught. A few very prolific offenders indicate that they are not put off by anything. Most are early school leavers. Few indicate that they have been abused or deprived, but most indicate that they have had limited parental supervision in the course of growing up (Anderson and Linden, 2002; Fleming, Brantingham and Brantingham, 1994; Fleming, 2003; Jenion and Brantingham, 2008; Tremblay, Clermont and Cusson, 1994).

Car theft clusters at certain times of the day and clusters in and around major activity nodes such as shopping malls or high streets and along major traffic arteries. Older models of certain makes appear to be the most often stolen and fairly simple techniques are used to enter and start the cars (Clarke and Harris, 1992; Dauvergne, 2008; Fleming, Brantingham and Brantingham, 1994; Wallace, 2003).

This brief summary of findings from a fairly extensive international literature suggests that car theft prevention strategies should operate at primary, secondary and tertiary levels and should include both criminality prevention and crime prevention approaches. The research literature on young car thieves in particular suggests a model of criminal action that might be usefully understood through person–situation interaction theories such as crime pattern theory (Brantingham and Brantingham, 1993, 2008) or situational action theory (e.g. Wikstrom, Clarke and McCord, 1995; Wikstrom and Svensson, 2010). Both theoretical approaches suggest that some social development interventions at young ages might prove fruitful and that a variety of situational interventions could be very effective.

A promising social intervention, based on the available facts about young car thieves, might be provision of long-term, educational day care for all children. Such a programme should enhance educational preparedness so that children arriving in primary school will do better in the classroom, will not subsequently drop out, and therefore will both learn better self-control (Gottfredson and Hirschi, 1990) and develop a stronger sense of morality (Trasler, 1962; Wikstrom and Svensson, 2010). In addition, because they will be spending more of their day in school they will not find themselves in so many unsupervised situations in which they will be tempted to steal cars.

The point here is not to assert that this is the best or only form of social development intervention that might be undertaken but rather to suggest that this is a plausible and perhaps even likely criminality prevention programme given what is known about the characteristics of young car thieves. But if the programme were to start as a service for two- to four-year-olds today it would be ten to twelve years before we could expect to begin to see substantial results: most persistent car thieves first become involved in car thefts when they are thirteen to fifteen years old. That would mean that the programme would have to start up and run through two or three complete election cycles before we could begin to judge whether it was paying off in reduced numbers of potential car thieves. Today's politicians and, for that matter, today's taxpayers might well become impatient – making the day care programme vulnerable.

Coupling the social intervention – day care – that must be protected for a long time in order to realize the crime reduction payoff with situational prevention interventions that have been proven to work in the near and medium terms could buy political patience with and continuing support for the long-term programme. In the medium term a comprehensive programme could mandate changes in vehicle design features such as lockable steering wheels, steel steering column shrouds, and steel pins in ignition locks and bring in new regulations requiring that immobilizers be installed on all new cars. Such changes are known to reduce car theft (Mayhew, Clarke and Hough, 1976; Clarke, 1991) but their impact grows over a three- to five-year period as more and more of the fleet is effectively theft-proofed from all but the most sophisticated, instrumental car thieves. Near-term, nearly immediate car theft reductions can be gained by simple situational modifications at car theft hot spots: the introduction of parking lot attendants (Webb, Brown and Bennett, 1992) or highly visible security guards (Barclay et al, 1996) or through public education programmes advising drivers to park their cars in their garages and close their garage doors and not to leave spare keys in their cars. Such a comprehensive programme will yield immediate and medium-term crime reduction payoffs that can provide the political cover that permits us to sustain the long-term intervention until we can tell whether or not it works.

Ron Clarke's career in policy and research, in defining situational prevention and finding concrete examples of successful situational projects and programmes; in developing the crime prevention treasure trove that is the popcenter.org website; in husbanding a generation of researchers when research into situational prevention was academically *unfashionable* (and often rejected out of hand by many criminologists) has made it possible to give consideration development of temporally bundled prevention programmes of the sort we suggest. It is itself a bundle of ideas, projects and programmes that has unfolded over time – some paying off very quickly, others taking time to mature. It has allowed a radical suggestion to mature into a conventional wisdom and, by the way, has resulted in a lot of prevented crimes.

Notes

1 Research on cohorts repeatedly shows that only a relatively small portion of a birth cohort is ever likely to commit a criminal offence (e.g. Philadelphia (Wolfgang, Figlio and Sellin, 1972), Tower Hamlets (West and Farrington, 1973), Canada (Carrington, Matarazzo and deSouza, 2005)).
2 It is worth considering the fate of America's 'War on Poverty', grounded on Cloward and Ohlin's (1960) differential opportunity theory. See Moynihan (1969).
3 See Wikstrom, Clarke and McCord (1995) for a slightly different idea about integrating crime prevention strategies.

References

Anderson, Jeff and Rick Linden. (2002) 'Summary report: pilot study of juvenile auto theft offenders'. Unpublished manuscript, University of Manitoba.

Barclay, P., J. Buckley, P.J. Brantingham, P.L. Brantingham and T. Whin-Yates. (1996) 'Preventing auto theft in suburban Vancouver commuter lots: effects of a bike patrol'. *Crime Prevention Studies* 6: 133–61.

Brantingham, Patricia L. and Paul J. Brantingham. (1993) 'Environment, routine and situation: toward a pattern theory of crime'. *Advances in Criminological Theory* 5: 259–94.

Brantingham, Patricia and Paul Brantingham. (2008) 'Crime pattern theory'. In Richard Wortley and Lorraine Mazerolle (eds) *Environmental Criminology and Crime Analysis*. Cullompton: Willan Publishing.

Brantingham, Patricia L., P.J. Brantingham and W. Taylor. (2005) 'Situational crime prevention as a key component in embedded crime prevention'. *Canadian Journal of Criminology and Criminal Justice* 47: 271–92.

Brantingham, Paul J. (2010) 'Domains of crime prevention'. In B. Fisher and S. Lab (eds) *Encyclopedia of Victimology and Crime Prevention*. Beverly Hills, CA: Sage Publishing.

Brantingham, Paul J. and Frederic L. Faust. (1976) 'A conceptual model of crime prevention'. *Crime and Delinquency* 22: 284–96.

Carrington, P.J., A. Matarazzo and P. deSouza. (2005) *Court Careers of a Canadian Birth Cohort*. Ottawa: Canadian Centre for Justice Statistics, Statistics Canada.

CCJA (Canadian Criminal Justice Association). (1989) 'Safer communities: a social strategy for crime prevention in Canada'. *Canadian Journal of Criminology* 31(4): 366–401.

Clarke, R.V.G. (1980) 'Situational crime prevention: theory and practice'. *British Journal of Criminology* 20: 136–47.

Clarke, R.V.G. (1991) *Preventing Vehicle Theft: A Policy-oriented Review of the Literature*. Edinburgh: Scottish Office.

Clarke, R.V. (1992) *Situational Crime Prevention: Successful Case Studies*. New York: Harrow and Heston.

Clarke, R.V. (1997) *Situational Crime Prevention: Successful Case Studies* (2d edn). New York: Harrow and Heston.
Clarke, R.V. and J.E. Eck. (2005) *Crime Analysis for Problem Solvers in 60 Small Steps*. Madison, WI: Center for Problem-Oriented Policing. www.popcenter.org.
Clarke, R. and P. Harris. (1992) 'Auto theft and its prevention'. In M. Tonry (ed.) *Crime and Justice*, Vol. 16. Chicago: University of Chicago Press.
Clarke, R.V. and R. Homel. (1997) 'A revised classification of situational prevention techniques'. In S.P. Lab (ed.) *Crime Prevention at a Crossroads*. Cincinnati: Anderson Publishing.
Cloward, R.A. and L.E. Ohlin. (1960) *Delinquency and Opportunity: A Theory of Delinquent Gangs*. New York: The Free Press.
Cornish, D.B. and R.V. Clarke. (1986) *The Reasoning Criminal: Rational Choice Perspectives on Offending*. New York: Springer-Verlag.
Cornish, D.B. and R.V. Clarke. (2003) 'Opportunities, precipitators and criminal decisions: a reply to Wortley's critique of situational crime prevention'. *Crime Prevention Studies* 16: 41–96.
Cozens, P.M., R.H. Neale and J. Whitaker. (2003) 'A critical review of street lighting, crime and fear of crime in the British city'. *Crime Prevention & Community Safety* 5(2): 7–24.
Dauvergne, M. (2008) 'Motor vehicle theft in Canada, 2007'. *Juristat* 28(10). Ottawa: Statistics Canada.
Fleming, Z. (2003) 'The thrill of it all: youthful offenders and auto theft'. In Paul Cromwell (ed.) *In Their Own Words: Criminals on Crime* (3d edn). Los Angeles: Roxbury Publishing Company.
Fleming, Z., P.L. Brantingham and P.J. Brantingham. (1994) 'Exploring auto theft in British Columbia'. *Crime Prevention Studies* 3: 47–91.
Gottfredson, D.C. (1987) 'Examining the potential for delinquency prevention through alternative education'. *Today's Delinquent* 6: 87–100.
Gottfredson, M.R. and T. Hirschi. (1990) *A General Theory of Crime*. Stanford, CA: Stanford University Press.
Jenion, Gregory and Paul Brantingham. (2008) *Project 6116 National Study of Youth Offender Involvement in Auto Theft Final Report: British Columbia 2004–2005*. Windsor: NCE Auto21.
Lab, Steven P. (2004) 'Crime prevention, politics, and the art of going nowhere fast'. *Justice Quarterly* 21(4): 681–92.
Löbmann, Rebecca and Uwe Verthein. (2009) 'Explaining the effectiveness of heroin-assisted treatment on crime reductions'. *Law & Human Behavior* 33(1): 83–95.
Lösel, Friedrich, Mark Stemmler, Stefanie Jaursch and Andreas Beelmann. (2009) 'Universelle Prävention der Entwicklung dissozialen Verhaltens: Kurz- und Langzeiteffekte eines familienorientierten Programms'. *Monatsschrift fuer Kriminologie und Strafrechtsreform* 92(2/3): 289–307.
Lutzin, S.G. and R.C. Orem. (1967) 'Prevention through recreation'. In W. Amos and C. Wellford (eds) *Delinquency Prevention: Theory & Practice*. Englewood Cliffs, NJ: Prentice-Hall.
Maris, Peter and Martin Rein. (1967) *Dilemmas of Social Reform: Poverty and Community Action in the United States*. London: Routledge & Kegan Paul.
Mayhew, P., R.V.G. Clarke and J.M. Hough. (1976) 'Steering column locks and car theft'. In P. Mayhew, R.V.G. Clarke, A. Sturman and J.M. Hough (eds) *Crime as Opportunity*. Home Office Research Study No. 34. London: HMSO.

Mazerolle, Lorraine, Rebecca Wickes and James McBroom. (2010) 'Community variations in violence: the role of social ties and collective efficacy in comparative context'. *Journal of Research in Crime & Delinquency* 47(1): 3–30.
Moynihan, D.P. (1969) *Maximum Feasible Misunderstanding: Community Action in the War on Poverty.* New York: The Free Press.
Perreault, S. and S. Brennan. (2010) 'Criminal victimization in Canada'. *Juristat* 30(2). Ottawa: Statistics Canada.
Poyner, B. (1993) 'What works in crime prevention? An overview of evaluations'. *Crime Prevention Studies* 1: 7–34.
Scott, M.C. and H. Goldstein. (2005) *Shifting and Sharing Responsibility for Public Safety Problems.* Problem-Oriented Guides for Police, Response Guide Series No. 3. Washington, DC: US Department of Justice, Office of Community Oriented Policing Services. www.popcenter.org.
Shaw, C.R. and H.D. McKay. (1969) *Juvenile Delinquency and Urban Areas: A Study of Rates of Delinquency in Relation to Differential Characteristics of Local Communities in American Cities.* Chicago: University of Chicago Press.
Sherman, L.W., D.C. Gottfredson, D.L. MacKenzie and J. Eck. (1998) 'Preventing crime: what works, what doesn't, what's promising'. National Institute of Justice Research in Brief. Washington, DC: National Institute of Justice (NCJ 171676) (July).
Trasler, G. (1962) *The Explanation of Criminality.* London: Routledge & Kegan Paul.
Tremblay, Pierre, Yvan Clermont and Maurice Cusson. (1994) 'Jockeys and joyriders: changing patterns in car theft opportunity structures'. *British Journal of Criminology* 34: 307–21.
Tseloni, A., J. Mailley, G. Farrell and N. Tilley. (2010) 'Exploring the international decline in crime rates'. *European Journal of Criminology* 7: 375–94.
US House of Representatives Committee on Natural Resources. (1994) *Urban Recreation & Crime Prevention.* Washington, DC: US Government Printing Office.
van Koppen, M.V., C.J. de Poot and A.A.J. Blokland. (2010) 'Comparing criminal careers of organized crime offenders and general offenders'. *European Journal of Criminology* 7(5): 356–74.
Wallace, M. (2003) 'Motor vehicle theft in Canada – 2001'. *Juristat* 21(1). Ottawa: Statistics Canada.
Webb, B., B. Brown and K. Bennett. (1992) *Preventing Crime in Car Parks.* Crime Prevention Unit No. 34. London: Home Office.
Welsh, Brandon C. and David P. Farrington. (2004) 'Surveillance for crime prevention in public space: results and policy choices in Britain and America'. *Criminology & Public Policy* 3(3): 497–525.
West, D.J. and D.P. Farrington. (1973) *Who Becomes Delinquent?: Second Report of the Cambridge Study in Delinquency Development.* London: Heinemann.
Wikstrom, P.-O.H. and R. Svensson. (2010) 'When does self-control matter? The interaction between morality and self-control in crime causation'. *European Journal of Criminology* 7: 395–410.
Wikstrom, P.-O.H., R.V. Clarke and J. McCord. (eds) (1995) *Integrating Crime Prevention Strategies: Propensity and Opportunity.* Stockholm: National Council for Crime Prevention Sweden.
Winchester, Stuart and Hilary Jackson. (1982) *Residential Burglary: The Limits of Prevention.* Home Office Research Report No. 74. London: HMSO.
Wolfgang, M.E., R.M. Figlio and T. Sellin. (1972) *Delinquency in a Birth Cohort.* Chicago: University of Chicago Press.

Index

3D prototyping 56
5Is framework 54–5, 62n.7–8

absconding: approved schools 18, 35, 172–3; environmental factors 35; and motivation 37–8, 43n.1
academia: and the police 116; and public officials 120
administrative criminologists/criminology 17
affordance, concept of 178, 179
agency, human 31
agglomeration economies 152
aggression, generating 209
Albany, University of New York 16
America: problem-oriented policing 94; research 95 *see also* individual place names
analysis: of crime 96–7; of crime/benefits of 99–101; improving police capacity 100
Andresen, M.A. & Felson, M. 228
anger 206, 207
angry violence, structure of 205–10
antecedent events, and escalating illegal behaviour 221
anticipatory crime prevention benefits 150
anti-psychiatry movement 27n.4
antisocial predators 190
appliance theft 151
approved schools 27n.1, 34–5; absconding 18, 35, 172–3
Asch, Solomon 175, 176
Ashworth et al. 178
assessments, problem-oriented policing 112–13
AT CUT PRICES 199
auto theft 25, 37, 52, 218, 220, 247–8 *see also* car trafficking

Baltimore 145; public surveillance cameras 135–6, 139
bars, and reducing crime 205
baseball bats, as weapons 178
Beat Health study 144
Becker, G.S. 168
Become a Problem-Solving Crime Analyst: In 55 Small Steps 100
behaviour: and the environment 34, 35; and interaction 185; and situational changes 179
behavioural contagion 176
behavioural perspective 35
behaviours at crime scene 216
Belli, R. & Freilich, J.D. 221
benefits, diffusion of 101
Bernasco et al. 227
bias, in evaluations/assessments 113–15
bidirectional causation 185
big-science evaluation 123
Bikeoff project 55–6
Bittner, E. 81
border control 220
Boston 145, 152–3; Boston Gun Project 66, 73, 74, 98, 125; youth violence 66–8
bounded rationality 150
Braga, Anthony 67
Brantingham, P. & Brantingham, P. 227
British Crime Survey (BCS) 24–5, 47
British Journal of Criminology 172
Brixton riots 24
Brody Report 18
Brody, Stephen 18
broken windows theory, and diffusion processes 151
Bullock et al. 201
burglary: classification of 41; and co-offending 228; Dorset 229, 233,

236; offender decision-making 227; Sweden 108–9
Burrows et al. 21
Burton, R.V. 175

Cambridge Institute of Criminology 17, 33, 41
cameras, CCTV 20–1, 23, 131–9
Campbell, Donald 124–26
Canada, human rights 245
cap-and-trade 221
car exhaust suicides 161–2 *see also* suicide
car locking campaign, Plymouth 21
car parks, and vehicle crime 25
car security 52
car theft 25, 37, 52, 218, 220, 247–8 *see also* car trafficking
Car Theft Index 52
car trafficking 197–8, 199
case studies database 217
causal inference 124
CCTV 20–1, 23, 131–9
CDRPs 23, 26
census data, and hotspots 229, 234
Center for Problem-Oriented Policing 25–6, 80, 85, 102–3, 127
Changing Behaviour to Prevent Crime 26
Character Education Inquiry 174
Charlotte 101, 151
Charlotte-Mecklenburg Police Department 96
Cheah et al. 167
CHEERS 82
Chicago: focussed deterrence strategies 68–9; gun markets research 75; public surveillance cameras 135, 136–7
child pornography 219
children and parents, and criminality prevention 245–6
child sexual abuse 219
choice architects 179
choice perspective/choice model of crime 39
choices, of offenders 38–9
choice structuring properties: of crime 41–2, 196; trafficking 200–1, 202
Cincinnati Initiative to Reduce Violence 71
Circular 8/84 22–3, 24
CLAIMED 55
Clarke, Ron: background of 32; after *Crime as Opportunity* 176–7; and crime prevention 192; development of SCP 174; evaluation for everyday life (EEL) 126–8; Home Office Career 16–17; and John Eck 100; the man/his work 46–51; model of prevention 184; and social psychology 175, 177; and suicide 160; and transnational crimes 194–5; in the US 95
Clarke, R.V. & Goldstein, H. 151
Clarke, R.V. & Harris, P.M. 218
Clarke, R.V. & Lester, D. 165–6, 168
Clarke, R.V. & Mayhew, P.M. 218
Clarke, R.V. & Newman, G.R. 219
Clarke, R.V. & Weisburd, D. 142–3, 144–5
Clarke, R.V.G. and Hope, T. 41
classification of offences, situational 41
cliff-edge 125
coaction 176
coal-gas, suicides 20, 161, 162, 218
coerciveness 34
co-evolution 58–60
cognitive behaviour therapy 23
Cohen, L.E. & Felson, M. 190, 196
collective efficacy, and crime patterns 148–9
Community Development Corporations (CDC) 122
community development programs 153
community empowerment 152
Community Oriented Policing Services (COPS Office) 26, 101–2
computer-aided design, buildings 57
conceptual practice, problem-oriented policing 109
configuration knowledge 57
conformity 176
Conran, Sebastian 26
co-offending 228–9, 231
Co-ordinating Crime Prevention Efforts 21
Coping with Burglary 41
Cornish, D.B. & Clarke, R.V. 190, 191, 213, 215–16, 226
Cornish, Derek 17, 48, 196
counter-terrorism 221
CPTED 19, 54
CPU 22 *see also* PRG
CRAVED 52, 60, 98, 103n.2, 194–202
crime: choice-structuring properties of 41–2, 196; and criminality 240–1; measuring 24; new 219; organized 220; probability of 188

crime analysis, and policing/crime prevention 99–101
crime analysts 26
Crime and Disorder Act (1998) 23
crime and disorder reduction partnerships (CDRPs) 23, 26
crime and place, tight coupling 144–50
Crime and Police Effectiveness 16
Crime as Opportunity 19–20, 36, 37, 38, 40, 174–5
crime as opportunity 39–40, 176
crime at place, and routine activity theory 148
crime attractors 227
crime-commission process 42–3
Crime Concern 23
crime detection, Dorset 229
crime displacement *see* displacement
crime events 34–6
crime generators 227
crime hot spots *see* hot spots
Crime in Public View 20–1
crime mapping 57
crime pattern formation, mathematical model of 228
crime patterns, and collective efficacy 148–9
crime pattern theory 125, 247
Crime Policy Planning Unit 16
crime prevention: anticipatory crime prevention benefits 150; broad meanings of 240–2; Circular 8/84 23; and crime analysis 99–101; and criminality prevention 241; and hot spots 238; long-time-to-payoff 245; more police on the ground 21; multi-agency aspects of 244; perceptions of 31; place-based 154; police interest in theories 98–9; policy 21–2; political palatability of 241–6; primary/secondary/tertiary 242; publicity campaigns 21; responsibility for 22; and SCP 19; Sweden 108–9
Crime Prevention and the Police 21
Crime Prevention Studies 66, 88, 126
Crime Prevention Through Environmental Design (CPTED) 19, 54
Crime Prevention Unit 52; and SCP 42
crime rates 47
crime reduction 22–3, 49, 176; and public surveillance cameras 133–4
crime reduction payoffs, prevention programmes 247
Crime Reduction Programme 23–4
crime reduction programmes, and situational prevention 246–9
crime risk, geographical variance of 226
crime scenes, behaviour at 216
crime science 50
crime-site locations 227
crimes of omission 221
crime-specific focus 217
crime-specific information 30–1
crime-specific offending 41
CrimeStatIII 232, 238n.2
crime theories 83
crime theory, and effective policing 97–9
crime triangle 98
crime trips 231, 233, 234
Crimewatch 48
criminal career, research 241
criminality, and crime 240–1
criminality prevention: and crime prevention 241; political palatability of 243–6; primary/secondary/tertiary 242; targeting parents/children 245–6
criminal justice, and federal agencies 122
criminal justice efficiency, and public cameras 132–3
criminals, skills/experience of 38
criminocclusive design 54
criminologists 48
criminology: environmental/situational 47; practitioners art 32–36; and psychology 33–4; reforming 49–50
crisis intervention services: and suicide 166
CRITIC 56
criticisms, of SCP 19, 40
Croft, John 36
Cutting Crime Strategy 26
cybercrime 218–9

data refinement 100
decision-making 206–7, 208–9; manipulability of 180; offender 227; and violent offenders 206
defective delinquent differentiating tests 174–5
defensible space hypothesis 20
Deisenhammer et al. 167
delinquency 189
deprivation, and crime 47
Design Against Crime (DAC) 52–4; research centre 59
Design and Technology Alliance against Crime 26, 53

Designing Out Crime 19, 21
designing out crime 23
deterrence, and diffusion processes 150
deterrence strategies, pulling levers 68
diffusion of crime control benefits 101, 132, 142–4, 150–4, 226
discouragement, and diffusion processes 151
discourse analysis 57–8
disinformation, and crime prevention 150–1
displacement 40, 101, 133, 142, 226; and choice-structuring properties of crimes 41–2; and crime prevention 154; evidence 143–4; and hot spots 143–4, 238; limits of 196; offense 155n.1; and place 145; and suicide 161; and target area impacts 153–64
Dorset, burglaries in 229, 233, 236
draw on design 54–5
drinking situations, and crime 205
drug markets: and diffusion processes 152; focussed deterrence strategies 69
drug trafficking 195, 197–8, 199; New York 201, 202
dynamics, of criminal events 60

Eck, John 95, 100
ecological theories, social disorganization 148
Economics and Resource Analysis Strategic Policy Team 26
Effectiveness of Sentencing, The 18
effectiveness, police 94
Eisner, M. 114
Ekblom, Paul 25, 190
Elements Contributing to the Occurrence of a Criminal Event 39
elephant poaching 220
ELT 35, 36, 39–40
endangered species, market reduction 220–1
environment: and absconding 172–3; and behaviour 35; and offending 34
environmental crime prevention 19
environmental criminologists 121; and problem-oriented policing 81
Environmental Criminology and Crime Analysis (ECCA) 50, 95
environmental management 21
environmental perspective, and suicide 163–4
environment/learning theory *see* ELT

evaluation for everyday life (EEL) 126–8
evaluation(s): big-science evaluation 123; justice policy 119–28; problem-oriented policing 108–16; of public surveillance cameras 131–9; SCP 83, 94; social policy initiatives 121–4
evidence-based administration 126
EVIL DONE 52
excuses, removing from offenders 73–5
expressive violence 207, 208
external situational factors 213

far-right extremists, and tax refusal 221
federal agencies, and criminal justice 122
federal programs 121, 122–3
Felson, Marcus 196
Felson, Richard 205, 209
5Is framework 54–5, 62n.7–8
focussed deterrence strategies 65–6; drug markets 69; emergence of 66–9; to individual offenders 68–9; and SCP 70–5, 76; social service component 74
Foresight programme 23, 52
four pillars, terrorist opportunity 219
free bonus effects 142
free rider effects 142
fundamental attribution error 177–8, 180

gain, and offenders 205, 207
gambling, structural characteristics of 41–2
Garland, David 22
Geographical Information System (GIS) 232
geography, and crime risk 226
Germany, steering column locks 20
Gibson, J.J. 178
Gill, M. & Clarke, R.V. 199
goals, of offenders 207
Goldstein Awards for Problem-Solving Excellence *see* Herman Goldstein Award
Goldstein, Herman 65, 67, 81, 95
Goldstein's theory of policing 81
governance 81
Green, L. 151
Grippa clip 55
Groff et al. 146, 147
guardians, as offenders 71
Guerette, R.T. 220
Guerette, R.T. & Bowers, K.J. 143, 153
gun control laws, and suicide 162
gun trafficking 197–8

gun violence 72 *see also* Boston Gun Project; Kansas Gun Project

halo effect 142
hard/soft SCP 216–17
Hartshorne, H. & May, M.A. 174, 175
hate crime 221
Hayes, Gary 95
Head Start 246
Heal, Kevin 21
Herman Goldstein Award 80, 85, 86, 87, 95–6, 99–100, 111
heroin trafficking 197–8, 199, 202
high-criminality individuals 188
high-criminogenic situations 188
High Point 71
Home Office: and DAC 53; Ron Clarke at 16–17
Home Office Research Studies (HORS) 20–1; Study 35 174
Home Office Research Unit *see* HORU
homicide reduction, Chicago 68–9
homicides, focussed deterrence 71
Hong Kong 162
HORU 16–17, 33, 36 *see also* RPU
hot products 25
Hot Products 52
hot spot policing 132, 146; and displacement 143–4
hot spots 145, 146, 227–8; burglary 236; and car theft 248; identification/examination of 232–7; juvenile crime 148; prolific/occasional offenders 233, 238; subcritical/supercritical 228; and victimisation 229
housing projects, and crime 152
human agency 31
human interest, of crimes 31
human motivation, and rational choice 216 *see also* motivation
human rights 245, 246
human smuggling 220

ideal final result discourse 59
identity theft 219
Improving Evaluation of Anticrime Programs 126
impulsivity 189; and suicide 166–7, 168, 169n.4
incentives, place managers 87–8
income, reducing offenders 72
Indermaur, D. 186
innovation 58–60
IN SAFE HANDS 52, 199

instrumental practice, problem-oriented policing 109
instrumental violence 207–9
intelligence-led policing (ILP) 89
interaction, and behaviour 185
interactions: as interdependent relationships 187–9; as reciprocal relationships 185–6
International Association of Crime Analysts 101
Internet crime 218–19
intimate handlers 72
iteration 55
ivory trafficking 197–8

Jersey City Drug Market Analysis Experiment 144
Jersey City Violent Crime Places experiment 144
Jill Dando Institute 25, 26, 52, 101
Jones, E.E. & Harris, V.A. 177
Journal of Experimental Criminology (JEC) 126
journey to crime 231, 233, 234
joyriding 247
justice policy, evaluations 119–27
juvenile crime, hot spots 148

Kansas City Gun Project 144
Kaplan et al. 166
Kashden et al. 166
Kennedy, David 66–7, 98
Kingswood Approved School 16, 34–5
Kingswood Controlled Trial of Residential Treatment for Delinquents 16, 17–18
Kirkholt Burglary Prevention Demonstration Project 25
Kleiman, M.A.R. & Smith, K.D. 151–2
Klein, Naomi 180
knowledge, configuration 57
Knutsson, Johannes & Tilley, Nick 124
Koslowsky et al. 166

law enforcement, norms and narratives 74
Law et al. 162
law inforcement, legitimacy of 75
Laycock, Gloria 21, 49, 52, 82
learning: of offenders 24; in SCP 22–3
learning theory of suicide 163
legitimacy, of law inforcement 75
Lemieux, A.M. & Clarke, R.V. 220
Lester, D. 163, 165, 168
Lester, D. & Yang, B. 168
libertarian paternalism 179–80

lichen conjecture 88, 89
Lipton et al. 174
London Metropolitan Police, problem-oriented policing 95
London Underground, CCTV 21
long-time-to-payoff, crime prevention programmes 245
loose coupling 145
Los Angeles, public surveillance cameras 133
low-criminality individuals 188
low-criminogenic situations 188
Lowell 72
Lucifer Effect: How Good People Turn Evil, The 177
Lynam et al. 189

mapping, crime 57
MARC project 52–3
market reduction, endangered species 220–1
Martin, D.N. 35
mathematical model, of crime pattern formation 228
Mayhew et al. 20–1, 39, 40
Mears, D.P. & Bhati, A.S. 152
medico-psychological model 33
Mexican border control 220
Mexico 192
migration 220
Milgram, Stanley 175, 176
Ministry of Justice 26
Minneapolis 145
Mischel, Walter 184
Model Cities initiatives 122
Modifying criminogenic products: what role for government 53
modus operandi, graphic illustration of 56
Morgan Report 23
motivation, offender 36–7, 40, 75, 216
Mr Big 201
multi-agency partnerships 23, 244
multiplier effect 142, 153
mundane offenders 190, 191

National Deviancy Conference (NDC) 17
National Institute of Justice (NIJ) 100
National Research Council 68
natural surveillance 20
neighborhood self-control 152
Newark Police Department 100
Newman, G.R. & Clarke, R.V. 218–19
Newman, Graeme 51, 102
Newman, Oscar 20

New Realists 17
New York 2, 95, 201, 202
Nick Tilley Award 111
No Logo 180
non-acquisitive violence 207
non-situational measures 85–6
Not Well Advised 121
Nowicki, Dennis 96
Nudge 179
nudgeability 179–80

Oakland Specialized Multi-Agency Response Team (SMART) intervention 151
occasional offenders, and hot spots 229, 233, 236, 237, 241
O'Connor, Alice 122
offenders: choices of 38–9; decision-making 206, 227; disposition 216; focussed deterrence strategies to 68–9; and gains 207; goals of 207; likely offenders 190; motivated 75; organized crime 241; out-designing 59; prolific/occasional 227, 229, 231; reasoning 226; spatial decision-making 227, 237; types of 190, 216, 226–7
offending 96; crime-specific 41; and victimisation 24
offense displacement *see* displacement
offenses, situational classification of 41
Operation Ceasefire 66, 67–8
Operation Identification 108–9
opportunity 36; concept of 212–13; crime as 39–40, 176; reducing techniques 213; types of 213
opportunity-reduction 39, 40, 43
Ordnance Survey data, and hot spots 229
organized crime 220; offenders 241; and SCP 195
Outsmarting the Terrorists 51

Panel on Improving Information and Data on Firearms 68
parents and children, and criminality prevention 245–6
parrot trafficking 194, 197–8, 199, 201
partnerships, multi-agency 23
pattern-matching 124, 125
Pawson, Ray & Tilley, Nick 124
Pease, Ken 49, 51
penal efficacy 174
perpetrator techniques, graphic illustration of 56

personality theorists 34
personality traits 184, 189
person-situation interaction, and SCP 184–92
person-situation theories 247
person × situation effect 189, 190
Philadelphia: drug markets 152; public surveillance cameras 134; Temple University 16, 95
Pires, Stephen 194
place and crime, tight coupling 144–50
place-based problem-solving 86–7
place managers, reducing crime 87–8
Plymouth 21
poaching, elephants 220
Police Executive Research Forum (PERF) 95
Police Research Group 22
policing: and crime analysis 99–101; and crime theory 97–9; function of 81; improving 89
policing strategies, lichen conjecture 88
policy units 26
political crime 51
political palatability, of crime/criminality prevention 243–6
politics, and crime 31
POP Guides 101–3, 127–8
positivism 17
precipitation-control strategies 215
precipitators, behaviour 163
predatory offenders 191
prevention programmes, time scales of 247
prevention strategies, car theft 247
prevention techniques 221
PRG 22
primary crime prevention 242, 246
prisons, and suicide 163
privacy rights 217
probation hostels: and desistance from crime 173; re-offending 18
Problem-Oriented Guides *see* POP Guides
problem-oriented policing 22, 81–2; academic origins 97; contexts for conducting 111–12; and criminological theory 97–9; early developments 94–5; evaluation of 109–16; evidence-based 127; instrumental/conceptual practice 109; and SCP 65–6, 86, 88, 89, 95–7, 115–16
Problem-Oriented Policing Conference 85, 95

problems: defining 82; as management function 86–90; at places 77–8
problem-solving 116n.3
programme design, crime/criminality prevention interventions 244
prolific offenders 228–9, 231, 247; and hot spots 233, 236, 237, 238; management programmes 245
properties, of offenses 196
property crime, and anger 205
provocation, reducing 73
provoked offenders 190, 191
proximal factors 37
psychoanalysis 32
psychology, and crime 32–34
public housing projects, and crime 152
publicity campaigns, crime prevention 21, 150–1
public surveillance cameras, evaluation of 131–9 *see also* CCTV
pulling levers 66, 68, 70

radical behaviourism 34
radical non-intervention 27n.4
randomised controlled trials 50–1
Ratcliffe, Jerry 89
rational choice: and human motivation 216; theory of 48, 125, 131–2, 151
rational choice perspective (RCP) 36, 42–3, 191
reasoning offenders 226
reconviction rates, and residential treatment regimes 35
recorded crime 47
Reducing Offending 23
reform, of offenders 50
regulators, behaviour 164
rehabilitation programmes 23, 35, 174
rehabilitative criminology 18
re-offending, probation hostels 18
replication 126
Reppetto, T.A. 40–1
research: American/British 95; applied 119; criminal career 241; early agenda 17–18; Home Office 26; and policing 21–2, 100; and SCP 80–1; social 17, 119–21; suicide 161–2
Research and Planning Unit *see* RPU
residential treatment regimes 35
responsibilisation 22
rewards, reducing offenders 72–3
risks, increasing for offenders 70–2
Robber's Cave experiment 175

Index   259

Rockford 69
Ross et al. 177
routine activity theory 98, 125; and crime at place 148
RPU 16–17, 22 *see also* HORU
Rutgers University 95

Safer Cities 23
Safer Places 56
Sam Houston State University 95
San Francisco, public surveillance cameras 134
SARA technique 22, 43, 54, 82, 85, 88, 109
scanning, analysing, responding and assessing *see* SARA
Schiphol fly 179
Schmidtke, A. & Schaller, S. 166
Schneider, J.L. 220
School of Criminal Justice 49–50
science of crime 89
SCP case studies database 217
scripts/script clashes 60–1
Seattle 145, 146–8
secondary crime prevention 242, 246
security products 54
self-control 209
serotonin, and suicide 168
Sherif, M. 176
Sherman et al. 145
Short et al. 228
Simon et al. 167
Sinclair, I.A.C. 4, 173
situational action theory 247
situational analysis, of crimes 65
situational changes, and behaviour 179
situational classification, of offences 41
Situational Crime Prevention: Case Studies 99
Situational Crime Prevention (SCP): academic origins 97; background 15; core mission of 39–42; criticisms of 19, 40; development of 18–21, 94–5; early publications on 19–21; evaluations 83, 84; evidence-based 127; explained 82–3; integration into mainstream 22–4; intervention possibilities 242–3; scope of 83–5; term 18–19; theoretical evolution of 212–17; theory to practice 36–9; twenty-five techniques of 214, 217
situational factors, suicide 163, 165 *see also* suicide
situational interventions 243

situationalism 184
situational measures 85; addressing problems with 85–6; suicide 163
situational policing 22
situational prevention model, two-stage 212
situational risk factors 52
skills/experience, of offenders 38
Skubak et al. 70, 73
small-claim/small scale interventions 125
SMART intervention 151
Smith et al. 150
smuggling, human 220
social deprivation, and crime 47
social development interventions 247, 248
social disorganization, ecological theories 148
social policy initiatives, evaluating 121–4
social problems 32
social psychology, and Ron Clarke 175, 177
social science research 17, 119–21
social service component, focussed deterrence strategies 74
sociological accounts, offending 33–4
Sparrow, M. 81, 82
spatial decision-making, of offenders 227, 237
specificity model, personality 189
Spelman, W. 145
spillover effect 153
standard deviational hotspots (STAC hotspots) 232
Stanford Prison Experiment 175
State University of New York 16, 95
steering column locks, Germany 20
Stephens, Darrel 96
street code, challenging 74
street violence 74
stresses 37
strong situations 189
subcritical crime hot spots 228
substitution, and suicide 161
subways, suicide in 162
suicide: coal-gas 20, 40; decision to commit suicide 165–7; and irrationality/impulsivity 168, 169n.4; learning theory of 163; and opportunity 160–8; prevention 160–1, 164; restricting access to a method 164; and SCP 218; theory of 165
suicide bombers 164
Suicide: Closing the Exits 160
super controllers 97–8

supercritical crime hotspots 228
Surrey Police, problem-oriented policing 95
surveillance: natural 6; and territoriality 20
Sweden, crime prevention 108–9
Swedish National Police Board 109
Szanton, Peter 119–20

Tackling Vandalism 20
Taniguchi et al. 152
target area impacts, and displacement/diffusion 153–4
target hardening 216–17
tax evasion 221
tax refusal, and far-right extremists 221
Taylor, R.B. 145
techniques of neutralization 74
Temple University 16, 95
temporal bundling, and auto theft interventions 247–8
territoriality 20
terrorism 219
tertiary crime prevention 242, 246
Thaler, R. & Sunstein, C.R. 179–80
theft, targets of 25
Theory of Inventive Principles 59
theory of suicide 165
therapeutic community approach 17–18
therapeutic regimes 50
think thief 53–4
third parties, and instrumental violence 208–9
third-party policing 87
Thomson, D.E. 153
3D prototyping 56
tight coupling, crime and place 144–50
Tilley Awards for Problem-Solving Excellence 80
Tizard, Jack 34
Townsley, M. & Sidebottom, A. 234
trafficking: car 197–8, 199; and CRAVED 195–202; heroin 197–8, 199, 202; ivory 197–8; parrot 194, 197–8, 199, 201
training: crime analysis 101; problem-solving 80
trait differences 189
Trasler, Gordon 173
TRIZ 59
truancy 21
Tuck, Mary 25

twenty-five techniques, of SCP 214, 217

UK Design Council 53
United States *see* America; individual place names
University of New York 16, 95
unrecorded crime 24
urban crisis 119
Urban Institute (UI) 134

vandalism: buses 20; Manchester schools 21; and motivation 39; telephone kiosk 20–1
vehicle crime 25, 52, 218, 220, 247–8; car trafficking 197–8, 199
victimisation 24–5, 108, 229
victims, potential 149
violence: and anger 205; conditions for 209; expressive/instrumental 207, 208; honorable exit from 74; irrational 207; non-acquisitive 207; street 72, 74
visualization, and design 56–7
VIVA 196
voters, and crime prevention 245
voting participation, and high crime trajectory 149

wars, on crime; drugs etc. 31–2
Washington 152–3; public surveillance cameras 135, 137–8
wealth, and crime 47
weapon priming effect 179
weapons trafficking 197–8
weighted displacement quotient 153
Weisburd, D. & Green, L. 154
Weisburd et al. 144, 145–6, 148, 149
Welsh, Brandon & Farrington, David 133
Weyrauch et al. 166
Whitehead et al. 199
Whitelaw, William 22
wildlife crimes *see* elephant poaching; ivory trafficking; parrot trafficking
Williams et al. 167
Wortley, R. 5, 163, 213, 215–17
Wortley, R.K. & Smallbone, S.W. 219

young offenders, and car crime 247–8

Zielenbach, S. & Voith, R. 152
Zimbardo, P. 176, 177